PETER BROOK AND
THE MAHABHARATA

Critical Perspectives

Edited by

David Williams

London and New York

First published 1991
by Routledge
11 New Fetter Lane, London EC4P 4EE

Simultaneously published in the USA and Canada
by Routledge
a division of Routledge, Chapman and Hall, Inc.
29 West 35th Street, New York, NY 10001

Phototypeset by Intype, London
Printed in Great Britain by
T J Press (Padstow) Ltd, Padstow, Cornwall

British Library Cataloguing in Publication Data
Peter Brook's Mahabharata : critical perspectives.
1. Theatre. Brook, Peter
I. Williams, David
792.95

Library of Congress Cataloging in Publication Data
Peter Brook's Mahabharata : critical perspectives / edited by David Williams
p. cm.
Includes bibliographical references and index.
1. Carrière, Jean-Claude, Mahabharata. 2. Carrière, Jean-Claude–Stage history.
3. Brook, Peter. I. Williams, David
PQ2663.A78M3436 1991
792.9'2–dc20   91–8195

ISBN 0–415–04777–3
ISBN 0–415–04778–1 (pbk)

To the memory of Brenda Williams
(1927–1988):

The unreal has no being,
The real never ceases to be.
(*The Mahabharata*)

Rage, rage against the dying of the light . . .
(Dylan Thomas)

And if you cannot be saints of knowledge, at least be its warriors. They are the companions and forerunners of such sainthood . . .
(Nietzsche, *Thus Spake Zarathustra*)

Peut-être me direz-vous: 'Es-tu sûr que cette légende soit la vraie?' Qu'importe ce que peut être la réalité placée hors de moi, si elle m'a aidé à vivre, à sentir que je suis et ce que je suis.
(Baudelaire)

CONTENTS

Part V Staging an epic: *The Mahabharata* in production

LIST OF ILLUSTRATIONS

Photographs of the original French-language production are marked with an asterisk; all others are of the subsequent English-language version.

PREFACE

Peter Brook's epic theatre work, *The Mahabharata*, attracted massive public interest during its short touring life in the late 1980s, and subsequently in a five and a half hour film version televised worldwide. Most of the critical matter it generated, however, failed to address in detail a number of central issues, notably: the relationship of the body of Brook's work with his International Centre of Theatre Research; the multicultural structure of the company, and its repercussions for scenography; the problematics and politics of an interculturalism in this instance; and, more specifically, the relationship between this production and Indian culture and performative forms. This book seeks to discuss all of these areas, as well as to describe the nature of the working process and to detail the technical and logistical problems engendered by touring a production of this size and complexity.

The first part aims to contextualize the production in relation to the body of Brook's work with the Centre. The second part provides first-hand accounts by many of those directly implicated in the collaborative process of bringing the production to fruition – director, writer, designer, lighting designer, musicians and actors. Part II provides detailed analyses of elements of *mise-en-scène* and scenographic discourses, while the subsequent part offers a diversity of critical perspectives – post-colonialist, socio-cultural, post-modernist, etc. The final part gives production details of the Avignon première (1985), the world tour English-language version (1987–8), and the film version, and details production logistics and economics in relation to two venues during the world tour: a 'found' theatre in New York, and a granite quarry in the hills above Perth, Australia.

Necessarily the problematics of interculturalism explored here form the core of the book, notably the complementary contributions by Rustom Bharucha and Maria Shevtsova, and my own account of the specifics of the scenography. The latter also attempts to provide a counterbalance to those critics who have too readily dismissed this work as cosmetic experimentation or reductive cartoon of a culture.[1] Indeed, my intention to engender debate in this complex area has to some degree determined both the structure and contents of the book. My espousal of pluralism, like Brook's, is not modish; in this context, it is the requisite means for eliciting meaning. Different perspectives set alongside one another implicitly offer the exchange of dialogue, and in turn invite further dialectical discussion. These are by no means the final words: they are simply essays in the true sense of the word – initial endeavours to map out terrain, exploratory attempts at clarification.

As this book is intended primarily for theatre specialists and more general readers, I apologize forthwith to Sanskrit scholars for omitting all diacritics in what follows. In addition, I have standardized alternative spellings in all quotations used (e.g. Krishna rather than Krsna, Shiva rather than Siva, etc.).

NOTE

1 See, for example, Liza Henderson, 'Brook's Point', *Theater* (Spring, 1988), in which she describes *The Mahabharata* as a reduction of 'the soul of a formidable culture to the level of a clichéd children's bedtime story' (p. 37) – as reductive and mono-dimensional an account of the project as *Plays and Players'* misleading tag – 'Air India's version of *The Hobbit*'.

ACKNOWLEDGEMENTS

The realization of this book would not have been possible without the cooperation in various ways of the following: at Routledge in London, both Tony Morris and Helena Reckitt for their enthusiastic and generous encouragement; at the CICT in Paris, in particular Peter Brook, Nina Soufy and Bruce Myers; also Jean-Claude Carrière, Maurice Bénichou, Malik Bowens, Alain Maratrat, Vittorio Mezzogiorno, Yoshi Oida, Toshi Tsuchitori, and the casts and crew of both French- and English-language versions of *The Mahabharata*; Dr Georges Banu at the University of Paris for his encouragement, and Professor David Bradby at Royal Holloway and Bedford New College, University of London, for his critical contributions – both fine scholars and valued friends; Professors Bob White and Gareth Griffiths in the English Department at the University of Western Australia, for their commitment to supporting this research project; Associate Professor David E. R. George at Murdoch University, Perth, and Barry Laing, for his valuable critical input; Dr Maria Shevtsova at the University of Sydney; Henry Boston, Kay Jamieson and Tony Reagan for the Festival of Perth; the 1988 Adelaide Festival of Arts, in particular Rob Brookman and the late Paul Iles; in Glasgow, Neil Wallace; in Sicily, Taormina Arte, Taormina; in India, the Sangeet Natak Akademi (Delhi), Sri B. V. Karanth (Mysore), Dr Attili Krishna Rao (Waltair), Rustom Bharucha in Calcutta, Yaduendra Sahai of the City Palace Museum (Jaipur), Anant Pai at Amar Chitra Katha (Bombay); in Kerala, the Kathakali Kalamandalam (Cheruthuruthy), K. N. Panikkar and the members of Sopanam, the Margi Kathakali School and the C. V. N. Kalari Sangham (Trivandrum); Ahmad Abbas, Craig san Roque, Shomit Mitter; my dear friends in England, Lightning Edwin and Mr P.; finally, and above all, Rachel Williams, not only for her help with the typescript, but also for sharing this journey with me from the very beginning. Needless to say, any weaknesses or inaccuracies in this book should be ascribed to me, rather than to any of them.

DAVID WILLIAMS
Perth

Part I

INTRODUCTION

1

THEATRE OF INNOCENCE AND OF EXPERIENCE

Peter Brook's International Centre
An Introduction

David Williams

THE GENESIS OF THE INTERNATIONAL CENTRE

In November 1970, Brook and his producer and friend Micheline Rozan received substantial and unprecedented funding – in large part from the Ford, Gulbenkian and Anderson Foundations and UNESCO – to help them establish an International Centre of Theatre Research (CIRT) in Paris. The group would include theatre practitioners from diverse cultural origins, including Japan, Africa, the USA., Britain and France. In collaboration with them, Brook hoped to be able to eschew the conventional channels and forms of commercial theatre, which he considered to entail a corruption and compromise of all that was valid and 'alive' in theatre practice. By exploring a more extended range of processes and conditions, perhaps they would be able to find a way to 'evolve something up from a seed: not to add things together, but to make conditions in which something can grow'.

For many years Brook had dreamt of being in a position of total subsidy, unencumbered by the crippling commercial demands and prevailing ideological impositions peculiar to the 'glamour-circuit' of showcase theatres. By the mid–1960s, as one of a triumvirate of directors with the Royal Shakespeare Company, he was becoming increasingly convinced that 'the present set-up of the theatre, with its formal institutional apparatus, provides the wrong arena for *communication, ceremony* and *involvement*': three central words that would recur in Brook's theory and practice, delineating the parameters of his exploratory work since 1970.

During an initial three-year period at the genesis of the Centre, this work was deliberately structured according to Brook's notion of 'a rhythm in and out of life'. A centrifugal outward movement 'into life', like anthropological fieldwork, was to take the group out of their private laboratory environment on a major investigative excursion every year: to Iran, Africa

3

and America respectively. These collective journeys were considered supreme exercises in the validation of research work behind closed doors, the public testing of the efficacy of 'work-in-progress', as well as an infusion of a new dynamism and stimuli through exchange: contact with new forms, the gathering of performative data and first-hand experience. The fundamental aim would be to explore –

> what the conditions were through which theatre could speak directly. In what conditions is it possible for what happens in the theatre experience to originate from a group of actors, and be received and shared by spectators without the help and hindrance of shared cultural signs and tokens?

The Centre's initial work was structured around a series of questions that intrigued Brook. They are avowedly essentialist and humanist – idealist in formulation and concern, signalling Brook's intuitive sympathy with Jung's foregrounding of a mythopoeic sensibility, to the detriment of a rationalist or materialist discourse. Can certain elements of theatre language pass directly between cultures without being filtered through the channels of any single culture's shared linguistic codes? Could the simple relationship of, for example, a sound and a movement be charged with a 'poetic density' touching a chord in anybody and everybody, generating one of those moments at which, in Arthur Koestler's words, 'eternity looks through the window of time'? Is there a tonal consciousness common to humankind? Are there archetypal 'deep structures' of a vocal or gestural kind – dynamic, instinctive and intercultural? If a genuinely collective expression of what was 'essentially human' in experience could be elaborated, Brook's utopian ideal of universal communication would be vindicated.

In its practice, therefore, the group would have to elevate above verbal text what were traditionally considered to be secondary elements of expressivity, although in reality they comprise the root components of a 'performance text': corporeal gesture, vocal tone and texture, paralanguage, proxemics, the affective and spatial dynamics of both sound and movement on an individual and collective level, etc. As a unit, their task would be to locate the specificity of theatre processes and languages, asking: what animates human beings in relation to their culture? what is at the origin of human needs for and manifestations of 'make-believe'? what situations are dramatic in human terms, while remaining areas of true exploration? is the impulse to make theatre an organic necessity, or an obsolete anachronism?

ORGHAST

During their first year, the CIRT group created *Orghast*, an experimental musico-poetic theatre piece for the Shiraz Festival in Iran, a self-consciously 'holy' work made up of esoteric mystical abstractions, both vocal and gestural. With its original point of departure in the myth of Prometheus, this darkly Manichean work was performed in an invented language of musical phonemes developed by the poet Ted Hughes, as well as in certain dead languages: Ancient Greek, Latin and Avestan, the hieratic religious language of the Parsee fire prophet Zoroaster. This project may be seen as an attempt to go back to the very source of language as incantatory sound, when an act of communication was synonymous with an act of communion. As Ted Hughes said,

> If you imagine music buried in the earth for a few thousand years, decayed back to its sources, not the perfectly structured thing we know as music, that is what we tried to unearth.[1]

One of Brook's recurrent ideals has been to locate what, in a theatre language context, can be conveyed and received as music, that invisible and mysterious language that seems to have an ability to surmount barriers imposed by social, linguistic and cultural forms. It can communicate directly on an affective pre-rational level, fusing form and content indissolubly. Means and meaning are inseparable; music is resolutely irreducible and untranslatable.[2]

Some of those present in Iran felt *Orghast* to be a significant development in both contemporary music and theatre language. In terms of the latter, it represented a liberating movement from representational to abstract, fifty years in arrears of similar trends in painting. However, Brook freely admitted the experiment was constrictive, that form and location – the awesome ruins of Persepolis – precluded certain potential emotional responses. There could be no room, for example, for the joy and release of laughter.

AFRICA AND IMPROVISATION

The second journey, in 1972–3, was a three-month trip in jeeps across the Sahara and North West Africa. Brook intended to place the members of his group in a position of vulnerability where the challenge would be greatest, and therefore the possibility of development richest. In the absence of the safety net of complicity that stems from sharing cultural matrices with an audience, an equivalent would have to be found on each separate occasion. For a radical pragmatist such as Brook, yesterday's 'truth' may very well be meaningless today, and a theatre event can only ever pulsate with energy and vitality if it is a meeting point. Brook was asking his performers to abandon accreted technique and begin again from as close as possible to a neutral zero point; in this heuristic process, nothing could be taken for granted. So they would simply arrive unannounced in a village, define a work/play space by laying out their carpet and then begin to perform. With only the most skeletal scenario or a simple object – a shoe, a stick, a box, bread – as the starting point for improvisation, the actors were obliged to find a way of coaxing a shared frame of reference into being, within the fury and passion of live performance. All theoretical questions became immediate in the heat of the moment.

In place of highly prepared 'polished' work, improvised forms were deemed to be absolutely necessary. On a daily basis, each member of the group was asked to confront his/her responsibility to create *ex nihilo*, entering the empty space to meet the 'moment of truth'. Naked, defenceless, alone, each actor was obliged to 'seize the current, ride the wind, deal with the forces that are there at that time and only at that time'. In this way, he/she would be forced to expose almost everything to the critical spotlight at the same moment, or at least those qualities that Brook believes to be of paramount importance: courage, powers of concentration and imagination, ability to strip away blurring parasitic impulses and to communicate with clarity, sense of rhythm in a collective, openness to one's immediate external environment and access to one's inner life.

All it takes is all you have . . .

Like Zen calligraphy or Japanese Kendo, the sink-or-swim predicament of improvisation can exist as a sensitive instrument for gauging and validating an expression of unhesitating spontaneity. It can short-circuit the gap between concealed inner impulse and external public action. An actor becomes responsible for actively exploring the unknown in the middle of life. A deliberate and practical response must be made – intuitively, instantaneously and repeatedly. For Brook, any aprioristic theoretical or dogmatic approach must be deadly:

> The training of an actor is like that of a Samurai. It may last for years and years, and lead up to one sudden confrontation. The only rule is that one is never prepared for the situation one really meets.[3]

Brook's conception of the process for the group seems to share certain structural and thematic qualities both with Grotowski's Taoist-based *via negativa* and with Jung's process of individuation.[4] This training was never intended to be an amassing of techniques, but rather a process of unlearning and uncovering. Through sharing experience in Africa, engendering a sense of 'common history', Brook believes his actors were able to some degree to regress (or rather progress, for this is an explicit instance of the paradoxical *reculer pour mieux sauter*) to what Brook has called a state of 'innocence' – a state of ur-wholeness and natural creativity, present in childhood but lost in the passage to adulthood. The ideal is of 'inner ripening' through *nunc fluens*: a direct opening and response to present reality, immersion in present process through a reawakening of a long-dormant spontaneity, as a means of nourishing and releasing 'authentic' creativity and individuality.

Such is the loose and in some ways reactionary conceptual theory. One may be excused for feeling somewhat sceptical about whether or not Brook and gang in fact 'found themselves' in the desert, following the well-trodden path of an army of mystics and prophets in myth and history, as well as of the birds in *Conference of the Birds*. The literalization of the metaphor of desert as forum for self-confrontation irritated some as pretentious. At the same time, the lack of any verifiable evidence that the group's foray into African culture involved a real exchange enraged others, who immediately wrote off the entire exercise as symptomatic of a radical utopianism, even of a neo-colonialist ethos. A word of caution: such a journey is inevitably misleading and meaningless if read in a vacuum, removed from the context of the ongoing work with which it was continuous and complementary. Like *Orghast*, it accounted for only one specific area of experimentation in an expansive range, a fine band of colours in an as yet largely unexplored spectrum. At the time, it was much too early (and easy) to dismiss this project on the basis of third-hand gossip and Brook's own more evasive or woolly pronouncements.

Nevertheless this one journey remains the most central collective experience to date. Africa has left a profound and visible imprint on all of the Centre's subsequent productions. Brook has suggested that certain celebratory and unifying encounters in Africa refined the actors' sense of what a relationship with an audience could be – the uncovering and sharing of submerged links, the joy of participating in a moment of revelatory creativity. On a more prosaic level, the practical nature of the research work undertaken there has coloured the very fabric of the actors' craft in subsequent formal productions. For example, one characteristic of all of the public work at the group's Paris base since 1974 is the minimization of scenic means, the creation of location and social realities through suggestion and the manipulation of simple everyday objects. Like popular theatre forms around the world, much of the Centre's work has taken the form of a stripped 'poor' theatre using metonym and synecdoche to actively engage audiences' creative imaginations. In the African 'carpet shows', objects were employed as a means of centring and focusing collective improvisation, the object itself serving a minimal supportive role. At the same time, it existed as a source of marvel, a stimulus to the imagination – raw material whose potential demanded to be explored in play.

One such example was a 'Shoe Show'. An old shoe thrown on to the empty carpet inevitably creates interest and demands development. As the power of focused attention infuses life into the inanimate, the object assumes a numinosity, and is free to be mobilized and undergo an endless series of transformations. When an 'old hag' puts on the shoe to become 'young and beautiful', an element of protean 'magic' accredited to the object by the space is realized in concrete terms. In almost all of these improvisations, the object was displaced from its habitual functional usage or apparent referential content, and redefined. A shoe might have become musical instrument, drinking vessel or weapon; a stick could be used as telescope or flute or to externalize an inner impulse, such as revenge or jealousy. The serious play of make-believe released an object's evocative resonances. As in children's games, it could participate fully. In turn, the actors reawakened their propensity for play, their ability to juggle with simple realities to create something entirely and surprisingly new. The use of objects in this way, as multi-transformable 'neutral' tools, has become an integral component in the group's performative idiom. Scenographically, this kind of suggestion and ellipsis comprises the very life-blood of the production of *The Mahabharata*, for example.

THE USA

In 1973, the Centre group travelled to the USA, where they lived and worked with Luis Valdez's El Teatro Campesino in California, performing in theatres, in fields, from the back of pick-up trucks. As had been the case in many of the 'carpet shows' in Africa, their source material was *Conference of the Birds*, a twelfth-century Sufi *Pilgrim's Progress* by the Persian poet Farid Uddin 'Attar of Nishapur: a lengthy philosophical and religious fable allegorizing the human condition and mankind's search for truth and meaning within themselves. The group successfully found a point of contact with the politically militant *campesinos* in the birds' commitment to their journey, their struggle and search through experience.

Their next stop was at the Chippewa reservation in Minnesota, where they were shown ceremonies, rituals and the poetry of American Indian sign-language. Then on to New York, where 'rough' improvisatory excursions to the streets and parks of Brooklyn were balanced with the final improvised versions of *Conference*, the form and content of each version determined by individual members of the group. After the final night-long session at the Brooklyn Academy of Music, Brook quietly outlined the creative point at which they had arrived, an outline that suggests a political agenda – a shared sense of ethical and moral responsibility to the supra-personal imperatives of a collective approach to the elaboration of theatre language:

> The clarity we achieved tonight could never have arisen through theory, but only through the experiences we have gone through together. We are trying to make work about theatre and about life.

It has to be true in a theatre form, and yet be something far beyond theatre . . . The work only becomes meaningful when we serve something other than our egos. This is when theatre takes on the promise of something more than just a poor thing in which to get involved[5]

None the less, the type of research undertaken in private during this first three-year period – the painstaking clarification and distillation of forms, the relentless pruning and discarding of whatever is deemed inessential – had proved intensely demanding. Evidently, there can have been very little real sense of collectivity in the early stages. Initially many of the actors had felt insecure and confused, finding no substantial point of contact with prior experiences. Fear of the unknown, the unforgiving requirement for them to place themselves in positions of 'risk' as the only means to go beyond themselves, coupled with a total lack of any clearly defined goals, had left many at first feeling profoundly disoriented. The New York director and actor Joe Chaikin, a participant for only a few weeks at a time, described it to me as 'like vertigo'. In addition, the nature of the 'fieldwork' was painful to the actors as human beings. For Brook as theatre 'scientist', who once described to me the group in Africa as 'guinea-pigs', even a failure can be informative; for the actors, it could only ever be a 'moment of total disgrace', in Bruce Myers' words. For more than two years, the process seemed to promote fission rather than fusion: the individuals concerned had little time for reflection upon and assimilation of the flood of experience into which they had been tossed, both behind closed doors and on the journeys. Brook's working regime simply did not come to a halt – and to this day he is still notorious for persevering indefatigably when those around him have fizzled out. It was only after the trip across America, with the temporary separation and the subsequent establishment of a core group at a new base in Paris, that the imprint of these initial areas of research was to become apparent in public performance.

A PERMANENT BASE: LES BOUFFES DU NORD

The nature of the Centre's formal theatre work has been determined to a significant degree by the discovery by Brook and Rozan in 1974 of a derelict nineteenth-century theatre, Les Bouffes du Nord.[6] Formerly a theatre of some prestige and history, it had been out of use as a theatre since 1950, then finally abandoned in 1952 when the building was gutted by fire. To this day, it remains largely as it was found, for it closely matches Brook's ideals. Although eviscerated and in a state of decay, the spirit of the theatre's past survives intact. This *espace trouvé* is above all a place marked by life, a silent witness to the withering passage of time. Immediate impressions are (deliberately?) contradictory, for the interior

9

seems to be at some indeterminate mid-point between demolition and renovation: a luminous weatherbeaten shell bearing the traces of an incomplete transition from an old to a new order of reality. As such, it has provided an ideal space thematically for *Timon of Athens* (1974), *The Ik* (1975), *Ubu aux Bouffes* (1975), *Measure for Measure* (1978), *Conference of the Birds* (1979), *The Cherry Orchard* (1982) and *The Mahabharata* (1985), all of which are concerned with worlds in transition.

Despite the building's suggestions of a contrived 'radical chic', it has been in no way artificially 'distressed'. At the same time, little attempt has been made to conceal what evidence of the theatre's former splendour lingers. More than 50 feet high, the towering and unadorned back wall is scarred and pitted by the wear and tear of the years, like an aged and leprous human face. At the time of *Timon*, the only trace of what was the stage and its machinery was a wide horizontal band traversing the base of the wall and a dark square stain above: the frame of the old stage picture, like a faded photographic negative or a Turin shroud recalling a dead form of theatre. The present playing area, originally the front stalls and stage, forms an earth-covered empty space of great depth. The full horse-shoe shape of the ground floor benches – located on the same level as the performance space – and of the three crumbling rococo balconies above, invest the theatre with a spatial concentration and a direct relationship with spectators. The structure is as dynamic and potent as the configuration the group had encountered repeatedly in Africa, on the carpet at the centre of a circle of villagers: a vibrant elemental bowl of focus.

Above all, the Bouffes reflects Brook's desired economy of means, his growing asceticism in a move towards a 'poor' theatre, within which the actor is free to communicate intimately and directly. Brook believes that the central lesson learnt in Africa was the imperative to reinject human content into theatre practice at every level – to place human being in relation to human being in form, content and space. In all of the Bouffes performances I have attended, the spectator is treated with respect, as active participant and even co-creator of a fluid theatre language. Brook has described his work at the Bouffes as an attempt to rediscover something of theatre's lost role as affirmatory and celebratory oasis, both social and spiritual meeting place. His ideal remains a shared space, literally and metaphorically, within which to 'reunite the community, in all its diversity, within the same shared experience'; in other words, to make theatre *necessary*, and potentially a modern-day *fiesta* enabling a community to taste *communitas*, to become 'whole' for a moment. In an ongoing search to uncover conditions permitting a continually supple and envolving relationship with an audience, he has come to believe that the theatre event is richest when audience, performance group and indeed work performed are made up of disparate elements – a mixed group made only provisionally homogeneous within a common experience.

Figure 1.1 The interior of the Bouffes du Nord. (CICT photograph)

Despite the essentialist and utopian assumptions underlying so much of this (for which Brook has received substantial personal criticism over the years), the tone of this theatre of myth and archetype is never nostalgic or escapist, and the form is ever evolving and provocative. A number of the less sympathetic commentators fail to tease out the ideological implications and repercussions of certain verifiable aspects in the work, from the company structure and make-up, and the actor-based working process, to the explicitly non-hierarchical relationship to any spectator visiting the Bouffes.[7] These are all clear political choices that should be read and accredited as such. I believe that the Centre's theatre practice remains confrontational, although sometimes admittedly in a rather politically insulated (and at times myopic) sense. However, rather than being mystical or quietist in impulse, it offers a compelling and recurrent provocation to individual and personal action in social contexts *beyond* theatre, for both actors and spectators.

TIMON OF ATHENS

The new base was opened to the public for the first time in October 1974, with a starkly uncluttered production of Shakespeare's *Timon d'Athènes* (*Timon of Athens*). Although one of the least performed of Shakespeare's plays, arguably it is one of the most pertinent thematically and structurally. In a stripped and polished French version by Jean-Claude Carrière, formerly a close collaborator and screenwriter for Luis Buñuel, the kernel of this difficult work was made available to a much wider contemporary public than perhaps ever before. All of its 112 performances in Paris were sold out, and it was subsequently awarded the Grand Prix Dominique for best production of the year, as well as the Prix du Brigadier. The production also attracted significant critical praise in France, although inevitably a small number of 'bardolatrous' purists and conservative journalists from the other side of the Channel immediately condemned Carrière's efforts on principle, as an act of vandalism.

Ever the humanist, Brook chose to see *Timon* in terms of 'commitment in a human situation'. Timon 'faces the profound liberal dilemma', and fails. Like the birds in *Conference*, he finds himself faced with the unknown; unlike them, according to Brook, he 'dies in confusion. He has not reached any point of transcendent understanding'. For Brook, the fable's 'universal' quality investigates the nature of the relationship of the individual to society, rather than the individual himself. The production implicitly posed, and left unresolved, a number of questions. Is our society reaching a point of no return similar to that of Timon's Athens? In our position of crisis and change, what must be saved and what destroyed?

At first the work to liberate the life of a text created certain difficulties for Brook's actors, all of whom were highly proficient after their African experiences in freer, more improvisatory forms, yet lacked appropriate and recent textual experience. In polar contrast with what Brook had encountered at the Royal Shakespeare Company in Stratford, here the shared experiences of the preceding three years had encouraged an opening towards certain 'areas of sound, rhythm, movement – the concrete nature of what seems abstract'. And throughout the Centre's work, Brook has attempted to reappraise what he considers to be the pseudo-profundity and inevitable vulgarity of an exclusive emphasis on psychological sub-text, and on creation through the limitations and distortions of a bastard-ized vision of Stanislavskian emotional memory. Instead, he has proposed an interpretation of 'non-interpretation' in which what is communicated is primarily the direct physical conviction of the actors, their *presence* and *individuality*. It is surely no coincidence that the company members' work has sometimes been mistakenly received as amateur, a fact that their director (if not the actors themseves) happily embraces as a compliment.

THE IK

The second Bouffes production made explicit the anthropological under-tones of much of Brook's work since the inception of the Centre. *Les Iks* (*The Ik*) was an adaptation of Colin Turnbull's study of the demise of a Northern Ugandan tribe, *The Mountain People*. Brook believes that this material offered the possibility of a radical multi-textuality, for it fused 'a personal experience, objective facts and poetic, mythic elements'[8] – the empiricism of an anthropological field study as well as an allegorical vision of our own condition and predicament – with Turnbull's own horrified journey into the liberals 'heart of darkness' as the point of union.

In performance it became a collision of discourses: the story of an African tribe's auto-destruction told by actors of five different nationalit-ies. As in all of his work, Brook chose to present it as a parable about us. The production constructed and foregrounded implicit parallels with contemporary social problems in the post-industrial urban West:

> The Ik survive at a cost – and so do we. The parallels are alarming. For me it's the pefect metaphor, something which exists on two levels – real in the sense of life as we know it, and real in the deep sense of myth.

For Brook, in this instance the actors' work could be based neither exclu-sively on a dispassionate relating of documentary facts, nor on total imper-sonation. Nevertheless during an intensive period of study, they copied in minute detail the postures and expressions of the Ik as recorded in Turnbull's photographs. While others observed, corrected or criticized, an actor would improvise the action or movement preceding and succeeding the single moment captured on film. Through this strictly physiological

13

and plastic reprocessing of material, it was hoped that the actor would gradually make contact with echoes of his/her own experience, eventually tasting somatically and organically 'the reality of that hunger: not from an emotion, but from an exact sense inside himself of what it meant to be standing in that position with that part of your body sagging and with that part of your mouth open'.

A mass of material drawn from episodes in Turnbull's book was thrown up in improvisation. At one point, the actors even built and lived in an Ik stockade within the theatre. Although much of this material was necessarily discarded later in the refining and writing processes, it had served its purposes of enabling them to a certain extent to 'become' Ik. One of Brook's apparent goals had been to employ this approach of 'saturated naturalism' to enable a racially mixed group of actors, using ordinary clothes and no make-up, to transcend their appearances and represent a recognizable essence of Ik-ness (the 'myth').

It soon became apparent that, as a reflection of the company's lack of ideological focus, this was a problematic and seriously flawed piece: there is simply too critical a distance between a constructed performative model of the 'reality of hunger' and the reality itself. And with hindsight it is perhaps understandable that a number of critical commentators were unimpressed. For this project, the fruit of a theatre company cushioned by subsidy, seemed to be an expression of an amoral Hobbesian nihilism, even of a deep-seated misanthropy, the entire work hovering on the brink of obscenity: in reductive terms, like making a cautionary tale about the dissolution of human values in Thatcher's Britain, using the egotism and materialism of the starving in Ethiopia as metaphorical narrative parallel. An essentialist and formalist reading of such material *as myth* was bound to infuriate many. As Albert Hunt, a former collaborator of Brook's in the late 1960s, suggested in an account of his own responses in *New Society*, in such a context the 'myth' had become a radically different discursive construct, a new 'text':

> Listening to the applause that burst out in the crowded Bouffes after the last Ik had vomited up his last sack of relief grain, and then dragged his twisted limbs into a hole at the back of the stage, I couldn't help thinking that Brook, the miracle worker, had pulled it off again. He'd made the Ik enjoyable.[9]

JARRY'S *UBU*

An entirely different quality of enjoyment underpinned the third work to be added to the Centre's repertoire, *Ubu aux Bouffes*, a production which none the less clearly coincided with the *Weltanschauung* represented in the cycle of Bouffes productions. In some ways, Ubu is an Ik. His

14

conception of reality is mono-dimensional. His world, the very antithesis of that in *Conference*, is one of extreme materialism and unadulterated egotism: reduced to its lowest common denominator, the world as stomach. For Brook, the primary value of Jarry's work lay in the way in which such content had been treated. By stylizing Ubu's amoral monstrosity, disintegrating language and exploding traditional forms – all of which are compressed within Ubu's abusive catchphrase, 'Merdre!' – the play as a whole is tilted off balance, and consequently taken far outside the parameters of social documentation.

The company successfully found a resonant equivalent for Jarry's anarchic linguistic primitivism in the playful manipulation of found everyday objects, a working process already outlined above in relation to improvisations in Africa. Bricks, sticks and so on were dislocated from their normal limited referential frame, new (temporary) functions endlessly redefined for them by the actor. The general tone of this 'rough' production was one of comic invention and vaudevillian celebration, its frenetic rhythm reminiscent of silent movies. During one sequence, for instance, Ubu rode on top of an enormous industrial cable spool – '*voiturin à phynances*', a royal state chariot, bulldozer and war machine – which was employed to devastate a fragile peasant dwelling. Some of these peasants were 'crushed' as the spool ran over them, emerging in its wake flattened into the ground: an image from Keaton or *Tom and Jerry*. During a scene of winter snowfall, Ubu tossed a fistful of confetti into the air above his head, teeth chattering audibly as it floated down over him. In similar style, the Russian offensive and bombardment of Ubu's army – just two actors in accordance with Jarry's specifications – were suggested by dropping a large number of silver rubber 'superballs' from the balconies, these tiny 'bombs' bouncing exhaustingly on the concrete floor and back into the auditorium, the image as a whole syncopated and underscored by Toshi Tsuchitori's driving percussive battery.

CONFERENCE OF THE BIRDS

After successful international tours of *The Ik* and *Ubu*, an adaptation of Shakespeare's *Measure for Measure* by Jean-Claude Carrière, a film version of G. I. Gurdjieff's semi-autobiographical *Meetings with Remarkable Men*, shot on location in Afghanistan, and a fleeting return to the RSC at Stratford for a muted new production of *Antony and Cleopatra* with Alan Howard and Glenda Jackson, Brook felt compelled to go back to 'Attar's *Conference of the Birds*. The thematic elements of struggle and search; the thirst for a beyond, a 'something more'; the intercultural bird idiom as reflection of humankind's inner aspirations, one's desire to extend oneself into 'flight' – for Brook, all offered the possibility of a theatre of myth and poetry.

15

Continually returned to as source material for free improvisatory work throughout the 1970s, *Conference* had become a symbol of the collective work for the members of the group: the focal point for a development of a commitment to their own ideals, a provocation to push further into new uncharted territory. At the end of the first decade of the Centre's existence, it was felt that the poem remained the only viable material offering the possibility of approaching Brook's cherished ideal of a multi-textual density ('totality') in theatre language. It was a natural choice for a production which would be a fusion, and in some ways a summation, of the diverse areas of investigation undertaken to that point.

Brook publicly justified the Centre's determination to stage *Conference* in terms of its 'objectivity' (Brook-speak for universality) and its 'inexhaustible richness':

> There are very few masterpieces in the world that have gone beyond subjective experience, that really touch something, that involve a real witness of man's essential experience . . . *Conference* has always been a challenge because it goes beyond one's capacity to penetrate it completely. Nobody can completely take hold of it, so that as something to work on it's inexhaustible.[10]

The production that emerged traced 'Attar's pellucid narrative by means of a lyrical and eloquent theatricality. Brook studiously grounded the performance vocabulary in an array of popular theatre/storytelling techniques and conventions. So for example the group made use of masks and puppets, to ease the multi-transformations demanded of the actor *qua* storyteller. Brook was convinced that certain ancient Balinese masks were denser, more 'essential' expressions of a 'human truth': a means of accessing poetry and music in contrast to the prose of the face. Their intensification of psychological states through simplification took them from the specific to the 'universal'. Masks were also displaced from conventional usage, and were used for example as puppets – extended at the end of an arm wrapped in evocative material, tiny subtle hand or arm movements amplified in the object to animate it as individualized 'character'. When a beggar represented in this way was executed, the actor simply bent his wrist and the mask plopped to the ground. I remain convinced that the performance language elaborated here forcefully vindicated some of Brook's more apparently contentious claims, for all was immediate, naive and mobile.

In 1980 the company travelled to New York and the Adelaide Arts Festival in Australia, performing three of their major works – *Ubu, The Ik* and *Conference*. On the final day in New York, all three were presented as a continuous sequence, an explicit statement of the relationship of the parts to a thematically coherent whole. Here was a body of work to be considered together, or even, as Brook told Margaret Croyden of the *New*

York Times, simply as one three-part play. As a trilogy, these plays comprise a lucid reflection of the Centre's aesthetic, social and ideological concerns:[11] *Ubu*, an explosive 'rough' work about callous and murderous inhumanity that bobbed along with the playful violence of an animation or a children's game; *The Ik*, a sparse study of a dying tribe, played out by the brittle human debris of the material and spiritual wasteland Ubu leaves in his wake: a sad and bitter song of disillusion and defeat; and finally *Conference*, with its starting point in a recognition of the implications of an Ik world – an account of an arduous journey, both literal and metaphorical, in search of sense, self and understanding; a glimmer of optimism, the world as it could be.

When read in this way, Brook and his actors were proposing a critique by recounting an epic fable that admitted mankind's greatest enemy to be mankind itself, yet ultimately rejected the despair of nihilism and even outlined a way forward. The mythical journey we have shared in this critique has taken us from the desolation of rampant materialism and egotism towards reintegration, harmony and healing. It is a restorative movement towards life – an itinerary later echoed in another three-part play, *The Mahabharata*.

LA TRAGÉDIE DE CARMEN

Over the next few years, the members of the Centre dispersed to pursue their own work around the world; some of them would never return. Meanwhile Brook staged a handful of productions in which the experiences shared and ideas developed within the Centre were conveyed to and further evolved by new groups or performers. There was a crisply observed new version of Chekhov's bitter-sweet masterpiece *The Cherry Orchard*, with Brook's wife Natasha Parry as Ranevskaya. Performances of smouldering physicality and energy fully complemented the text's rhythmic montage of minutely observed emotional changes to present us with a satisfying illusion of the movement of life itself. Audiences flocked to the Théâtre Montparnasse to see Brook's production of the boulevard comedy *Tchin-Tchin*, co-directed by Maurice Bénichou, an integral member of the Centre as performer; the production starred Natasha Parry and Marcello Mastroianni. Brook also found time to co-write with Carrière the screenplay for Volker Schlöendorff's *Un Amour de Swann*: a single episode of obsessive love extracted from Proust's mammoth *A la recherche du temps perdu*, but in some ways a miniature reflecting the whole.

Finally Brook directed a revolutionary new version of *Carmen*, his first opera work for thirty years and a sell-out wherever it has played in the world to date. Almost a quarter of a million people have seen it live, surely some sort of record in opera? The production flouted every convention one cares to name, and there were a few predictable accusatory cries of vandalism and tinkering. However it brought a radical new vitality – and audience – to opera, the genre of pompous elitist immutability *par excellence*: in Brook's experience, 'a prehistoric monster'.

During the preparatory period, Brook had led his performers in strenuous daily movement sessions for ten long weeks. Not only did he want to free the singers from gestural and vocal cliches by establishing an organic relationship between voice and movement – one of the cornerstones of his work with the Centre. In addition, he insisted on the need for their bodies to be shocked back into a state of alertness, in which voice, thought and gesture could assume a fresh integration. And in the re-embodied *Carmen* that emerged, performers endeavoured to engage their entire physiologies to sing. Song itself came to seem the most natural and appropriate form of expression – crystalline, transparent, a dense poetry of the soul whose emotional marrow communicated instantly. Here was an uninsulated language of passion.

Although Marius Constant's sinewy score made melody immediate and active, Brook chose to prioritize the dramatic/narrative line above the musical line at every level. There were no choruses, no star system. Each 80-minute performance involved only four young singers and two actors, although, for the piece to be presented nightly like a play, it was necessary to prepare three casts in parallel. In the end ten singers from a company of twelve alternated performances. The conventional orchestra pit was abandoned as an insurmountable barrier separating audience and performers. The orchestra itself was reduced in size to a fifteen-piece chamber ensemble, as if this were a 'chamber opera', then split into two parts placed visibly (and stereophonically, using the back wall as sounding board) *behind* the singers. This freed the singers from the usual obligation to take their leads from a conductor. Instead the orchestra supported and fed their work – a total revision of the traditional spatial and hierarchical relationship.

The acting style was as direct and elemental as the performance area itself – an arena filled with red sand: a bullring, the scorched earth of Andalusia, the 'bowl of living human focus' that Brook had experienced in African village squares. The event's characterizing components were movement, energy, physical contact and intimacy. The performers sat or lay down, made love, fought, rolled in the dirt; all the while able to sing *mezzo voce*, as if the arias were *lieder*. Ritual and magic coloured every relationship. An anonymous gypsy hag traced a circle of ochre powder around Don Jose and Carmen as their love was consummated. Three tiny votive fires hissed and crackled at the circle's rim – an ambiguous multi-textual configuration, for the image of plenitude and harmony in union was offset by darker undercurrents: the funerary rites of Africa and India sprang to mind. Was the circle protective or imprisoning? For in Merimée's

18

Spain 'l'amour' is almost synonymous with 'la mort', and fate too is cyclical and ineluctable.

EPIC STORYTELLING: *THE MAHABHARATA*

Since the late 1970s, much of the creative energy of Brook and certain core Centre members had been devoted to realizing a theatre adaptation of the world's longest narrative poem, a 2,000-year-old Sanskrit heroic epic, *The Mahabharata*. For Brook and Carrière, this had been an epic undertaking in more ways than one. At eighteen volumes and almost 100,000 verses in its full form, in the west *The Mahabharata*'s size alone has spawned a number of statistical comparisons with western epic poetry, the jaw-dropping brand of comparison much beloved of journalists looking for instant copy. Fifteen times the length of the *Bible*, we are told; eight times the length of *The Iliad* and *Odyssey* combined; more than thirty times the length of *Paradise Lost*!

Rather more fruitfully, some commentators have preferred to treat the epic as a repertory, even a library, rather than as a single book.[12] Alongside *The Ramayana*, it forms a central compendium of Hindu culture, an encyclopaedic storehouse recording myth, edificatory legend and history, political, legal and religious doctrine, as well as moral and philosophical discussion. In addition to the *Bhagavad Gita*, it contains the famous stories of Savitri, Nala and Damayanti and Shakuntala, even a version of *The Ramayana*. It is little wonder, then, that in India and throughout South East Asia it has become the common source for the bulk of the dramatic material of dance drama, storytellers, popular folk players, puppet shows, films and even strip cartoons.

To this day it is considered by Hindu scholars and public alike as the most substantial work of imagination their culture has ever produced. In *The Literatures of India*, Edward Dimock attempts a rather breathless analogy with western culture:

> One would have to imagine something like the following: an *Iliad*, rather less tightly structured than it now is, incorporating an abbreviated version of *The Odyssey*, quite a bit of Hesiod, some adapted sequences from Herodotus, assimilated and distorted pre-Socratic fragments, Socrates by way of Plato by way of Plotinus, a fair proportion of the Gospels by way of moralizing stories, with the whole complex of two hundred thousand lines worked over, edited, polished, and versified in hexameters by successive waves of anonymous church fathers. In the Western tradition this seems incredible. In the Indian civilization, *The Mahabharata* is a fact.[13]

The CICT version was premiered at the 1985 Avignon Festival in France as a twelve-hour cycle of three plays, each self-contained part titled to

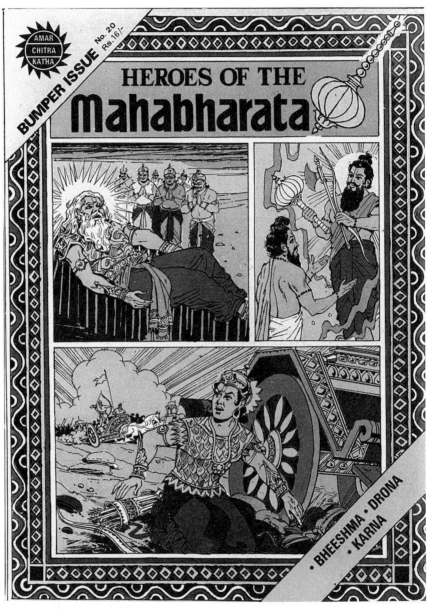

Figure 1.2 An edition of the Amar Chitra Katha cartoon *Mahabharata*, published in Bombay, India.

reflect its central narrative content: *The Game of Dice, Exile in the Forest, The War*. Although both Brook and Carrière had been reading and working on translations of the epic poem for almost a decade, and Brook himself had been aware of it through the *Gita* since the mid-1960s, the limpid and restrained French text by Carrière that emerged had been almost three years in the writing. The closed rehearsal period itself, including a journey to India for everyone involved in the project, had lasted more than six months. Subsequently, an English-language version, in Brook's own translation and with the production to some degree recast and reworked, toured the world in 1987–8, playing in six countries on four continents. Finally a five-and-a-half hour film version, shot in studios near Paris, was released in late 1989.[14]

The Provençal city of Avignon is renowned for its medieval papal palaces, its bridge and its granite quarries. Typically, Brook chose to reject conventional festival venues in favour of a remote amphitheatrical quarry on the banks of the Rhône south of Avignon, the towering cliff face texturally reminiscent of the Bouffes' pitted and ravaged back wall. Brook believes that such places offer a concentrated elemental bowl organically linked to natural surroundings, a found space resonating with the spirit of a civilization's relationship to its environment. It was Anstey's Hill quarry, the site of the Centre's Adelaide Festival programme in 1980 (and perhaps before that the desert ruins of Persepolis used for *Orghast* in Iran) that first instilled in Brook a taste for such spaces. To stretch a metaphor, here is a director who has fossicked through the scree of the world's cultures, digging deep into the bedrock of theatre forms in the hope of exposing an ore: a living theatre language, radical in the etymological sense of the word (a return to roots), of and for our time. Despite the accessibility of forms elaborated, the Centre's experimentation has never been cosmetic.

A series of quarries (in Avignon, Athens, Perth and Adelaide), a boathouse on the shores of a Swiss lake, a film studio sound stage in Los Angeles, a disused transport museum in Glasgow, the newly renovated Majestic Theatre in Brooklyn, the Bouffes du Nord – these diverse spaces and others chosen as tour venues for the production, whether inside or in the open air, share a number of common qualities: first, a dynamic spatial configuration facilitating the possibility of a direct, immediate and fluid relationship with an audience; second, a starkness and economy of means; third, a palpable quality of weathered textured humanity, the location itself as literalization of the passage of time, bearing visible traces of its past – in the case of the buildings, most of them late nineteenth-century industrial designs, their former function now redundant, an anachronism; finally, their settings outside or on the fringes of the conventional cultural geography of a city, most requiring a certain effort to be reached –

the 'extra-ordinary' journey as act of literal and metaphorical displacement becoming an event in itself.

In the tradition of heroic romance, the central narrative of the Epic (as it is called in India) is encrusted with countless loosely related episodes. In a rather excited description, Herman Oldenberg manages to convey something of the poem's scope and size, as well as of its allure:

> Besides the main story, there are veritable forests of small stories, and besides, numberless and endless instructions on theology, philosophy, natural science, law, politics, practical and theoretical knowledge of life. [It is] a poem full of deeply significant dreamings and surmisings, delicate poetry and schoolmasterly platitude, full of sparkling play of colour, of oppressive and mutually jostling masses of images, of show-ers of arrows, of endless battles, clash after clash of death-despising heroes, of over-virtuous ideal men, of ravishing beautiful women, of terrible tempered ascetics, adventurers and fabulous beings . . . [15]

Brook and Carrière endeavoured to chisel free a viable narrative spine from this sprawling material. In essence, their resultant text traces the story – a collision of dreams – of two warring families, the misguided and venomous Kauravas (the 'sons of darkness') and their exiled cousins the Pandavas (the 'sons of light'). The narrative takes us from their magical origins in some fabulous pre-historical Edenic 'golden age' to their apoca-lyptic mutual destruction during an eighteen-day battle: from Genesis to Revelations.

The attraction of such material for Brook is readily comprehensible, on the level both of richness of dramatic content (what could be more dramati-cally compelling than the end of the world?) and of underpinning arche-type and myth. He maintains that, as a vision of a society in discord teetering on the very brink of auto-destruction, this 'great poem of the world' (the inferred meaning of the Sanskrit title) affords us the closest mythological reflection of our present reality. Brook has repeatedly and consistently sought to locate that quality Eliot described as 'the present moment of the past'. For, as Irving Wardle has pointed out, Brook shares Ottomar Krejca's radical conviction that theatre can embrace the modern world only by 'retreating' from it and re-enacting past narratives.[16]

Like *Conference*, the production was presented as a fable of desolation, reconciliation and healing, a mythic journey from disruptive division to reintegration. Here was a morality play or cautionary tale alarmingly pertinent to a divided post-nuclear world. *The Mahabharata* has been called a 'Doomsday Epic', and indeed, when Robert Oppenheimer saw the first murderous flash of a split atom, he immediately recalled a passage from this mythological holocaust: the blinding vision in the *Gita* of Krish-na's *visvarupa*, Arjuna's theophany as Krishna reveals his universal form to his disciple. In all of Brook's productions with the Centre, myth becomes concrete and immediate. It is implied that we are all in some ways Ubu, Ik, Kaurava and Pandava.[17]

At the heart of the Sanskrit original, and of Brook's production, is the celebrated *Bhagavad Gita*, Hinduism's most influential devotional work, within which the archer and warrior-yogin Arjuna, demi-god son of Indra and heroic prince of the Pandavas, discusses with Krishna the necessity and propriety of war. Krishna, an avatar of Vishnu, suggests that the real conflict is with the self on the 'battlefield of the soul'. One's ultimate responsibility must be to struggle incessantly for the preservation of the light of *dharma*: the law of personal conduct, truth and understanding that has to be respected to ensure balance in the cosmos as a whole. When it is located in the context of an ongoing agonistic narrative, the *Gita* is a very different entity from the one championed by Gandhi and others. And the problematic interpretation of and apparent contradictions within the theory and practice of *dharma*, discussed in detail in Chapters 6, 13 and 14, provide much of the philosophical substance and dramatic tension both in the original epic and in the Centre's production. Ultimately, while the poem resolutely refuses any easy answers – either politically, psychologically or morally – this Doomsday Epic never becomes a Book of Despair. The original *Mahabharata* itself repeatedly claimed to be a beneficial poem: all who hear it will be somehow cleaner, better.

'Listen to stories', Vyasa advises the child, our representative, 'it's always pleasant and sometimes it improves you.' At its most basic level the performance is self-consciously framed as the recounting of a story by a group of mixed nationality to an assembled ring of spectators. Brook has differentiated between an 'actor', who fully inhabits an imaginary character, sinking his/her own personality in an act of identification and self-transformation, and a 'performer', a Piaf or Garland who becomes fully charged only as his/her individuality blossoms under the focused spotlight of an audience's attention. Brook has encouraged the Centre members to amalgamate the two in the skilled storyteller, who retains the actor's capacity for transformability and psycho-physical empathy, and at the same time remains unencumbered by the superficial trappings of naturalistic impersonation and celebrates his/her individuality. The ideal relationship with one's role(s) in a storytelling framework can be related to both Brecht and puppetry: 'distanced without distancing', the storyteller can either foreground the role or slide towards a state of 'transparency' and 'invisibility' by effacing the role and prioritizing his/her function as narrative tool, available to serve the needs of the particular moment and context. In the production of *The Mahabharata* – the crystalline realization of the actor-as-storyteller *topos* – this presence/absence flux engenders an incessant movement between representation and presentation: a scenographic and affective oscillation between jolting savagery and dispassionate objectivity, incandescent passion and reflective observation.

THE POLITICS OF INTERCULTURALISM: THE CICT
MAHABHARATA AND INDIA

Brook proposes that *The Mahabharata* is 'anonymous', in the same way as the work of Shakespeare or 'Attar, an 'objective' expression of what is 'essential' in human experience, rather than the fruit of a subjective, and therefore 'incomplete', consciousness. Moreover as a *liber mundi* of 'universal interest', he has repeatedly claimed it belongs to the world, not only to India. Habitually in interview, at this point he backtracks and qualifies this contentious statement by adding the paradoxical and conciliatory – for Hindus – qualification that only India could have produced it.

Sadly Brook seems unwilling to confront the dangers concomitant with applying a culturally non-specific, essentialist/humanist aesthetic to such material. He has done himself a great disservice by never satisfactorily accounting in public for his production's relationship to Hindu culture in India, or teasing out the ideological repercussions of that relationship. Whether unwittingly or deliberately, in response to the media hype generated around the production Brook has often erected a defensive philosophical smokescreen of equivocating vagaries, within which there is a recurrent and disjunctive confusion between reductive simplification and reverential profundity. He has repeatedly laid himself open to understandable charges, not only of insensitivity but more damagingly of neo-colonialist paternalism and, in some circles, of cultural appropriation as theft (see e.g. Chapters 16 and 18 in this volume). This is an instance not of intercultural exchange, we are told, but of wholesale plunder or rape, for behind his 'mask' of tolerant liberalism Brook is authoritarian and self-serving. As the self-appointed representative of a 'universal culture', it is suggested, he has pillaged world culture in search of new territories, then planted his own imperialist flag in the flank of the quintessential Hindu work, a work so vast that it has never before been staged in its entirety. The fact that Brook set his sights on realizing just that can only be symptomatic of his megalomania, even of a 'Messianic paternalism, translating the mysterious into the banal for the grateful, exotica-starved homefront'.[18]

Some of this strikes me as an inappropriate and doctrinaire misreading of the production itself in the deceptive light of its inflated media attention ('the theatre event of the century', etc.), Brook's own unwillingness or inability to enter certain necessary conceptual debates and, above all, the immovable weight of the history of cultural hegemony. In response, one could suggest that Brook has only continued a process that has recurred throughout the lifespan of the Epic, a process of transposition and reinterpretation that has not only explicitly celebrated the material and brought it to a wider audience, but also infused the material with a new vitality. One thinks of the array of versions within India itself, from the recent highly popular synthetic Doordarshan TV series to the Amar Chitra Katha cartoons; of those evolving hybridized forms that have travelled with Hinduism throughout South East Asia, from Cambodia to Indonesia, even as far afield as Fiji or East Africa; or of politically and aesthetically radical 'transcreations' like the stunning Persian *Razm-nama* commissioned by the Mughal emperor Akbar in the sixteenth century.[19]

Alternatively one might look at the problem from a different angle and compare Brook's company's heterogeneous and discontinuous perform-ance language – a reflection of its structural make-up – with the imposition of a homogeneous traditional form on to appropriated mythological narra-tives; for example, recent Kathakali Kalamandalam versions of *The Iliad*, *King Lear* and even biblical and Koranic narratives performed in South West India, to the inevitable dismay of Kathakali purists with their unshakeable conviction that only Hindu Puranic and epic material can be 'appropriate'. Setting aside the fact that such experiments invigorate the Kathakali tradition, and are embraced as necessary to the continuing sur-vival of the form by many of its practitioners, doesn't the fact that there are both Christians and Muslims in Kerala (although one suspects few Greeks) make any difference? One would imagine so. Does it make any difference that Brook's company contains Hindus, not to mention Buddhi-sts, Muslims, Christians, Jews and others? Or does that in turn simply reflect, as some cynics have hinted, the extent of the villainous Brook's rapacious personal greed? The arguments can go round and round in circles. Brook is always going to be the 'villain' in such post-colonialist readings for the simple and unavoidable fact that he represents the eco-nomic, and *ipso facto* cultural, power and hierarchy of the west throughout the history of its relationship with Asia. Yet another instance of western entrepreneurs selling the marketable east to the west? Regrettably, the traffic has been almost exclusively one way.

While it is evidently fundamental in the context of a book such as this to address the serious accusations that have been hurled at Brook in the wake of this one project, at the same time I believe it is essential to preface the discussion by recognizing certain aspects of the Centre's work which are rarely mentioned in critical appraisal – to redress the balance somewhat by presenting both sides of the debate. For the issues are complex, and implications extend far beyond the parameters of this one instance. So, for example, it is surely germane to recognize the ideological repercussions of the Centre's multicultural company structure and working processes – in many ways an exemplary model – and to record their substantive impact upon the polyphonic performative discourses collectively elaborated here. Both the French- and English-language versions produced by the Centre bear tribute to Brook's skill as a director of actors and as multicultural catalyst. The English-language production, for example, involved a company of thirty performers and five musicians drawn from eighteen different nations.

Indeed, throughout the Centre's history, cultural difference and individuality have been cherished and celebrated within the work as sources of a creative friction, never homogenized or erased in the search for some imaginary theatrical esperanto. There is no question of the kind of patronizing tokenism implicit in suggestions of a UNESCO-style company casting policy, which anyone even vaguely familiar with the working processes will rightly reject as absurd. Productions have been marked by a consciously naive (in the *art brut* sense of the word) and textured mixture of styles, traditions, races and accents. Some may choose to detect recurrent evidence in productions of the group journeys to Africa, the Middle East, Asia and even Australia: alternatively one could just as well read this multi-/inter-textuality in large part as evidence of the creative input of culturally diverse individuals within the company. The performance style is 'open', discontinuous and self-subverting, endlessly remaking itself as it evolves to meet the demands of the moment: setting Brechtian techniques beside Artaudian shock tactics, combining storytelling skills with the hieratic physicality of Asian dance drama, knockabout cartoon humour and puppetry with the dynamism of martial arts. Its intellectual and affective impact stems from its non-homogeneity and its rigorous rejection of any formulaic stylistic criteria.[20] The only determinant in this hotch-potch of conventions – some perhaps borrowed directly, others invented and erased in an instant – is the popular theatre imperative for communication to be direct and effective. The ultimate sanction is that what works, works . . .

NOTES

1 Ted Hughes, in A. C. H. Smith, *Orghast at Persepolis* (London: Methuen, 1972), p. 45.
2 In *The Birth of Tragedy*, Nietzsche wrote, 'Music, an expression of the world, is in the highest degree a universal language.' Cf. the symbolist Walter Pater's celebrated assertion that 'all art aspires to the condition of music'. For a much fuller account of the work on *Orghast*, and indeed of the body of Brook's work both with the Royal Shakespeare Company and with his Paris-based Centre, please refer to David Williams' compilation *Peter Brook, A Theatrical Casebook* (London: Methuen, 1988).
3 Brook, in Peter Wilson, 'Sessions in the USA: A Chronicle' (Paris: CICT, 1973, unpublished), p. 25.
4 Jung himself had originally travelled to Africa to 'find that part of my personality which had become invisible under the pressure of being European' (*Memories, Dreams, Reflections*, London: Collins, 1977, p. 272).
5 Brook, in Margaret Croyden, *The Center: A Narrative* (Paris: CICT, 1980), unpaginated.
6 In 1974, to mark the intention to produce public performances at their new base, alongside continuing research in private, the Centre changed its name to

International Centre for Theatre Creations (CICT). However, since that time the acronyms CIRT and CICT have become fairly interchangeable, simply signalling different if complementary areas of concern.

7 A relationship that is non-hierarchical on two levels: first, on that of undermining any 'star' system or myth of theatre and performers – they share the same neighbourhood cafe as audience members, then enter the theatre through the same point of access – and second, on that of contact and engagement during the performance itself. One should also mention here the relationship fostered between the building and its company and their immediate community behind the Gare du Nord in Paris (free shows, Christmas and other events for local children, etc.), as well as that established through 'invisible' outreach work in other 'communities' (prisons, rehabilitation centres, new towns, immigrant workers' hostels, and so on); ticket pricing and distribution on standby for students, etc.

8 Brook, in Denis Cannan and Colin Higgins, *Les Iks* (Paris: CICT, 1975; French translation by Jean-Claude Carrière), p. 97.

9 Albert Hunt, 'Acting and Being', *New Society*, 20 February 1975, p. 468.

10 Brook, in Margaret Croyden, *The Center: A Narrative*, op. cit. (n5).

11 Typically, Brook chose to define all three as live performance in terms of celebration. The 'pure, rough, crude energy' of *Ubu* expressed the actors' 'celebration of energy', whereas the heightened naturalism of *The Ik* was a 'celebration of detail' (an unwitting reminder of the startling insensitivity of formalism!). Lastly, the intercultural resonances and accessibility of *Conference* offered a 'celebration of the possibility of crossing barriers'.

12 See, for example, Edward Dimock in *The Literatures of India* (Chicago: University of Chicago Press, 1974): '*The Mahabharata* became the founding library of Brahmin–Indian civilization. . . . In its eight centuries of formation it was to become the principal library of all texts that were written in the verse form called *sloka*, in the Sanskrit language, and in comformity with a growing Brahmanistic consensus. It is the massive effort of generations, nameless as generations, and grey like the consensus of generations' (p. 53).

13 ibid., p. 53.

14 For full details of cast lists, touring itinerary and film details, please see Chapter 20.

15 Quoted in C. R. Deshpande, *Transmission of the Mahabharata Tradition* (Simla: Indian Institute of Advanced Study, (1978), p. 6.

16 Irving Wardle, 'Brook and Shakespeare', paper presented at a conference in Taormina, Sicily, on the occasion of Brook's award of the Premio Europa per il Teatro, May 1989.

17 According to Eric Gould (*Mythical Intentions in Modern Literature*, Princeton, NJ: Princeton Unversity Press, 1981), myth and archetype need not be essentialist pre-existent structures, as they are for Jung and even Lévi-Strauss. Instead he suggests that they can provide a 'working proposition' in the process of interpretation. Rather than enacting reactionary nostalgia for lost Edenic origins, they can signal present absences, and operate as part of a radical critique.

18 From Liza Henderson's review of Brook's *The Shifting Point* ('Brook's Point', *Theater*, Spring 1988, p. 35 ff.). There have even been accusations of a deep-seated racism. See, for example, a virulent attack by Sadanand Menon printed in *The Hindu* ('Giving a bad name to interculturalism', 29 December 1989), which includes the following, re. Bhima's disembowelment of Duhsassana: 'what is reinforced (by having a black actor as Bhima) is a viewpoint that subconsciously pervades the narrative – the White West's conviction of the

"primitivism" of the African and the Asian, the racist stereotype of the "ignoble savage", of the black man's "natural" cannibalism. Now here is a filling in of our imagination and fantasy that is revoltingly negative, and in the Indian context positively crude. Obviously Brook lacked the guts to show a white man drinking human blood.'

Some might argue that Mr Menon's reading is itself implicitly 'racist', while at the same time it chooses to ignore the well-documented fact that a number of white actors were approached to play the part of Bhima. Indeed, the (white) American Andreas Katsulas was initially cast, only to drop out because of other commitments and be replaced by the Senegalese actor Mamadou Dioume: evidently skin colour was not a casting criterion. However, given the incidence in the past of racist representations of black people as cannibals, perhaps Brook should have been more aware of the possibility and indeed probability of such a reading here, as also in those episodes where black actors portray the demonic *rakshasas*. Menon is justified in responding only to what was included in performance.

It should also be added in this context that blackness *per se* is problematic in India. In many areas of Indian society, unquestionably it does carry overtly racist connotations of primitivism, just as lightness of skin can connote higher status and 'sophistication' – a reflection of the interconnection between economic power, cultural hegemony and geographic location. At the same time, the Sanskrit word 'krishna' means 'black', 'the dark one': in this context the connotative polar paradox is insolubly contradictory.

19 The *Razm-nama* (*Book of Wars*), a translation into Persian of *The Mahabharata*, is one of the most sumptuous of all early Mughal manuscripts. It was commissioned by Akbar in 1582. Now in the possession of the Maharaja of Jaipur in Rajasthan, and held in Jaipur's City Palace Museum, it includes 169 beautiful full-page colour miniatures.

20 See Roland Barthes, *Le Plaisir du texte* (Paris: Seuil, 1973, p. 10), in which he describes the 'pleasure' afforded to a reader by the coexistence (*cohabitation*) of antipathetic languages in collision.

2

A NARRATIVE SYNOPSIS OF *THE MAHABHARATA*

THE GAME OF DICE

A storyteller-poet called Vyasa announces to a child that he is going to tell him the history of his people, and that this story will constitute 'the poetical history of mankind'. Ganesha, the god with an elephant's head, arrives to offer his services as writer of this great poem. When questioned by the child, he tells his own story, explaining how he came to have the head of an elephant. Then he settles down to write.

Vyasa begins with the story of his own birth. He himself takes the part of his first protagonist, King Santanu, who falls in love with the river goddess Ganga: she bears him a remarkable son, called Bhishma.

Twenty years later, Santanu falls in love with another woman, Satyavati, the poet Vyasa's own mother. Her father, in agreeing to her marriage with Santanu, demands that their son become the future king. Santanu cannot accept, for he already has a son, Bhishma. Whereupon Bhishma, for the love of his father, vows to remain celibate so as never to have a child.

So Santanu marries Satyavati. They have a son, Vichitravirya, plagued by such poor health that he is unable to win a wife at a tournament, as was the custom. So Bhishma fights on behalf of his half-brother, and returns with three brides instead of one. One of them, Amba, is already secretly engaged. Bhishma allows her to leave, but her betrothed does not want her any more. Lost, alone and forlorn, she returns to Bhishma and demands that he marry her. Ever faithful to his vow, Bhishma refuses. Amba then swears that one day she will kill him. The gods however have granted Bhishma the power to choose the day of his death: he cannot be killed. Amba nevertheless swears that she will find a way to kill him.

The young king dies childless. Ganesha and Vyasa are profoundly worried: does this mean that the great poem of the world is over so soon, for want of protagonists? The young princesses must be given children. But who can father them? The only man in the family is Bhishma, and he has renounced women. So Satyavati asks her first-born son, Vyasa himself, to give children to the two princesses. The author of the poem

29

fulfils his duties, but the princesses flinch from contact with him, for he is filthy and smells. He then explains to them that they will each bear a son: however, the first will be born blind because the first princess closed her eyes when seeing him, and the second will be pale-skinned because the second princess blanched at his touch. The blind son is called Dhritarashtra, the pale one is Pandu. Pandu is made king, but before long he is cursed by a gazelle he killed while it was enjoying the pleasures of love: should he make love to either of his two wives (Kunti and Madri), he will die instantly.

Pandu goes to live with his wives in the mountains. Kunti, his first wife, informs him that she possesses a magic power. By reciting a secret formula, she can invoke a god at will and have a child by him. The mantra's power is put to the test straight away, and three sons are born to her. Yudishthira, the first-born, truthful and scrupulous, son of the god Dharma; Bhima, the strongest of men, son of Vayu, god of the wind; and Arjuna, an irresistible warrior, son of Indra. In turn Madri, Pandu's second wife, makes use of this power too. She gives birth to twin sons, Nakula and Sahadeva. Thanks to his two wives, Pandu now has five sons directly descended from the gods: the Pandavas, the 'heart' of Vyasa's poem.

Meanwhile, following his brother's exile, Dhritarashtra has become king, despite his blindness. He marries Gandhari. When she learns of her husband's infirmity, she decides to cover her eyes with a blindfold which she will never remove. Then, after an abnormally long pregnancy and an extraordinary birth, she becomes the mother of one hundred sons, the Kauravas. The first born is called Duryodhana. Sinister omens of disharmony and violence greet his arrival into the world: he brings with him hate and destruction.

One spring day Pandu dies, because he prefers love to life. Madri joins him on the funeral pyre. The first age of the world – its childhood – is coming to an end. In the future lies a terrible war – incomprehensible, universal. Satyavati, the poet's mother, disappears into the forest forever.

Bhishma, by now already an old man, decides to bring up the two sets of cousins, the Pandavas and the Kauravas, together. But everything tears them apart: ever since their youth they have quarrelled and even tried to kill each other. Enter Drona, a prodigious master of arms, who discovers in Arjuna a singularly gifted archer. Drona promises to make him the best, not shrinking from asking a young rival of Arjuna's, who also yearns to be Drona's pupil, to cut off his thumb, thereby forfeiting his skill and strength.

Arjuna's superiority is soon contested, in the course of an archery tournament, by an extremely dangerous newcomer, called Karna. Welcomed by Duryodhana and consecrated king by him – the Kaurava prince recognizes in him the most useful of allies – Karna swears eternal friendship. However, as we learn from Vyasa, Karna is in reality Kunti's first-born child, the result of her union with the Sun long ago. So he is in fact the unknown brother of the Pandavas, against whom he will one day fight to the death.

The five Pandavas marry. A careless phrase of their mother's obliges them all to share one woman as their wife – Draupadi, paragon of women: she binds them together irrevocably. And as increasingly dark omens gather in the background, Krishna makes his appearance. It is said he may be an incarnation of the god Vishnu, the preserver, come down to save the earth from chaos. On his advice the Pandavas present themselves to the blind king. Ignoring the protestations of his brother Bhima, Yudishthira accepts a worthless part of the kingdom, in the hope of averting a war which all now feel to be unavoidable.

Several years pass happily. Yudishthira could well believe that Vyasa's great poem has come to an end: but this is only the beginning. He must now be crowned king of kings. His coronation ceremony elicits a sudden violent outburst from a young prince, Sisupala. Krishna uses his prodigious disc, a miraculous weapon, to cut off Sisupala's head.

Duryodhana, the eldest of the Kauravas, cannot stand Yudishthira's wisdom and power. He follows the advice of his uncle, the cunning Shakuni, an infamous dice player, and invites Yudishthira to a game, knowing full well that gambling is his cousin's one weakness. Yudishthira accepts. Carried away by the intoxication of the game (and for other secret reasons), he loses all that he possesses: his lands, his kingdom – even his brothers, even himself, and eventually even Draupadi, their joint wife, who is dragged before the company by her hair. She is about to be stripped naked when she invokes Krishna, who comes to her rescue. She swears that one day death will avenge her. There will be a war, a war without mercy.

It is perhaps in order to avert this war that Yudishthira agrees to a final game, a kind of double or quits. Once again, he loses. The Pandavas and Draupadi are condemned to spend twelve years in exile in the forest, and a thirteenth year in an unknown place, disguised so that no one may recognize them. They leave. Vyasa describes their departure to the blind king and queen.

EXILE IN THE FOREST

While the Kauravas grow increasingly uneasy in their palace, the Pandavas have withdrawn into the forest in hiding. There they encounter Amba, who had earlier sworn to kill Bhishma: she is still searching desperately for someone to perform the impossible task. A mysterious voice in the forest tells her that nothing can outwit death 'except death itself'. She leaves.

Draupadi and Bhima reproach Yudishthira for his inaction and resigned passivity. Since it is obvious that Shakuni cheated at dice, wouldn't it be better to stand up and fight? Yudishthira flatly refuses. He will keep his word: he resolves to follow his *dharma*. (*Dharma* is the moral obligation which each and every human being should recognize and follow; failure to do so could endanger the course of the cosmos as a whole.) Arjuna then leaves, aiming for the highest mountains to look for the divine weapons they will need one day. He entrusts his brothers with caring for Draupadi.

As night falls, Bhima keeps watch while the others sleep. There then appears a *rakshasa*, a creature of the night. She falls madly in love with Bhima, who fights and kills her venomous brother. Bhima and the magical creature than have a child, who is called Ghatotkatcha: he swears to come to the aid of his father whenever necessary.

Meanwhile the Kauravas have come right into the forest. Duryodhana's vicious brother, Duhsassana, wants to destroy the Pandavas once and for all, but they are saved by Vyasa himself.

In the palace, the two mothers, Kunti and Gandhari, are increasingly worried. Kunti tries to persuade her unacknowledged son Karna not to take part in the war, but she fails.

Duryodhana wants to know the reasons for Arjuna's journey. Having evoked him by magic, he is able to watch as Arjuna fights with a mysterious hunter, who turns out to be the god Shiva himself. And Shiva gives Arjuna the supreme weapon, Pasupata, which is capable of destroying the world. And that is not all: Arjuna goes on to tell Karna about his journey in the celestial spheres. He has perfected knowledge of this weapon in the company of his father, the god Indra. Moreover, during his travels in the distant skies, a seductive creature (an *apsaras* called Urvasi) approaches Arjuna and offers herself to him. When he refuses, she curses him: one day he will lose his virility and he will be like a woman. His enemies, magically enabled to witness this scene, ask themselves whether it isn't at that precise moment that they should attack and destroy him.

One day, the Pandavas, still in exile, brush with death, 'killed' by the waters of a poisonous lake. However Yudishthira brings his brothers back to life by correctly answering the questions which the lake puts to him. They must now find a place to hide *dharma* for one year: Vyasa tells them to choose the disguise of their most secret desires.

Meanwhile Karna, who has promised Duryodhana victory, decides he too must acquire the ultimate weapon. The dangers grow ever closer, ever more threatening. Krishna, who has come to join Vyasa in the forest, is anxious, as is the boy to whom the story is being told.

For many months Karna serves an all-powerful hermit, Parashurama, the destroyer of warriors. As a reward, he bestows upon Karna, whom he takes to be a servant, a formula for the supreme weapon. But Karna reveals himself to be a warrior by an excess of bravery – he does not cry out when a worm bores a hole into his thigh. The hermit curses him and predicts that he will forget the secret formula at the moment he wishes for the weapon: and that will be the moment of his death.

According to the conditions of the game of dice, the thirteenth year which the Pandavas are to spend in disguise has now arrived. Yudishthira (who presents himself as a poor brahmin), his brothers and Draupadi (who pass for wandering servants) all find refuge at the court of King Virata. There they tell the story of Bhima's meeting in the forest with his half-brother Hanuman, the miraculous monkey god, whose tail he was not even able to lift. At this point, Yudishthira announces the coming of a dark age, the age of Kali: *Kaliyuga*.

A general in Virata's court, called Kitchaka, becomes infatuated with Draupadi. He goes to great lengths to possess her, even threatening her life. Draupadi implores the mighty Bhima to help her; so he goes in her stead to a secret rendezvous, and pulverizes the over-amorous general.

Meanwhile Duryodhana has launched an attack on Virata's kingdom. The king entrusts his troops to his young son Uttara, who declares he has no driver for his chariot. Draupadi – she seeks war at all costs – points out Arjuna as the world's best charioteer despite the fact that he has disguised himself as a transvestite dance instructor. Arjuna cannot refuse to fight and is decisively victorious. The Pandavas reveal their true identities, somewhat before the agreed time. Before leaving Virata's kingdom, they listen to Vyasa recount the ancient story of an earlier destruction of this world – a world which nevertheless remained alive and whole for more than one hundred years in the stomach of a single child.

War draws even closer. Duryodhana refuses to give his cousins back their kingdom because they came out of hiding before the appointed time. He tries to win Krishna's support, as does Arjuna. Arjuna chooses Krishna himself, alone and unarmed, allowing Duryodhana to have all of Krishna's armies. When Arjuna asks him to drive his chariot, Krishna accepts.

In the Kaurava court, the blind king, who is intimidated by his sons, also senses the imminence of war. He asks the elderly Bhishma, an unparalleled warrior, to take the supreme command. Bhishma reluctantly accepts, but on one condition: that Karna does not fight. Although very displeased, Karna bitterly agrees to fight only after Bhishma's death.

Krishna arrives as an envoy, in a final attempt to safeguard peace. He speaks to Duryodhana who does not listen to him. He reveals his universal form, which is only visible to those who have eyes to see. He talks with Bhishma, who is tied to the Kauravas, then with Kunti, who does everything in her power to push her sons into war. Finally, he speaks to Karna, going so far as to reveal to him the fact that he is the brother of those with whom he intends to fight. But Karna was abandoned by his mother in his very first hours of life; furthermore he senses the end of this world.

He will fight alongside the Kauravas, even though he can already foresee their defeat and his own death.

THE WAR

Just as the battle is about to start, Arjuna falters at the sight of his relatives, now his sworn enemies. He breaks down and refuses to fight. His charioteer Krishna addresses him as they pause in the no-man's land between the two armies. This is the celebrated *Bhagavad Gita*, the guide to firm and resolute action. Arjuna regains his fortitude, and his conch-shell sings out once more.

The battle begins, but it is impossible to overcome Bhishma. One evening in the camp, Bhishma receives a visit from the ghost of Amba. She has come to inform him of her death: she says that she threw herself into the fire and that she is now reborn as a man, called Sikhandin. After nine days of bloody fighting, the Pandavas come to Bhishma: they tell him that, unless he is killed in the war, the carnage will carry on until the end of the world. When asked how he can be defeated, he advises them to place Sikhandin in the front line, from where he will be able to fire freely at Bhishma.

The next day, confronted by Sikhandin, he makes one final challenge. But his will to live leaves him, and he abandons his weapons. An arrow strikes him; but it has not been fired from the bow of Amba-Sikhandin, who has suddenly forgotten all reason for hating Bhishma: it has been fired by Arjuna. Bhishma does not actually die until much later. He remains lying on a bed of arrows until the very end of the battle. Karna now takes up his weapons to enter the fray, and Duryodhana rejoices.

Drona, the master of arms, takes command. He positions the armies in a formation known only to him, the iron disc of war, which nobody knows how to break open – nobody apart from Arjuna. If only Arjuna can be diverted away from the central battle, Drona promises victory.

Karna is on his own at night. Kunti approaches him (she knows that he now intends to fight) and tries to persuade him to join the Pandavas. She confesses that she is his mother, and asks his forgiveness. But Karna is inflexible: he will fight against his brothers. However, he does promise Kunti that he will only kill Arjuna, for, as he says, one of them must die. In this way, she will still have the same number of sons after the war.

Arjuna has a second wife, Krishna's sister Subhadra. They have a 15-year-old son, Abhimanyu, who, by listening to his father while still in his mother's womb, has learnt to force an entry into Drona's battle formation, the iron disc. As Arjuna has been called to a diversionary battle far away, Yudishthira entrusts Abhimanyu with the task of opening a breach in the disc. Abhimanyu succeeds brilliantly. But when Bhima and Yudishthira try to follow him into the opening, they are stopped by the magic power of a single man, Jayadratha, and the breach closes behind the young Pandava. In spite of his bravery, Abhimanyu is killed.

Vyasa recounts to Yudishthira the origin of death, which he says 'kills no one'. At which point Arjuna returns to the camp. Inflamed with rage and grief at the sight of his son's body, he swears to kill Jayadratha before sunset on the following day. He solemnly swears to throw himself into the sacrificial fire, should he fail. Even Krishna is alarmed by this terrible oath. On the next day, Jayadratha is heavily guarded, and Arjuna is unable to reach him. It takes an extraordinary trick by Krishna – he causes a momentary eclipse of the sun – to enable Arjuna to kill Jayadratha, and thereby save his own life.

The following day, Karna hurls himself into the battle, fighting with immense skill and ferocity. He possesses a magic lance, the gift of a god, which will kill any living being but can be used only once. He keeps it in reserve – for Arjuna. To dispose of this lance, Krishna calls upon Ghatotkatcha, son of Bhima and the *rakshasa*. He appears immediately to defend his human family. During the night, he fights an epic battle against Karna, who can destroy the demon only by resorting to his magic lance. Ghatotkatcha is killed, but Krishna dances for joy. With his lance now expended, Karna is vulnerable and Arjuna can kill him.

First, it will be necessary to kill Drona, an invincible warrior, surpassing even Arjuna himself. He can be beaten only through knowledge of his weaknesses: his love for his only son Aswhattaman, and a curse which hangs over him. Bhima slays an elephant, also called Aswhattaman, then deceitfully tells Drona of the death of his son. Suspecting a lie, Drona asks Yudishthira for the truth: is his son dead, or not? In order to safeguard his armies, Yudishthira is forced into telling a half-life, which distresses him. Drona senses his energy and strength leaving him, and acquiesces to death. At Duryodhana's request, Drona's son Aswhattaman launches the most fearsome weapon in his arsenal to avenge his father's death. Krishna succeeds in finding a means of protection against this weapon: deflected from its target, it disintegrates and disperses harmlessly in the endless skies.

Now it is Karna's turn. He sets out for battle as the Kaurava commander, weighed down by bad omens: his charioteer, a troubling figure, may be the god Shiva himself. He spares Yudishthira, as he had promised Kunti, and forces Arjuna to retreat. Terrorized by Karna, Yudishthira insults Arjuna who, consumed with rage, threatens to kill his eldest brother. In spite of Draupadi's efforts, the Pandavas are being torn apart by discord and despair.

Meanwhile Bhima, who is seriously wounded, sees Duhsassana coming towards him. Earlier, Bhima had sworn to drink the blood and eat the guts of this avowed enemy. This he now proceeds to do, while Draupadi washes her hair in the dead man's blood. Duryodhana asks Karna to avenge his brother Duhsassana, and he finally meets Arjuna in the decisive confrontation. By seizing Karna's chariot wheel and holding it fast, the earth itself determines his death. Karna tries to invoke the ultimate weapon, but the magic words escape him. He dies, just as the hermit's curse predicted.

It is now the turn of Duryodhana, who refuses to surrender to the very end. He hides in the waters of a lake, which he has solidified by magic. He only emerges from its depths to fight Bhima, who kills him by treacherously striking him on the legs. As he lies dying, Aswhattaman tells him how he sneaked into the camp of the victorious Pandavas to perpetrate a hideous and futile massacre, leaving the Pandavas without any heirs. Duryodhana dies contented.

Bhishma, close to his end, is carried back onto the battlefield. The Pandavas discover that Karna was Kunti's son, and that he prized loyalty to Duryodhana more highly than brotherhood. Whereupon Yudishthira determines to renounce his bloodstained throne, and to withdraw into the forests. Draupadi urges him to stay and continue. Bhishma reveals to him that, even in the midst of the most extreme misfortune, man always clings on to a glimmer of hope, a 'taste of honey'. Then Bhishma himself dies, for his hour has now come. The blind king Dhritarashtra, overwhelmed by rage, tries to crush Bhima to death in his arms, but Krishna has foreseen this final outburst. He substitutes a corpse from the battlefield in place of Bhima.

Now that all her sons are dead, Gandhari's eyes are so charged with grief that, by looking under her blindfold, her emotion sears the flesh of Yudishthira's foot. She curses Krishna, whom she holds responsible for all of the tragedy that has befallen them: he shall be killed by a passing stranger. Krishna calmly accepts this curse, then tells her that a light has been saved, even if she cannot see it. And Yudishthira agrees to reign.

Thirty-six years have passed, and it is now Krishna's turn to die, very simply, mistakenly killed in the forest. Before dying, he has had time to save the child carried in the womb of Abhimanyu's young widow. From him is descended the boy to whom this great story is being told.

The blind king, Gandhari and Kunti are on a riverbank: they speak of the past, of the war that remains etched into their memories. The king orders his wife to remove her blindfold, just this once before dying. She tells him she has taken it off, but she leaves it in place, ever faithful to her vow. Then all three walk towards a fire that has broken out in the forest.

A much older Yudishthira arrives at the entrance to paradise, carrying a dog in his arms. His brothers and Draupadi, who left the earth with him, have fallen from the mountains into the abyss along the way. A gatekeeper tells him to abandon the dog if he wants to enter paradise. Although he refuses, he is permitted to enter, for this was a test. In paradise, 'the inconceivable region', further surprises await him. His enemies are there, smiling and contented. His brothers and Draupadi, on the other hand, seem to be in a place of suffering and torment. Why? Yudishthira asks himself these final embittered questions, before eventually finding repose from this 'last illusion' in peace and harmony. Ganesha closes the 'great poem of the world', its last page now complete, and gives it to the child.

NOTE

The interested reader is referred to the 1951 English version of *The Mahabharata* or to van Buitenen's 3-volume translation (1973, 1975, 1978).

Part II

PRACTITIONERS' ACCOUNTS

3

THE PRESENCE OF INDIA
An Introduction

Peter Brook

One of the difficulties we encounter when we see traditional theatre from the east is that we admire without understanding. Unless we possess the keys to the symbols, we remain on the outside, fascinated, perhaps, by the surface, but unable to contact the human realities without which these complex art forms would never have arisen.

The day I first saw a demonstration of Kathakali, I heard a word completely new to me – *The Mahabharata*. The dancer was presenting a scene from this work and his sudden first appearance from behind a curtain was an unforgettable shock. His costume was red and gold, his face was red and green, his nose was like a white billiard ball, his fingernails were like knives; in place of beard and moustache, two white crescent moons thrust forward from his lips, his eyebrows shot up and down like drumsticks and his fingers spelled out strange coded messages. Through the magnificent ferocity of the movements, I could see that a story was unfolding. But what story? I could only guess at something mythical and remote, from another culture, nothing to do with my life.

Gradually, sadly, I realized that my interest was lessening, the visual shock was wearing off. After the interval, the dancer returned without his make-up, no longer a demigod, just a likeable Indian in shirt and jeans. He described the scene he had been playing and repeated the dance. The hieratic gestures passed through the man of today. The superb, but impenetrable image had given way to an ordinary, more accessible one and I realized that I preferred it this way.

When I next encountered *The Mahabharata*, it was as a series of stories told to Jean-Claude Carrière and me with passionate enthusiasm by a remarkable Sanskrit scholar, Philippe Lavastine. Through him we began to understand why this was one of the greatest works of humanity, and how, like all great works, it is both far from us and very near. It contains the most profound expressions of Hindu thought, and yet for over two thousand years it has penetrated so intimately into the daily life of India that for many billions of people the characters are eternally alive – as real

Figure 3.1 Peter Brook during rehearsals at the Bouffes du Nord. French-language production. (Photographer – Gilles Abegg)

as members of their own family, with whom they share the quarrels and the questions.

Jean-Claude and I were so fascinated that, standing in the rue St André des Arts at three o'clock in the morning after a long storytelling session, we made a mutual commitment. We would find a way of bringing this material into our world and sharing these stories with an audience in the west.

Once we had taken this decision, the first step was obviously to go to India. Here began a long series of journeys in which gradually all those preparing the project took part – actors, musicians, designers. India ceased to be a dream and we became infinitely the richer. I cannot say that we saw all its aspects, but we saw enough to learn that its variety is infinite. Every day brought a new surprise and a new discovery.

We saw that for several thousand years India has lived in a climate of constant creativity. Even if life flows with the majestic slowness of a great river, at the same time, within the current, each atom has its own dynamic energy. Whatever the aspect of human experience, the Indian has indefatigably explored every possibility. If it is that most humble and most amazing of human instruments, a finger, everything that a finger can do has been explored and codified. If it is a word, a breath, a limb, a sound, a note – or a stone or a colour or a cloth – all its aspects, practical, artistic and spiritual, have been investigated and linked together. Art means celebrating the most refined possibilities of every element, and art means extracting the essence from every detail so that the detail can reveal itself as a meaningful part of an inseparable whole. The more we saw of Indian classical art forms, especially in the performing arts, the more we realized that they take at least a lifetime to master, and that a foreigner can only admire, not imitate.

The line between performance and ceremony is hard to draw, and we witnessed many events that took us close to Vedic times, or close to the energy that is uniquely Indian. Theyyam, Mudiattu, Yakshagana, Chhau, Jatra – every region has its form of drama and almost every form – sung, mimed, narrated – touches or tells a part of *The Mahabharata*. Wherever we went, we met sages, scholars, villagers, pleased to find foreigners interested in their great epic and generously happy to share their understanding.

We were touched by the love that Indians bring to *The Mahabharata*, and this filled us both with respect and awe at the task we had assumed. Yet we knew that theatre must not be solemn and we must not allow ourselves to become crushed into a false reverence. What guided us most in India was the popular tradition. Here we recognized the techniques that all folk art has in common and which we have explored in improvisation over the years. We have always considered a theatre group as a multi-headed storyteller, and one of the most fascinating ways of meeting *The Mahabharata* in India is through the storyteller. He not only plays on his musical instrument, but uses it as a unique scenic device to suggest a bow, a sword, a mace, a river, an army or a monkey's tail. We returned from India knowing that our work was not to imitate but to suggest.

Jean-Claude then began the vast undertaking of turning all these experiences into a text. There were times when I saw his mind reaching explosion point, because of the multitude of impressions and the innumerable units of information he had stored over the years. On the first day of rehearsal, Jean-Claude said to the actors as he handed them nine hours' worth of text: 'Don't take this to be a finished play. Now I'm going to start rewriting each scene as we see it evolve in your hands.' In fact, he didn't

43

rewrite every scene, but the material was constantly developing as we worked.

Then we decided to make an English version and I set out to prepare a translation that would be as faithful as possible to Jean-Claude's gigantic achievement.

In the performance, whether in English or in French, we are not attempting a reconstruction of Dravidian and Aryan India of three thousand years ago. We are not presuming to present the symbolism of Hindu philosophy. In the music, in the costumes, in the movements, we have tried to suggest the flavour of India without pretending to be what we are not. On the contrary, the many nationalities who have gathered together are trying to reflect *The Mahabharata* by bringing to it something of their own. In this way, we are trying to celebrate a work which only India could have created but which carries echoes for all mankind.

NOTE

Originally published as a foreword to the CICT French text of *Le Mahabharata* (Paris,1985); subsequently reprinted in English in *The Mahabharata* (New York: Harper & Row, 1987, and London: Methuen, 1988).

4

THE LANGUAGE OF STORIES

Peter Brook interviewed by Georges Banu

THE LANGUAGE OF STORIES

I think that today people are just beginning to recognize, in a clear and simple way, the quantity of languages that exist. Particularly in theatre, where it has become a cliché to say that other aspects of experience, and not only words, form a language: the language of the body, and so on. And it tends to be forgotten that a story itself is a language. We tend to take a story as an end in itself, something simply to be told and heard, without realizing that the very principle of myth is in the telling of a story and the full experience of its charm (in other words, quite simply following the plot, wondering who these people are, what they are going to do, what's going to happen). At the same time, we receive impressions which taken together express something which couldn't be expressed in such a profound way uniquely through spoken or written language.

In the theatre a clear example can be seen in the indefinably potent fascination that the early work of Robert Wilson provoked. His work allowed us to see that a continuous flow of images is a language. And in our century there have been many experiments in cinema and theatre in which, by removing the narrative element, people have endeavoured to communicate by means of a flow of imags with no clear anecdotal thread linking them.

In some ways, *The Mahabharata* is a culmination of a whole series of experiments that I have made – like all experiments, a way of returning to a source. We have come back to the fact that the best way of making the contents of *The Mahabharata* available is to follow the story. In *The Mahabharata* itself, we are often told something which seems rather strange to us: if you listen to this story, you will be somehow different by the end; the very fact of listening to the story will make you virtuous, etc. It is in this sense that a true story contains within it an 'action'; and in *The Mahabharata* this action goes beyond any analysis of contents. It's very difficult for the western mind to accept this idea of a mythical language. We accept it to a certain point, but ultimately at another level

45

we think it is about this or that. In fact it's exactly the opposite. The 'this' and 'that' are approximations which become more precise when the apparent precision of analysis gives way to the precision of the image, the flow of the story as it unfolds.

A TRAVELLER INVOLVED IN STORIES

I have spent all my life travelling. When I began to work, I felt more like a traveller involved in theatre than a director who travelled to relax or better himself. I think that there has been an entirely natural movement in these journeys. I have spent a lot of time in Europe, Africa, the United States, South America, and my exploration of the east has happened progressively through the Middle East, Afghanistan and into India. Today I would very much like to go further. I have not yet been to South East Asia, China or Japan, but these are perspectives for the future.

ROOTED IN THE EARTH OF INDIA

If you want to compare *The Mahabharata* with *Conference of the Birds*, I would suggest that *Conference* as a story takes place on an imaginary level. The birds talk to each other, and their language is no more Persian than it is French. So it is situated in a fictional, vaguely 'Oriental' universe, to free it from any specific and familiar location. Also there is no realistic context in this story. And we used masks for the simple reason that it takes place in the imagination.

The Mahabharata is much meatier. It exists on two levels: that of *Conference*, the level of the imaginary, and that of *The Ik*, the level of what's grounded and rooted. Both are there. And as usual we're not trying to show, but to suggest. We are telling a story which, on the one hand, is universal, but, on the other, would never have existed without India. To tell this story, we had to avoid allowing the suggestion of India to be so strong as to inhibit human identification to too great an extent, while at the same time telling it as a story with its roots in the earth of India. If it were to be placed uniquely in the realm of the imaginary, it would both betray and diminish its vitality to some degree. Ganga, the first person to come on stage, is the goddess of a particular river which is central in the thought of all Indians. At the same time, for us, she is an actress making abstract theatre, in as much as she gives the impression of being a goddess who comes from the water, when she is in fact firmly on the ground, with her feet in the water of a stage stream.

CASTING AN EPIC

When we were bringing together the group of performers, as usual we did not set out with any schematic ideas in mind. We didn't cast in the spirit of UNESCO, saying that one country will represent such and such a thing. We worked by searching and 'sifting' (as it says in *Conference*). On this level, Marie-Hélène Estienne undertook an enormous amount of work, looking everywhere for actors; that took a lot of time. We held numerous auditions, we saw hundreds of people; we travelled a lot. We even went as far as Dakar to meet Senegalese actors. We also watched film rushes here in Paris to see African actors from other countries.

The necessity of having actors capable of speaking French reasonably well imposed certain practical limitations. In addition, we respected our usual criteriton: openness in the actor. He must be open internally to the subject matter, and externally to the collective work. As with *The Cherry Orchard* (but not at all like when we established the first group at the Centre, in 1970), here there were jobs to be filled: roles. For example, we looked everywhere for a Bhima, because it's quite rare to find a giant who acts well. We hesitated between several actors before discovering the one who now plays him. Initially we didn't imagine that Bhima would be an African, but we eventually found him in Dakar. And now, after extensive work on this role, Mamadou Dioume can see that all he has within him can serve the part – not only his external qualities, but what's deepest inside him, what comes from his roots.

As far as the Pandavas are concerned, it is made clear from the start that they do not share the same father. Here is a family that does not need to comprise a family in the same way as in *The Cherry Orchard*, for example. On the contrary, since they have different fathers, it's quite plausible that they should be very different from the point of view of race, culture and origin. That widened the horizon from the outset. From there, we tried to make of them a group, a coherent unit. We eventually discovered a certain natural logic: there is something which corresponds with each actor in relation to who he is and what his culture represents. From the very beginning, therefore, we wanted quite different kinds of people. And the fundamental meaning of the Pandavas echoes that of a Brothers Grimm story, *The Five Servants*, that we performed for children here in Paris. These five men have to live and work together because each one complements the others.

DESIGN: FINDING WHAT'S RIGHT, WHAT'S FRESH

Chloé Obolensky and I worked together for many months while we looked for a scenic base for the performance, how to stage it. As always, something which seems very simple is in fact the result of all sorts of abandoned projects: simple solutions never present themselves at the outset. We thought we would need several platforms to designate different areas, we thought about surrounding the performance space with water, and so on. Through a process of elimination we gradually arrived at something which retained the idea of an arena, but meant suppressing certain small anecdotal details in the Bouffes that we have used a great deal in the past: the doors, the lateral windows. When I work, two things are always present in my mind: find what is right for the piece, and find what is fresh. In fact we have exhausted certain of the Bouffes' possibilities – and it must never be allowed to become a museum. In addition to blocking the lateral openings, we wanted to give the crumbling beauty of the Bouffes (which, although this is the theatre's real beauty, had started to get rather sordid and dirty) a new, luminous quality, and this has meant some repainting. In some ways, given the reality of the Bouffes, we have had to reimagine it. And a scenographic base has been found in the elements themselves – water, fire, earth.

The fact of playing with and implicating the audience (by the actor penetrating the auditorium, for example) is an effect, and like everything else it wears itself out. It becomes something we've seen before, it loses its freshness. Beyond that there's also something else: in plays like *The Cherry Orchard* or *Carmen*, the image is sufficiently close to us today for the audience to be able to really believe that it shares this same world. It takes the tiniest provocation of the imagination for us to think we are in the same house as Ranevskaya. And of course that serves to heighten the play's proximity. But in *The Mahabharata*, the war, for example, has to be treated on two levels constantly. First of all, when necessary, one can play on the great proximity that close-up affords. At the same time, one must remember that this battle is in our world, but not all the time. Showing this war is not the same thing as showing a war from a contemporary or nineteenth-century work. If I had to stage *War and Peace*, I wouldn't adopt the same solution as far as the relationship between audience and war is concerned.

MUSIC: THE TASTE OF INDIA

At first I spent a lot of time searching around, because I felt that a nine-hour performance would need an unusually varied kind of music. I even wondered whether we needed a composer on this occasion. I looked everywhere, but apart from Richard Peaslee, I have never found a musician to parallel Jean-Claude Carrière in the writing area: in other words, someone who is a great specialist in his field and at the same time totally committed to what we are doing. (It's true, we did have just such a relationship with Marius Constant for *Carmen*, but Asian music is not his field at all). I saw Middle Eastern and Indian composers, but on every occasion either the composer was completely locked within the western tradition of scoring, or else he had nothing to suggest beyond what comes naturally in improvised music.

In the end, the richness of the music in this performance comes from the work of Toshi Tsuchitori, who carried out an enormous amount of preparation. He lived in India for two years, travelling by foot from one place to another, listening to all sorts of music. We have ended up looking for a form of music which is neither entirely Indian nor non-Indian, music which has a 'taste' of India. There was a lot of collective work to arrive at a certain tonal colour, which in fact is a direct result of the musicians' own avid research. For example, Kim Menzer spent three months in India learning to play the *nagaswaram*: he is now the only musician in Europe able to produce this sound. Kim is a wonderful player of wind instruments, but it took him three months to be able to produce the first sound from the *nagaswaram*.

A number of Indians worked with our musicians to help them find a point of access into the style. They also listened to tapes and records, and travelled to India with all of us. They were in exactly the same situation as the international group, in as much as they were both trying to reflect India through their own understanding and experience, to colour it with their own culture. That's why the music is neither Indian nor non-Indian. Above all, it's theatrical, for it has to respond to the needs of the perform-ance. It serves the same material, *The Mahabharata*. So the contents of this poem link the performance of racially mixed actors, the music of racially mixed musicians and the work of technicians. Through collabor-ation, theatrical aim and necessity gradually become clear at every moment, and we are able to find what sustains them.

STORYTELLING: THE TROUBADOR AND THE CHILD

By looking closely at Indian theatre (and we have had to remain open to Indian ways of telling the story), it became immediately apparent that we would have to completely eliminate classical Indian art at every level: in the style of acting, dance, song and music. Because it is an art only accessible to those Indians who have devoted themselves to it for several generations. On the other hand, we saw that there was another style of theatre in India, another way, just as Indian, of telling *The Mahabharata* story: it exists everywhere, for it's popular. This popular style is exactly like our own, what we call a 'carpet show' in our terminology. It's like *Ubu* – the same way of playing, the same atmosphere. And we believed that, in order for *The Mahabharata* to be simultaneously very close to our audience and at a certain distance from it, we would have to begin from a 'low' point as opposed to a 'high' one. In other words, we would have to find a starting point at a level of very natural contact.

49

A far as Vyasa is concerned, we could have plumped for a realistic relationship to the story by presenting him as an impressive old guru, a yogi of at least 70 who would tell us the story. But I don't know any actor capable of doing that, and we would have been obliged to remain permanently at that level. The other possibility was to do something which comes from our own work: to introduce a storyteller who is on our side, a Frenchman close to the French audience. Along with Ganesha (Maurice Bénichou is French as well), he establishes a direct contact with the spectators from the very beginning of the performance. Early on in rehearsals, we even started the play with these two, not as characters, but as people talking with the audience. Although that has since been modified, the initial idea was for them to speak directly with the audience. We subsequently found it more touching to see Vyasa addressing the spectators accompanied by a child. People arrive for something rather solemn and grandiose, and on the contrary at the very beginning they find a very human, very simple atmosphere. But then the actor performing Vyasa gradually becomes something else. In the middle of the play, he becomes a character in it.

The child is there to receive, and to give us what's in *The Mahabharata* itself. It is a story 'told to' someone. In the original *Mahabharata*, in fact the story is told to a young king who is in the process of sacrificing all the snakes in the world. This massacre is interrupted when he is told the story of his ancestors so that he will understand what lies before in the future. The whole of *The Mahabharata* is told so that a young man can prepare for life. We didn't want to follow this literally. In a certain kind of academic theatre, you would have a young king as in the original story. But if you start with a young king, everything is at such a distance that you won't be able to identify with it, or be touched by it. A child touches us directly. And it is clear that this child's role is to listen to the story. We watch as he listens and asks questions. We sense that for the child in all of us there is a lesson of great immediacy to be learnt in these fabulous adventures from another era.

A POSITIVE ATTITUDE

Today it's impossible to pretend that we are not in an age when the destruction of the world exists incessantly around us. It's not up to me to suddenly point out to people that the world is in danger; it's all too obvious. But like everyone else I am conditioned by our century. This is why *The Mahabharata* is something to be heard today. When you read in the paper about what's happening in Beirut, you see in a very shocking way what you already know, but nothing helps you to understand what you can do, how to feel and be if confronted with that. Today nobody can do a thing to stop or influence the course of events. It's an illusion to think that marches, speeches, books, art can change an immense movement that's sweeping the world. You can struggle on and fight, but it must be freed from the illusory belief that it will in any way block this relentless mechanism.

In *The Mahabharata*, there is a constant appeal to a positive attitude. *The Mahabharata* tells a story which is as dark, tragic and terrible as our own story today. But tradition allows us to see on every page, in every word, that the attitude when confronted with that situation was not negative, not Spenglerian. There is no pessimistic despair, nihilism, empty protest. It is something else. A way of living in this world in a catastrophic predicament without ever losing contact with what enables man to live and fight on in a positive way. But what does 'positive' mean? It's a word that takes us back to our starting point, and in a very concrete way that points us to the epicentre of the *Bhagavad Gita*: should you reject and withdraw from confrontation, should you act, or what? That question 'or what?' is on everyone's lips today, and although the *Mahabharata* provides no answer, it gives us immense food for thought.

NOTE

From an interview with Georges Banu, originally published in *Alternatives Théâtrales*, no. 24, July 1985. Translated by David Williams.

5

THEATRE, POPULAR AND SPECIAL, AND THE PERILS OF CULTURAL PIRACY

Peter Brook interviewed by David Britton

I saw The Mahabharata *at the Los Angeles Festival earlier this year; an unforgettable experience. It may be seen as three separate three-hour plays or one nine-hour marathon of three acts. I chose the latter and found myself drawn into what is, on the surface, a mythological tale of two divinely begotten families warring for the crown of the country. Brook's orchestration of voice, movement, music and design ensures that the fundamental issues of* The Mahabharata, *the relationship between man, God and the earth, are always present. Yet what surprised me was that despite the spectacle – for* The Mahabharata *is spectacular – and despite the unfamiliar territory of eastern mythology, I found myself caring desperately about the fate of the characters. So when I interviewed Peter Brook in New York a few days later, I began by asking him why the personal story depicted in* The Mahabharata *was so compelling.*

The language of dramatic imagery is a language which is deceptive, because it is naive on the surface, like 'the universe began as an egg' It seems to be the hilt of primitive naivety, like what in Australia are called – I think in slightly contemptuous terms – the Aboriginal fairy tales and the Aboriginal dreams. I'm not at all sure that word 'dream' is the right word. I'm sure there is a deeper and richer word that could correspond to the Aboriginal experience. But, whatever it is, on one level this seems very naive, which in itself is a virtue because what is naive is accessible to everybody.

However, on the other side of that muddle are levels which cannot be put into words. So in a way your experience is exactly what has to happen if a myth is told to someone who is interested in it. You go along with it because one can't resist the simple, accessible level of someone saying 'this is a story about. . . '. Then gradually you get caught up in it and the myth begins to work in the way a myth is supposed to – which is to evoke things in one's subconscious. Gradually by the flow of it, almost like music, by unfolding in a certain order, one is touched in a certain way.

As a director, how aware are you of pursuing that combination of the naive and the profound in a production like The Mahabharata? *Or is it something which, if you do all the other things in theatre correctly, simply happens?*

Both have to be there. One has to be naive and innocent and open, and on the other hand in no way pretend that those other levels are not there. One looks for them consciously but one realizes that the real magic of theatre is that, however much one looks for them in rehearsal and however much one looks for them conceptually, it is only in the movement of performance – because it is an alchemy between performance and audience – that they come to life. That's why all performances have to come, exist and then vanish. At the end of a good performance (and this is what all our actors have to come to terms with) you have a good feeling for a quarter of an hour afterwards. Then you really know you've nothing to lean on; that the next day you really have to begin again and that with a new audience the whole process has to be repeated, and it is only if the process really is repeated that they can come into existence again.

Following that theme, I have just come from Los Angeles, from seeing The Mahabharata *performed in a Hollywood sound stage. You originally staged it in a quarry in Avignon and it will be performed in the open air in Australia. How much does the different venue affect what people perceive as the performance; and how do you make allowance for that?*

Well, I think nothing is more satisfying than to settle down to a dish of raspberries with cream and sugar. It's still a dish of raspberries but it's so much better. I think that's what *The Mahabharata* is. As a work it is much stronger than any of us; stronger than our attempts to make a good or bad performance, so even if we give a bad, tired performance – which can easily happen – *The Mahabharata* is still there and can easily come through. We can play in a better or worse venue and still the raspberries are there. Certainly a film studio is a neutral venue. It doesn't give anything to us and in fact is very difficult for sound because it's designed to be anti-acoustic. For our musicians it's a very painful time because they want to be intimately attached to the actors, because the musicians have worked with them for so long, and there are many times when they can't hear them well enough. They are very delicate, these traditional instruments, and they can't feel the resonance of their instruments. These are real difficulties. . . .

The quarry is a particularly good site for us because normally in a quarry the acoustics are marvellous. The stones are a very good reflecting surface and the relation between the earth, the fire and the water, which is fundamental, carries on upwards. When we play indoors, we have that as far as the back wall, but whatever the back wall is, it isn't part of nature, as in a quarry. People who don't know our work have invited us to play in a Greek amphitheatre. Well, that would be useless because a place must have the right association . . . It's been suggested that we go to India and play in front of a temple. None of that is relevant. What is relevant, because it is a very ancient work, is sheer nature, sheer rock. Quarries are an ideal place to play, yet maybe we would never have thought of a quarry had it not been for *Conference of the Birds* which, in fact, we played originally in a quarry in Adelaide. That was our first.

Fire, earth and water are visually very strong in The Mahabharata. *Why do they have such significance?*

They are characters in the story. Think of some great dramas about children in which the presence of their parents is vital in understanding what happens to the children. In the same way this story comes out of an outdoor society, a very highly developed society, a society in which the constant elements behind the people and behind the events are the relationship with the sky, with the earth, water and fire. To tell the story without these elements, on the boards of a theatre or on a carpet as we have done, would be leaving out central characters.

The themes of The Mahabharata *are universal: good and evil, peace and love, hatred . . .*

I think you won't find an Indian who would accept that good and evil, which are very western Christian terms, come into Indian thought. There is clearly a powerful distinction in *The Mahabharata* between right and wrong, and one of the great interests for us, if we open ourselves to *The Mahabharata*, is to find a work that smashes concepts, and we can say that almost all our concepts, good and evil, good and bad, right action, wrong action, fate, destiny – these are all very superficial, ill-considered. Very early in life we lock ourselves into a certain, very little-digested, sense of what these words mean and we don't question them any more, and one of the big experiences in *The Mahabharata* is to jumble up, shake, put through a mixer and give back these terms so that one really sees that there is a gap between them and living experience. *The Mahabharata* is about conflict in all levels, conflicts between this and that, this being passionately opposed to that, meaning something that, in human terms, is considered right and necessary against something in human terms that's unnecessary and destructive, and yet, all within a universal meaning.

Now if I were to develop those themes I could only do that through the cold, abstract language of intellectual concepts. *The Mahabharata* talks very precisely about the earth in terms of passionate, human interaction by very, very difficult, opposed beings in very tense situations. But if one follows it, not only closely with one's mind, but allows oneself to be moved by it, one finds that good and evil are replaced by understanding and ignorance. The highest point that the human being can reach is understanding, the lowest point he can reach is ignorance, but there are reasons, some of these inevitable reasons, why somebody can understand more and somebody can understand less. But within understanding, actions become right; somebody of a certain quality in *The Mahabharata* can only speak the truth. So that whatever they say, even if they say what, in someone else's mouth, would be meaningless, takes on a ring of truth. The person is of such quality that he cannot say something irrelevant. On the other hand, a self-indulgent, stupid person can even be capable of very fine actions at certain moments, and yet the net result of this can be unhealthy and destructive, even to the point where it says in *The Mahabharata* that, if a king is good, then the crops are good and the weather is good. One looks at our planet when there is no longer a good king or a good leader anywhere, and the first thing one sees is that, in *Mahabharata* terms, the weather is bad, disease has spread, there is hate, families crumble, crime flourishes; that these are, in *Mahabharata* terms, not related to the menacing idea of a battle between good and evil, but a much greater battle between understanding and ignorance, and that our planet today is covered with the darkness, not of the devil, but the darkness of stupidity, the darkness of ignorance.

Into this comes the most exceptionally difficult concept for any western person to face, which is the concept of destiny and fate. The west is brought up to think that half the world are a lot of orientals who sit looking at their stomachs and doing nothing and abdicating all adult responsibilities because they say, 'Kismet, it is fate', and this is, in fact, another part of western blind ignorance, becaue that isn't at all the real oriental understanding of fate. To understand what this notion of fate and destiny is, and how it is in no way in contradiction with freedom and free will, one has to enter openly into this world of *The Mahabharata*, which expounds ideas in front of which our mind not only boggles, but has to boggle. If it refuses to boggle it has no way of receiving what these apparently contradictory concepts are saying, because they're saying it is only through accepting what seems at first sight to be contradiction that something else can be understood. Now *The Mahabharata*, in the way that every dramatic work has to do, puts the spectator in front of living contradictions, because in dramas you sympathize with one side and you sympathize with the other. The more you do that the more you want both sides to win and the moment you want both sides to win, you're in trouble yourself, which is a very good thing.

In attempting to show that to western audiences you've chosen an international cast, people from all over the world. Why did you do that?

To increase the sense of contradiction. Our aim within the company is to make a little model of what could be possible, which is people so different, made not to understand one another, actually reaching understanding because they're working for a common project, so the audience wants to feel this fundamental harmony. On the other hand, at one and the same time one wants to feel the essence of drama, which is an interplay between very strongly contrasted people. This is what, I think, helps to give an impression of universality, again not universality as a weak liberal intellectual concept, but as a reality of people so different struggling with and against one another through what is life.

In your English version you've used very direct language and, frequently, very direct humour, in quite a popular style. Was this an intention to make the appeal in itself direct to an audience which is, at the same time, attempting to grasp concepts which are way beyond normal understanding?

This, I've always felt, is what theatre is about. Theatre is not a lecture, theatre is not a religious ritual, theatre is not a sermon. Theatre is something happening in the market place. It is a coming together, a rich area of concentrated meaning between many, many diverse elements, and that's why the movement within a theatre experience must be constantly between the popular and the special. If everything is just heavily popular to please the audience, you rapidly sink below the lowest denominator. Popular that self-consciously sets out to be popular all the time is very limited. At the same time, something that aspires to be special can easily become precious and all the tragedies of the over-intellectual and the over-refined are there.

But I think that in all good theatre processes there is a constant pendulum movement. There is a coming and going between the level where vulgarity has its firm place and there is a direct popular humour that makes it possible for one to live together, act as an audience, and feel that one's part of the same world, because nothing puts people more naturally onto the same level than humour. And, out of that and through that, one goes places. One goes places and some of them are mysterious and intense and very special; and you try not to stay there too long, because if you stay there too long, like anywhere, you are no longer welcome and get turned out. So before outstaying your welcome, you drop back into that level where everyone feels at home.

The production has been described as Shakespearean. How do you feel about that?

Well, some years ago I did a production of *King Lear* and a journalistic cliché spread that this was Shakespeare in the light of Beckett. For me it was the other way round. I found that the very extraordinary quality I greatly admired of Beckett can already be found in Shakespeare. And I say in exactly the same way that the extraordinary quality of Shakespeare can already be found in *The Mahabharata*, so that it really depends in which direction you point your time machine. By that I mean – What is Shakespeare? We know that Shakespeare was a great rewriter, he hardly ever invented a plot. He took old stories and rewrote them and the uniquely Shakespearean touch was to break open anything that seemed schematic, stories that seemed to have good people and villains, for instance, and humanize them. Humanizing them meant going away from simplified epic figures and filling them out so that every Shakespearean character actually goes beyond judgement. And today it's at last recognized that if you approach a Shakespeare production judging your character, whether you're a director or actor, you lose the essence. The essence is to try to find the inner justification that each character has for himself and then you put them together and you see that much more complex strands arise.

Now, the extraordinary thing is that in the period of human history when the great myths and epics arose, in general, myths and epics cast in a heroic mould tended to be very sparse on human contradiction; that, on the whole, epic characters were heroes and villains. The very special characteristic of *The Mahabharata* – what struck Jean-Claude Carrière and myself – was that there, in *the Mahabharata* were this range of characters all developed, in the round, in the full complexity of human beings. Which is why I think they've lasted to this day; that in India they are today living characters in the way that, for us, Falstaff is a living character, and Hamlet. To Indians today Arjuna or Karna are characters in that way, fully in the round, who they perceive as brothers, as human beings. And so that way I think *The Mahabharata* is Shakespearean.

What we see in this production is something much more than a piece of exotica or Indian nostalgia and I think that's very important, but the danger is, isn't it, that you could be accused of cultural piracy, of plundering another culture, for presentation to a western audience. That's obviously something you must have considered, and worried about. What line did you take, how did you decide what to do on that issue?

To me it's a meaningless question because once you start on that you can say, with no limit to parochialism, why should an Englishman, for instance, touch *Carmen*? Which, luckily, nobody said. But when we first did *Carmen* in Paris we did expect that somebody would say, 'That is a great French masterpiece, what is an Englishman doing with it?' And it goes on forever until you come to a pure Nazi ethic where you ban all but pure German works. On the other hand, I think cultural piracy is what the English have done without any hesitation over a hundred years in India, which is to take their objects and without paying for them put them in British museums. That is piracy.

What happened in *The Mahabharata* is that here is a very great work which all the pirates have ignored because there was no cash to be made out of it. You steal a Buddha from a temple and you can resell it, as people are doing all over the place. *The Mahabharata*, one of the great works of humanity, to this day remains a name that most people in the west haven't heard, a totally unknown work, apart from a few scholars and specialists. And yet it is a work of the greatness of the works of Shakespeare, of the greatness of the great Greek epics, a supreme religious work as well, totally unknown. Now, all the Indians with whom we have been in touch are deeply touched, deeply moved to find that today, after a hundred years in which every educated Indian was forced to know the works of Shakespeare and Molière and Racine, otherwise he wasn't a gentleman (and when no educated Englishman, even having lived in India for half his life, was expected to have known *The Mahabharata* to be passed off in his club as an educated man), to find that today there are a group of people from many countries who have spent a long time, with all the care and respect they can, to say that this is a work that belongs to mankind and should be known. Why has nobody accused the west of cultural plundering because it reads *The Odyssey*? Why should *The Odyssey* be known and *The Mahabharata* be just totally neglected? I think the Indians, who would be the first to be sensitive to anything being taken away, don't see this as stealing but as an opening.

In the wider world of theatre at the moment, what are the things that excite you and what are the things that depress you?

One of the themes I've stressed all my life is I don't believe any generalizations about the theatre can exist; that theatre is such a vast term that it's like saying 'the world' and it's like saying 'What's exciting you in the world?' I mean, the world is such a mixture, one can be excited by one thing and depressed by another. And the theatre is so much – there's so little continuity, there are no traditions except dying ones – and so, in the theatre one can only talk about particular events. You see something and you like it, you see something else and you don't like it, and that's all one can say.

NOTE

Originally published in *Westerly*, no. 4, December 1987. David Britton is a playwright, critic and ABC radio presenter based in Perth, Western Australia.

6

WHAT IS NOT IN *THE MAHABHARATA* IS NOWHERE

Jean-Claude Carrière

The writer Jean-Claude Carrière, who has a PhD in history from L'Ecole Normale Supérieure, has been involved in theatre and film for over twenty years. A lengthy period of collaboration as writer with the director Luis Buñuel resulted in six feature films, including *Belle de Jour* and *The Discreet Charm of the Bourgeoisie*, as well as Buñuel's autobiographical book *My Last Breath*. He has also written screenplays for Louis Malle, Pierre Etaix, Milosz Forman (*Taking Off*), Volker Schlöendorff (*The Tin Drum*); and, more recently, for Daniel Vigne (*The Return of Martin Guerre*), Wajda (*Danton*) and Phillip Kaufman (*The Unbearable Lightness of Being*, based on Milan Kundera's novel). His first play was produced by Micheline Rozan in 1968. At present, he is president of FEMIS, the new French School of High Technology, dedicated to the arts of Image and Sound.

His collaboration with Peter Brook began in 1974, with a translation of *Timon of Athens*. He also adapted *Measure for Measure*, *Conference of the Birds*, *The Cherry Orchard* and *The Tragedy of Carmen* for Brook.

The Mahabharata is one of the world's greatest books. It is also the longest poem ever written. It was written in Sanskrit, and is more than 100,000 stanzas long – about fifteen times the length of the Bible. The first known written versions of it, made up of ancient stories, go back to the fifth or sixth century BC. These versions continued to be made for seven or eight hundred years, until in the third or fourth century AD they took on a more or less definitive form. Throughout this time of composition, additions of all kinds were made – up until the twentieth century – with variations depending on the province of origin, traditions, interpretations, or the various groups of writers involved. In the Indian tradition, *The Mahabharata* is simply called 'The Epic', and it is the masterpiece of the very rich literature of the Sanskrit language. The poem is at the origin

59

of thousands of beliefs, legends, thoughts, teachings, and characters which even today are part of Indian life.

Yet it was entirely unknown in Europe until the eighteenth century. The first edition of the *Bhagavad Gita*, a section of the poem, was published in London in 1785 in a translation by Charles Wilkins, and in

Figure 6.1 Jean-Claude Carrière. (Photographer – Gilles Abegg)

Paris in 1787, translated into French by M. Parraud. The first European to immerse himself in the entire poem was a Swiss Army officer of French extraction, Colonel de Polier, who lived thirty adventurous years in India, also in the late eighteenth century. In the nineteenth century a French orientalist, Hippolyte Fauche, undertook the colossal task of translating the whole epic into French. Only two hundred people subscribed to buy the work. After many long years of labour, Fauche died. His work was taken up by Dr L. Ballin, who also died before it was finished. But this translation, which is very beautiful in many ways, is often incorrect or incomprehensible. In any case, it is incomplete. There is no complete French version of the world's greatest poem.

One evening in 1975 Philippe Lavastine, a remarkable professor of Sanskrit, began telling the first stories of *The Mahabharata* to Peter Brook and me. We were completely enchanted. For five years we met regularly, Peter and I listening to the poem without reading it. I took notes, and in 1976 I started a first version of the play. Advice and encouragement subsequently came from a number of quarters, particularly from Madeleine Biardeau, author of several works on Hindu culture, and finally we began to read. At first we read separately – Peter Brook read in English and I read in French – and finally we began a long, slow study together, comparing translations, with the help of Marie-Hélène Estienne. After these studies, which we pursued for almost two years, we travelled to India a number of times. We gathered all kinds of images and impressions – images of dance, film, puppet theatre, village celebrations and plays. Although, so far as we know, there has never been a complete adaptation of *The Mahabharata* (the film-maker Satyajit Ray worked on one for many years, but had to give up for lack of funds), many episodes of the epic poem are very alive today in both India and Indonesia. They are often played, in a variety of fashions, and the stories are told in picture form, which can be found all over the country.

We read a great deal during this time of research, and some of it was most revealing. I'm thinking particularly of several short plays by Rabindranath Tagore, freely adapted from The Epic, a brilliant essay by Irawati Karve called *Yuganta*, and a long series of the *Krishnavatara* (the 'descent' of Krishna) edited by K. M. Munshi, all of which gave us precious keys to meanings, and made possible a more subtle, deeper and in a way more realistic development of certain characters.

The Indians with whom we talked about our project responded warmly, once they got over their initial amazement. The notion that their great Indian epic would at last be played in the west intrigued and interested them. We received the advice of professors and the benediction of saints. In Calcutta we met a hospitable and enthusiastic man, Professor P. Lal, who was finishing a complete translation into English verse of *The Mahabharata*, which he called a 'transcreation'. He too was most encouraging, convinced that the great Indian poem could speak in different voices to the rest of the world.

Maha in Sanskrit means 'great' or 'complete'. A *maharaja* is a great king. *Bharata* is first of all the name of a legendary character, then that of a family or a clan. So the title can be understood as 'The Great History of the Bharatas'. But, in an extended meaning, *bharata* means Hindu, and, even more generally, man. So it can also be interpreted as 'The Great History of Mankind'. This 'great poem of the world' tells the story of the long and bloody quarrel between two groups of cousins: the Pandavas, who were five brothers; and the Kauravas, of whom there were a hundred. This family quarrel over who will rule ends with an enormous battle where the fate of the world is at stake.

The events told in *The Mahabharata* most probably have a historic source. Most specialists are agreed on this point. Indian tradition places the great battle of Kurukshetra in the year 3200 BC. Some historians see in the poem a reasonably faithful reflection of the wars between the Dravidians and the Aryans of the second millennium BC. Others maintain that the correct interpretation of the poem is entirely mythological. Still others point out the importance of the books of teaching of The Epic – political, social, moral and religious – and see *The Mahabharata* as a long treatise of royal initiation. Commentators point out that all the pages that maintain the superiority of the Brahman caste – and there are a great number of them – were added much more recently. We chose not to pay a great deal of attention to any of these comments, however interesting they might be. As far as we were concerned, this immense poem, which flows with the majesty of a great river, carries an inexhaustible richness which defies all structural, thematic, historic or psychological analysis. Doors are constantly opening which lead to other doors. It is impossible to hold *The Mahabharata* in the palm of your hand. Layers of ramifications, sometimes contradictory, follow upon one another and are interwoven without losing the central theme. That theme is a threat: we live in a time of destruction – everything points in the same direction. Can this destruction be avoided?

I began the final draft in Autumn 1982. I continued throughout 1983 as well as 1984, when research began with the actors, as well as the music composition. When rehearsals began, in September 1984, the play was written, but there was as yet no definitive structure. Throughout the nine months of rehearsal, incessant changes were made. For a long time we had no idea how lengthy the play would be, how many playing hours we would need, or even how many plays were involved.

From the beginning it seemed obvious that we would have to set aside most of the secondary strands of the story, although many of them are very beautiful. The storytellers of *The Mahabharata* liked to arrest the mainstream of the action for a while to tell another story, like a little backwater, which illustrates or comments upon the main actions. Some of these stories go on for over fifty pages; for instance, the rivalry between Drona and Drupada, or the loves of Nala and Damayanti. Some are shorter, such as the cunning and courageous Savitri's snatching her husband from death. Some, on the other hand, take only a single page – the love of Arjuna and the daughter of the king of snakes. *The Mahabharata* even contains a shorter version of the other great Sanskrit epic, *The Ramayana*.

At various times we tried a very dramatic beginning, in the middle of the conflict. But each time it seemed to us that the fabled origins of the family, the adventures and desires of distant mythic ancestors, were absolutely necessary, even if that meant forty minutes of playing time before the appearance of the principal characters. It became obvious that we needed the storyteller/author, Vyasa, even though the characters he creates sometimes escape him (he is both their author and their father), and even though Ganesha and later Krishna dispute the reality of his inventions. Eventually a clear line began to appear, which led from a mythic tale of demigods told by a storyteller, to characters who became more and more human and who brought with them the theatre as we understand it.

In *The Mahabharata* there are sixteen main characters. Each of them has a distinct and often complex personality and a particular story which is part of the main action, with varying degrees of importance. We left out only one of these, Vidura, half-brother of Pandu and Dhritarashtra, but a half-brother born of a servant and consequently unable to exercise royal power. Vidura is a wise, moderate, sensible man whose narrative importance is minor. What he brings to the poem, and it is almost always a purely verbal contribution, has been incorporated into other characters: Bhishma, Yudishthira or Vyasa himself.

Krishna presented us with a special problem. Today it is almost impossible to separate Krishna from his immense later legend, which continued to develop up to the Middle Ages. But in *The Mahabharata*, at least in those parts of the poem generally thought to be the earliest, nothing clearly indicates that he is an avatar, one of the earthly incarnations of Vishnu. He is a man who tires, who ages. Sometimes he is 'surprised' or 'distressed' by the things that happen. Mysterious and bloody revolts destroy his city. And he dies killed by a hunter in the forest – an abrupt death, briefly told.

Some commentators, such as Norbert Klaes in *Conscience and Consciousness*, maintain that in the original *Mahabharata* Krishna is simply Vasudeva, the best and highest of men, of whom only one is alive at any given moment. Not a god. Yet the poem describes some of his prodigious acts. Krishna lengthens Draupadi's dress indefinitely. He creates an illusion which makes his enemies believe that the sun has set before its time. He possesses an invincible weapon, a disc, which he uses to decapitate Sisupala. But, above all, just before the battle he gives his friend Arjuna the *Bhagavad Gita*, the famous text where he appears as a divinity and shows his 'universal form'. Man or god? It is obviously not up to us to decide. Any historical or theological truth, controversial by its very nature, is closed to us – our aim is a ceratin dramatic truth. This is why we have chosen to keep the two faces of Krishna that are in the original poem, and to emphasize their opposite and paradoxical nature.

In order to adapt *The Mahabharata*, to transform an immense epic poem into a play, or three plays, we had to draw new scenes from our imaginations, bring together characters who never meet in the poem itself – all this within the context of deep respect for the shape and sense of the story. Each of these characters has a total commitment, each probes in depth the nature of his actions, each considers his *dharma*, and each confronts his idea of fate. So we had to make it possible for each of these characters to go into his own deepest places without interposing our concepts, our judgements or our twentieth-century analysis, in so far as that is possible. In the second play, which involves long years of exile, we had to find some way of concentrating fast and fluid action in space and time without destroying its energy or its mystery.

As far as the writing itself is concerned, we dropped the notion of archaic or old-fashioned languages, because they carry with them a stream of inappropriate images and associations from our own Middle Ages or ancient tales. On the other hand, it was impossible to tell this story in modern, familiar or even slangy language. But the polish of French classic or neoclassical language was, of course, equally impossible. So we settled on a simple, precise, restrained language which gave us the means to oppose or juxtapose words which ordinarily are never used together. This careful choice of language led us to a problem which would be repeated in the stage decor, the music, the costumes, the colours, and the props: one might call it 'the Indian-ness'. I had to write in French without writing a French play. I had to open my language to rhythms and images of Asia without being caught in the other trap, the opposite one, of merely providing local colour or the picturesque.

While we kept the names of characters, we found equivalents for most of the Sanskrit words. There were two exceptions: one was *kshatrya*. In ancient India it was the name of a caste, which is untranslatable unless one attempts a kind of forcible assimilation, which would be a colonization by vocabulary – words like 'noble' or 'warrior' and certainly 'knight' simply would not do. The other untranslatable word is *dharma*, a concept at the very heart of the poem: 'truth', 'justice', or 'duty' fall short of the mark. *Dharma* is the law on which rests the order of the world. *Dharma* is also the personal and secret order each human being recognizes as his own, the law he must obey. And the *dharma* of the individual, if it is respected, is the warrant of its faithful reflection of a cosmic order.

Indian tradition says: 'Everything in *The Mahabharata* is elsewhere. What is not there is nowhere.'

NOTE

Originally published as an introduction to the CICT French text of *Le Mahabharata* (Paris, 1985); subsequently reprinted in English in *The Mahabharata* (New York: Harper & Row, 1987, and London: Methuen, 1988).

7

THE BRIDGE OF SAND

Jean-Claude Carrière interviewed by Georges Banu

THE WRITING PROCESS: THE SEARCH FOR A LANGUAGE

For both *Conference of the Birds* and *The Mahabharata*, I tried to adapt my writing as closely as possible to the original work. *Conference* is more of an initiatory poem than an epic, whereas *The Mahabharata* is in truth an immense epic poem. Even without one wanting it to be, the tone would necessarily adapt itself.

A second difference concerns India. In *The Mahabharata*, India exists at every level, and you have to ask the question: what role, what emphasis should be given to India? In fact in the final performance it's present at every level, and to an infinitely greater degree than Persia in *Conference*, a work which is much further from the earth, much freer from realistic contingencies. That is what allowed us to use Balinese masks, more stylized costuming. *The Mahabharata* does not allow that; it's very difficult to imagine it performed with Japanese or Korean masks, or with western elements.

The third difference arises from a rather subtle writing problem that I will try to explain. With *Conference*, I had almost no western reference points, there was no danger of comparison with this or that model in our own culture. It remained an Oriental fable removed from any historical reality, and that allowed me a certain linguistic freedom. With *The Mahabharata*, from the outset I have tried to recognize the enormous danger of it being compared to western tragedies in whatever form: whether classical tragedies or, even more dangerous, romantic dramas.

Very few western writers have taken their inspiration from India, but Victor Hugo did it superbly in some of the poems in *La Légende des Siècles*. The temptation was (and in fact it was my initial dream) to write *The Mahabharata* as Victor Hugo would have written it. This dream was very quickly dispelled; as soon as one tries to introduce a French poetic style – and this is what happened with the translation of *The Mahabharata* in the Second Empire – one lapses into a sort of sub-Hugo, which is inevitably conventional, pretentious and uninspired. It's unavoidable. Feeling very aware of that, I abandoned my initial attempts to write in verse, in false verse. None the less a trace of this still remains, for the prose in the play is rhythmic. The search for a language took much more time than with *Conference*.

I began very humbly by re-reading enormous amounts of French poetry and theatre. I then progressed through a process of elimination, with the aim of removing anything which might have produced a precise reference to the west. Christian terminology, for example, 'sin', 'soul', 'eternal life', 'redemption', 'incarnation' – all of these words had to be immediately excluded, because they evoke other images we wanted to avoid. A second category of words to eliminate: medieval language – 'noble', 'cavalier', 'knight', 'suzerain', 'fiefdom'. Keeping these words would be like superimposing our own Middle Ages on to the Indian characters.

A third category: vocabulary that might be called classical or neoclassical. Whoever writes the English version will come up against the same problems, because even in Shakespeare there are words which were once very powerful, but are weakened today. Some words become worn, corrupted, wrinkled and old, they fade and wither, words which may be potent in Corneille or Racine, but have no strength for us today; for example, 'afflicted', 'torment', 'wrath'. They are unusable because they inevitably bring to mind the sub-products of neoclassicism. A fourth category: the pompous flowery vocabulary of the nineteenth-century Parnassian poets. All those pseudo-ancient words in Flaubert's *Salammbô* or in José-Maria de Hérédia. In other words, local colour transposed into French, all surface gloss and bejewelled formal splendour. By eliminating them, I wanted to avoid superimposing a ghostly presence on to the play and its characters, a presence which can attract attention to itself through the subtle interplay of words and associations.

Once all of these categories have been eliminated (as well as modern language, which goes without saying), you're left with a very simple vocabulary. You rediscover words which have not diminished in force at all: 'heart', 'blood', 'death' – three very simple words which are fundamental to the play. These words still remain fully alive, and they're not in any of the linguistic categories I have just described. By taking these three words and about twenty-five others (for example, *'déchiré'*, – 'torn' which I really like), and linking them with unusual adjectives that I've often found in the mannered vocabulary of the seventeenth-century Baroque poets (that is where French language, more archaic and not yet coded by classicism, is the mot interesting), one discovers quite surprising and forceful associations. For example, one character in the play says, 'If in the depths of your heart you desire defeat . . .' – *'coeur profond'* is unusual without being artificial.

A BENEFICENT POEM

In undertaking this long-term adventure, we have continually forced our-selves not to arrive before we had even set out, to proceed calmly and slowly, only ever doing what seemed possible. *The Mahabharata* as a poem sings its own praises in an abundant fashion. From the very begin-ning, it tells us: 'I am the world's greatest poem, and whoever reads this poem will emerge from it happy, purified . . .' and so on. No poet has ever said that before. We tried to take it quite literally: *The Mahabharata* is a beneficent poem. If you tell or listen to this poem, it will do you good, it will make you better . . . And in my own experience it's true. I have put an enormous amount of work into it, I have written more than the total length of the poem, but every time I come back to it I experience a revitalizing feeling. Never once have I grown tired of it.

We all agreed to tell the central story while preserving its fantastic origins. We could have let them go by the board, but you lose so much – you miss out on the fabulous magical thrust in the story. On the other hand, we did decide to sacrifice the secondary stories. The main characters tell them to each other, sometimes reiterating the events of the principal story; they're another way to describe what's happening to the central characters. For example, the famous story of Nala and Damayanti was cut because it repeats the game of dice. Similarly, in the characters' early years, certain episodes are used twice. For example, there is an earlier period of exile in the forest; the Pandavas come back from it only to return there again. And Arjuna wins two tournaments . . . We also cut out the books of teaching. When Bhisma is old and dying, he speaks for about 300 pages on the duties of a king, the organization of society, etc. It's inconceivable on stage, and not that interesting anyway; it refers to a society which is completely foreign even to contemporary Indian society. Finally, I deliberately pruned everything that happens after the battle. There are still thirty-six more years in which quite a number of things happen. Scholars consider this section of the poem, which was added on much later, to be the weakest. And it's very difficult to regenerate the performance's dynamic after the battle. For this reason I concentrated everything into three short scenes: the death of Krishna, for he has to die; the deaths of the blind king Dhritarashtra and his wife Gandhari beside the river (a scene I had to invent, the poem simply says that they left for the forest); and, third, Yudishthira's journey to paradise.

FROM STORYTELLING TO DRAMATIC ART

The section we start with, detailing the characters' mythical origins, is crucial to the work of the storyteller. As in all traditional cultures, the storyteller reminds those people he is addressing of his origins. Vyasa is both author and father to his characters (literally – he makes love to the two princesses so that his poem can continue). Initially we are interested in the figure of the storyteller, but later, as these characters of divine origin gradually become more human, they interest us more. In general, we find interesting what is near to us. From the point at which these characters take on a greater substance, the writing changes: we move from a mythical narrative to theatre, from storytelling to dramatic art.

It's exactly what we saw in India, where we sometimes felt as if were were witnessing the birth of theatre. You couldn't tell whether the person in front of you was a priest or an actor; in fact he is both at the same time, or one about to become the other. Within the body of the performance, I tried to show this movement while at all costs retaining the storyteller and the child to whom he tells his story. But, from that point onwards, the story is self-generating. And, when someone asks Vyasa for help, he replies: 'No, now you are alive, I can't do anything more for you.' In the third part, he is sometimes afraid of dying. . . .

One of the fundamental concerns of our work is to maintain a sense of wonder, to preserve in an honest way our capacity to feel astonishment and wonder when confronted with beautiful unknown stories. The importance of stories in the east is incomparable with the west. A group of Indian anthropologists were able to record 17,000 stories in one small Rajasthani village of 350 inhabitants. The storyteller is an essential and central figure in eastern society, as much as a soldier or a baker. They understand perfectly that no society can survive without its own myths being told to it. This reflects Vyasa's central role as storyteller in our *Mahabharata*.

The patron saint of storytellers is Scheherezade. She risks losing her life if she fails to capture the interest of the king, the absolute power. The storyteller's voice must never be interrupted. When you launch yourself into *The Mahabharata*, it seems as though you'll never be able to finish, as though it's a poem without an end, still in the process of being written by itself. Two French writers who tried to translate it failed; they died before reaching the end. An old allegory represents the storyteller as a man who stands facing the sea, talking to it. He tells a story, the sea listens. When he has finished one story, he drinks a glass of water and carries on. And so on. This very simple story ends with a thought: if one day the storyteller is silent or silenced, no one knows what the sea will do.

THE WRITER'S WORK

Working in the conditions that exist with this group in Paris – able to write with twenty-five people, refining and reworking as and when necessary – is the greatest luxury imaginable for a theatre writer. We are convinced that both Shakespeare and Molière wrote in this same way. Although I put together some rough drafts at the very beginning, I didn't really start to write the play until after our first trips to India. And, once rehearsals were underway, I made countless modifications. At first Peter and I would work on the text together, then we invited the actors' participation and, particularly after the group journey to India, they started to defend their characters to me: not the parts, the characters. There was then a lot of work with the public. Their reactions are fascinating because one gets to see what interests them, what's missing. Sometimes a single phrase is sufficient to alter the shape and tone of a whole scene.

In rehearsal, we begin by looking at a scene with the actors – once, and then a second time. Often we are not happy, so we ask: is it because of the scene itself (in which case it has to be rewritten), or is it because of the actors' work? And there's no absolute answer. Sometimes it's one, sometimes the other. The penultimate part of the writing process is carried out collectively. But for the last part I'm as alone as I was at the beginning, because at a certain point you must decide to work on your own, as a writer. However, the passage through collective writing is indispensable, and I consider it to be a supreme luxury.

THE PATH OF *DHARMA*

One of the most profound themes in *The Mahabharata*, and certainly the one that touches me most deeply, is that of the destruction of *dharma*. At the very beginning, Vyasa says: 'I wrote this poem to inscribe *dharma* in the hearts of men.' He tosses out this invocation knowing full well that the human species has already entered an age of inevitable destruction: *Kaliyuga*, the age of Kali. It's not something that people can change; it's their destiny. This period of time lasts several thousands of years; it began with *The Mahabharata* and we are now bang in the middle of it. You cannot alter it, but, within the cycle of destruction and decay, something can be saved.

That's Krishna's precise role in the poem, his mission if you like. If you allow destroyers to go on destroying, they will indeed destroy everything. On the other hand, if one arrives at a point of crystallization within oneself with regard to *dharma* – the very task for which we were born – it is possible to save something, to alleviate some of the destruction.

Indian thought is very complicated, it refuses any utopia as far as human beings are concerned. It does not tell you where happiness is, how to

reach it. It's very difficult to follow the path of *dharma*. It's not enough
to entrust oneself to God, as in Christianity. Indian thought makes no
naive concessions to human nature. It has no illusions concerning our
deepest desires and motives, our *coeur profond*. So the task in hand is
very hard. It's extremely difficult to say anything, given man's motives
and desires and the fact that we are living in an era of cosmic destruction.
That's why the descent of a god, with his incredible powers, is needed.
Krishna shows us that, in order to save *dharma*, in fact you must not
respect it – but if you make that into a general rule for everyone, then
you're lost. For this reason Krishna's role is essential; in some way he
must remain ambiguous and esoteric and die in the end. Gandhari curses
him for having resorted to tricks and lies, but something will have been
saved. The battle for *dharma* has to begin again every day; that is the
poem's fundamental meaning. *The Mahabharata* is an astonishingly proud
poem, but it's entirely without vanity. It represents a whole world, but
it offers no solutions.

THE BRIDGE OF SAND

I'm very fond of one story we left out. A very fervent young man decides
that he is going to receive knowledge directly from the gods. So he
undertakes extraordinary penances, for the gods can refuse nothing to
such a person. He goes up into the Himalayas and decides to remain on
one big toe for however long it takes. The gods are thoroughly fed up
with him. They tell him that this is not how to obtain knowledge; instead
he should work, learn and search for masters. But he will hear nothing
of it and continues his penances.

One day, although he is absorbed in the strictest ascetic austerities, he
sees an old man carrying an enormous sack of sand on his back pass by.
The old man puts the sack of sand down on a nearby river bank, and
drops a fistful of sand in at the water's edge. The strong current immediately sweeps it away. A second handful disappears just as quickly as the
first. Although he's deep in meditation, the young man notices this strange
activity, and after a time asks the old man: 'What are you doing?' 'What
do you mean, what am I doing?' 'Well, what are you doing?' And the
old man replies: 'I'm building a bridge.' 'You're building a bridge of sand
in the great river? That's totally absurd. Can't you see that the current
sweeps away the sand you put in the water every time?' 'Well, it's no
more absurd than what you're doing,' replies the old man, who immediately reveals himself to be a god.

In our work on *The Mahabharata*, this image of the bridge of sand has
haunted us.

NOTE

From an interview with Georges Banu, originally published in *Alternatives Théâtrales*, no. 24, July 1985. Translated by David Williams.

8

FLUIDITY AND OPENNESS

Chloé Obolensky interviewed by Georges Banu

Born in Athens of Greek parents, Chloé Obolensky was educated in England and France. Her first theatre work was as assistant to Lile de Nobili. She has subsequently designed sets and costumes for both plays and opera, collaborating with Gian Carlo Menotti, Mauro Bolognini, Raymond Rouleau and Franco Zeffirelli. She is the author of *The Russian Empire: A Portrait in Photographs*, published internationally.

She designed costumes and sets for Peter Brook's productions of *The Cherry Orchard* and the costumes for *The Tragedy of Carmen*. For *The Mahabharata*, she designed costumes as well as all the scenic elements and properties.

I believe today that design means creating possibilities for a continually moving and evolving set of images that need have no consistency, no stability, no architecture, but which spin out of the actors' themes and play on the audience just at the moment when they unfold. They should parallel the rich and formless impressions of the world we live in. Yet behind this is the call to classicism, the constant wish to give form, to impose order again. But what form? Whose order?

(Peter Brook, *The Empty Space*, 1968)

My starting point is always in documentation. For *The Mahabharata*, I started by going to India with Brook and Carrière. It was an extraordinary trip lasting one month. It was only after my return that I put together detailed documentation of what seemed important to this project. Little by little things filtered through. Subsequently I went back to India, this time with my assistant Pippa Cleator, to look for fabrics and objects, and to note down design cuts and styles. So, for example, we spent a long time working on drawings at the Calico Textile Museum in Ahmedabad. Obviously, it would be ideal to be able to go back: we all feel the need to, we're still looking, still modifying.

For me the interest of collaborating with Peter Brook stems from his wish not to fix an image, but to preserve in scenographic terms the same

72

possibility of evolution that the actors and even Jean-Claude Carrière have at their disposal. It's a question of developing constantly, for the preparatory period is empirical rather than analytical. Of course, that can engender certain technical difficulties: we have to produce costumes and three-dimensional objects, and their realization demands a different period of time. But in the end you get there.

Figure 8.1 Chloé Obolensky. (CICT photograph)

Every subject demands its own solutions. What is interesting here is the progressive evolution towards an ever greater precision. Initially, any possibility was open to us. At one point, for example, we thought of creating a multi-levelled floor for the space, breaking it up with little low

73

walls. Although it was an interesting solution, its extended use throughout all three plays would have been impractical. (Only two baked earth platforms survive: one for Vyasa the storyteller, one for the musicians.) Besides, given the multiplicity of types of action, any solution which risked becoming closed or restrictive had to be avoided. Fluidity and openness must be preserved at all costs. We really needed a strong base on to which forms and colours could be inscribed, like a bass part sustaining the various melodies in a piece of music. We wanted to be free to play with ideas, allowing them sufficient room to take seed, breathe, before determining any fixed element.

One of our first decisions revolved around our theatre. As far as the Bouffes is concerned, we came to the conclusion that the theatre's walls would have to be reworked. We hesitated for a long time between a very white space and a warm reddish or orchre space. Eventually we chose the latter solution because we wanted to change the atmmosphere of the theatre without interfering with its true nature. Above all, however, we wanted a place that would be complete: unique and unified, with no separation between playing space and auditorium; a shell within which the imagination could be stimulated – active and free to follow the birth and erasing of any situation.

We introduced beaten earth, which is in fact an Indian element, but it complements the Bouffes' atmosphere in a very natural way. Next came water – one brings the other with it; fire follows on quite naturally. In conjunction with the theatre's architecture, these three elements have such immense evocative power that they are sufficient in themselves. And we have avoided too arid or ascetic an ambience with the suggestive use of mats and lengths of material: timeless and simple.

The costumes presented a real stumbling block. We tried out a great number of designs – some sewn, some not – before adopting the present direction. Again, it was a question not of undertaking some sort of archaeological reconstruction of the costumes of ancient India, but of finding what could both evoke India and best lend itself to our purpose and subject matter. My only guiding principle: suggestion and evocation rather than illustration. And we also needed to respect the meaning of a story which is both ancient *and* contemporary. It's an extremely delicate process.

One thing that is truly beautiful to see in India is the way in which certain items of clothing are used constantly: the big rectangular scarves (*schotti*) that they wash at the water's edge in the day are used as covers when they go to sleep at night. Now that's just what we are looking for: a rigorous economy, and incredibly strong and stark simplicity – but a simplicity which must never smack of poverty.

The vast majority of fabrics used are Indian. These are cottons you no longer find in Europe. As far as designs are concerned, we started from authentic cuts, mainly borrowed from examples in the Musée de l'Homme in Paris, from the Victoria and Albert in London, from the Calico Textile Museum in Ahmedabad and from Benares. The cut of the *kurtas*, the cloaks and the dimensions of the scarves were all taken from originals, and, for example, from studying similar forms in the cave frescoes of Ajanta. I don't believe in abstract forms in costume design. A form is the result of a process of evolution, and certain essential forms remain unchanged with the passage of time. I have always found authentic cuts much more interesting than so-called 'transposed' designs.

For the costumes in *The War*, we needed to establish a double image: of warriors both in ceremonial dress and in fighting gear. Our costumes combine the breastplates of Northern India and the huge pleated skirts that crop up in so many cultures in both Asia and Europe. For divine, quasi-mythical or heroic characters, we deliberately set out to avoid description in costuming, leaving the actor free to evolve in accordance with dramatic situations. Nevertheless, the appearance of certain specific characters (let's say Shiva, the hunter, in *Exile in the Forest*) had to relay immediately the strange world from which they have emerged.

People say that once you have heard certain sounds, you never forget them. I would suggest that the same is true of the visual element. You must take into account what is happening in the streets, avoiding solutions which automatically run the risk of provoking associations which are alien to the performance (for example, in this case, the trace of India in hippy clothes). But having said that, once an element is right, it's right: and you must not be afraid to use it.

NOTE

From an interview with Georges Banu, originally published in *Alternatives Théâtrales*, no. 24, July 1985. Translated by David Williams.

9

SENSITIVITY AND LISTENING

Toshi Tsuchitori interviewed by Georges Banu

Toshi Tsuchitori was born in Japan in 1950. He began learning traditional Japanese drums as a child, later taking up percussion to play free jazz. In 1975, he travelled abroad for the first time, as solo composer-musician with an experimental theatre group directed by Yoshi Oida. In New York and Paris he collaborated in free improvisation with such artists as Milford Graves, Steve Lacy and Derek Baily.

He has been integral in the Centre work since 1976, providing music for *Ubu*, *The Bone* and *Conference of the Birds*. His research into ethnic music for *The Mahabharata* took him to Africa, Asia and the Middle East. He has also undertaken research in musicology and musical archaeology, making recordings of prehistoric music-stones and ancient bronze bells; he is currently preparing a book on this subject.

Tsuchitori: The relationship that exists between music and dramatic action in *The Mahabharata* is one based upon sensitivity. There is a fundamental difference between using pre-recorded music and live musicians. The relationship is no longer between human being and material, but between human being and human being. And an interpersonal relationship is fundamental to our working practice.

Obviously the musical references in *The Mahabharata* are to India. But over the last five years I have looked just as hard for other kinds of music, notably those that I have studied personally during my visits to different countries: these include Nepal, Bali, Sri Lanka, Indonesia and Africa as well as India itself. That's why we use music material and instruments from very diverse sources: Africa, Japan, Iran, Australia and so on. Our main instruments are the *ney*, a Turkish flute; the *kamantche*, a sort of Iranian violin; and the *nagaswaram*, a Southern Indian cousin to the western oboe. For my part, I play about thirty percussion instruments of all shapes and sizes, many from the east, some invented. In their application here, however, all of these 'tools' lose their individual cultural connotations: in that way, the audience is never made to feel blocked by the orginal cultural resonances of elements employed in performance.

Figure 9.1 Toshi Tsuchitori during rehearsals at the Bouffes du Nord. (Photographer – Gilles Abegg)

The end result has more than a taste of India, and yet we have neither a sitar nor an Indian musician. Like the actors with their diverse origins, the musicians are able to find a meeting point in suggestion.

The four musicians I am collaborating with are classically trained: two Iranians, a Turk and a Dane – Peter was very keen to have one European. Their background is in pure music; they have no theatre experience. So it was necessary to get them to understand the importance of the relationship I have just described in order for them to be able to implement that kind of fluid organic interrelationship: a quality of sensitivity between the actors and themselves. Initially, all they would do was play music, and still more music. . . . there was no possibility of collective improvisation: each one could only play 'his own' music. But eventually our collaboration bore fruit, and now it's quite different. They truly *play*, both with the actors and the action. And with growing directness and vitality, they are able to experience the relationship that *has* to exist between music and action – in such a way that changes and developments at the present time are not only of a purely musical nature; they are also organically related to the dramatic action.

Brook: In order to understand the music of theatre, one must recognize what differentiates it from non-theatre music. In theatre music, a relationship must be established between sound and silence: the vibration of sound in relation to silence. Moreover, movement is always related to something else. In the theatre, one cannot limit oneself to seeing only the actors' work, or the dramatic action, or indeed the music. A performance is an energy, functioning within and redefining silence as well as space. A movement in space is affected and determined by numerous elements (story, situation, intention, emotion, etc.), all of which give rise to different sorts of dynamic and mobility. Music is an integral part of such movement. And in fact the only musician I know who has fully understood this is Toshi: he possesses that fundamental 'beat'.

The musical work begins by listening to the nature of accomplished movement. The relationship is constant, and not only with the story. So when the actors display too low an energy level, the music is unable to participate in an effective way, whatever the structure of the action. In a relationship with an energy, a certain kind of music will always be possible. In order to discover it, to plug into it, it is absolutely essential that the musicians' quality of listening be developed. They are obliged to be attentive not only to silence: they must also be highly sensitive to space, and its evolving dynamics. They must watch it closely.

Tsuchitori: Listening also entails remaining vigilant to, and respecting, any musical event whatsoever.

Usually, Peter Brook and his actors leave a substantial amount of room for improvisations. Is it the same case with the music?

Tsuchitori: This question is always very difficult to tackle. There are as many ways of envisaging improvisation as there are kinds of music. When I play my own music, for example, I apply my own way of improvising; but on the other hand, when I play with jazz musicians, it becomes necessary for me to adopt *their* laws of improvisation. Nevertheless, apart from the musical sequence accompanying the *Bhagavad*

Gita episode in *The War* (a composition by Subramaniam), almost all of it is improvised to some degree, the only truly fixed element being the moment of intervention. We follow the scene, rather than individual actors. Nothing is either routine or automatic.

Do you take part in The Mahabharata *not only as a musician, but as an actor as well?*

Tsuchitori: I never separate actor from musician. As far as I am concerned, when the actor's work is good, the music is good: I am able to draw on his work, and join with him in it. I become implicated in the action.

Brook: In our work, if the execution of something is not good (which can always happen of course!), it produces a substantial and perceptible loss on the level of rhythm: everything coincides at this low moment. One cannot define rhythm; but nevertheless one can state that at the heart of a fine performance there is always rhythm.

NOTE

From an interview with Georges Banu, originally published in *Alternatives Théâtrales*, no. 24, July 1985. Translated by David Williams.

10

MUSICAL BRICOLAGE

Vincent Dehoux

Vincent Dehoux is a French musicologist who was engaged by Tsuchi-tori and Brook as musical consultant for *The Mahabharata*.[1]

The set of the 'bricoleur's' means cannot therefore be defined in terms of a project. . . . It is to be defined only by its potential use, or, putting this another way and in the language of the 'bricoleur' himself, because the elements are collected or retained on the principle that 'they may always come in handy'. . . . The 'bricoleur' addresses himself to a collection of oddments left over from human endeavours, that is, only a sub-set of the culture . . . In this continual reconstruction from the same materials, it is always earlier ends which are called upon to play the part of means . . . Once it materialises the project will therefore inevitably be at a remove from the initial aim . . . Now, the characteristic feature of mythical thought, as of 'bricolage' on the practical plane, is that it builds up structured sets, not directly with other structured sets but by using the remains and debris of events.[1]

The texture of the music in *The Mahabharata* undoubtedly evokes the aesthetic of India's various musical forms. There is no need to look very far for confirmation of that: the very presence on stage of certain kinds of instruments and the sonorities that emerge from them are in themselves revelatory. And something of an Indian influence is reflected in the actual music's style as much as its 'colour'. Given the fact that none of the musicians are of Indian origin, one may be forgiven for thinking that the work they undertook was built around as faithful an imitation of that aesthetic as possible. However, what kind of results could one hope for from a few months of work on a form of music which demands years of study? And furthermore, if that were the case, what freedom of action and degree of imaginative engagement would be available to the musicians?

As we shall see, the musical style of *The Mahabharata* does not in reality stem from reproduction or imitation. It is in fact the consequence of a process of reconstruction. Indian music did not act as a starting point for the musicians. They came towards it progressively, and I would even say quite naturally. It is therefore necessary to outline briefly the nature of this approach.

Work commenced with as open as possible a study of all traditional music forms in the world. We listened to a vast array of musical and sound patterns from all kinds of sources. Our aim was quite simply to *listen*, attentively but free from ulterior or aprioristic thoughts; in other words, with no overriding concern to fashion links with *The Mahabharata* itself. And indeed we were not searching for a particular musical style; quite the contrary. We were on the look out for original sound qualities, irrespective of structure and above all of an initial categorization of 'rough' and original sound combinations. Evidently there was no question of learning the organized language of a particular music (in this case, *a fortiori* Indian music), but of uncovering simple elements we would latch on to and record for the impact they communicated using a minimum of means. This return to fundamental sources could not be subordinated to the obligation to realize a fully structured project. Its *raison d'être* is really understandable if one is willing to see within *The Mahabharata* what Jean-Claude Carrière has called 'the Great History of Mankind'.

So, throughout the long period of listening, we were waiting for manifestations of certain illuminatory signs of a 'primary music', taken together (and without us planning it in any way) constituting an unusually rich range: our own patrimony. Our discussions reflected these first exploratory steps: we talked about the density of breath, qualities of timbre, the function of rhythm, and so on.

As the musicians tried to reproduce the musical fragments we had retained, a second stage in the work began: manipulation. This took all sorts of forms and configurations: we would attempt to reproduce particular musical patterns and sequences; these would then be imitated, rhythmically structured in different ways, arrangements modified, and so on. All of these experiments offered us a way of engaging in some sort of dialogue with our chosen fragments; a collective dialogue, which could never remain for long untouched by the individual musical practice of each of the musicians. Through imitation, reproduction and above all modification of any particular structure, each individual's 'signature' would inevitably emerge, in such a way that manipulation of this kind became a profoundly personal matter. Then musicians regrouped according to certain affinities (of culture or instrument), integrating newly acquired material into their personal work. As a result, from that moment onwards, musical activity diversified in a number of different directions. In addition to each musician's personal training and study in relation to the production, collaborative liaison with the actors focused largely on vocal work and learning certain instruments (horns, conches), as well as tentative application of accumulated musical baggage to action on stage. It was at this time that a meeting with a group of Indian musicians from Rajasthan occurred – a meeting which was to last several weeks. It took the form of workshops, essentially concerned with instrumental practice; it enabled the musicians to study new instruments as well as adapting their own skills to the style of a specific popular Indian musical idiom. In a similar vein, intermittent encounters with the Indian violinist L. Subramaniam allowed them to extend their initial explorations of the erudite aesthetics of Indian music.

Eventually, in possession of certain strengths and enriched by such collective experiences, the musicians came face to face with the actors' work. From then on, the gradual application and definitive ordering of the music became a collective endeavour: certain choices were made, experiments incessantly reassessed, progressive refinements facilitated. I do not want to relay the details of this final area of exploration; to my mind, what is vitally important here is to outline a way, one kind of approach, and not to describe its ultimate specific materialization.

One might characterize such an approach as *artisanal* in terms of the sort of progression roofing tilers follow: each new phase of work sketched in before the preceding phase has in reality come to an end, successive goals at the same time serving in turn as new points of departure. Any notion of precisely structuring the path we followed never became an issue, and in that way the process was never one of construction. In truth, there was never a question of inventing from predetermined schema of any kind. Instead, our concern was to bring together existing elements by elaborating to as great a degree as possible fresh combinations to which they lent themselves. One might say that, in order to realize the music of *The Mahabharata*, we applied the principles of 'bricolage' to musical fragments from around the world.

NOTE

Originally published in *Alternatives Théâtrales*, no. 24, July 1985. Translated by David Williams.

1 Claude Lévi-Strauss, *The Savage Mind*, Weidenfeld & Nicolson, London, 1966, pp. 17–22.

11

MALLEABILITY AND VISIBILITY

Jean Kalman interviewed by Georges Banu

The lighting designer Jean Kalman is also a freelance journalist, cameraman and writer of poetry. His only previous collaboration with Brook was on *The Cherry Orchard*. This interview was conducted shortly after the Paris premiere of *The Mahabharata*.

In an article published recently in the Journal de Chaillot, *you said, 'light can only intervene in a given space, even if it is empty'. Lighting is not involved from the very beginning of a project; it arrives later on in the process, putting finishing touches to a process generated by a director. Henri Alekan once said that in cinema lighting comes first, to which Antonioni replied that it was his vision – the eye of the director – that came first: he was the one to have first seen the island in L'Aventura. In theatre, perhaps even more so than in cinema, lighting really only stems from and augments something that has already been elaborated.*

It's possible to have quite specific images of desired lighting effects, a particular lighting style in mind; but nevertheless I think that in general lighting can only occur in relation to a particular performative or spatial proposition. For *The Mahabharata*, I was the last to arrive: I only started work in February. That did not cause any problems. I feel a need for speed and urgency in whatever I do. At the Bouffes du Nord, I am in a particular situation, because I am very familiar with this space; a space that, as is always the case with Brook, is the performance space itself. And thanks to Chloé Obolensky's work, the space is even more simplified than usual: with certain doors, windows and passageways erased, it appears almost virginal. But that makes it all the more difficult on the level of lighting.

Of course it would have been possible to entrust the invention of space throughout the production solely to the actors, as was the case with *Ubu* or *Conference of the Birds*. However, for *The Mahabharata*, Peter Brook wanted to feed and sustain the actors' creation of space with the help of lighting. Lighting would have to facilitate and ensure a rapid succession of interiors, exteriors, palaces, battlefields, and so on. Perhaps that is not immediately visible, in as much as rather than employing signs to designate specific spaces – the vault of an arch for a palace, for example – it seemed to me more appropriate to bring into play an overall spatial structure. To signify night in lighting, bluish light is the most commonly used; but sometimes it is more interesting to imagine warm amber-coloured nights which draw their legitimacy from an overall structure. In comparison with the movements of settings and objects, light has a greater degree of mobility. It enables a free and easy passage from one location to another, in a way that is almost *immaterial*. And that's what we have exploited.

But apart from this level of topographic information, doesn't light also intervene in relation to the actors and their roles?

Well, of course lighting has a variety of functions. Outside of any pre-occupying concern for realism, it can concentrate and focus very intensely: as, for example, in the *Bhagavad Gita* sequence, when Arjuna hesitates before taking part in the battle, and Krishna helps him to overcome his moment of weakness. I would suggest that light can act as a 'magnifier' and transmitter of messages, a 'speaking trumpet' (*porte-voix*), as Pierre Saveron, Jean Vilar's lighting designer, once said. Another instance in this production when light intervenes and impinges to breach the parameters of realist day/night conventions occurs when a nocturnal demon reveals her beautiful aspect in a sudden burst of love . . .

We did want to respect the passage from night to day, without ever elaborating a temporal structure that would be too restrictive. Malleability has been the fundamental rule: I have endeavoured to avoid a design 'style'. On another level, I was looking to convey the heat of India. To my great regret, I have been unable to actually go to India, but everything led me to imagine light in which heat dominates. Real heat.

We are talking about the lighting in this production as if it's a matter of course, forgetting – or at least pretending to forget – that Brook has always been a champion of the full wash, that is to say of purely functional lighting, maximum lighting that implicates and incorporates both auditorium and playing space conjointly.

To paraphrase Barthes, I would say that full lighting is the *degré zéro* of lighting, and that this zero degree can be more aesthetically satisfying than a great deal of so-called 'subtle' lighting; at least of the kind that is based on pointless embellishment or on an aetheticism clogged with wilfully aprioristic contrivances. It can be very beautiful to represent the unfolding of time as an inexorable movement, set apart from the action of human beings. But at the same time one must never take oneself for Chronos, indifferent to what really makes theatre – the actors and their relationship with an audience. The fundamental question remains: should light be used to isolate the actors, or, on the other hand, to bring them closer to the audience? Adopting the role of 'magnifier' at least takes this question into account.

In the Journal de Chaillot, *you said: 'I realize that I cannot conceive of a truly white light. How unconscientious can you get!*

Yes! I haven't resisted the corruption of colour. And – dare I say it? – neither has Peter Brook. It was amusing when a lighting designer from the Royal Shakespeare Company paid us a visit during a rehearsal. Almost scandalized, he exclaimed: 'Oh Peter, but you are using colours.'

I worked with amber, blue and green. On stage and sometimes surreptitiously in one's memory, green produces the sensation of a colour without one perceiving the light as coloured. It's similar to the spices one might use to lift a dish. The colours I use are selected in such a way that the eye integrates them very quickly as non-colours, so that light is a transparent patina for an image – both present and absent. As I have already suggested, in general nights are reflected in blues. This use of blues and ambers to represent cold and warmth accords with a convention which is based on a physiological reality. In my work, however, I have become increasingly aware of the extent to which it is possible to reverse this evidence, that a night in the theatre might just as well be warm as cold.

What are the particular demands that Brook makes during rehearsals? What input does he have?

What he asks for primarily is full visibility of faces. And I have tried to respect that to the letter, by means of full-wash front lighting. So, for example, I have used 'svobodas', those low tension units which produce a very powerful directional light; they are positioned at head height, 3 or 4 metres in front of the actors. Initially, suggestions that were made often included references to cinema. I think that is because cinema tends to prioritize the visibility of faces in 'natural' light – in other words, by means of lighting whose technical reality is not in evidence. Such a demand is somewhat problematic in the Bouffes, where equipment is open and visible. At the present time, these cinematic references have faded into the background to the extent that we are now concentrating on specific concrete details.

With as complex a narrative as this, one of the roles of the lighting is to participate in its clarification: it must sustain the story at every moment. The first part of the production is structured around an epic discourse, and that's when full-wash lighting comes into play. The lighting begins to evolve as soon as the protagonists start to assume specific identities. The movement from storytelling to drama engenders a transformation on the level of lighting.

The Mahabharata *is not presented as non-localized: clear references to India impose themselves. These are neither concealed nor denied.*

It's the warm atmospheres that have imposed themselves, and perhaps also a certain softness. In my mind I make connections with films and photographs, but I don't think that that is immediately perceivable in performance. So, for example, for the game of dice, I remembered Satyajit Ray's *The Music Room*, because I detected in it, particularly in its peculiarly soft and gentle atmosphere, a similar encounter with the tragedy of fate. On other occasions, it might have been a photograph of the greenish interior of a temple, with a single ray of sunlight cutting across it. I think that in the end India is reflected in the search for a certain visual pleasure and enjoyment.

What was your thinking behind the placing of lighting sources in the theatre? To what extent does that have an effect on one's perception of the space?

The very first question that always has to be asked in the Bouffes is: where are we going to place the lamps? There is no grid as in other theatres, and the space is very constricting. For example, the only back-lighting we have is a single 5kW projector, which is never really fully integrated into the decor, although it's more or less alright; however, if there were two of them, it would be unbearable. As is always the case, the major lighting choices are positional – even more so in the Bouffes, where the placement of lamps always establishes a tension in relation to the theatre space. It would be enough to seriously discourage any lighting designer if they were to go into the Bouffes one afternoon, before any lighting sources had been installed, with the only light coming through the glass in the roof: one wouldn't want to add anything at all.

One of the major decisions I made, and to some it may seem mistaken, was to put nothing at all on the rims of the balconies, except on the first one. Previously there have always been clusters of lamps positioned along them, like warts. Although everyone had become entirely used to them, it seems to me that the Bouffes is much more beautiful as it is now. The formal purity of the roundness of the auditorium has been rediscovered and re-emphasized. However, this decision entails a major limitation of possible lighting vantage points. In current practice, frontal lighting in the theatre comes from an angle of 40 to 60 degrees, which means that one rarely has that sparkle in actors' eyes, that absolute point of clarity that one strives for as a photographer, and without which a look seems to be dull and flat. In order to obtain that quality, we have had to retain those light sources on the first balcony, which is slightly above head height.

Brook is rather reticent with regard to technology. At the Bouffes, we simply have a small memory board with sixty-four circuits and relatively little equipment. Any new request for equipment is as exhausting as running an obstacle race. Sometimes it's rather a shame. One often imagines that inventiveness and *bricolage* can make up for what's missing, but I don't believe that. They are only stimulating in so far as one is compelled to find fresh responses called for by a production. So, for example, using wires and pulleys, we made up some sliding shutters to go in front of the 5kW projectors; these devices enabled us to modify both colour and diffusion of light according to the needs and dynamism of a scene.

As a spectator, I have to confess that during The Mahabharata, *I noticed a fair number of the kind of modulations you are describing, but that ultimately the impression I received was rather of coherent unified lighting. The light itself seemed to reflect Brook's taste for totality.*

Isn't that how it should be? Achieving variety without ever losing sight of the continuity. Mustn't the multiplicity of effects always be harmonized fully within an overall unity? Such lighting can offer us a mental image of India through this epic story.

NOTE

From an interview with Georges Banu, originally published in *Alternatives Théâtrales*, no. 24, July 1985. Translated by David Williams.

12

ENERGY AND THE ENSEMBLE
Actors' Perspectives

ANDRZEJ SEWERYN (DURYODHANA, YUDISHTHIRA)

Interviewed by Martine Millon

Born in East Germany, Seweryn has acted in almost forty films in his parents' native Poland, starring in a number of Wajda's films. After graduating from the National School of Drama in Warsaw, he worked as a stage actor at the Athenao. Since 1980, he has been based in Paris, working in theatre with such directors as Chéreau, Regy, Serban, Sobel and Vitez. *The Mahabharata* is his first collaboration with Peter Brook. He played the role of Duryodhana in the French-language production, then switched to Yudishthira for the world tour – his first English-speaking role.

What initially struck me in Brook's approach was the fact of working for ten months before the premiere, a period of very intensive and specific work on the body. Brook wanted to awaken everything in us – every cell, every finger. There was also a great deal of work on breathing and the voice, as well as exercises in learning how to enter a rhythm almost unconsciously. Much of this reminded me of my early years at theatre school in Warsaw, although here it was infinitely more precise, and as a result more clearly understood by me. Brook makes much greater demands. He directs with extreme precision.

During the trip to India, in fact we worked on only one or two occasions. Once we had come together as a group, we were given specific tasks to fulfil. On one occasion, at a temple in the forest, Peter asked us all to go out into the woods and to bring something back. Some people gathered leaves, others found dry branches and flowers; I brought back a handful of earth. We put all of this material in one corner, then began to work on an exercise with our eyes closed. While I was involved in this, I suddenly became aware of a strange presence. Opening one eye, I saw an Indian woman approach the little altar we had built: she knelt in front of it, prayed and then left. For me, that was one of the most remarkable moments of the entire journey. Quite simply it had proved to us that God is everywhere. Incidentally, on one of our last days in India, Peter asked us not to tell other people about our experiences on the trip. Not because they are 'secret', but because they are difficult to recount; and it is only right that something shared by us should remain between us. As a collective experience, the journey helped cement the group. We finally became a unit after five months of work.

Figure 12.1 Andrzej Seweryn as Yudishthira in 'The Game of Dice'. (Photographer – Gilles Abegg)

In his work on Hindu myth, George Dumézil always refers to Duryod-hana as 'bad' in inverted commas, as opposed to the 'good' Pandavas. However, we were interested primarily in understanding Duryodhana's motivation: we wanted to discover his humanity. It is a European tendency to be intrigued by evil; goodness is somehow less interesting. I merely exploited that impulse to make of him someone we can understand. And in India we found out that the Sanskrit language possesses no word for 'evil' . . .

Duryodhana is a victim of his fate, he is condemned to be what he is: he fulfils his *karma*. The destruction of the world is never his goal. He believes that he is defending his kingdom. He is an idealist, who loves

89

those that are on his side. In the end, he *becomes* a destructive force, an agent of annihilation, although he has been a good king. His mother pays homage to him at his death: 'I have seen the earth governed by you,' she says. His flaw is that he sees no need for the gods, something which becomes eminently clear when he informs Krishna and Arjuna that he has no need of Krishna, only of his armies. Then he deliberately turns his back when Krishna manifests his 'universal form', so as not to see it. He represents a world without God. He remains convinced he will succeed on his own in realizing what he wants to do, despite the fact that his opponents are the sons of gods. Perhaps he is unaware of that fact.

Duryodhana is a solitary character, always set in opposition to everything and everyone: to his father, his mother, Bhishma, Drona. 'You all hate me,' he says. He does, however, exclude himself from many things, in particular from an open vision of the cosmos. Nevertheless, he does go to the very end of himself; at least he is consistent. And this most hated of characters is the only one to die happy.

One of the difficulties of interpretation must be to make him human without working psychologically, in a Stanislavskian way . . .

What do you mean by psychology? What is the Stanislavski system? There is a great deal of linguistic confusion in this area. At the school where I trained in Poland, we were steeped in Stanislavski's method: I am the product of that school and that approach. If I am to play a human being, and not some inanimate object, how can I bring it to life without psychology? It seems that here in France, psychology primarily implies slowness . . .

It always suggests attenuated, in half-tints, on a small scale. Whereas in this production performances are grand, on an epic scale, sketched with broad strokes. They are based on energy and clarity . . .

But that is precisely what I mean. In the absence of psychology, you could never achieve that degree of clarity. In order for every hundredth of a second to be infused with life, as Peter would say, you must know what life is. Perhaps we should call it 'life', rather than 'psychology'.

Our process has been to start with enormous complexity and end up with simplicity, thanks to what I would call 'psychology' and what Peter would call 'detail'. Our initial aim was to free the body of its own inner obstacles, then to follow a similar process in relation to the voice and pronunciation. The ideal state that Peter refers to as 'transparent' is very difficult to attain; occasionally, for a minute or two in a performance, it flows unimpeded by blockages.

Broadly, we have used two sorts of improvisation: first, what I would call 'pure' improvisation, and second, improvisation rooted in the text or narrative contexts. Pure improvisations have opened me up enormously:

they oblige me to forget one of my tendencies, which is to concentrate too much on form. I have achieved things that have surprised me, I have felt utterly free. Ensemble work is another crucial element in this area. And fortunately I have been able to find my place and role in the group's work very quickly. After a month and a half, I knew where I stood. I think it was largely the others who helped me on this level. They began by locating me in terms of my areas of sensitivity and insensitivity, something which filled me with a sense of security I really needed. Until that point, I had been scared – to tell you the truth, I'm not sure of what. Perhaps of not being rich enough to be a true partner.

What one learns here is that this is not only a job, or a craft. One also comes to recognize what is human, and what it is to be human. I hope that we have become – I almost said 'better' – more demanding of ourselves, more disciplined, more open and respectful of others. Theatre can become a way of life. I would love to go on living with this group. We see each other for fourteen hours a day at work, but I would like to live with them outside of the theatre as well. I would also like to see them again as they were during the trip to India. In that way, I could get to know new and different facets, and that would nourish our work.

NOTE

From an interview with Martine Millon, originally published in *Alternatives Théâtrales*, no. 24, July 1985. Translated by David Williams.

VITTORIO MEZZOGIORNO (ARJUNA)

Interviewed by Maria Shevtsova

Born in Naples, Mezzogiorno originally studied law. Although he started his career as a theatre actor in Italy with Eduardo de Filippo, Vittorio Mezzogiorno is best known as a film actor, taking major

Figure 12.2 Vittorio Mezzogiorno as Arjuna in 'Exile in the Forest'. (Photographer – Gilles Abegg)

roles in Rosi's *The Three Brothers* (for which he was voted best actor in Italy, 1980), Beneix's *The Moon in the Gutter* and Chéreau's *L'Homme Blessé*. The French-language version of *The Mahabharata* marked his return to the theatre. In order to continue playing Arjuna during the world tour, he was obliged to learn English.

How long did it take you to get used to Brook's way of working?

Well, it took an awfully long time, and I'm still getting used to it. We spent ten months rehearsing for the French production. I have now been with Brook for about four years and, to tell the truth, his methods are still not completely familiar to me. It isn't as if working with him has become simple, although it is still extremely fascinating.

How did it feel going from Italian to French, then to English? I know you had to learn English . . .

Yes, but I also had to learn French. It's only that French wasn't totally new to me because I had already made some films in France. Just the same, I had to do a great deal of work in order to perform in the theatre in a foreign language. The ten hard months of rehearsal for the French version included work on my diction. I had a smattering of French, but it's obvious that performing in the theatre in an acceptable fashion is altogether a different story. As for the English version, I was sent to study the language. Since I had never taken English at school, I had to start from the beginning.

I like English much more than French, and have the feeling that it is probably more beautiful to perform in because its words are stronger. I get the impression that every word in English is carved out of stone. It has been intriguing to discover how the same ideas can be expressed with totally new sounds. I think that English has given my work greater solidity. I can't be precise, but my impression is that sounds coming from a different language require different gestures and movements.

As I was watching the performance the other night, it occurred to me that you would be wonderful in Shakespeare . . .

I have absolutely no idea about that. I have never performed Shakespeare, but must say that, having had this experience in the theatre, I would love to make contact with Shakespeare's characters. I have been reading an extremely interesting essay that was sent to me here in Adelaide, on the close similarity between Arjuna and Henry V. As a friend of Falstaff, Henry had a dissolute youth, then became a king fully aware of his sovereign role. Perhaps Henry is the first of Shakespeare's characters I would like to study, starting with when he was a prince in *Henry IV*, parts one and two. Brook has promised to tell me which of Shakespeare's characters he thinks would suit me best. The fact that I asked him probably hides my secret desire to reach into this world.

From the point of view of cultural interpretation, what were the main problems and difficulties of the actors, all of whom come from diverse ethnic and cultural backgrounds, but together encountered a classical Indian epic poem?

I can only speak about my own problems, not about those of the group as a whole. This was completely new material, and each one of us had to deal with it according to his or her own nature. Some read a good deal. Others devoted themselves entirely to work on their bodies. I had to interpret the first thing that came to hand – a great warrior. I worked body and soul on the physical exercises. In order to perform the role of a warrior, I had to prepare my body to get the appropriate results. Then I read parts of *The Mahabharata*: not all of it was available in translation. I read interpretative essays. In other words, I tried to combine both physical and intellectual work.

I was fearful at the beginning and inhibited by the idea of playing Arjuna, because it is extremely difficult for any actor to deal with this kind of unblemished hero. I have always tried to find the key to a character by looking for his weaknesses, weaknesses that invariably motivate his actions. For instance Karna, Arjuna's illegitimate brother, is always motivated by the fact that he was abandoned. This has tarnished his life. Consequently he is always tense, overwrought, caught in an atmosphere of hatred and revenge, and always eager to get results. He is driven by a will to conquer mountains. I could not approach Arjuna from this angle. In fact, I could not broach Arjuna from any side.

Arjuna was psychologically very difficult for me. Being imperfect, I did not know how to perform a perfect hero, a demigod. Bit by bit, I found a way to free myself from the block of inhibitions and obstacles facing me. I am still trying, despite having worked on Arjuna for more than three years. I am now in the process of finding my freedom not so much by looking for a way to play a demigod as by discovering the possibilities of what could be like a demigod in me. In other words, I have to look for Arjuna's qualities in me. I have to bring Arjuna closer to me so as to be more truthful on stage. I have to be myself, with my own impulses. I have discovered – and I may seem to be stating the obvious here – that Arjuna is a human being; in the end this was the only way I could perform him.

I firmly believe that an actor can only give what he has. He cannot go outside himself or beyond himself. I always thought this was true for film, and now I'm discovering it's just as true in theatre. I can only dig deep into myself and draw on the well inside me. These considerations have become necessary because, at the beginning, beat my head as I might,

I had no idea where to turn. In every situation and scene involving Arjuna, I keep in mind that Arjuna has his own story to which I give my own impulses. In this way I have a greater chance of touching spectators.

But Arjuna's not only an invincible warrior. A warrior might well be a mere brute, whereas Arjuna really loves women. In Virata's court, he succeeds in transforming himself into a woman – not by chance, I'm positive – and into someone well versed in music and dance. These things are hidden inside him. What is interesting about Arjuna in his double identity is that being a woman means giving life rather than taking it away, which is what a warrior does. The fact that he turns into a woman makes Arjuna two-sided, a complete being.

By stressing how you looked for Arjuna within yourself do you mean to suggest that you didn't look for him as much in the framework of Indian culture?

It was perhaps a matter of consecutive journeys. That is, I first looked for cultural information, and then, having that as a basis, was able to go into myself. I don't know exactly whether, while I was looking for my route to freedom, I actually changed direction at a certain moment, or whether the two processes were necessary and complementary.

The whole company spent time in India, an absolutely non-intellectual period in the sense that each one of us did what he or she wanted. We didn't make any intellectual preparations, or study specific things here and there. We breathed in India. We absorbed impressions. I seem to have understood that this too, this lack of intellectualism, is also a constant feature of Brook's work.

You have said that each of you brought something from your own nature, but nature is also impregnated by society. How do you think that you have contributed to the production as an actor of Italian culture?

I don't know to what extent my nature is Italian. It is bound to be in some way, but I don't know how I actually carry Italian qualities. There is probably what could be called an Italian vitality in me, perhaps a certain mental agility. There probably are scenes in which spectators can discern my Italian hinterland, or, more accurately, a landscape belonging to Napoli and the south of Italy in general. This question could probably be answered more easily by someone watching me perform in such a heterogeneous group. It would probably be clearer to someone watching from the outside. Perhaps I could ask you?

I realize that the question is difficult, that this type of question can generate superficial ideas, stereotypes and 'folklore' images in the pejorative sense of the term. But I would say that southern Italy contributes to your work in how clearly you articulate emotions and how you accompany them with open, eloquent gestures. There is a great deal of physical articulation in everything you say and do. Also my impression is that your rounded diction wasn't learnt in a drama school. It seems that your energy, inner energy as well as external expression, has a southern (I would really say Neapolitan) tone. Naples is an extremely dynamic city where everything buzzes with life. So I cannot imagine this energy coming from you as being, say, Parisian energy, which I think has a sharper quality . . .

You see, your question should be answered by those in a position to do so.

Do you think that working with actors of multiple nationalities and cultures is essential for realizing Brook's objective of creating a 'universal' theatre, a theatre accessible to everybody?

Brook automatically realizes it by putting together people of different colour and nature. For all the diverse languages spoken by the actors in it, our production has its own particular language which anybody can understand. Obviously the choice of actors from so many different races and nationalities contributes to the scope implied in the idea of 'universal' theatre.

As an actor, what else have you learnt from your work with Brook?

I think that an actor continues to learn all his life. I wanted to have this experience with Brook because I felt I had a lot to learn. Being a film actor with precious little groundwork in theatre, I needed it. I'm learning that I have a body and can use it consciously. I'm learning to use my voice a little better. I always had it, but was not aware of it. Many of Brook's exercises are elementary: placing your voice, for example, or finding your body's equilibrium. These are absolutely essential.

The work we do with Brook is very detailed. Brook worked on my becoming conscious of my body, and on the fact that I express myself with my whole body. Performing means being right there with your mind, body and words in the same instant. I'm saying something that seems to be quite natural, but it isn't. These three things *have* to be united. You are only ever really saying a line if your thoughts are in your words and, at the same time, your body is following what you are saying.

How did your experience in film help you in your collaboration with Brook?

I had many of the vices of film actors. For instance, I was used to not thinking about how I spoke because I knew my voice would be dubbed afterwards – this happens in Italian films. I also had other bad habits derived from how angles were shot. I would say to myself, 'I know my face is being framed', or 'Now it's my whole body, now up to my belt', etc. In short, I was used to performing in bits and pieces – and always without thinking of my voice, because I often spoke in one language while the other actors replied in another. In the theatre with Brook, at last I have had to act with all of me, all at the one time, in a determined space.

And this was another aspect of the work I found extremely difficult, for the simple reason that I was not at all used to performing with my whole being. In the theatre, a change of space can be conjured up in the imagination. In *The Mahabharata*, the imagination must rule. At one moment you are in a forest. Somebody comes in, puts a carpet on the ground, and it's no longer a forest: it's a palace. A thousand spaces are created in this way; the changes are realized far more easily than in film.

Have you noticed any differences in how audiences have responded to The Mahabharata according to which city you are performing in – say, Paris, Perth, New York or Adelaide?

The difference I noticed most was in America, when we first arrived there. I got the impression that people there were not disposed to listening attentively to something for a long time. So they struck me as people who combined superficial with immediate responses. Their reactions were more lively, and also let's say more childlike than those of European audiences. In Europe generally I felt a great degree of concentration, particularly on the narrative. Here in Australia there seems to be a mixture of the two. People listen with interest and also have lively, childlike responses – in that they laugh readily, for example.

Do you see a parallel between the war that takes place in the Mahabharata and the nuclear age in which we live?

This link is made repeatedly in *The Mahabharata* whenever someone is appalled by the possible destruction of the world. Vyasa, the author of the poem, says, 'It has already happened': it has happened and it can happen again. My own impression of *The Mahabharata* is that this kind of great sacrifice is unavoidable, as if it were the destiny of the human species, in its very nature.

Although he is born to be the greatest of warriors, Arjuna has a horror of war; that is, he is horrified by the task conferred upon him. He fulfils his calling. He arms himself with destructive weapons, but does not use them – he does not want to use them, consistently refuses to do so. His psychological collapse before the war occurs because he does not want to destroy his family, which is humankind. So Arjuna always has this terrible possibility before him and always seeks to escape from it, even if he is ultimately forced to face it: Krishna drags him by the hair to do what he has to do.

And yet war there is in The Mahabharata, even if Arjuna does not want it.

Precisely: that's exactly what I meant when I said that the sacrifice was inevitable. Nobody wants war, least of all Arjuna's brother Yudishthira, who is destined to be the best of kings. He is also the one who has to call upon a universal massacre; yet he is still the best of kings. So the earth needs him to govern, although he is the one who will carry humanity to destruction.

NOTE

From an interview conducted in Italian by Maria Shevtsova on 27 February 1988, during the visit of *The Mahabharata* to the Adelaide Festival. The translation is also by Maria Shevtsova.

MALLIKA SARABHAI (DRAUPADI)

Mallika Sarabhai is now recognized as one of India's finest classical dancers. She made her screen debut at the age of 16, subsequently featuring in almost forty films. With her mother Mrinalini, a highly respected performer in her own right, she is co-director of the Darpana Academy of Performing Arts in Ahmedabad, Gujarat. She has undertaken research into folk performing arts and has a PhD in Arts Management. *The Mahabharata* was her first collaboration with Peter Brook: she was the only Indian member of the company. She was obliged to learn French for the original production, which also marked her first professional acting role.

'Maha' in Sanskrit and in most Indian languages means 'great'. 'Bharata' is alternatively defined as either the race that lives in India, or mankind, because we think that everyone originally came from India, or India itself. So *The Mahabharata* is really 'the great India', or 'the story of mankind', the story of the original men and women, our ancestors.

India is a country in which most things are orally transmitted; they have come down from one generation to another. *The Mahabharata* was a series of stories which were probably first told three or three-and-a-half thousand years ago. The basic structure is built around the kinship ties of a ruling family divided into two. At the same time as the kernel of *The Mahabharata* was being created, Hinduism was developing in a philosophical fashion, and was being recorded in written form for perhaps the first time. So somewhere along the way story, religion, philosophy and moral history all became wrapped into one.

In India we are brought up with *The Mahabharata*. It is the source of our popular heroes and heroines, our popular music, our bedtime stories, our parables on morality, our values. You can go into a very remote area of North Eastern India, for example, where there are still tribes which haven't really changed in hundreds of years, and they will sing songs to Krishna, or perform stories with characters from *The Mahabharata*. On the other hand, you could go to a completely different part of the country, and they will do puppet shows or traditional shadow puppetry with these same characters. So in India it is very difficult to escape these stories anywhere, in any epoch, in any art form.

There is an odd situation in the publishing industry in India. The greatest success story of any comic strip is something called Amar Chitra Katha, which is based entirely on *The Mahabharata* or *The Ramayana*. It is difficult to understand this in a western context where religion is set so much apart: it is something you go to church to practice. It is not like that for us. For example, if there is one child in a school who is very strong or very large, the other children will compare him with Bhima. In

Figure 12.3 Mallika Sarabhai as Draupadi in 'Exile in the Forest'.
(Photographer – Gilles Abegg)

India when you talk of Draupadi or Krishna or Bhima in the middle of a completely contemporary conversation, you still know exactly who you are talking about. And that is the extent of *The Mahabharata*'s contemporaneity in India today.

Unfortunately, because of the all-pervasive quality of *The Mahabharata* in India, most of us take it for granted. Unless one is a scholar of Sanskrit or of Hinduism, a scholar in fact working on *The Mahabharata*, one rarely sits down and actually reads it. When I first came to work on Jean-Claude Carrière's version, I felt that the script was so incorrect in many ways: all of the women characters in particular had been incredibly badly written. So just in order to fight for the existence of the woman I had come to play, I delved into every version of *The Mahabharata* that I could lay my hands on. I was forced to study it as I had never done before.

In the course of rehearsals, gradually certain things were added or cut out. I would quibble, or defend some detail quite ferociously. I would talk to Jean-Claude about it, and he would explain to me that a European audience, deprived of any frames of reference for *The Mahabharata*, would understand it more clearly this way. I still don't agree with everything. After the game of dice, for example, when Yudishthira has lost everything including his wife Draupadi, the queen Gandhari declares, 'Like any woman, Draupadi does not distinguish herself from her husband. She comprises a part of him, she is him.' As far as I am concerned, that is deeply shocking. An Indian woman steeped in *The Mahabharata* would never speak in that way!

In India we believe that the five Pandavas represent the five senses. Now, if the five Pandavas are the five fingers of a hand, the palm is Draupadi; that is how it becomes a strong fist. Without the palm, the fingers would be completely separate, they would never be united. In each husband, one can see one human quality taken to its greatest extreme: the mind, the feelings, strength, knowledge, wisdom. Individually each one is but a part of a totality, but when united they become the complete human nature, the complete Purusha.

As far as the terrible war that is the central subject of *The Mahabharata* is concerned, I know that it simply puzzles and perplexes many westerners. It seems very clear to me: you have to cut off a gangrenous limb. When evil reigns, one must fight to the death to put an end to it. And in our work, we discovered that the epic cuts across everything: time, colour, race, language. These same issues have continued to confront human beings over millennia.

I knew very little about Peter Brook's work beforehand. I knew from Indian newspapers that he was making a nine-hour theatre version of *The Mahabharata* in French and English. I had met him briefly once when he had come to Ahmedabad to study costumes at my family's costume museum. I didn't like him when I met him at first; I found him extremely rude – he says he was very unwell, which I am willing to believe! Then one day in 1984 I received a telegram, saying that Peter was in India and wanted to fly down to see me. When Peter arrived with Jean-Claude, Chloé and the gang, I was recovering from the most terrible attack of hepatitis, and I was five months pregnant. I hadn't been able to get out of bed for five months because of the hepatitis. Obviously I knew he would offer me something if he was coming, but I had no idea that he would offer me the one role that there was no way I could refuse . . .

I found the theory that went into the costumes very fascinating. Chloé managed to take elements that, to somebody who knows India, were very definitely Indian. The colours that she used, for instance – white and off-white, saffron, red – are all so Indian. The fact of using design elements that were Indian, developed and even made in India, yet putting them together in a jigsaw that's completely different, makes the end results Indian and at the same time non-Indian. It was very important to avoid making it into an 'ethnic' production.

As a director, Peter's working process is organic. I must confess that at the beginning it was very difficult for me. Many things seemed odd to me, even wrong. Now I understand how Peter meanders and manoeuvres, how he uses detours to arrive at the polar opposite of the starting point. The directions he gives are entirely contrary to what an Indian would do, but he gets to the truth. Peter does not let you fall back on any clichés, or any predetermined understanding. This means that he forces you to peel away the outer layers of a character, to find the basic silence and nothingness within. At those times when he thinks the work is not leading anywhere, Peter can be very precise, very cutting: even very hurtful and sometimes unreasonable.

During the rehearsal period, I discovered a particularly strong link with the African and Asian actors. Somewhere there was a conscience and a consciousness that I shared with them and that I had to explain to the western actors. Often when I had to take on the role of sole Indian in the group and explain why certain things were or were not done, one of the Africans would understand it immediately. Similarly, when it came to why some things were respectful and others weren't, without any apparent logic to them, the Balinese or Japanese or Senegalese actors would understand immediately. But for instance a German actor might say, 'I don't think that's true'. For me, it was a great joy to discover this connection.

In my conversations with Peter, I have often asked him why he works with an international group. One of the things he said is that if we can create something that is harmonious in such a small group of mixed races and cultures and colours, then the world has a chance.

Although all of my life I have been a closet feminist, or perhaps more accurately a humanist, living with Draupadi radicalized me. It has made me take up certain positions, and has caused me to change the thrust of a lot of the creative work I am doing. I might be an Indian woman, but I think I am primarily a woman of my times. And Draupadi for me is the epitome of what a contemporary woman's role-model should be. She is an entirely modern woman. She is both very strong and at the same time vulnerable. She is just, and she wins respect through her behaviour. She accepts the suffering brought about by her husbands, but not passively. Her compassion and gentleness give way, when necessary, to something else – she tells her husbands just how worthless they are if need be. She possesses a sort of spiritual grace . . . Living with her has been a revelation.

There were definite stages in the development of the play, the first being those rehearsals when Jean-Claude Carrière sat in and the entire play was rewritten several times over. But the play became strongest to my mind once we had performed it in Australia in the open air. Somehow, transferring it from small enclosed stages to a location where you could look up and see the sky – where the wind could blow you away at any stage, where you were holding on to things while talking about the destruction of the world – suddenly it made the play very rich and powerful. Of course, for me, moving from French to English was already like coming home. Going from the play to the film, which I loved making, was even more so.

I have to say completely unequivocally, both as an Indian and as a woman, that had I not felt that this representation was right, had I felt at any time that there was anything of which I should be ashamed and for which I would have to apologize to Indians, then I would have left. I think the fact that I was involved in the French version, then chose to come back to do the English tour and then again for the film, was the greatest compliment I could pay.

NOTE

This text conflates two interviews, the first published in *Théâtre en Europe*, no. 8, 1985, the second recorded for a documentary film, *Making the Mahabharata* (R. M. Associates, 1989). Translated by David Williams.

SOTIGUI KOUYATE (BHISHMA, PARASHURAMA)

Interviewed by Martine Millon

The descendant of a long line of *griots* (the West African storyteller-historian caste preserving and transmitting oral culture), Sotigui Kouyate was born in Burkino-Faso. He has worked for many years as a dancer, singer, actor, choreographer, musician and composer, even finding time to play professional soccer (up to international level) until 1966. He is the founder of the National Ballet Company of Upper Volta, the Volta Theatre Company and an instrumental ensemble. He has appeared in many African, German and French films, most recently *Black Mic-Mac* (1986). *The Mahabharata* marked his first collaboration with Brook; he learnt English from scratch for the world tour. Continuing his collaboration with the CICT, he played Prospero in Brook's production of *The Tempest*, which opened at the Bouffes du Nord in September 1990.

Figure 12.4 Sotigui Kouyate as Bhishma in 'The War'. (Photograph courtesy of Adelaide Festival of the Arts)

Before we went to India, we were grounded in the work. We had to weld a unified group out of the twenty-five actors and musicians, all from different cultures and nationalities. We wanted to establish a coherent unit, who talked the same language, metaphorically speaking. There were

104

countless exercises involving the voice, listening, performance skills, led by either instructors or Peter himself; and there was training in martial arts.

Starting in September 1984, this preparatory period went on for five months. During that time, we read Carrière's translation, which was reworked endlessly, as well as another translation of the entire epic. *The Mahabharata* offered a wholly new universe for us. The more we steeped ourselves in it, the more we wanted to know about it. And it was at that point that the journey to India occurred. If we had left any earlier, it would merely have been tourism, as opposed to continuing research, direct first-hand experience.

You cannot describe India; it is something that one experiences. And yet it has a number of points in common with Africa: the way of life, famine, the sun, nature, vegetation. If you restricted yourself to the land and nature, you might get the impression of being in Africa. And the way of relating to people is very close to my own experience, my own people. Indians are tactile contact people, full of human warmth: they intermingle. It is almost impossible for a foreigner to perceive the different religions and castes.

It is difficult to say whether this journey helped me create the character of Bhishma, because my conception of this character is still evolving and being reassessed daily. I would not claim to have mastered him. I am still exploring certain points of access, certain approaches to him. There's something in *The Mahabharata* you can never finally grasp and fix – and this is nothing to do with it being a Hindu story: I am only beginning to understand how far this poem goes beyond Hinduism. It is universal, and it echoes my own life and experience closely. By birth I am a Moslem, and although I am not practising, I remain a believer. I can detect the spirit of my religion within *The Mahabharata*.

Bhishma is the figure in the poem who most strongly embodies religion. That's why it is so dangerous for me as an actor: it is very difficult to know how to embody a god. And yet I believe that everyone retains a divine element within themselves, and that is what one must strive to disinter from oneself for this role. By searching inside oneself for what is divine, one ends up thinking the whole world could be divine. At the same time, one must retain one's humanity. Search for the god within the man, and the man within the god: for Bhishma is both god and man.

In that sense, the journey to India did help me. Everything is religious over there. Indians' profound respect for and attachment to their religion makes it a vital part of life, a cohesive force. At the same time, recognizing that *The Mahabharata* is not limited to just one society frees and opens it to a greater degree. The further you go, the further there still is to go: it's like the Himalayas. For me, this is a journey whose end remains out of sight. I have set out, I am on my way, but as yet I think I have done no more than find the right direction.

Although each one of the other members of the group has their own approach, I don't think there is a great margin of difference in ways of conceiving things. As I have already said, the most difficult problem initially was to constitute a group able to speak the same language, as opposed to individuals locked within private worlds. One cannot speak the same language if one does not have similar sensations. The journey to India helped bond the group through common sensations and experiences. You can't keep such sensations to yourself: that's what opening up is all about. *The Mahabharata* is a story we tell to others. What I have within me and what the others have within them are pooled and shared, and that helps. You see the welcome others give to what you make available to them. And if it is not well received, perhaps it's bad; or you didn't know how to express it; or your partner was not open and available.

Bhishma's death is very particular – serene, almost leisurely. There seems to be no interruption between his life and his death, no clear break . . .

Bhishma gives all the time, right up to his deathbed. He has awaited universal destruction in this battle in order to show man's attachment to life – he tells the story of the drop of honey. On the very threshold of death, man is tempted by the drop of honey and forgets the danger: the taste of life infuses and animates him as far as death's door. Bhishma's death is a lesson in living.

At one and the same time, Bhishma is a sort of priest (he remains celibate), a moral authority above the mêlée, and a warrior who ends up fighting against those he wants to win. He's quite a complex and contradictory character . . .

Aren't they all in *The Mahabharata*? Although in *The War*, Bhishma is the only one to keep his white robe intact, unblemished, even though he fights. He has a separate status, a glorious divine reality.

To my mind, performing is being. And with Brook I have learnt more in six months than in twenty years, particularly on a human level. His working methods and advice have given me the means to extend and develop what I have within myself. He allows the actor freedom – *demands* it. The actor must reach deep within himself, to try to discover what there is inside of which he's unaware – or perhaps that he senses, but does not possess enough courage or will to express. With infinite calm, gentleness and patience, Peter guides you in this direction; so much better than a director *showing* it to you. And outside of the work, he takes time to talk with each individual. You are at liberty to talk about personal worries and problems just as much as, on a more professional level, about your blocks. He has also allowed me to understand that one never truly arrives at a definite summit: it's the life of the ongoing journey that matters.

Preparation consists primarily of liberating an actor from his blocks. Everything must flow, free of obstacles. Simultaneously, and at every moment, one must find a tranquillity, serenity and balance in oneself, *and* a strength, an energy. The most essential thing I have learnt from Brook is the ability to overcome obstacles – a kind of liberation that isn't so much a matter of technique, of the kinds one learns in schools. One must be able to confide one's difficulties. Even entrusting them to someone else instills confidence. At that point, Brook will not present you with the solution, but will ask, 'What do *you* really think about it?' And he finds those elements that are necessary to bring you to a position of freedom; from there you can go where you want. That's what is really marvellous. If he simply said to me, '*That's* what you must do', I would set about mechanically imitating him. I would have to force myself to feel what he had told me. On the other hand, by only pointing out the direction to me, I discover and respond. Brook has cleared the path, but my creativity and engagement is truer, it remains organically part of me. And in the future I will know where to start to arrive at that point.

In fact, paradoxically, Brook gives us everything, even though every-thing comes from us. He leads and guides us like a father bringing his children together, helping them to understand themselves, to be aware of themselves, to love and express themselves.

To tell you the truth, outside of the theatre I am bored. At the moment, we spend fourteen hours a day working together, and when we go home, we phone each other. It's like a huge family. After working in this way, it is going to be very difficult to work elsewhere. There will be an immense sense of loss and nostalgia.

NOTE

From an interview with Martine Millon, originally published in *Alternatives Théâtrales*, no. 24, July 1985. Translated by David Williams.

YOSHI OIDA (DRONA, KITCHAKA)

Interviewed by Martine Millon and Olivier Ortolani

Originally trained in Noh theatre, then an actor in Japanese film, television and theatre, Yoshi Oida left Japan in 1968 to work with Peter Brook on *The Tempest* at the Roundhouse in London, Brook's first experiment with an international company. Their collaboration has continued since that time. Oida has been involved in all of the Centre's major productions and journeys, and is recognized as one of the cornerstones of the collective work. During the late 1970s, he staged some of his own productions, drawing much of his inspiration from traditional Japanese culture. Performances included *Amse Tsuchi, Interrogations, The Tibetan Book of the Dead* and a version of Dante's *Divine Comedy*.

Peter Brook's theatre is a living theatre, a theatre for today. In his search for such a theatre, he has undertaken an enormously difficult task, because all theatre is continually under threat of death – at the hands of theory or of cheap and vacuous entertainment. Peter always asks himself the same questions: 'What is theatre? What is it for us today? Does it possess certain fundamental characteristics? Where does its power lie?' He refuses to imitate things that others have already done, only looking at past styles and concerns in order to reappraise them and to develop something fresh and unknown. He undertakes research. Anyone who does not involve themselves in research has to ask themselves why they are involved in theatre at all. For the money? Maybe for the prestige? But these can only ever lead to an impasse.

During the rehearsal period, Peter never says to us, 'You must do it this way'. He does not force us to do anything. Instead of intervening, he requires us to be responsible and present, leaving almost everything up to us, with a remarkable degree of patience. Instead of saying, 'Now I want you to do this movement', or, 'Now you have to turn to the left', he waits until the actor himself has discovered the appropriate response. Peter encourages the actor to discover precisely what it is that is required of him, what is right at that moment.

Improvision holds a central position in our work; it has a crucial role to play. There are two general conceptions of improvisation. The first, commonly applied, is of a rather romantic woolly kind. It suggests that anything can happen in improvisation, that participants are utterly free. The second conception is one to which we subscribe. It maintains that certain obligations, 'rules' or 'laws' if you like, are necessary for the success of any improvisation, for spontaneity and discipline to coexist. In the Japanese Noh theatre, for example, every physical movement is predetermined in a fixed way, every single step is specified. Within the

Figure 12.5 Yoshi Oida performs the death of Drona in 'The War'.
(Photographer – Gilles Abegg)

109

confines of this very strict framework, however, actors are free: they can improvise.

For us, improvisation cannot mean proceeding aimlessly and at will. It is a tool for forging a living organic connection between actor and audience. Peter requires us to discover this level of communication in a practical forum. In rehearsal the audience is made up of the other actors. Between those who create and those who watch, there can exist something alive, and we are trying to locate this vitality. In every evening's performance, narrative, text and *mise-en-scène* are identical – but it is imperative to discover a fresh life in each performance. Otherwise theatre assumes the qualities of something like a computer. It loses any sense of immediacy or fascination, and dissipates in boredom. In reality, improvisation necessitates pinpointing and responding to the particular life that circulates between actor and audience at that moment in the theatre. In one way of course, even during performances of *The Mahabharata*, there are still elements of improvisation. The work is never completely fixed, and Peter has always wanted us to retain some of the freedom of improvisation. If true improvisation remains a goal, then the preparatory work might perhaps be seen as an apprenticeship. Once body, voice and spirit are freed, once one has found one's character, only then can improvisation begin.

The three-month journey in Africa that we undertook in 1973 has had an enormous impact on our research. In Africa, we were confronted with audiences who were wholly unfamiliar with our kinds of theatre. Of course, before we left, we worked on a performance for an imagined audience, but the reality there bore no resemblance to our expectations, and the performance simply did not work. We were forced to invent everything anew, from scratch. One day, one of the actors suddenly had a great idea: he took off his boots and put then in the space in front of the spectators, who immediately started to show interest. In Africa, just as in Japan, boots represent wealth, culture and status. From then on, a point of contact – an understanding – existed between our audience and us, and we were able to begin improvising. Someone put the boots on, then walked to and fro, displaying their immense power and wealth. People immediately understood, and loved what was going on. Similarly our singing often met with great enthusiasm, but reactions were hardly ever the same: nothing was predictable. Whenever we performed songs from the depths of our hearts, brimming with emotion, spectators would respond positively. When we played modern music, communication fell apart. In the end, it became apparent that only clear simple performances would be accepted. Complex ideas, or rather the products of any intellectualization, stood no chance at all.

Just as this trip to Africa helped us discover the basic language of *The Conference of the Birds*, so too a two-week journey to India allowed us to crystallize something in *The Mahabharata*. Inevitably we were exposed to Kathakali and other forms of classical Indian performance, but our intention was not to borrow elements from these forms. Our fundamental concern was to try to learn and experience at first hand, both physically and spiritually, something of the richness of Hindu culture. Personally I did find much inspiration in Kathakali for the character of Kitchaka. But the primary intention of the journey was for us to gain impressions and personal responses to help us on our own individual inner paths. One day for example, from a boat on the Ganges, I saw some bodies being cremated; it made a profound impression on me. Peter wanted to avoid any kind of intellectual or scholarly explanations of what we saw. He felt that that kind of knowledge wouldn't help us as actors in this performance at all.

Peter did not aim to create a unified style of performance for *The Mahabharata*, because of the nature of the mythology he wanted to represent. The Africans and the Japanese will each tell the story in their own way, although the demands of a general balance forbid me to remain too Japanese. And whereas for *The Ik* I had to become physiologically and psychologically involved in something quite alien to me – Africa – in *The Mahabharata* nobody has set out to imitate anything specifically Indian. And *The Mahabharata* is easier for me than certain other texts – Shakespeare, for example. I can dig out the meaning of a character such as Drona much more immediately than, say, that of Hamlet or Macbeth. As an Asian, I have certain innate affinities with the culture that produced this epic; it is more possible for me to find a way in to this world. In western culture, with its roots in Plato and Socrates, logic and the law of cause and effect predominate. Japanese culture, on the other hand, has many of its sources in Indian rather than Greek culture. So I come to this material already equipped with a particular quality of understanding.

Given the differences in cultural background and approach to performance within the company, Peter has tried to create a harmony or balance by integrating the different elements and perspectives. Collaborating with actors of mixed nationality forces one to find and expose what is essential – more authentic relationships. The difficulties we encounter working as a group teach us to be more direct on stage, to find a way of communicating with all sorts of audiences. And anyway it's much more interesting for an audience to be presented with strong differences between the nationalities.

The friction caused by the presence of different cultures within our group is very exciting. In a homogeneous group, for example consisting uniquely of French actors, there is a reduction in tension. In such a performance, less will happen between two actors than in this group, where national and cultural differences set up a vibrancy and richness of contrast. Contrast in theatre is always a source of invention and vitality.

Of course The Epic itself is full of clearly differentiated archetypes, popular and recognizable. But the mixture of westerners, Asians and Africans in the company also has the effect of obliging the spiritual heart of the work to pass as much through the body as through words. Westerners use the body to a lesser degree than Asians or Africans, but they can construct whole philosophical worlds by means of words. In performance, both possibilities must be present and active.

When we began rehearsals in September 1984, each actor had to discover their own characters and to find their places within the ensemble. Initially it was necessary to find some common ground – a playground, if you like – without in any way eliminating the specific cultural identity of each individual there, with backgrounds in classical French or traditional Japanese theatre, Albanian or Indian dance etc... During the training period, we studied various martial arts, notably *kung fu*, in order to locate the spirit of combat. We practised vocal exercises with the musicians under Toshi Tsuchitori's direction, Aboriginal and American Indian chants and cries, and elaborate rhythm exercises to learn how to mobilize each part of the body spontaneously and in a unified way.

When we came to the text, some scenes were initially approached in the individual mother tongue, in order to free certain actors from the difficulties they experienced with the French language. Originally I had intended one day to be able to speak French and English faultlessly, but much to my regret I am unable to do so. However in this context, if I were in fact able to speak French or English without a trace of accent, certain disadvantages would arise. My way of speaking would become conventional, it would standardize. For example, when I say in English, 'The sky is blue', the phrase is more loaded with meaning and is perceived with greater dynamism than if an Englishman had said it.

The work on *Orghast* in 1971 enabled us to understand that there are three aspects of language and delivery. First, muscularity; second, the exchange of information; and third, the magical energy at the heart of something like a *mantra*. When I speak in my mother tongue, I sometimes forget its musicality and energy. In a foreign language, on the other hand, I pay much more attention to these two aspects. In our work we endeavour to override the reduction of language, its diminishment uniquely to the level of intellectual informational exchange. When language is charged with energy, theatre is invested with a greater richness.

Conference of the Birds was more difficult for actors to perform than *The Mahabharata*. Roles in the earlier work were not substantially characterized, apart from the Hoopoe, and as a performance its spirit was more mystical and religious. *The Mahabharata*, on the other hand, goes beyond a purely religious point of view. There is room for everyone to interpret it in their own way. Whereas *Conference* was a difficult and even severe text, *The Mahabharata* is more accessible, more like a children's show.

In the process of creating a role it is important to remain aware of one particular characteristic of theatre. In contrast to painting or sculpture, which only account for the dimension of space, the art of theatre is realized both temporally and spatially. For the actor, this means that his character must develop during the course of a performance. And when a performance lasts nine hours, the evolution from first to last appearance is potentially enormous. Inevitably this requires an actor to ask himself, 'How can the audience's interest be stimulated by the development of my character?'

In *The Mahabharata*, I was required to play two roles that are polar and yet complementary – Drona, a master warrior , and Kitchaka, a comic figure. I tried to portray Drona as a spiritual being, whereas for Kitchaka I really went to town, treating him as a farcical character – so for the former as little theatrically as possible, and for the latter as overtly theatrical as possible. Kitchaka is a lecherous old man, and the entire episode is dealt with in a comic spirit, containing as I have said certain allusions to Kathakali. Right now I would like to approach him in a more serious way, as a young general in possession of real power. Perhaps I will try out just such an interpretation when we return to work on this episode.

I feel that the ironic and even cynical attitude of Drona, the martial arts master, owes something to Zen Buddhist teaching. I think it is originally more of a Chinese attitude, certainly not a very Indian characteristic. In response to his disciple's question, 'What is God?', the Chinese priest might say, 'God is shit!' In my performance, Drona behaves as a cynic. Irony enables us to communicate a more complex indirect truth, a truth difficult to convey using only logic; the kind of truth each individual can interpret differently.

I once tried playing Drona as someone totally serious, devoid of irony. When I asked Peter which interpretation he preferred, he told me, 'If you play the character with irony, there will be more room to act than if he's only ever serious.' At one stage, I tended to transform Drona into too much of a Samurai. Peter simply said, 'Be human, don't turn him into too much of a stereotype, find some variation . . .' Having known me for almost twenty years now, Peter has been able to encourage me to play Drona as a multi-faceted character.

Drona is primarily a *brahmin*, a sage and priest. He has only become a warrior to finance his son's education. I recognize Drona's wisdom, serenity and simplicity in Japanese Buddhist masters. Drona's death is tragic, violent – and beautiful: the death of a Samurai. It was Peter who found for me the gesture of pouring blood over my own head. At the age of 40, I began to think about death. The attitude I take in this performance reflects what I understand by death, the relationship between body and spirit at that precise moment. I take up a meditation position, and await death without feeling any fear. I try to go beyond the body, to separate body and spirit. If my body must die, I will let it die. At that moment when he sits in the yoga position, Drona abandons his body, he throws it away, then struggles to keep his spirit alive. And at that very moment, someone physically kills his body. If one day I find myself in the middle of a desert with nothing to eat, I think that is how I could die.

In an Indian comic strip version of *The Mahabharata*, Drona can be seen adopting this yoga position at his death. When you get to a certain age, and you have a certain experience and wisdom, you know how to detach yourself from your body while keeping your spirit alive. You can accept the transitoriness of existence without pain. I believe I understand Drona as a character fairly well. His behaviour when confronted with death ties in with my own conception, although of course he is stronger and more intelligent than I am. Perhaps I will become better by embodying him?

At the same time it is rather a mysterious death: why does he decide to die? Even before learning of the death of his son, he says, 'My death is near'. However, in my interpretation Drona also tempers his feelings with irony. His death seems tragic, but perhaps that is not the case in his eyes. In a sense, he's happy. Going beyond the body is a catharsis. It produces great joy.

NOTE

This text combines extracts from an interview with Martine Millon (originally published in *Alternatives Théâtrales*, no. 24, July 1985) with part of an interview with Olivier Ortolani, included in his book *Peter Brook* (1988). The translation from the German is by Petra Evers and from the French by David Williams.

Part III

PRODUCTION – SCENOGRAPHY

13

THE GREAT POEM OF THE WORLD

A Descriptive Analysis

David Williams

Nel suo profondo vidi che s'interna,
legato con amore in un volume,
ciò che per l'universo si squaderna:
La forma universal di questo nodo
credo ch'i'vidi, perche più di largo,
dicendo questo, mi sento ch'i' godo.
(Dante, *Il Paradiso*, Canto XXXIII)

On a rainy Saturday in March 1986, I was able to immerse myself in the marathon version of Peter Brook's and Jean-Claude Carrière's *The Mahabharata* at the Bouffes du Nord, Paris. All three parts in this epic cycle were presented as a continuum.[1] A marathon for performers – that is how they referred to it – and spectators. The performance began shortly after 1.00 p.m. and finished at 11.00 p.m., with substantial pauses between the separate parts – the equivalent, I am told, of staging the Bible in about 40 minutes.

In contrast with the other great Sanskrit epic, *The Ramayana*, which Hindu scholars have labelled *kavya* – an illustrative romance couched in elegant court poetry – *The Mahabharata* is described as *itihasa*, a history or chronicle: literally, 'thus it was'. The root of the Greek word *istorin*, from which we derive 'history', suggests travelling to find out for oneself; and indeed the performance invited an immersion in experience. In addition, I felt it to have been the ultimate refinement and crystallization of the Centre's ongoing work, and in some ways a summation of distance travelled.

My primary aims here have been to contextualize the production in relation to the original Sanskrit *Mahabharata* and Hindu culture in general, as well as the body of Brook's work with the Centre; to discuss the nature of Brook's interculturalism in practice; and above all to detail *mise-en-scène*, narrative structure and something of the production's dizzying intertextuality. It contains countless points of contact with epic literature inter-

117

culturally – in particular with the Sumerian *Gilgamesh*, the Norse Sagas, *Beowulf*, the *Niebelungenlied*, *La Chanson de Roland*, the Homeric and Shakespearean canon – as well as with Hindu symbology and iconography, and a host of performative forms from around the world (although in production they are rarely foregrounded or made specific). I believe it is important to retain some record of the original production's scenography, for the text that has been published only hints at the nature of the performance text: here, more so than ever, is Barthes' 'network with a thousand entrances'. Despite the surprisingly central status of the word in this production, Carriére's dialogue comprises just one discursive component amongst many.

NOTE

1 Zeami's *johakyu* writ large, and an echo of the three great strides (emblematic of the three positions of the sun, at dawn, noon and sunset) that Indian tradition suggests Vishnu needs to pass through and reclaim heaven. See Francis Fergusson in *The Idea of a Theater* (Princeton, NJ: Princeton University Press, 1949, p. 18), in which he proposes a tripartite structure for 'a tragic rhythm' of action. These parts, in some ways reminiscent of the components of initiatory paradigms, are *poiema* (purpose), *pathema* (passion/suffering) and *mathema* (perception) – the terms are borrowed from Kenneth Burke's *The Philosphy of Literary Form*.

THE GAME OF DICE

We that are young shall never
see so much nor live so long.
                                                    (*King Lear*)

He that came seeing, blind shall he go:
Rich now, then a beggar: stick in hand,
Creeping his way to a land of exile.
                                        (Sophocles, *Oedipus*)

Before the performance starts, the fight for seats. No empty *politesse* here, just launch yourself into the fray. Luckily, there is still an empty seat on the central benches downstairs. Having scrabbled in to claim my territory, I sit back to watch the continuing onslaught, horribly pleased with myself. Many crushed feet and angry exchanges later, Peter Brook suddenly, and surprisingly, emerges at the front of the playing space. Those still without seats, now immobile alongside the diminutive figure of Brook in the space, echo the calls for hush. Brook puts a question to the audience, an old favourite of his: 'What is the difference between theatre and life?' He goes on: 'In this case, the people coming from life – you, the audience – are not rehearsed. The actors who will play for you today have spent a long time rehearsing battles, an epic war. And meanwhile, before the perform-ance even gets underway, an unrehearsed battle is taking place in the auditorium, for the best seats and positions. Please be calm: allow the only battle to take place on stage.' Laughter, applause, and miraculously a sense of calm. Before we know it, the performance has begun.

Vyasa (Alain Maratrat), a bearded ascetic in rags, an immortal *rishi*, appears from beyond the river. The yellow clay markings of Vishnu surround a glistening blood-red *tilak* on his forehead. He is primarily a storyteller, a troubadour, a poet in the original meaning of *poesis* – a creator. He carries a copy of an ancient stringed instrument, rather like a *tambora*. Suggesting musical accompaniment, it is also a multi-functional object to be used in the course of narration by this poet-magician. The son of Satyavati ('truth'), he was conceived in *maya* between the shores of a river: illusion comes naturally to him.[1]

The elephant-god Ganesha (Maurice Bénichou), the jovial and propitious 'remover of obstacles', is invoked in India before any undertaking – a letter, a book, a journey. This tutelary deity of the *limens* (in himself a liminal being, between the divine and human/animal spheres) is also the divine patron of literature and the arts: a god embodied. Here he will act as Vyasa's scribe, his amanuensis. Piercing a hole with his thumb in a fresh mango, he dips his pen (the tip of his broken tusk) into a natural inkwell; this poem will be written in mango juice. The elephant's head mask fully covers the actor's own head. It is ornate, bejewelled, a plaything

119

– the storyteller's device to locate the character. As soon as it becomes redundant, it will be removed, manipulated at arm's length for a brief moment (like some of the masks in *Conference of the Birds*), then abandoned.

Vyasa and Ganesha immediately establish a direct contact with the audience, like the narrator's in Indian Kuttiyattam: intimate, comic, human. And the child to whom they tell the story – innocent, intelligent, demanding clarification – is instantly located as our point of entry into this world, for he is our representataive.

There follows a sequence of invented rituals to generate enactment of the story – like *holi* in India: a spray of richly coloured powders in the air and on the bare earth, vermillion, gold, as well as rice, garlands of flowers, leaves, and a splash of ochre beside the pool at the front of the space. The child had drunk from the pool when he first appeared; it is a 'natural' property, to be exploited and incessantly redefined within the story. The edge of the pool is now stained, evoking further resonances: an echo of Ganesha's own violent beginnings – he describes how he was decapitated by Shiva while defending his mother from the god's amorous advances – and an omen of the bloodletting to come. The water reddens and settles, now tarnished as a source of purification, blessing and refreshment.

An exposition of the 'origins of the human race' now commences. Ganga (Mireille Maalouf), realized through the invocation and formally introduced, locates herself in the pool. Her submerged feet suggest emergence from the water: as the river goddess, Ganga Ma (Mother Ganges), she is inherently part of it. She tosses her first seven children into the water – now the Ganges, a locus of liberation and deliverance, for her offspring are *vasus* (a class of Vedic gods), cursed to be born of mortals. The babies are suggested by simple manipulation of her long floating shawl, clasping a tiny bundle to her breast. As she unfurls the material to abandon each baby in turn, its tip touches the surface of the water to produce a tiny splash.

The oath of Bhishma (Sotigui Kouyate) is structurally and stylistically similar to a number of other scenes of parallel content, such as the gazelle's curse of Pandu, for example; all significant moments with deleterious *karmic* consequences are foregrounded and framed as such. So much of the drama of this *Mahabharata* stems from this unresolved tension between individual free choice and imprisoning predetermination. Although almost all of the characters are unwilling to accept the ineluctability of fate, here the eighth son of Ganga (a lone *vasu* trapped in the mortal world – is he aware of his past reality?) swears never to know the love of a woman: an altruistic vow of chastity, the brahminic *brahmacharya* – a blameless oath with formidable repercussions. For this reason, he is henceforth to be called Bhishma, 'the Terrible', an extension of his earlier name, Devavrata, 'he whose vow is Godly'. Fatality, determination – an invisible 'law' is

Figure 13.1 'The Game of Dice'. Ganga (Mireille Maalouf) drowning one of her new-born children in the pool (the Ganges): on the right, Vyasa (Alain Maratrat); seated, in the background, Ganesha (Maurice Bénichou). French-language production. (Photographer – Gilles Abegg)

121

made palpable in a moment framed as 'heightened reality', a 'moment of truth'. A low-level fresnel on a diagonal illuminates the actor's full face, like cinematic lighting, while a didgeridoo throbs and pulses to a rhythmic gong counterpoint.

Ganesha crosses off a page in the hefty tome he uses to record Vyasa'a tale – and we accept an instant leap of twenty years in the narrative, to King Salva's rejection of the young princess Amba (Pascaline Pointillart). Salva (Georges Corraface) wanders alone in meditative solitude, whispering penitences to the accompaniment of the chant of a musician in his wake. A way of life is immediately created, separated from the front of the space by the river – Salva is in a different geographical and spiritual 'space' by the back wall. Salva's nobility is established by a simple metonymic swathe of rich material around his neck, pure white with delicate gold needlework. According to Brook, his treatment of Amba shows him to be 'the perfect macho shit' . . . In the original *Mahabharata*, he will eventually meet with his 'just' deserts, when Krishna (his cousin) slices him in two with his discus, for having ransacked Krishna's city, Dwaraka, during his absence.

The death of Satyavati's son, Vichitravirya (unnamed here), is signalled by dipping the corner of a vivid scarlet silk cloak in the river, to the mournful cry of the *nagaswaram*, a brash and viscerally agonizing cousin of the western oboe or shawm: a voluminous wail of despair. Kim Menzer, the Danish instrumentalist who plays the *nagaswaram* throughout, claims that it took him three months to find a note during a period of concentrated study in Madras. In Indian culture, mainly in the southern states, the instrument is used to attract people to weddings or political rallies: never for funerals. Throughout this performance it is used at moments of great public celebration or mourning. In creates an awesome sound that fills the space, makes the hair on one's neck prick up.

As Vichitravirya died without issue, his half-brother Vyasa is obliged to enter his own story and 'generate' the protagonists of his fiction by making love to three princesses – a bizarre Pirandellian blurring of the interrelationship between creator and created, a singularly modernist device in a 2,000-year-old epic. To signal the moment of birth of Dhritarashtra, Pandu and an unnamed third brother, three rush mats are held up by concealed figures behind. Their silhouettes are visible, an imminent potential reality.[2] As Vyasa describes him, Dhritarashtra (Ryszard Cieslak) slowly lowers his screen to reveal himself: compositionally, a split-screen cinematic convention. His blindness is conveyed immediately and minimally, as he fumbles tentatively for the top lip of the screen, and an onlooker passes a hand in front of his unseeing eyes. The screen/mat focuses and frames the character's head and shoulders. It is also a storytelling convention established to convey directly a 'magical' revelation of birth, the introduction of a major protagonist: again a different 'order of reality' made palpable.

Ganesha and the boy observe with us, commenting and querying. They are directly allied with us. The boy is an 'everyman', involved and implicated as a spectator on stage, further focusing our attention on the storytelling element as a continual present. He is also the direct issue of these protagonists, the survivor, the possible future. The performance becomes a journey of initiation into experience, a complex morality, an educative and revelatory process resolutely irreducible to any pat formula or dogma. He must observe, listen, share the journey's cycle from Genesis to Revelations, then draw his own conclusions. The receiver of the story in the original *Mahabharata* was a young prince, Janamejaya, Arjuna's great grandson, the story itself used to bring to a halt his sacrificial slaughtering of all of the world's snakes. Brook's version foregrounds the storytelling aspects of the performance, and strips away the distancing insulation of high rank (prince) and culturally specific act (snake sacrifice): the child is more immediate, closer to us.

Pandu the pale (Tapa Sudana) has a fine layer of chalky make-up on his cheeks, rendered all the paler by Tapa's jet turban and beard. In a trice, he signals his nobility through a simple device, wrapping a piece of cloth around a stick, which is then held up as a mark of regal office. As he pursues two gazelles, he unwraps part of the material, and in his hands it becomes both a bow and the reins of a hunter giving chase, in some ways reminiscent of the stylized metonyms of Chinese Opera. The hunt is a formal, if comic, dance, its dynamic in Toshi Tsuchitori's percussive rhythms. The gazelles themselves offer an image of an innocent harmonious relationship with a natural environment. They gambol around the space with unfettered joy, bearing sprigs of foliage in their mouths. The leaves are taken from them on their deaths.

Kunti's invocation of the god Dharma and the birth of the Pandavas produces a flurry of ritual activity, some of it clearly invented 'play', some apparently 'authentic' – using the forms and trappings of ritual, but generalized and neutralized by deracination from sources in specific cultural contexts. From one point of view, meaningless exotica, decoration. From a less cynical perspective, the Centre group is multi-racial, containing members of a number of strongly ritualistic cultures – Balinese and Indian Hindu, Shinto, African griot-animist, etc. Certain aspects of these diverse cultural forms have been tapped for a vocabulary, and some will inevitably brand this process 'orientalism', in Edward Said's politicised sense of the word.

Furthermore, underlying the sequence is a strong sense of theatricality, of the actors' celebrating the act of theatre itself, using whatever comes to hand, natural properties (the root vocabulary of all ritual activity). Fire, water, earth. Earth, the source of all, is a 'mother' constantly touched in respectful supplication. Natural juices – a coconut is smashed open, its milk sprinkled on the pool for Dharma to bathe in, and in a circle around the boy who kneels on a carpet in the central area, signalled as 'other' by its being surrounded by tiny votive candles and petals. Flashes of fire from magnesium powder, tossed into the air above the flambeaux, explode with a dull roar. The boy awaits palms up, hands extended in a position of meditative yogic calm. He is the agent of invocation, the focal locus of an act of sympathetic magic. Vyasa hands him a sword, then a bow and arrow, then a club – all apparently toys. There is immense visual excitement, while at the same time music and mantras fill the air. A whirlpool of simultaneous activity draws us in, invites us to select what we watch.

Suddenly the Pandavas appear at the base of the back wall, emblematically presented, already in their adult forms. Demigods all, like Hesiod's or Homer's Trojan heroes: **Yudishthira**, his sword drawn – a simple white tunic for the son of Dharma, the future 'king of kings'; **Bhima**, son of the wind god Vayu, an enormous mace on his shoulder; **Arjuna**, son of Indra – the world's finest archer, a bow in his hand; **Nakula and Sahadeva**, the twin deities, the Ashvins. The only sons of Madri share the same cloth drape, like Siamese twins. The family bonding is concretized visually and spatially. It appears that the Pandavas collectively compromise a human microcosm, the individual and different facets of one ideal being, like the Hindu Maha Purusha, the primeval 'cosmic man'. As a unit, they are interdependent, complementing each other. Five is Shiva's number; and there are associations with the five elements in Hindu cosmogyny, the five senses and other quinary groupings symbolic of wholeness.[3] In addition, the actors playing them in some ways reflect the multicultural pluralism of India itself. The scene also provides an example of Brook's repeated application in a scenographic context of cinematic depth of field/ deep focus – it is for this reason that Michael Billington has referred to Brook as the 'Greg Toland of theatre'. The form of the Bouffes invites such techniques, and they will recur throughout the performance. Here we look through the dynamic movements of those invoking the Pandavas to the effect of that invocation – a distant 'magical' vision of them realized, 'conjured up', and at the same time patently and literally there.

The arrival of Gandhari (Mireille Maalouf) for her marriage to Dhritarashtra. Pomp, celebration and acclamation in movement and music, a majestic public procession created with simplicity and understatement. A stately queen, draped in luxurious trappings, is borne in on the shoulders of her attendants. Indian or African parasols lend height to the image: synecdoches of palatial vaults, scalloped arches, caparisoned palanquins, and metonymic suggestions of a particular way of life. The reveller-celebrants carry huge curling Indian brass instruments, like Tibetan horns. One of them at the front 'becomes' an elephant's trunk, the swaying rhythm of its progress rippling back through the body of bearers. The image, somehow more evocative than a dozen real elephants, is constructed instantly and with economy, then just as quickly dismantled as the ensemble disperses and the joyful illusion evaporates. For Gandhari's husband is blind, a state she determines to share. An agonizing moment in her first meeting with Dhritarashtra: he gropes and fumbles, eager to discover the form and face of a spouse never to be visible to him. Conducted in an all-embracing silence, his discovery of her blindfold is profoundly moving.

Gandhari's pregnancy. Vyasa and the boy, 'stage managers', visible agents and operators of narrative devices, sweep her away behind a hand-held curtain – a convention borrowed in a redefined form from the diaphanous *tira sila* of Kathakali, Kuchipuddi, Yakshagana, Kuttiyattam and a host of other Indian dance-drama forms, in which it acts as a membrane between the diurnal world and a magical beyond. The cloth curtain is used to great effect throughout this production. Its 'operators' remain unconcealed, and yet they are 'invisible', like the *zukai*, the puppeteers in Japanese Bunraku. Here it is above all a means either of focusing or of clearing the space, 'wiping the slate clean', leaving a void demanding to be filled anew. Brook has been using this device in various guises for a quarter of a century: for example, a bath towel was held up in similar fashion to introduce Charlotte Corday's third and final visit to Marat's house in *Marat/Sade* (1964).

The birth of the Kauravas is an ominous and agonizing process, in stark contrast with the ritual order of their cousin's birth. After a two-year pregnancy, the birth itself eventually has to be forcibly provoked by an act of violence. A servant strikes Gandhari's distended stomach with an iron bar, until a large black ball drops with a thud from her skirts. Cold and hard, it rolls across the earth into the pool – the very dirt and mud in which Duryodhana, the first born, will meet his death. The ball sits there, immobile, unwanted. Vyasa suggests fracturing it into one hundred pieces, then placing each fragment in an earthenware jar before sprinkling them with fresh water: a century of sons will emerge!

As a servant drags off the sphere to begin this strange process, another instant temporal leap (the equivalent of a cinematic jump cut) takes us to Duryodhana's birth. This event is greeted by the hideous and jagged ululations of a jackal, a cosmic warning of the disorder he will bring, an omen ignored by Dhritarashtra who is delighted at the birth of a son (like Laius in Aeschylus' *Septem*). Another 'moment of truth', at which the subsequent carnage could have been avoided, drifts past. However, within the confines of an implacable fate, Dhritarashtra, progenitor of the 'sons of darkness', is only following what he believes to be his own *dharma* – an elastic and slippery concept, endlessly unfixable. Broadly it refers to a natural law that upholds and sustains the universe. On a personal level, it means individual duty, order and truth. Truth to personal *dharma*

125

(*varnashrama dharma*), it is suggested, will sustain social order, and indeed a wider ecological balance in the cosmos as a whole (*sanatana dharma*). If *dharma* is respected, micro- and macrocosm are indissoluble.[4]

At the very moment of his birth, Duryodhana (Andrzej Seweryn) emerges in the throes of a nightmare, yelling incoherently. A grotesquely disturbing Goyaesque figure scurries across our vision, wrapped in a torn blood-red cloth. An amorphous, deformed shape – headless, faceless, trailing the lining of his mother's womb as a shroud . . . A foretaste of the age of Kali, with which Duryodhana will come to be associated.

A radical change of environment and atmosphere takes us to the lyrical Edenic oasis of **Pandu's love for Madri** (Tam Sir Niane). A harmonious relationship with their forest surroundings is conveyed in the measured simplicity of their movements and of the musical accompaniment. In addition there is Madri's respectful symbiosis with water, now again a true source of sustenance and renewal. Pandu's death is rendered poignantly comic by a distended 'boing' from one of Toshi's invented percussion instruments. The five musicians, visible to one side throughout, participate fully, as in so much Asian theatre – sustaining the narrative, punctuating the evolving dynamic, observing the actors' work closely. The relationship between them and the performers is fluid and organic. They also provide a further level of focus, observing and responding with us, extending the circle of complicity and shared invention.

Madri's self-immolation (*sati*) on Pandu's funeral pyre is simply suggested by Vyasa burning a bundle of sticks he carries. A synesthetic appeal is made to all of our senses – tiny crackling sounds, the bitter smell of smoke, the hypnotic aerial dance of the sparks. Fire retains its primal mystery, purity and ferocity, and is here another active element in this protean play of elements. Then all is once again swept away behind the floating curtain, and the episode comes to an end with Vyasa's ominously prescient speech, announcing the chaos that is to come: 'The earth has lost its youth which has gone by like a happy dream. Now, each day brings us closer to barrenness, to destruction.' The beginnings of a separation from the sacred, the end of spring – *mundus senescit*: the stage is set for the entry of humankind into the realm of History.

Another twenty years pass in a flash: we are simply told so by Vyasa. From here on, as dramatic intensity heightens, the stories are increasingly self-generated. In general, Vyasa, Ganesha and the boy will appear only when their presence is necessary to the continuation or clarification of the narrative. The simple alienation device of the storyteller-observers in the outer frame of the performance is gradually dispensed with, as we 'descend' from the enchanted magical plane of a pre-historical 'golden age', a mythical time peopled by fabulous beings, to a more recognizable human level, characterized by familiar conflicts of jealousy, pride and ambition. The myth is made concrete and present as a theatre of suffering and violence, a theatre of war driven by the same impulses that underlie all collisions of dreams and intent. (For Jung, every individual was the locus of a continual battle between mythical time – restorative – and historical time – desctructive.)

Figure 13.2 'The Game of Dice'. The archery tournament for the young cousins, supervised by Drona (Yoshi Oida, in black). Bottom right, Bhima's 'uprooted tree' frames the configuration. (Photographer – Gilles Abegg)

A dispute between the young Pandava and Kaurava cousins boils over, all one hundred of the latter conflated into the two central representatives (like Jarry's suggestion for Ubu's army): the first born, Duryodhana, and the eldest of his 99 brothers, Duhsassana – Seweryn and Corraface respectively. The confrontation, here merely sparring but presaging future violence, is brought to an immediate halt by a mysterious warrior-brahmin, Drona. Who is he? Where does he come from? The motives he has for engaging the support of these young warriors, as described in the original *Mahabharata* (his desire for revenge on a neighbouring king, the father of the future Pandava bride Draupadi), are never clarified in this production. In many ways, he remains an unknown quantity, but it is never

127

distracting. A central guiding principle of Carrière's work becomes apparent: whatever is not directly related to the central spine of the narrative is either dispensed with, distilled or circumvented.

Drona sets up a test of archery skills, a tournament to find the outstanding warrior. Both Arjuna (who *is* that star performer) and Drona are set apart by their costumes, the latter in the black priestly robes of a martial arts master. Further Samurai resonances are inevitably read in the guttural vocalizations and sinewy physicality of the Japanese actor Yoshi Oida. The mechanics of bow and arrow are based on sleight of hand and simple child-like suggestion. The bow is an unstrung bamboo stick, the arrow a thinner bamboo length. As an archer takes aim and fires, the arrow is swished through the air in a blur and pulled out of sight behind him. We follow, in anticipation, its invisible flight to the target, our eyes arriving as the goal is 'struck'. In *The War*, the victims snap arrows from behind them and clasp them to chests, necks, thighs, etc.; in this way, arrows can be caught 'in mid flight' in hands or mouths, then tossed aside or snapped with comic brio. Here the effect is as farcical. As Arjuna fires an arrow into the sky, Vyasa visibly lobs an impaled dead bird (recognizably artificial) into the space. Bathos is one way of coping with, and staging, extraordinary heroic feats. However, the archers' firing position – solid base, imperturable balance and focus – clearly stems from familiarity with real weaponary of this kind. The posture also contains something of the contemplative heroic attitude in classical Indian painting (for example, Mughal miniatures) and sculpture (see, for instance, the cave sculptures at Ellora, and the *Mahabharata* bas-reliefs in the Khmer temple of Angkor Wat, Cambodia), as well as of classical dance (notably Bharata Natyam).

Drona and Ekalavya, master and servant/pupil. Fanatical devotion to his master causes Ekalvya to set up idols. He sculpts a statue of Drona, quite simply Yoshi himself 'chiselled' from the air around him, immobile – a statue – but watching, aware of this misdirected zeal: echoes of Pygmalion and Aphrodite. Drona demands that Ekalavya chop off his own thumb; an agonizing moment, though all is discreetly suggested. Drona's determination to exact insurance for the future reflects an expedient and unflinching prudence he will share with Krishna.

Vyasa informs us that the lamp has been extinguished by the wind, as he openly snuffs out the flame, and Arjuna (Vittoria Mezzogiorno) is shrouded in darkness. This scene proposes an image of the perfection of a spiritual craft, for Arjuna the archer shoots 'blind', like the Zen master in Eugen Herrigel's *Zen in the Art of Archery*. Here the darkness is his blindfold, as it will be when he kills Jayadratha in *The War*. First, a moment of intimacy in great proximity to the spectators, a 'close-up' held for a meditative period of concentration during which he makes his inner thoughts available to us with gentleness and modesty. Then he takes aim in silence and unleashes an arrow into the darkness – a mysterious whipping sound, created by the *analapos*, a spring attached to a soundbox, an invention of Tsuchitori's friend Akio Suzuki: an otherworldly aural effect for the magical bow Gandiva. Instantly, full lights shoot up to reveal the court at the back of the space in all of its pomp and finery. Having assembled silently in the darkness, the company now cheers and applauds as a bird-kite with an arrow lodged in one of its wings floats down into the centre of the space from a great height and an unspecified source – it has been released from the tip of a towering scarlet banner. Someone catches it before it hits the ground. We have shared Arjuna's own 'journey', from the moment of concentration, immobility and blindness to sudden illumination and glorious sight: from darkness and silence to an explosion of sound, colour and light – the spiritual *satori* of the Zen archer 'firing at himself'. With the lights now full on, Arjuna performs other tricks and feats – for example, hitting one of the struts of a spinning wheel with an arrow (a distant allusion to the final chariot confrontation between him and Karna in *The War*?).

The arrival of Karna (Bruce Myers) now instigates a rapid series of spatial redefinitions engineered by Brook, a master of proxemics. Karna's challenge to Arjuna clearly prefigures their pivotal confrontation on the battlefield of Kurukshetra much later. The four corners of an inner square of focus, the arena for their combat, are marked out by the four red banners, held erect. As Kunti faints, for she has recognized her first-born son, the banners are laid flat along the edges of this square to define a new, more intimate space and focus: the onlookers remain outside its perimeters, immobile and silent. A flashback re-enactment of Kunti's love-making with the sun god Surya, father to Karna, is visible only to the privileged few – the boy, Vyasa, the spectators – but not to either Pandavas or Kauravas; this will become a rich source of dramatic and tragic irony. Once again the scene is stage managed by Vyasa: so, for example, his words 'I stop all motion' signal the temporal manipulation that enables the generation of the flashback.

A 'flash-forward' back to the present and the confrontation between Arjuna and Karna, the latter now seen in a different light – a demigod hero, brother to the Pandavas. The actor-spectators are reanimated, they complete the circle of focus around the central locus of collision. When the fight is cut short, the spatial configuration is broken down again and redefined, as Duryodhana makes the outcast Karna a king: a vivid *tilak* on his forehead (at the point of the highest of the six yogic *chakras*), a gilded white swathe hung around his neck. After an exchange of threats and maledictions – the establishment of enmities and alliances, for two camps are forming before our eyes – Karna leaves protected by the 'invisible' Surya (Clément Masdongar), the god's red cloak creating a shield behind his son. This is the 'mysterious aura', the ineffaceable stigmata of his origins, that Duryodhana perceives around Karna. Three of the banners follow him out, one is left flat to mark out an area of focus for the scene's end: lying parallel to the river at the back, it throws our attention forward to the front of the space. Then it too disappears. The sequence as a whole offers an exemplar of Brook's notion of 'living illusion'.

Duryodhana has shown some humanity in welcoming Karna to the fold, but this is a benign blink in the narrowing focus of his vision. In truth his motives are rooted in self-interest: expediency and additional strength. Rivalries and destinies are being suggested with ever-increasing clarity. We already sense the inevitability of impending tragic confrontation. Like the house of Atreus, a family will be fragmented.

An entirely new space immediately illustrates **Pandava domesticity**. Four fawn rush mats are unfurled across the central area; the very process of unrolling produces a tiny hissing sound. Four candles along the nearside bank of the river delineate the perimeters of their dwelling. The new bride Draupadi (Mallika Sarabhai, the only Indian in the cast) enters from the darkness beyond the river, across the bridge: a tender lyrical appearance. The five brothers take her as their joint wife, forming a circle, their hands conjoined with one of her's in a central pile, the tactile union further bonded with a garland of marigolds. Draupadi (often linked with the goddess Sri, 'prosperity') remains the focal point throughout the scene, relationships concretized spatially in relation to her. Similarly in Hindu culture she is sometimes described in terms of a 'palm' uniting the five 'fingers' of the Pandavas. As a structural unit, they are inseparable, complete.

For the new polyandrous family's first night of shared sleep, all five brothers lie side by side, Draupadi at their feet, Kunti at their head. The bedroom itself has been established by laying one carpet on the floor, an idyll lit and enclosed by a small oil lamp at each corner. Structural and affective echoes of Carmen's 'union' with Don Jose in Brook's 1981 production underpin this image of repose, infinite harmony, balance, plentitude, shared interdependence: an oasis of ordered calm before the storm.

We step outside the narrative for a moment as the boy questions Vyasa on the battle that is to come; a jarring reminder almost inconceivable alongside the image of family bliss before us. Suddenly we hear Krishna's flute in the distance (in reality the Turkish musician Kudsi Erguner's breathy *ney*, a wooden flute, played visibly from stage left), and a low-level diagonal beam of light suggests the eminence of the divinity described: a mystical presence as the source of illumination. Is Krishna the avatar of Vishnu, descended to earth to restore *dharma*?[5] Vyasa seems to suggest it, but in performance the tension between his humanity and divinity will lurk unresolved. For an actor in this context, his trickster aspect must be foregrounded, and he will be necessarily low-key, humanized (how do you play gods?): an equivalent to the version of Jesus portrayed in Renan's Life of Christ. Here the attempt is to portray Krishna as a Vasudeva –

an exceptional man, given to worries and occasional flashes of anger, as well as a scheming and expedient pragmatist, and finally a mortal who in turn must die. At the same time, on a vertical axis, he is the source of miraculous feats and the agent who engineers each individual's realization.

Bénichou/Ganesha – for his elephant's head has long since been removed – describes to the boy the richness of the Hindu universe (in reality a 'pluriverse') and the complementary trinity at the heart of the pantheon, then goes on to relate mythical episodes from the life of Krishna. The words radiate, set up resonances in our imaginations on a sonic level alone: nothing is illustrated. He stands behind a saffron curtain held in front of him at waist height by Vyasa and the boy: there is already a suggestion of Krishna's presence in the yellow colour of the material, for all Hindus in itself an auspicious association with Vishnu/Krishna. A moment of puppetry, as Bénichou holds the Ganesha mask at arm's length just above the curtain, his 'final curtain' before he disappears from sight. Having referred to his exploits and prestigious powers, and underlined that he is a man, Ganesha bids the boy (and us) –

Watch carefully. His action is subtle, mysteriously clear. At the same instant, they say, he can be everywhere – here, there – he is water and the trembling of a leaf, he's you, he's fire, he's the heart of all that's invisible.
The Boy: Is Krishna you as well?
Bénichou/Ganesha/Krishna: Naturally.

An irony, for he is storyteller and incarnation, scribe and character inscribed. A moment of gentle comedy prepares the ground for the subtle smiling irony that characterizes this Krishna. As in a conjuring trick, the curtain is then whipped away to one side to reveal Krishna sleeping peacefully, leaning on one arm, smiling – an allusion to classical Indian iconography (cf. the many images of Vishnu reclining asleep on the serpent Ananta). The flute we have already heard in the distance is now lodged in the crook of his arm. Then the curtain is draped over his body – an instant bedcover; in the foreground, garlands of brightly coloured flowers, the whole image illuminated with crisp clear light.

The Pandavas, asleep in the background until this moment, awaken and watch from the shadows, and the narrative's central alliance is immediately established. Throughout the epic, Krishna will protect and assist the Pandavas – a relationship similar to that of Mars and Aeneas' Trojans in Virgil's *Aeneid* (there are a number of striking parallels). Kunti is Krishna's aunt, sister of his father Vasudeva. And later the bond will be strengthened when Arjuna marries Krishna's sister Subhadra.

It would be impossible for any western actor to attempt to embody Krishna: in India people talk of Krishna 'playing' the actor . . . Here Bénichou plays Ganesha playing Krishna within Vyasa's story. There is a

Figure 13.3 'The Game of Dice'. The first appearance of Krishna (Bruce Myers) in iconic position, abandoned at his feet the mask of Ganesha. In the background, three of the Pandavas. (Photographer – Gilles Abegg)

double distancing between actor and role, as densely textured as the polyphonous sliding structure of discourses in Weiss' *Marat/Sade*. Krishna will later ask Vyasa, 'Which of us invented the other?' These Brechtian/storytelling techniques of estrangement or alienation offer the possibility of multiple and mobile perspectives, engendering an ever-evolving relationship between audience and action.

Another piece of coloured cloth is laid on the bare earth, a change of light, including the relocation of the four lamps from the Pandava household – and we are in **the Kauravas' home at Hastinapura**. The blind Dhritarashtra plays chess on his own, his only means of ordering or impinging upon reality: his game dovetails meta-textually with the conflict of the powers of light and darkness that we see unfolding before us. At a moment of panic (the Herculean Bhima – Mamadou Dioume – roars with rage and comically threatens the Kaurava sons with an uprooted tree!), the old king knocks the table and scatters the pieces all over the floor. Disorder returns, he is incapable of taking charge, of truly acting. A tragic image of impotence as he scrabbles around in his darkness for pawns and queens.

The creation of the Pandava palace, the Mayasabha at Indraprastha, 'the city of the gods'. Vyasa informs us that it is being constructed by 'Maya's invisible workers', thereby ironically explaining away and theatricalizing any incongruity of the actors' dropping roles to redefine visibly the space on stage. There is of course an element of meta-theatrical self-consciousness in equating the actors with 'workers of illusion'. Pure white strips of material are unrolled, almost covering the base matting. Then a number of white cushions or bolsters are positioned in a symmetrical horseshoe, two banks of candles flicker beside the river – and the space resonates with suggestions of luminosity, peace, tranquillity and order. The candles promote a depth of field, conveying the size and simplicity of the palace, as well as its relationship to the environment (the river). But there is something fragile underlying this radiant light. The barely perceptible peeling scars and distant shadows of the back wall evoke an undercurrent of impermanence, decay and menace.

The investiture of Yudishthira (Matthias Habich) as 'king of kings' – *samraj*. White material is draped over the cushions to suggest a regal atmosphere, and a simple emblematic cloth is hung around Yudishthira's neck. In his hand he holds a single red flower (an unwitting echo of Don Jose's red carnation? This tale is another 'tragedy of *karma*', Brook's description of his own *Carmen*). When young Sisupala (Clovis) violently interrupts the proceedings, the flower drops from Yudishthira's fingers and lies abandoned, forgotten. Sisupala and Krishna confront each other across the central space, the others looking on from behind. With half-closed eyes and the suggestion of a smile, Krishna unleashes his magic disc – his *chakra*, Sudarshana. The missile and its trajectory through the air are suggested in light and sound, an eery whistle from the musicians. A tiny flicking gesture from Krishna, and Sisupala's head drops to his chest before he collapses, 'decapitated', to be dragged away, his feet trailing like a dead bull's. The red flower remains in the centre of the white wash, a tiny splash of blood – a minimalist refinement of the clichéd cinematic symbolism of red wine spilling on to and staining a wedding dress or white linen tablecloth.

In the original *Mahabharata*, the nature of the enmity between Krishna and Sisupala, the king of Chedi, is complex. Krishna has abducted and married Sisupala's betrothed wife, Rukmini, despite the fact that he is in fact Sisupala's cousin. Furthermore, Sisupala, sometimes portrayed as an incarnation of the demon Ravana, is a devotee of Shiva, and is perhaps therefore antagonistic towards Krishna/Vishnu. Carrière's distillation leaves us with a sulky petulant troublemaker in Clovis' Sisupala; their animosity remains largely unexplained. However, the confrontation has obliged Krishna to reveal his divine powers for the first time, and there is an echo of the familial conflict to come in this slaughter of a cousin. 'It will have blood, they say, blood will have blood' (*Macbeth*).

Arjuna questions Vyasa as to the story's outcome: 'Do you know the end of your poem?' – 'I'm not sure it has an end.' By inference, we are still living it today. The characters' existential awareness of their reality as fictional 'enacted' beings also serves as a further storytelling device: some of the audience's own questions and interests are voiced in this way. The boy is now specifically designated as the survivor, a concrete glimmer of hope and future continuity. This story has a clear didactic quality; it is almost a morality play. The lessons of our collective ancestral past must be confronted and assimilated. We are still responsible, humanity's survival is in our hands.

The same spatial arrangement is retained for **Duryodhana's furious entry to his own home**, but immediately he kicks two bolsters apart with intense violence. So disarray and disharmony are reflected spatially: rupture and fragmentation are made visible in this disturbance of symmetry – the introduction of an anarchic, uncontrolled element into the scenic configuration. He is wracked with jealousy and bitterness. Gandhari tries to appease him by offering him a bowl of fruit: we have already seen a similar bowl being enjoyed in tranquillity by the Pandavas. He rejects her offering, hurling the bowl and its contents as far back as the river – a dump, like a Venetian canal. Food offered and rejected, the ordered mutuality and communion of shared sustenance refused: an archetypal image of fragmentation and impending disorder (one thinks of all those ruptured Shakespearean banquets).

A secret meeting between Krishna and Bhishma offers an ironic juxtaposition with the preceding scene, in which Duryodhara claimed he had nothing to fear with Drona and Bhishma unearringly allied with him. A single lamp defines the nature of both meeting and location – covert, only possible in the secrecy of darkness: in this way the misgivings both feel at the mounting tension and increasing omens are made apparent. Which is worse – the destruction of their people, or the destruction of *dharma*?

The scenic configuration for the **game of dice** (for the narrative now takes us into the second book of the *Mahabharata*, the *Sabhaparvan*) involves a re-establishment of formal order in the space, but once again not of perfect symmetry. An unresolved and dynamic spatial tension stems from this asymmetry, while the focal point is clearly located in the central gaming table – a forum for confrontation.

Figure 13.4 'The Game of Dice'. Duryodhana celebrates Yudishthira's loss at the gaming table – similar in design to the traditional Indian pachisi board. In the foreground, from left to right, Shakuni (Douta Seck), Duryodhana (Andrzej Seweryn), Yudishthira (Matthias Habich). In the background, from left to right: the blindfolded Gandhari (Mireille Maalouf), Dhritarashtra (Ryszard Cieslak) and, on the far right, the young boy (Lutfi Jafkar) complete the circle of focus in silence. French-language production. (Photographer – Michel Dieuzaide)

Initial wagers are made: gilded necklaces, pearls, beads, shells. An element of deliberately naive theatricality is foregrounded here, for these objects are all explicitly imitations, playthings. As the tension increases, spatial relationships remain fluid, constantly redefined. At first, everyone remains seated, but with further Pandava losses and the loutish and vituperative Duhsassana tirelessly scheming at one side, individuals gradually rise to their feet to watch more closely. The musicians' percussive rhythms are repeatedly syncopated with a similarly rhythmic interjection by Shakuni, the wily Kaurava diceplayer, Gandhari's trickster brother: 'I've won.' A comic colouring to his relish heightens the sense of impending loss. When the Pandava brothers are wagered away, they step outside of the central space and into the Kaurava camp, like captured chess pieces. Stripped of their status, they are therefore stripped of their emblematic robes and neckscarves: a pile appears to one side. Silence and immobility for the final throw of the dice. Finally Dhritarashtra is forced to ask, 'Who has lost?' A pause as the actors freeze around the table, the dice invisible to us: we too are blind. Only Arjuna has seen Shakuni cheat, but even the world's greatest archer misses anything illegal in the replay. The *magister ludi* Shakuni tacitly invites Duryodhana to throw the last dice by dropping them into his palm, assuring him he cannot lose, but at the last moment the Kaurava prince places the dice back in Shakuni's hand. He fails to trust his luck in a situation he cannot afford to lose.

Draupadi's invocation of Krishna. A further change of light focuses attention on her full face, while Carnatic music suggests her inner mantra. Krishna appears to her, invisible to all others: once again, the spectators are in a privileged position. For the miracle of the inexhaustibly reproducing sari – Draupadi can never be forcibly stripped – she stands together with Krishna in tranquil immobility, in contrast with Duhsassana's frenzied wrenchings and tuggings. Comically, he is forced to give up, collapsing exhausted and bemused. Her curse of Duhsassana and the Kauravas is delivered to the distant cry of an enraged beast.

The Pandavas en route to exile. The gaming hall remains half-visible in the unlit forward section of the playing space. Only the back wall is fully lit as the Pandavas trudge along the far side of the river, specks of dust kicking up in their wake. The preceding space – the gaming hall – and its events are still fully present in their minds, as in ours: the cause of their present predicament. From our perspective, we look through that cause to effect. They disappear accompanied by Toshi's harmonium drone and plaintive song, adapted from the Bengali writer Rabindranath Tagore's Nobel Prize-winning volume of poems *Gitanjali* (Toshi had studied Rabindra Sangeet in India on one of his many preparatory journeys). Interwoven with the images of final departure and enforced banishment, the song colours all: a sense of immense loss, a yearning for despoiled innocence never to be recovered.

Vyasa recounts the final moments of the Pandavas' leaving – their ominous attitudes, etc. – to the blind king. The die is now cast but the story is just beginning. A bloodbath seems inevitable: revenge for outrages suffered at their cousins' hands. The spectator closely follows the narration to the blind king in his/her imagination. On an associative level, the words are invested with a heightened charge, for they exist as the only reality available to Dhritarashtra: the quality of word as sound, colour, image, taste is amplified. An appeal is made, through empathy with the blind king's predicament, to the spectator's imagination. Like blind Gloucester, we are able to 'see it feelingly' with him. This further illustration of Dhritarashtra's dependence upon others – his inability to act, his horror at his own weakness and irresponsibility, their repercussions – also serves to provide a naturalistic rationale for the 'suggestive' art of the storyteller at this precise moment: so an impulse for the form exists in the narrative itself.

The final image: Vyasa and Bénichou/Ganesha/Krishna return to the gaming table, the source of the exile and inexorable resultant conflict. Accompanied by the musicians, Bénichou sings an Indian folk song, 'The Song of Maya' (illusion), as they play their own game of dice. While their gentle lyrical humour affirms the song's content by reframing the game as 'play', the song itself in some way accounts meta-textually for what we have just seen (a 'song of illusion'), as well as for this temporary hiatus in the performance.

NOTES

1 Vyasa is traditionally accredited as author/compiler of all eighteen Puranas (lesser epics), as collector and arranger of the Four Vedas, and indeed as creator of Vedantic philosophy. His generic name means 'the arranger', and repeatedly in this performance quite literally he 'arranges' the construction of narrative representation. The word *'vyasa'* is still used in India today for any storyteller.

Maya, as David R. Kinsley points out in *The Divine Player* (Delhi: Motilal Banarsidass, 1979, pp. 10–14), is more than illusion or ignorance. 'For *maya* is also the power of the absolute, or the power of the gods. [It] is more than simply a negative concept, more than simply illusion. In the *Rig Veda, maya* means power, or the ability of the gods to change form and to create. *Maya* is the supernatural ability on the part of the gods to extend themselves.' In its earliest context, '*maya* meant the wonderful skill of the gods . . . It is as a vehicle of the gods' display, as their means of revealing themselves, that *maya* may be understood as the *lila* of the gods. For *maya* is their means of creating and sustaining the phenomenal order, and *maya* is always mysterious, unpredictable and bewitching. The gods are great *mayins*, great magicians, and the created order is the result of their trickery. They have conjured the world into being, and they similarly conjure it out of existence' (ibid p. 13).

2 The unnamed brother is the illegitimate Vidura, whose name signifies 'knowing much'. The wise counsellor is absent from this version, the only major protagonist to have been supplanted, most of his role now allocated to Bhishma.

3 According to Georges Dumézil, the Pandavas collectively represent the *locus classicus* of 'the ideology of the three functions . . . the conception according to which the world and society can live only through the harmonious collaboration of these three stratified functions'. The functions are: sovereignty (Yudishthira); force – *danda* (Arjuna and Bhima, twin aspects of this quality, like Odin and Thor, with his hammer, in Scandinavian myth); and fecundity (the twins, an undifferentiated union, who specialize in breeding livestock). This hierarchy of functions represents the king and his specialized auxiliaries (see Dumézil, *The Destiny of the Warrior*, Chicago: University of Chicago Press,

1968, p. 5). In terms of *danda*, Arjuna, the warrior-*yogin*, seems to be a representative of brahminic spiritual power (cf. Achilles), whereas Bhima represents temporal *kshatrya* power (cf. Heracles).

4 Cf. G. J. Held on the central conflict in The Epic: '[it] concerns two parties representing the two halves of the cosmos . . . we have here to do with a cosmic ritual i.e. an event in which the entire cosmos is understood to participate' (*The Mahabharata, an Ethnological Study*, London: Kegan Paul, 1935, p. 332).

In *The Shifting Point* (New York: Harper & Row, 1987, p. 163) Brook describes *dharma* in the following way: 'What is *dharma*? That is a question no one can answer, except to say that, in a certain sense, it is the essential motor. Since it is the essential motor, everything that accords with it magnifies the effect of *dharma*. Whatever does not agree with it, whatever opposes it or is ignorant of it, isn't 'evil' in the Christian sense – but negative.' He goes on to point out the problematic (if inevitable) contextualization of The Epic in western 'readings', in terms of a reductive good/evil polarity, a diminution of complex Hindu syncretism: '*The Mahabharata* cuts to shreds all the traditional Western concepts, which are founded on an inessential, degenerate Christianity in which good and evil have assumed very primitive forms. It brings back something immense, powerful and radiant – the idea of an incessant conflict within every person and every group, in every expression of the universe: a conflict between a possibility, which is called *dharma*, and the negation of that possibility'.

5 Meher Baba: 'The Avatar appears in different forms, under different names, at different times, in different parts of the world. As His appearance always coincides with the spiritual regeneration of man, the period immediately preceding His manifestation is always one in which humanity suffers from the pangs of the approaching rebirth . . . Humanity grows desperate. There seems to be no possibility of stemming the tide of destruction. At this moment the Avatar appears. Being the total manifestation of God in human form, he is like a gauge against which man can measure what he is and what he may become.

'He is interested in everything but not concerned about anything. The slightest mishap may command His sympathy: the greatest tragedy will not upset Him. He is beyond the alterations of pain and pleasure, desire and satisfaction, rest and struggle, life and death. To Him, they are equally illusions that He has transcended, but by which others are bound, and from which He has come to free them. He uses every circumstance as a means to lead others toward Realisation. The Avatar awakens contemporary humanity to a realization of its true spiritual nature, gives liberation to those who are ready, and quickens the life of the spirit in His time' (from *Discourses*).

I am indebted to the Jungian psychologist Craig San Roque for pointing out this passage to me as pertinent to the discussion of Krishna and of his role in *The Mahabharata*. See the *Bhagavad Gita*, IV, 6–8, for further discussion of the avatar.

EXILE IN THE FOREST

This above all – to thine own self be true:
And it must follow, as the night the day,
Thou canst not then be false to any man.

(Hamlet)

But where there is danger, there grows also what saves.

(Holderlin, *Patmos*)

The narrative is now fully self-generative, so there is no need for Vyasa and Ganesha to set us on our way. Centre stage, the musicians set up jagged percussive rhythms which immediately locate the gnawing unease in **the Kaurava camp**. Duhsassana awakens from a nightmare with a scream, to disturb his equally troubled brother. Merleau-Ponty's celebrated caveat hangs unvoiced on the air – 'We struggle with dream figures and our blows fall on living faces.' A low diagonal light casts ghastly deformed shadows behind them on the side wall: the darker aspects of their psyches stick with them, haunt them.

As the narrative moves into Book 3 of the *Mahabharata*, an immediate transposition to the forest exile of the Pandavas, 'wanderers in the scorching and barren wilderness of this world', to borrow a phrase from Dostoevsky's Grand Inquisitor. Draupadi's hair is now loose, tangled and natural. Yudishthira and Arjuna are both stripped to the waist, warrior-ascetics whose lives are worn down to simple constitutive elements – rags, sticks, stones, pots: the austerity of *The Ik*. Draupadi creates an altar with a single stone centrepiece, garlands, candles, mango leaves and petals. Religious observance and devotion (*bhakti*) continue, as a wife assures the gods' protection of her family. After Tsuchitori's initial song, a direct narrative bridge to the end of the last section, the nature of their forest existence is established in silence. An elemental way of life, involving two different kinds of fire – votive candles and open fires in the bare earth, tiny tenuous *foyers* of sticks and twigs for warmth.[1] Yudishthira also performs his own *puja*, creating two concentric circles of red powder around a jug of water: a prayer for sustenance.

Therefore we are presented with an immediate vision of a world of great simplicity, religious devotion, respect for and interdependence with the natural world. At the same time, the implied way of life is difficult, impermanent. Underlying this aesthetically satisfying reduction to the elements is a quality of privation, profound unhappiness and threat: hence Draupadi's *cri de coeur*, challenging Yudishthira to action. His mute acceptance of *dharma* smacks of passivity to her, she is frustrated and embittered by the sterility and hopelessness of inaction. The original *Mahabharata* often refers to Draupadi in exile as 'having husbands, but like a widow'. Compare her frame of mind with Sita's in Valmiki's *Ramayana*

139

during her forest exile, which she feels to be a delightful romantic dream. *The Mahabharata* is so much more contradictory and less idealized.

Arjuna recognizes the inadequacy of wandering aimlessly ('As the true method of knowledge is experiment, the true faculty of knowing must be the faculty that experiences' – Blake). He must search, learn, develop his skills and acquire new ones: he must 'live more abundantly', as Hesse would have said, by becoming a Nietzschean *Überganger* (a self-sur-mounter). His solitary departure recalls the journeys in both *Conference* and Gurdjieff's *Meetings with Remarkable Men*, as well as Gilgamesh's quest for ancestral wisdom: *solvitur ambulando*. This is a recurrent theme in Brook's work with the Centre: the searcher and the search, the impera-tive to extend one's boundaries, to find understanding by confronting and embracing experience – a process described by the Sufis as 'making a journey to the outer horizons' which corresponds to 'a journey to the inner horizons'. In one way, the forest is a metaphor, as much a spiritual and initiatory landscape as Dante's 'Dark Wood', or Gilgamesh's 'The Country': a locus of retreat as a symbolic death, facilitating a subsequent ontological 'rebirth'.

The remaining Pandavas sleep, their shelter a blanket suspended between two sticks embedded in the earth, their only light an open fire: a tiny pocket of humanity engulfed by darkness. The shelter also serves to focus a defined space: a cinematic screen, a frame in front of which Bhima sits on guard. The sudden appearance of two flesh-eating demons, *the rakshasas*, introduces Manichean elements of the primal human predicament: fire, darkness, the Beast – the latter a homologous motif in diverse mythological discourses, a component of archetypal 'initiatory' narratives. There are explicit echoes of tribal Africa and Australia in these masked 'devil' figures, a representation that has inevitably been read as racist, serving to underline and reinforce dangerous received ideas about tribal cultures. Brook locates the *rakshasas* in relation to shamanistic animism, or the pagan notion of chthonic *genii loci* – the protectors of places and the places themselves (cf. the Humbaba in *Gilgamesh*). One of them is covered in animal pelts, a faceless shadow with bells on her ankles; the other boasts a spray of menacing spines, like an outsized porcupine. The union of Bhima and Hidimbi – now transformed into a beautiful woman (Tam Sir Niane) – is narrated by her from Bhima's shoulders: they blend and merge, a two-headed beast.

The *rakshasa's* brother Hidimba (Clément Masdongar), returns to inter-rupt their love play and do battle with Bhima. In this scene of great dynamism and athleticism, the space is used fully, including the rungs up either side wall – and Masdongar in particular is a phenomenally compel-ling dancer. The noise awakens the Pandavas, who emerge bleary-eyed to observe this strange conflict; comically, they peer over the top of the blanket/shelter. Much of the energy of this titanic struggle stems from

140

Tsuchitori's percussive battery: the earth itself seems to shake. Eventually Bhima snatches the blanket to use as a weapon, ensnaring his opponent in it, then crushing him. A comic 'panto' death – the defeated *rakshasa* as 'dead ant', arms and legs rigid above him. Nothing is gratuitous, however, for this position enables him to be carried off forthwith in a familiar (cartoon?) position of captured prey, suspended by all four limbs from a stick: we have seen it in every Stewart Granger film. Further slapstick occurs in the instantaneous appearance of the son of Bhima and Hidimbi, fully developed physically if not in other ways – no gestation period here (a quality traditionally ascribed to *rakshasas* exploited for narrative dynamism). At this point, Ghatotkatcha is a lumbering gormless 'child' of immense strength, the curls of a wig sticking bolt upright on his head. Masdongar, who had played the dead *rakshasa*, returns to portray him as a lovable oaf, mumbling ill-formed cries of 'mama' and 'papa' to his astonished parents. Later he will be summoned to the battlefield, his awesome physical prowess used to erase the threat of Karna's sacred lance.

Figure 13.5 'Exile in the Forest'. In the foreground, the Kauravas invoke Arjuna by making a circle of fire around the pool – an iconographic link with Shiva Nataraja's circle of flame (*tiruvasi*): in the background, Arjuna is overcome by Kirata-Shiva (Tapa Sudana). (Photographer – Gilles Abegg)

The Kauravas arrive in the forest, dressed in warrior black costumes, the very antithesis of the semi-naked, ragged and unarmed Pandavas. Vyasa is forced to intervene to prevent imminent violence. His fictional creations now possess an independent life of their own. His intervention is necessary, he says, to avoid crimes against *dharma*. It is too early for the conflict, and at this time the odds are too strongly stacked in favour of the Kauravas. Like Krishna, Vyasa is apparently allied with the Pandavas, for they are purportedly the agents of *dharma*.

A neutral empty space is re-established quickly. Fires are starved with earth or doused with water, leaving tiny mounds of steaming, smoking sand; rugs and materials are removed. Another somewhere/nowhere created in a blink by the actors; while to one side–

> *The Boy:* Vyasa, I don't want to stay in the forest any more. I'm afraid.
>
> *Vyasa:* But you are no longer in the forest

The invocation of Arjuna by Duryodhana is a scene of startling beauty, using the simplest of pyrotechnic effects. As Duhsassana creates a circle of fire around the pool, Duryodhana lobs petals into the water with little respect: a hasty nod at ritual by someone the original text suggests may possess very real magical prowess.[2] The circle of flame entraps them, forcing them to watch a vision they have summoned up, but in fact will not wish to see. At the same time, a lateral line of fire parallel with the front edge of the river springs up from the sand: naked flame, writhing shadows, reflections on the surface of the pool. Duryodhana faces the spectators, Duhsassana and Karna look on aghast as Arjuna breaks through the back line of fire to enter the central space. There is a sense of transgression, even initiation, in the movement of this figure from another 'reality'. The back wall twists in the flickering light, its leprous scars like drifting mist through Arjuna's mountain retreat – he is near Mt Kailasa, the Hindu Olympus in the Himalayas. Later, in *The War*, these same plaster stains (the Bouffes' 'wounded aspect', as Micheline Rozan calls it) will conjure up, Rorschasch-like, momentary human faces and forms, like outlines branded into the walls and earth of Hiroshima.

Arjuna's battle with the hunter Kirata – Shiva in disguise – is a popular episode for representation in Hindu iconography and performing arts: it is also the subject of Bharavi's celebrated poem *Kiratarjuniya*. Here the Pandava's martial skills are no match for Shiva's cosmic powers. With prodigious acrobatic leaps and whirls, he scythes two tiny yellow flags through the air around Arjuna, producing the sound of distant muffled thunderclaps. A similar convention is used in Chinese Opera, but in truth the source of this image may well be in Indian lore. One of Shiva's traditional attributes is a yellow flag, attached to his trident, bearing the motif of the white bull Nandi; it is said to represent the necessity for dedication and patience when following the path of *dharma*.

Here Tapa Sudana as Shiva deflects, catches or shatters Arjuna's arrows, using the same convention as described above. Arjuna perceives the presence of divinity and hastily constructs an earth *lingam* (in its widest signification, an aniconic symbol of the wholeness of the Hindu universe), crowns it with a garland – a supplication to Shiva, as well as a reconstruction of the Hindu evening prayer *arati* – and the deity reveals himself. He sports an identical garland around his head, a trident in his hand. Shiva at his most martial, immobile in his traditional 'cosmic dance' position – *Shiva nataraja*, 'lord of the dance'. (The direct iconographic allusion must be recognizable to many in the audience: the Chola *nataraja* bronzes have become a virtual cliché of Indian culture in the west.) Arjuna's *mysterium tremendum et fascinans* is underlined by a repeated gasp of 'Shiva' by all those present – the Kauravas are still observing, spellbound; the use of rhythmic stycomythia for a radical elevation in status. Yet the actual moment of protean transformation has been made available and visible to us: the ludic self-consciousness of storytelling is rarely far away.

Figure 13.6 'Exile in the Forest'. Tapa Sudana as Shiva Nataraja. (Photographer – Gilles Abegg)

Shiva grants the kneeling Arjuna possession of *pasupata*, the ultimate weapon, or rather one of a number sought and employed in The Epic; associations with the arms race are unavoidable. Arjuna's hands are pressed together and held above his head in a *namaste* position of devotion, as

Shiva spins the tip of his trident along the outline of Arjuna's body, the blurred tip infusing him with numinosity, a palpable charge. In India, the three prongs of the trident (*trisula*) are said to represent bodily, worldly and heavenly suffering, as well as the interdependence of words, thoughts and actions: it is both destructive and protective, like Yahweh's staff. Some commentators propose that it represents a cosmic pillar holding heaven and earth apart, an *axis mundi;* and, like Krishna's *chakra*, the trident is said to have been moulded from shavings from the sun.

We turn back to the evident disillusion and despair of the Kauravas, entrapped in their dying circle, now an ominous black ring of scorched, sterile earth. Karna confronts Arjuna, despite the fact that they are in different fictive places and 'realities': such is the freedom of storytelling, unencumbered by the laws of causality and *vraisemblance*, the deliquescent materiality of the physical world. The two rivals (brothers) meet in an imagined no man's land, a mysterious liminal conjunction where the two 'worlds' overlap. Boundaries between reality and illusion blur and implode. An audience has no trouble reading or accepting this: in storytelling, 'truth' is clarity, an invitation to imagine . . .

Arjuna has evolved, he is enriched by the mountain penitence and search. The marks of an initiate/sage now colour his brow. He has travelled in different worlds, assimilated experience and understanding. Hence Madeleine Biardeau's description of him as 'the warrior-yogin',[3] for he has unified the powers of both *kshatryas* and brahmins. It is now his turn to relate a story to the Kauravas, literally a 'captive audience'. He re-creates a past encounter with **the nymph Urvasi** (Pascaline Pointillart), an *apsaras* from heaven. *Apsaras*, often sensuously represented in Hindu temple sculpture, are in some ways similiar to Valkyries, or the Irish Sidhe; in addition, traditionally they love to torment *rishis* rapt in meditation, or are sent to seduce them. Urvasi makes an extraordinary entrance, flitting across the stage, a trail of fire snaking through the sand in her wake: a comet's tail in the night sky. Tongues of flame flicker blue and gold across the sand and on the surface of the pool – for it too is now ablaze, in an instant transformed into its opposite but complementary element. This proves to be one of the most hypnotic and entrancing sequences in the performance as a whole. Like us, the Kauravas observe, but they are able to question, interject, dispute: they serve as our point of access. The scene also celebrates the coherence and potential resonance of doubling, for there is both an underlying logic and a continuity in the casting of roles. Here is a second rejected advance and vengeful curse from Pointillart (we look back to Amba). Compare this with, for example, Clovis' roles: Ekalavya, Sisupala, Virata's son Uttara and Abhimanyu are all variations on a theme.

As the fire dies, the scene fades and the space is freed to be redefined. Scenographically, nothing in this production is gratuitous, even the by-product of a pyrotechnic effect is embraced and exploited. A wash of light pinpoints the pool, now ringed with black charred sand, like kohl around a glistening eye. Something of the malignant Kaurava presence remains, and the pool is now a poisoned lake. (This movement seems to propose a scenographic equivalent for the match cut, that formal dialectic device in cinematic montage that links disparate scenes.) Then the booming voice of Dharma emerges from the periphery of the space, openly created by Maratrat/Vyasa to one side – he uses the sound box of his troubadour's instrument. The resultant hollow echo *suggests* a voice from afar (*vox dei*), but the actual process of representation – the mechanics of 'mystery', if you like – is made available to the spectators. Such a device expresses Brook's avowed determination since *A Midsummer Night's Dream* to show that there is 'nothing up our sleeves', to invite participation in the imagination by opening up and demystifying the creative processes of play.

Then Vyasa, as narrator, enters the central space to deliver the voice of Dharma. Once established, the echo device is abandoned as redundant: we move on, although by association Vyasa's ordinary voice carries within it something of its amplified resonance seconds before. Dharma poses a series of **initiatory riddles** to Yudishthira, who remains ignorant of the fact that their source is in fact his father.

Dharma: Give me an example of space.
Yudishthira: My two hands as one.
Dharma: An example of grief.
Yudishthira: Ignorance.
Dharma: Of poison.
Yudishthira: Desire.
Dharma: An example of defeat.
Yudishthira: Victory.

Dharma tests his own son, the agent of *dharma* on earth. Yudishthira stands alone, bare to the waist, addressing his responses to a light above our heads: defenceless, unarmed, such as he is. The final question and answer bring us back to the one inescapable collective given – mortality – and humankind's imperative to locate meaning within it:

Dharma: And what is the greatest marvel?
Yudishthira: Each day, death strikes and we live as though we were immortal.

The residue here of a Vedic tradition of contests of enigmas, these riddles resemble Zen *koans*, the gnomic paradoxes of the 'Valleys' in *Conference*, or Oedipus' confrontation with the Sphinx. Later, at the threshold of Paradise, a similar interrogatory process awaits the Pandava king, once again a lone survivor: he is to be tested throughout his journey.

A sudden transposition back to the Kauravas, now in possession of a fearsome armoury of real weapons – metal swords, shields, spears. As silhouettes, they are idealized, epic, virtual cartoons. Nevertheless they immediately convey the unmediated reality and horror of pain and death. And a stark dislocation is set up in our imaginations between their position of strength, armed to the teeth and fully prepared for battle, and the solitary figure of Yudishthira moments before, Christ-like in his semi-nakedness.

Krishna's return. Vyasa and the boy kneel by the pool, the dark ring now more or less erased: a brief hiatus in the narrative thrust as they discuss the story. Suddenly a tiny pebble splash in the water, the contemplative mirror disturbed by this image of life, perhaps a fish breaking the surface. And Krishna becomes apparent high on a side wall, hanging from a rung, his playful lob into the pool accompanied by the inevitable wry and enigmatic smile. The 'plop' precedes our awareness of Krishna's appearance, it is almost as if he had emerged from the pool. However his playfulness is only momentary as, full of foreboding, he admits to sensing a 'lake of dark water' within himself. He tells us this while gazing reflectively into the pool, its surface once more still and glassy, almost as if it had cued his utterance.

Parashurama, the brahmin hermit who is traditionally the sixth of Vishnu's ten avatars (Krishna is the eighth), is pursued by Karna. The latter is also in search of an 'ultimate weapon', for he had witnessed Shiva's gift to Arjuna. The hermit resembles a shaman, an Aboriginal elder or mendicant *Naga sadhu*. He shakes his stick and the axe that gives him his name. 'Rama with the axe' – a weapon with which a number of legends suggest that he broke off one of Ganesha's tusks, and despite which he lost a three-week long battle with Bhishma (also played by Sotigui Kouyate in this production). He sings a lament, his face and angular body stained with grey ash, his only garment a loincloth: a Giacometti sculpture infused with life. In this form, the West African *griot* Kouyate offers a direct if hybridized allusion to tribal cultural forms encountered in Africa, Australia and India: a funereal apparition wandering alone in search of his dreamtime ancestors, as well as a Shaivite holy man seeking empowerment deep in the forest. The echo of indigenous Australian culture is further strengthened by the use of a trio of didgeridoos. The musicians form a choral presence around Kouyate (interestingly only Tsuchitori has mastered the circular breathing technique). The image thus created is both radically 'other' and disturbing. Krishna, Vyasa and the boy observe from the shadows behind. As spectators, they help evolve the dynamics of space, never committed to a single, exclusive vantage point: a mobile focusing device.

The magical formula for the weapon is handed to Karna on a piece of bark, a fragment of living nature like the bark paintings used in Aboriginal

Figure 13.7 'Exile in the Forest'. Krishna (Maurice Bénichou) tells the young boy (Samon Takahashi) of his fears. French-language production. (Photographer – Gilles Abegg)

ritual.⁴ Parashurama had the bark concealed beneath a tiny pile of straw and grass, his bedding and environment: another minimalist metonymic adjunct suggesting a way of life. As Parashurama sleeps on Karna's lap, a 'worm' chews – or rather *drones* – its way into the flesh of the Kaurava warrior's thigh; it is 'injected' by Tsuchitori through a didgeridoo, like the venom from some outlandish mosquito. Later it will be suggested that the worm was divine retribution, sent on behalf of the Pandavas to foil Karna's search: he will forget the formula when he needs it – an addition to the already complex web of oaths and counter-oaths, all of which will be implemented. The *karmic* balance is now back with the Pandavas. Toshi's hovering presence suggests a *deus ex machina*. A Japanese, face hidden in his swinging hair, carries and plays a sacred Aboriginal instrument as if it were organically part of him: a bizarre polysemic image, the collision of discourses in this configuration curiously satisfying. The didgeridoo is employed throughout to introduce a textural 'otherness', a transcendent quality. Interestingly, it finds its place quite naturally in this elemental world, any precise textual/cultural reference insulated.

The court of King Virata (Andreas Katsulas), a new space once again established with clarity and economy. Its representation is based on what are by now familiar structural ellipses, which engage our imaginations to complete a suggested reality: Brook invites us to 'fill in the missing half of the equation'. Ropes at least 20 metres in length are attached to the domed base of the cupola in the theatre's ceiling. Two on each side suggest the dimensions of the imaginary palace within which we now find ourselves. They are employed to suspend a pair of swinging benches of the kind beloved by late medieval maharajas. A similar device was employed by Mnouchkine at the Cartoucherie de Vincennes for the scene of John of Gaunt's death in the Théâtre de Soleil's *Richard II;* here the resonance of a slightly opulent decadence is less hieratic. The musicians move to a carpet centre stage behind and between these benches, to enact 'musicians' within the fiction. As they begin to play, the perfect image of a court at ease, united in harmony, blossoms before our eyes. A number of oil lamps flicker while tiny candles on silver bases are set afloat in the pool, now an ornamental pond or lake. Mats with bolsters from a circle of focus around an inner central space lit more sharply than its surrounds: an empty space, latent, waiting to be filled, for the focus is centripetal. Tapa Sudana performs a short Balinese puppet entertainment for the court's delight. It seems to be the comic tale of a king losing his head, which culminates with the puppeteer pursuing one of the puppets (a *wayang golek*) off into the 'audience' on stage: it has taken on a chirruping life of its own. However, as is so often the case in this production, no sooner has the activity been established than it is erased, perhaps before we have had time to assimilate it fully, to linger over skills and details.

The arrival of the Pandavas, introduced to the playing space from

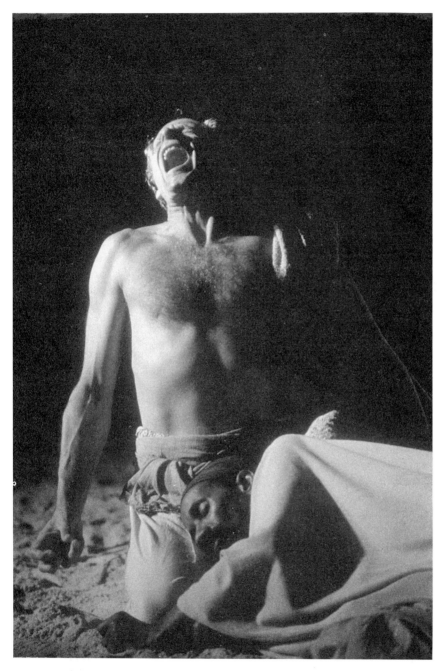

Figure 13.8 'Exile in the Forest'. The *kshatrya* Karna (Bruce Myers) screams silently as a worm burrows into his thigh; his *guru* Parashurama (Sotigui Kouyate) sleeps on his lap. French-language production. (Photographer – Gilles Abegg)

behind the river by the back wall – located as somewhere 'outside'. We watch them waiting nervously, preparing to convince the king (whom we have already seen to be amiable and warm) that he must take them in. For it is the final year of exile, and the Pandavas must disguise themselves, 'in accordance with their deepest thoughts', as Vyasa has said. In reality this means ludic carnivalesque inversions: Yudishthira as brahmin, a *sanyasin* – and, ironically, as dice teacher. Arjuna, like Achilles, is an effeminate eunuch or transsexual (Brihannada), it remains unclear which. Either one would suggest the very antithesis of his apparent status as *kshatrya:* the curse of Urvasi realized and the metaphorical impotence of exile, but also a holistic equilibrium, like Shiva's manifestation in a composite male/female form called Ardhanarishwara or Shakta-Shakti. During his five-year sojourn in Indra's heaven, where he learnt to use his divine weapons, Arjuna had received instruction from a *gandharva* – so he will teach dance. Bhima, a man of Gargantuan appetites, presents himself as cook. Sahadeva (the Iranian musician Mahmoud Tabrizi-Zadeh) will be a musician. And the loyal sustainer Nakula (Jean-Paul Denizon) a groom – comically he claims to know 'all the secrets and desires of cows'.

There follows a sequence of great comedy and lightness of touch. Andreas Katsulas' Virata is portrayed with great compassion as a very human king, worried by the expense but delighted with his new companions. Yoshi Oida's Kitchaka, with its roots as much in Japanese Kyogen as in Kathakali, is an arrogant, self-satisfied and vainglorious Samurai – a vain buffoon and laughable peacock, dolled up to the nines, with eyeliner and silk kimono. His suspicions are aroused when he hears that Bhima has been juggling horses in the yard . . .

The Pandavas tell stories to the king and court, animating the central focal space. The scene is underscored with dramatic ironies: the Pandavas as lowly servants mask their true natures; Arjuna used the disguise to implement Urvasi's curse; and Bhima enacts his own meeting with his half-brother Hanuman, the monkey god. Their counterparts are storytellers in village squares throughtout Asia and Africa, using whatever comes to hand to tell their tales, accompanied by two musicians behind them. Toshi finds an astounding range of percussive slaps and burps by beating an earthenware jug, similar to the *ghatam* of South Indian music. (A few moments later, when Kitchaka is found 'crushed' into a sphere, he uses his talking drum to mimic one of the actor's utterances: he then sustains an intelligible dialogue by modifying drum tension and pitch to mirror conversational intonation).[5] Such music from a visible source enjoys a position of extreme mobility and freedom in relation to the diagesis, while self-consciously acknowledging the fictionality of representation.

A sudden jarring change of tone occurs in the Pandavas' story – Hanuman's warning prefigures the *Kaliyuga*, the age of Kali ('The Black'), the fourth and final subdivision of the cyclical Hindu *Mahayuga*. Sanskrit scholars claim that the *Kaliyuga* will last 432,000 years, and at present we are only in the sixth millennium. At its end, it is said, world redemption will be possible only through its destruction by deluge, fire, and subsequent reconstruction. It is an era of mechanization, fragmentation, environmental sterility and violent carnage. Yudishthira's words are unaccompanied, they take flight in silence, painting an apocalyptic vision of a

Figure 13.9 'Exile in the Forest'. Kitchaka (Yoshi Oida) pleads with Virata's wife Gudeshna (Mireille Maalouf) to send him Draupadi; in the background, Toshi Tsuchitori. French-language production. (Photographer – Michel Dieuzaide)

bleak post-nuclear world. Echoes of the *The Wasteland*, as of the cosmic disorder and anarchy of pathetic fallacies in Shakespearian tragedy. Unaccommodated man on a blasted heath, locked within some endless nuclear winter; life as a metaphysical Beckettian farce, when seconds before there was joy and innocence . . . An affectively charged polar movement that reflects the performance idioms and textures in miniature, like an individual fragment of a shattered holographic plate: structurally, a discursive hypostasis.

For **Kitchaka's 'boudoir'** the ropes are pinned back behind the side walls, the swinging benches upended as wicker screens. Behind one of them, Kudsi Erguner plays a haunting melody on the *ney*. Oida warbles a hilarious lovesong, a pastiche with suggestions of Kyogen. An idiot seducer, he scatters powders and rice on the floor and, suggestively, on the bed (a length of material on the ground); finally an adolescent overdose of scent intended to wow Draupadi, or club her into submission. When she escapes, there is a change of light as Bhima clambers under the sheet and awaits Kitchaka – for it is now the following night, time for the 'secret' rendezvous with Draupadi in the dance hall: again temporal concatenation for narrative dynamism. Dramatic irony underpins and colours overt clowning as Kitchaka approaches the concealed shape, lingering with relish over his 'moment of glory'. As he slides his body under the sheet, his head remains framed above the rim of the material. We follow the dawning horror of gradual realization in his facial contortions. Eventually Bhima drags him out of sight, wraps him in the sheet and crushes him into a perfect ball, which he then rolls across the floor with his foot – the cartoon humour of *Ubu aux Bouffes*. And as with the *serio buffo* of *Ubu*, a darker undercurrent is present: Bhima's prodigious and merciless strength, a further death, a prefiguration of the treatment to be meted out to anyone who mistreats Draupadi.

Back to Virata's court, the airborn 'loveseats' down in an instant for a scene of ongoing everyday life. Gentle comedy as Arjuna teaches dance, mincing outrageously, as feminine as Desperate Dan in a tutu. Meanwhile Yudishthira is whooping Virata at dice, with comic brio. At the news of the Kauravas' raid – they have come to steal Virata's cattle – Arjuna/Brihannada is proposed as Virata's son's charioteer (a parodic distortion of Krishna's relationship with Arjuna during the forthcoming battle?). There is irony in the courtiers' scorn: 'what, *this* fey creature a hero?', fuller comedy in Arjuna's shy refusal. Presented with two shields, he appears dumbfounded: what could these possibly be for? Then a joyous moment of realization and recognition – when he holds them up at either side of his head, they become the most cumbersome earrings you have ever seen, an Amazon version of Zsa Zsa Gabor. Vittorio Mezzogiorno is loving this shift of textural gears, as is the audience which accepts this offer of some release from threatened danger in knockabout burlesque.

Figure 13.10 'Exile in the Forest'. Animating the inanimate, dynamism in stasis: Arjuna (Vittorio Mezzogiorno) fires on the invisible Kauravas, while his 'charioteer' Uttara (Clovis) executes a series of karate *kata*. In the top left-hand corner, one of the rope nooses used to suspend the swing-seats for Virata's court. French-language production. (Photographer – Gilles Abegg)

Confrontation with the Kauravas. The chariot is established using two industrial pallets, set up in profile. The forward one is supported by the young prince Uttara (Clovis) as he runs through an impressive display of karate *kata*, with Arjuna behind, immobile on the platform, firing his bow. Brook is fond of finding suggestive life in the abandoned debris of building sites. (One thinks of the electric cable spools used to such great effect as *voiturin à phynances*, war machine, throne, etc. in *Ubu.*) Here almost everything is suggested – horse, charioteer, chariot/fighting machine, pursuit, mobility – although in truth all is immobile, no enemy is in sight as yet. The dynamic stasis of the martial artist is used to invite

153

and then anchor a stream of imagined elements. Punctuating cries of the Hindi 'Achcha!' provide direct echoes of India, and at the same time energize the image.

The Kauravas eventually appear, watching, immobile, horrified vultures suspended from rungs high across the back wall and both side walls, scattered at different heights. Spatially fragmented as a unit, they seek refuge from the onslaught. Shadows with an ominous menace, their black capes flap lazily like those of the parasitic senators in *Timon*. Like us, the Kauravas recognize the denotative sound of Arjuna's bow, the *analapos* again visibly operated by Tsuchitori to one side: a vibrant chilling sound, which conveys the high-speed movement of an object through space, the spiralling friction of a missile. Drona and Bhishma – silent shadows – retire into darkness, refusing conflict. The Kauravas, transfixed by light in their eyries, look on as the victors return. The perspectival fluidity of this use of depth of field allows radically different and apparently incompatible images to be presented simultaneously. So the mood behind bleeds into the scene in front, colouring the triumphant court's rejoicing. Another *holi* celebration – garish clouds of powder and potions, a flurry of dance and music – then the image dissolves.

Another mood change for Vyasa's enigmatic fable, the story of Markandeya's initiatory journey away from the sterility, exhaustion and emptiness of mortal life through the mouth of a numinous and angelic child: we are not told here that the *puer aeternus* is Vishnu himself. The old man finds beauty, order, repose and life during the 100-year period he spends in the child's stomach. Then he is regurgitated/reborn back into this world, like Jonah from the whale. He emerges the same, but profoundly nourished and refreshed. Death to oneself, the myth suggests, enables contact with the infinite, out of time. This in turn is regenerative, immortalizing, in contrast to an endless imprisoning cycle of death and rebirth. There are similarities with Bottom's 'most rare vision', with the slave's night of love in *Conference*, or even with our epic immersion in this tale, and the perceptual transformation or evolution it claims it can engender.[6] The narration of Markandeya's tale employs a double narrative voice – Vyasa's and the boy's – both in the third person. However, although the anecdote is an illustrative or didactic aside in terms of the central narrative, the child storyteller also enacts the child in the story told. As Pandavas and courtiers listen attentively, the circle of focus is complete. The back wall, now empty and apricot in colour, remains fully lit, evoking a substantial sense of space, distance, infinite horizons and realities beyond.

Krishna's home. A monastic existence is conveyed with a scenic minimalism, an asceticism in decor that in purely naturalistic terms is both pertinent and resonant here: a piece of rush matting, a swathe of material for a mattress, a blanket. Duryodhana is already there, impatiently waiting for Krishna to awaken. He has chosen to sit on a small table by Krishna's head (the gaming table?), the Kaurava's disrespectful arrogance immediately established physically, spatially. When Arjuna enters, in stark contrast he lowers himself gently on to the bare ground at Krishna's feet in an attitude of humble devotion. Seen first by Krishna on awakening, its Arjuna who will be granted his desire. He recognizes Krishna's value to him in many more ways than uniquely as a charioteer. And, indeed, the Sanskrit word for charioteer apparently contains overt suggestions of 'leader' and 'guide': the martial configuration is a clear metaphor for a psycho-spiritual relationship.[7]

Figure 13.11 'Exile in the Forest'. Duryodhana and Arjuna seek Krishna's help in the coming battle. Left to right: Arjuna (Vittorio Mezzogiorno), Krishna (Maurice Bénichou), Duryodhana (Andrzej Seweryn). French-language production. (Photographer – Michel Dieuzaide)

Much of the growing sense of imminent, inevitable conflict is conveyed through the dynamic montage of scenes, their heightened speed. In addition, increasing exploitation of harsh low-level diagonal lighting casts long unnatural shadows, highlighting every facial tic, every bead of sweat on lips. **Krishna's final attempt at peace** is answered only by Duryodhana's obstinate and misplaced pride, his sulky short-sightedness: a chillingly rich performance by Seweryn. Krishna's sudden intense fury is profoundly shocking, given his tranquil smiling norm, his lightness in every situation. Forced to manifest his divine appearance (*visvarupadarshana* or *viratrupa*), and thus locate himself definitively as Vishnu's avatar, he turns his back to the spectators and stands behind a transparent cloth: then a flute accompaniment and sharpened area of light as Bhishma describes his cosmic form. Significantly, Duryodhana turns away, refusing to countenance the transcendent. This revelation comes as a prelude to the celebrated theophany contained within the *Bhagavad Gita*, at the beginning of *The War*. Here Krishna's purpose is to make peace – the revelation is public. Later it will be to make war, to strengthen Arjuna's resolve – a private revelation for the exclusive benefit of his disciple, when he will become seraphic rather than human: *Logos* incarnate, the word made flesh. The nature of these two episodes juxtoposes the two faces of Krishna: creative or restorative, as well as destructive (but this in turn is regenerative). In the *Mahabharata* and in Hindu iconography, the *visva-rupa* in itself exists as a *textum* containing a web of individual narratives, comprising a meta-history of the world from creation to destruction. Inevitably, and happily, in neither instance in this production is there any attempt to represent this divine form.

In order for him to perceive this vision (*darshana*), Dhritarashtra's sight is momentarily restored by Krishna. Cieslak's face is now ravaged, the radiant purity of his *Constant Prince* has crumbled with the passage of time. His face records his experience, like a map or a weathered stone. In this work, the paradigmatic Grotowskian 'holy actor' rarely demonstrates, almost nothing is explicit. He is an *expressive* actor, in the literal sense – inner impulses are squeezed out, as if under pressure, then embodied. It is a performance of tiny economical nuances, grasping the twin knettles that both Grotowski and Brook have consistently privileged for their performers: a 'deep libidinal surrender'[8] and a 'deep-breathing economy of organic form'.[9] An almost imperceptible increase in the brightness of the light on his face, a minimal hand gesture, a sense of focus in his eyes, a minor adjustment in the muscular tension of his lantern-jawed face, a real tear, 'And see, no longer blinded by our eyes' (Rupert Brooke) – and then he returns to darkness. Cieslak excavates for us an immensely tragic figure wavering on the very brink of decrepitude, disinterring echoes of Oedipus, Lear, Gloucester and Priam *inter alia*. He saws and spits his way through the text with a voice of rock and glass, his physical presence emanating what one critic had accurately described as 'blowtorch intensity'. Words become bitter balls of phlegm to be spat, or blows from a rusty hammer. Every utterance strikes percussively, then reverberates.

As Karna and Krishna embrace, the musicians' percussive cacophony grows to a climax. The carnage of battle is now unavoidable. **Karna** is also a tragic archetype – the 'outsider'. He is an ambiguous and contradictory figure, both illuminated by a personal sense of *dharma*, destiny, honour, pride and loyalty, and at the same time fuelled by bitter resentment and fury at his childhood abandonment to his fate in a river by his mother, like Moses, and his subsequent rejection by the Pandavas (his family).[10] Karna is one of a number of protagonists in The Epic of confused caste status: a *kshatrya* by birth, a *suta* by upbringing and in others' eyes. One thinks also of Bhishma, a *kshatrya* turned brahmin through his vow of *brahmacharya*, or of Drona and Aswhattaman, brahmins who are consummate warriors. Must they all perish for violating an ordered caste hierarchy? Are their deaths part of a ritual re-establishment of purity, harmony, order, *dharma*? – a notion that in the post-Auschwitz west inevitably carries associations of a reactionary ideology. Just as the Pandavas' possession of 'ultimate weapons', justified in terms of defending *dharma* – 'the right way' – from the forces of 'darkness' and ignorance, might be read as smacking of something akin to Captain America in conflict with the forces of Spectre ...

Karna is fired primarily by a sense of duty and of the significance of his role – a fire that is both obstinately dangerous and hypnotic. Here is a character born from a web of mixed motives and drives. In order to fulfil what he has determined and to meet allegiances made, he will have to deny his own origins; but then he has already been denied in turn. Karna's predicament is such that his only escape can be in death. Here he shows himself to be aware of what is at stake – the fate of humanity as a whole – in a feverish speech studded with grotesque images of cosmic decay and destruction: unnatural happenings, the omens of an apocalypse. Time and the world order are out of joint, dislodged from their axis. The immediacy of his nightmarish language contains echoes of *Macbeth* and *King Lear*, inter-textual chords that ring in our ears as the second part comes to an end without closure. A point of tension and irresolution demanding further development.

NOTES

1 The Hindu fire god Agni, the mediator between men and gods, is also known as Bharata, 'the sustainer', in Vedic literature. And incidentally Bharata is not only the ancestral forebear of these protagonists, and by extension the Hindu word for India, but also an ancient word for an actor. Cf. Bharata Natyam, the first word comprising the first syllables of the three primary categories in Sanskrit performance aesthetics: *Bhava* (expression), *Rasa* (flavour) and *Tala* (rhythm).

2 Cf. *Shiva nataraja*'s attendant ring of flame, the *prabha mandala*. In addition, a warning in the *Hitopadesa* springs to mind: 'The spirit in thee is a river. Its sacred bathing place is contemplation; its waters are truth; its banks are holiness; its waves are love. Go to that river for purification; thy soul cannot be made pure by mere water' – a warning Duryodhana consistently shows himself incapable of understanding. One might read much of the narrative, like *Hamlet*, in terms of 'maimed rites'.

3 Madeleine Biardeau, introduction and commentary on extracts from *Le Mahabharata* (Paris: Flammarion, 1986; translated by Jean-Michel Peterfalvi), p. 125.

4 Cf. the oldest existing *Mahabharata* manuscript, dating from no earlier than the tenth century, which was discovered in Kashmir, written on birch bark.

Or Bhasa's classical Sanskrit plays, which were found in 1912 inscribed on palm leaves: early media for recording significant elements of a culture that had formerly been oral. See also Edward C. Dimock in *The Literatures of India* (Chicago: University of Chicago Press, 1974, p. 12): 'the materials used for writing, birchbark and palm leaf, were very perishable. The rigours of climate, the heat and the humidity, and vermin threatened them. It has been remarked that 90% of Indian literature has been eaten by white ants . . .'

5 Memories of his solo performance at the Almeida Festival, London, in 1983, when one entire number was built around 'playing' a styrofoam cup he had found in the audience: magic in the everyday, the musician as virtuoso 'multi-vocal' performer in his own right as well as integral connotative constituent of the narratorial ensemble.

6 There are direct parallels also with a passage in *The Koran* (II 261):

And God had him die for a hundred years, then revived him and said:
'How long have you been here?'
'A day, or a part of a day,' he answered.

7 In the original *Mahabharata*, even before the war Drona proclaims, 'Where there is *dharma*, there is Krishna. Where there is Krishna, there is victory' (VI, 43.63).

8 Joseph Chaikin, *The Presence of the Actor* (New York: Atheneum, 1980), p. 20.

9 Henry James, quoted in George Steiner, *Language and Silence* (London: Penguin, 1979), p. 288.

10 The foundling figure is another archetype in mythological narratives: cf. the stories of Oedipus, the young Cyrus, Romulus and Remus, Iamus, etc. – of these, only Oedipus and Karna end in tragic *anagnorisis*.

THE WAR

Is this the promised end
Or image of that horror?
(*King Lear*)

The agents of force are the triumphant victims of the internal logic
of force, which proves itself only by surpassing boundaries – even its
own boundaries, and those of its raison d'etre . . . Above all [in Indian
fable] it is the warrior, on placing himself on the margin of the code,
or even beyond it, who appropriates the right to pardon, to break
through the mechanisms of hard justice: in short, the right to introduce some flexibility into the strictly determined course of human
relations – to pave the way for humanity.

(Dumézil, *The Destiny of the Warrior*, 1968)

The *Wanderjahre* of *The Odyssey* are over, the time for war (*The Iliad*)
is ripe. A huge Japanese drum pounded by Toshi Tsuchitori, centre stage,
signals the beginning of the final part. There are immediate signs of
something new in the ferocity of the music – a call to arms – and in
Toshi's martial costume: the musician as Samurai, the way of the drum
(*kodo*). At the same time, a fanfare of four immense Southern Indian
horns bellows from around the theatre at different levels. For most of *The
War*, the percussive undercurrent is constant, a concussing barrage that
locates the changing dynamic, supports the narrative thrust and feeds
tension. In many ways, music will be used to a similar effect as in
Mnouchkine's *Richard II*. Early in this section, a prevalence of conch
shells becomes apparent, an attribute traditionally associated with Vishnu,
Arjuna and victory (indeed Arjuna is often referred to as Vijaya, 'victory').
An actor mimes blowing into a conch on stage, while the sound is created
simultaneously and visibly 'in overdub' off.

As with Tsuchitori's, all of the costumes now have a military flavour:
the pre-eminence of the *kshatrya* – leather boots and gaiters, multi-layered
pleated skirts, simple tunics decorated with traditional patterns. Duhsassana
sports a *kshatrya* chignon. They resemble warriors from medieval miniatures, although references are deliberately non-specific both geographically
and historically – India, Central Asia, Anatolia, etc. Visually only the
saintly Bhishma is set apart, dressed as he is in a pure white robe. Even
though he fights at the very epicentre of the carnage, emblematically he
will remain unsullied.

It is at this point that bamboo screens are introduced for the first time,
mobile objects with limitless potential functions for the actor/*bricoleurs*.
These screens will serve as war machines, archery platforms, tents, shelters,
shields, beds, etc. Here they operate as a framing device for the disem-
bodied heads of the protagonists, sustaining a frieze behind. The warriors

adopt a configuration of confrontation, a perfectly symmetrical military 'V' formation, like an air-strike squadron. A sudden flourish, and the screens become two shelters, places of repose: Bhishma's has a roof, Drona's is without cover. This new configuration is constructed, then held in position, by the actor/warriors who have momentarily dropped their roles. The drum has now been positioned at stage right.

Figure 13.12 'The War'. Percussionist as warrior: from left to right, Tapa Sudana, Toshi Tsuchitori, Mavuso Mavuso. (Photographer – Gilles Abegg)

The perfect synecdoche for a chariot, a single naturalistic wooden cart-wheel, is rolled on by Krishna, Arjuna's charioteer.[1] Bénichou cracks a whip and mimes the horse's movements (another echo of Mnouchkine's *Richard II*), while Arjuna follows at a trot in his wake. A playful cartoon image, transparent and legible. Inevitably the wheel will be read as a metaphor, the shape of fate itself, the wheel of destiny – *karma* – the cycle of destruction and regeneration, although in truth it functions dynamically, as an *image* in Ezra Pound's sense of the word, something presenting an 'intellectual and emotional complex in an instant of time':

The image is not an idea. It is a radiant node or cluster. It is what I can, and must perforce call a VORTEX, from which and through which and into which ideas are constantly rushing . . . [2]

The wheel as *pars pro toto* conjures up an imagined chariot with infinitely more refined a lyricism than any 'real' chariot would in this context. At the same time, considered in terms of Pound's conceptual 'vortex', it suggests a diagrammatic representation of Hindu *samsara*, the round of existence – a vision of the shape of time, linked to the meta-historical pattern of a degenerative/restorative cycle of ages, in direct contrast to the apparent linearity of the narrative; the plenitude of a *mandala* or *orobouros*; a *chakra*, a *conjunctio oppositorum*; an archetype of the Self; an *imago mundi* . . .

Figure 13.13 'The War'. The *Bhagavad Gita*: Krishna (Bruce Myers) with his hand on the chariot wheel, on the left, and Arjuna (Vittorio Mezzogiorno). (Photographer – Gilles Abegg)

As the two opposing armies align themselves in a position of direct confrontation across the back of the space, Arjuna throws down his arms and expresses his famous misgivings to Krishna. His intense consciousness of self and surroundings obliges him to cease to act at the very moment when action must begin. The others remain silent, immobile, attentive, and slip out of focus in the background. This is the *Bhagavad Gita*, 'the Song of the Lord', the *Mahabharata's* own Upanishad: it is Hinduism's most sacred and influential devotional work, which forms the central chapters of Book 6 of the original *Mahabharata*, the *Bhishmaparvan*.³ Brook recalls first becoming aware of the *Gita*, and intrigued by its central question ('Shall I fight?'), during the preparation of *US* at the Aldwych in 1966.

Here the words of the sacred text are whispered by Krishna into Arjuna's ear. The Pandava prince then repeats fragments aloud, to the accompaniment of a single bitterly piercing note from the strings of a *sarod* and a muffled gong. Krishna/Bénichou sits on the wheel, momentarily alluding to the iconography of the *chakravartin* ('universal ruler'): the wheel is now flat on the earth (a minimally raised status, like the Kathakali Krishna during the *visvarupa* – on a stool – or those Gupta-period Buddha images, where he sits cross-legged on a wheel, symbol of the *dharma* he taught). Half-*conteur*, half-impersonator, much is third person description. We are left with an evocative compression of the heart of the *Gita*, and of course suggestion here inevitably entails reduction. One inference that emerges is that the conflict is firmly located on an inner spiritual plane, the 'battlefield of the soul'. We are told that only those actions performed without attachment (i.e. with a dispassionate lack of concern for results on the part of the agent) are free from the laws of *karma*. What is interesting here is that, in this agonistic context, the *Gita* is very unfamiliar – partisan advice to one combatant, far from Gandhi's more familiar (decontextualized) 'reading'.

As the lights focus increasingly on this central spot, Krishna again reveals his *visvarupa*, his universal form. Everything is left to our imaginations, stimulated by the resonance of Arjuna's enchanted and terrified description of the god's awesome cosmic dimensions, Mezzogiorno's facial expression and a plangent lyrical flight from the *ney*. Krishna remains immobile and impassive throughout this second theophany on the central axis of the wheel – *axis mundi*. As he returns to his human form, he steps back to earth from the wheel, smiling. Lights are now full up: let the pageant of battle commence. As Arjuna is 'reborn', the shadow of his bow takes on mythical proportions on the side wall. He blows into his conch with renewed vigour, determined afresh to confront the situation, to commit his energies.

The wall of shields (bamboo screens) evolves constantly, redefining their function and the space, altering the dynamics and tensions of the playing area as a whole: now ramps for archers, now the panels of a martial formation – one slides away to allow a single arrow shot, as in close-up, then slams shut again. On occasions, Brook uses a classic cinematic shot/reverse shot structure: at one moment we are behind one line, at the next behind the other. Finally, at the end of the first day, a camp shelter for the night is set up, with mats, flambeaux and shields focusing the locus of action. Drona's private prayer is a ritual centred around a bowl of fire. As in the Pandava forest exile episodes, fire offers a tiny comfort and a flicker of illumination in the teeming life of the night.

Amba has been reborn as Sikhandin (still Pascaline Pointillart). In this magical world, a woman can become a man, we accept it immediately, no further explanation is necessary. (In the original *Mahabharata*, Amba had deliberately tortured herself through penitences so as to force Shiva to grant her the means of revenge in the next life.) She challenges Bhishma, but he is spirited away to safety behind an instant wall of bamboo shields, the impenetrable *testudo* of Roman martial strategy, only to return seconds later borne aloft on a platform from which he can survey all. His height and stature designate his status and sanctity, which are renounced when he drops his arms and jumps to earth. The shields are lowered and angled to catch him when he falls – a deathbed. Significantly his body never touches the earth – he is cushioned and suspended. Compare this with the ignoble deaths in the mud and filth later experienced by Duhsassana, Karna and Duryodhana.

This scene is another of great spectacle and formal beauty. While still towering on his platform, Bhishma is whirled around the space mirroring Sikhandin, who aims unflinchingly at his avowed target. The spectator is offered a variety of perspectives on the linear axis of tension, the point of incandescence. The spiral movement perhaps also reflects Sikhandin/Amba's hesitation at the crucial moment in his/her life. The original *Mahabharata* literalizes this inner division at a later stage in The Epic, at the moment of Sikhandin's death at the hands of Aswhattaman's avengers during their noctural raid on the Pandava camp. He is shot between the eyes and hacked in two with a sword.

On this tenth day of the battle, in the end it is Arjuna, egged on by Krishna and shielded by Sikhandin, who fires at Bhishma. The entire scene is built around the cinematic technique of slow-motion, although a similar convention does exist in Asian popular theatre. As the arrow is unleashed, it is carried by Krishna – the agent of Arjuna's resolve and of *dharma* – slowly twisting through the air towards Bhishma's heart a few paces away: further parallels with the 'invisible' agents in puppetry in general.[4] By inference the predicament of the universe as a whole hinges on this one act. There is suspense in the extension of the instant between life and death, further concentrated by the silent immobility of those present and by the unsettling smile of Krishna (victim of his own prescience). The sequence provides a fragment of extemporal 'holiness' in the dislocation from habitual time of a 'moment of truth', like the deceleration of real time at the moment of a matador's delivery of the *coup de grâce*. The manipulation of the passage of time is hallucinatory in effect, the only sound a haunting pulse, like a heartbeat, from Tsuchitori's *analapos*. As the arrow strikes home – with childlike gravity, Krishna plants it in Bhishma's clothing seconds later – the onlookers erupt in a frenzy of cries

Figure 13.14 'The War'. The exploitation of a cinematic depth of field: Amba-Sikhandin (Pascaline Pointillart, right foreground) takes aim at Bhishma, Arjuna (Vittorio Mezzogiorno, left) at her side. French-language production. (Photographer – Gilles Abegg)

and movement, Bhishma collapses mortally wounded, and the baleful drone of the *nagaswaram* sings out, like the cry of a wounded elephant. Linear sequential time returns, the narrative pursues relentlessly, renewed.

Suddenly Bhishma is transfixed by a massive number of arrows, like Saint Sebastian, or Washizu, the Macbeth figure in Kurosawa's *Throne of Blood*, who is pinned to a wall by volleys of arrows. Here they are wedged in clumps in the deathbed around Bhishma by onlookers and by those supporting him. Arjuna fires two arrows in a cross for the dying man to rest his head, a 'warrior's cushion'. In the original *Mahabharata*, Arjuna also unleashes an arrow into the earth, piercing its flesh with such ferocity that a spring erupts for Bhishma's refreshment: a mite tricky here. The deathbed scene is a set piece of carefully composed beauty and harmony. Brook has a painter's sense of pictorial dynamics, here reminiscent of Uccello. At this moment of sanctity, formal positional relationships to the dying sage are established: Drona, for example, prostrates himself in the dirt at Bhishma's feet. Light emanates from his pure white robes as he is carried off with great solemnity.

Drona, his cropped hair now grizzled to suggest the passage of time, is ordered to take command of the Kauravas. His unwillingness is met with open hostility, the Kauravas surrounding and pressing in on him. 'The wheel stops on me, it's my turn now,' he concedes, resigning himself to meet the wheel of fortune, the kiss of death. He describes his disc to the Kauravas – an impenetrable battle formation, with echoes of Krishna's own disc; a spherical unit, as self-sufficient as any circle. He sprinkles a circle of water in the dust at his feet. It is only momentarily apparent before being soaked up by the earth. Within its circumference he traces a diagrammatic pattern, like the I Ching hexagram or a Tantric *yantra*. Rolling wheel, self-perpetuating circle – a potent motif for Brook, as for such others as Zen master Gibbon Sengai with his calligraphic circles and Jung with his *mandalas*.

Karna's song by the pool, in worship of the sun god, his unknown father, is an intoned nasal prayer, a gentle Hebraic plea from Bruce Myers, a compassionate actor of an intensely gaunt vocal and physical presence. Kunti emerges behind him unseen, places a candelabra with seven candles beside the river, then approaches her son with a single flaming torch. During this *pietà* beside the pool, the inevitable iconographic inter-textuality of a mother's tender care for her demigod son is explicit, if ironic. For this relationship of harmony is soon ruptured and rejected by the foundling Karna, just as formerly he had been rejected. In this seamless performance, Myers, a most tactile man, is always looking to refuse contact, to break free, to turn his back, to lock his arms across his chest: all Karna's natural instinctive feelings are displaced and suppressed.

Fluidity, speed and energy characterize all battle scenes, the dynamism of movement underscored by a percussive battery. 'All men are dancers,

Figure 13.15 'The War'. The deathbed of Bhishma. Left to right: Duryodhana (Andrzej Seweryn), Bhishma (Sotigui Kouyate), Karna (Bruce Myers), Dhritarashtra (Ryszard Cieslak), Gandhari (Mireille Maalouf) and Duhsassana (Georges Corraface); on the far right, Yudishthira (Matthias Habich). French-language production. (Photographer – Gilles Abegg)

Figure 13.16 'The War'. Warrior as *samurai*: the Kauravas in battle formation – the prelude to Drona's 'disc'. From left to right, Andrzej Seweryn, Georges Corraface, Yoshi Oida, Tapa Sudana, Bruce Myers. French-language production. (Photographer – Gilles Abegg)

and their tread goes to the barbarous clangour of a gong' (Yeats, *The Tower*). The recurrent use of cinematic changes of perspective and a full exploitation of space at all depths and heights mean that our interest rarely flags, as it does to some degree reading the interminable accounts of weaponry and carnage in the original *Mahabharata*. On a number of occasions here, a charged reality out of sight is suggested with sublime economy and lyricism: for example, the distant voices of armies marching in unison, conveyed in song and rhythm.

Abhimanyu's moment of decision, for he is a true son to Arjuna and nephew to Krishna – he will attempt to breach Drona's disc, he proclaims, standing in the very centre of Drona's water circle, now almost dry and barely visible: metaphorically, the precise location of his imminent demise. He purifies and blesses the tip of his spear by dipping it in the water by the pool, thereby investing it with a renewed status as locus of holiness and benediction.

Drona's disc, an impressive sight, is a sort of revolving maze (it is referred to as a 'labyrinth' in the original). Three spinning scaling ladders fill the space, each perhaps 8 metres in length, two Kauravas and Drona as the 'hinge pins' of these overlapping threshing circles. The tips of one of the wooden ladders slashes through the air inches in front of our noses. Abhimanyu's leaps and thrusts are built around the vocabulary of martial arts, in particular Karate and Kalarippayatt. Jayadratha's 'invisible wall', a boon obtained from Shiva, is a piece of bamboo of similar length to the ladders, vibrated by Katsulas from one end. Eventually, and predictably, Abhimanyu is surrounded and succumbs, penned in by a circle of five stick-brandishing Kauravas. There is a certain sculptural plasticity in the flight through the air of the layered skirts in the warriors' costumes: a swirling fluidity and lightness that bring to mind Sufi Mevlevi dervishes, as well as certain folk dances of central and southern Asia. Further spinning dynamism is also present here in the ensemble stick movements of battle, the canes used like the *jo* of Aikido or the swords of Kendo (an echo of the group's exercises with sticks since the early 1970s, almost a trademark of Brook's highly somatic approach and the group's shared experience – an authentic sense of a highly accomplished ensemble unit, their shared dynamic extending to the very tips of the sticks).

Abhimanyu's death – a 16-year-old child spreadeagled on the wheel of his own chariot. When all else fails, it is the only weapon left to him, as though the chariot itself has collapsed into matchwood, the wheel all that survives the might of a combined Kaurava onslaught. He raises it above his head to crush his enemies – a clear parallel with Krishna's *chakra*. The Kauravas lock their sticks through its spokes, as if this were a Morris dance, then wrestle it from his grasp, suspending it out of reach above his head. A boy against men, but a *kshatrya* death. Clovis falls surrounded by his weapons on top of the wheel – a further allusion to Drona's disc and the uncompromising wheel of *karma*, as well as a momentarily raised status in death. Tragically, the youngest of the major protagonists is the first to die. There follows a brief oasis of respectful tranquillity, a charged pause for breath after a scene of immense energy and excitement: the climax of silence. Like the Kauravas, we are aware of the repercussions.

Figure 13.17 'The War'. The Kauravas lock their sticks to immobilize Abhimanyu's wheel. French-language production. (Photographer – Gilles Abegg)

This episode offers an instance of Krishna's dispassionate expediency. His nephew Abhimanyu has been thrown into the battle so as not to distract Arjuna from combat elsewhere, indeed to further stiffen his resolve. Later Ghatotkatcha will be sacrificed in a similar way to free Arjuna and his brothers from threat. Krishna's morality is highly provocative in humanist ethical terms: the expendability of life as means to an end, the distancing of an individual death for the greater salvation of the whole. Mortality takes on a different hue in relation to personal and universal *dharma* – and, as has been suggested, here the two are indissolubly intertwined.

Vyasa narrates the story of death (absent from the English-language version). In an earlier golden age, 'the universe was free from destruction. But the creator, attentive to the complaints of the earth, decided that all living things had to have an end, and a new beginning. He created a black and red woman...' Vyasa's third-person delivery of the words of the creator Brahma are ironic, given his relationship to the protagonists, his own creation. This is perhaps the last enactment generated by Vyasa, and a real 'black and red woman' materializes for an instant in the background. Her tale of death and rebirth is central to our understanding of these events. The creator tells her to 'rid yourself of all love, of all hate. Strike down the living without any fear for death kills no one, creatures kill themselves and even gods die...' Draupadi adds that one should mourn the living rather than the dead. For a warrior, paradoxically it is only death that confers meaning on life: as Dumézil has pointed out, life in battle for a *kshatrya* seems to assume the character of an initiatory test for the life beyond. Those who live on continue to suffer without that resolution.

Arjuna returns from the battlefield to find his son. Lights full up on the back wall, a separate spatial zone for the tired but victorious warrior. Dark shadows in the foreground surround the corpse of Abhimanyu: a silent dumb-show of mourning. We peer through the silhouettes of death to a different space and light beyond, each separate constituent of the image *en somme* colouring the other, like overlaid slides. Arjuna is becoming increasingly stained and scarred by the battle. There is merely a splash of (overtly artificial) blood on his temples here, but with every new appearance there are further emblems of the despoiling effects of war. Indeed, all of the combatants – and none more so than Bhima, Duryodhana and Duhsassana, those most bestialized by the conflict – grow ever filthier: mud, blood, sweat stains. Arjuna, an altogether nobler being, will only ever reach a point where hands are bloodstained, temples are gashed. Compare this with Duhsassana's undoing at the hands (and teeth) of Bhima, or Aswhattaman's Macbeth-like scourge of the sleeping Pandava camp.

As Arjuna moves forward into the centre space, the lights come up on Abhimanyu's death scene – a literalization of Arjuna's own lacerating and tragic illumination. To the ominous throb of a didgeridoo, he swears to exact revenge by killing Jayadratha before dusk on the following day. Another song of lament from Tsuchitori as the body is quietly removed, the mother cradling her dead child's head.

The Kauravas look on in formation at the base of the back wall, Drona and his son Aswhattaman at their head. Jayadratha (Andreas Katsulas) is protected by a fortification, a seemingly impenetrable structure of bamboo screens and ladders. For Arjuna to survive, Krishna the trickster-god is obliged to perform a further miracle. Once again he manifests his divinity, by obscuring the sun prematurely – a simple lowering of the hand and the lights dim. We are happy to read the undisguised visual cue for the LX operator as 'magic'/*maya*. Arjuna and Krishna are allied spatially with the spectators. They stand close to us in the shadows, observing with us the distant celebrations of the Kauravas, for they believe it to be nightfall: the end of the day and of Arjuna – a parallel of the earlier 'blindfold' shot in the dark, as well as a prefiguration of Karna's eventual abandonment by the sun at the moment of his death. Arjuna's arrow strikes Jayadratha in the neck, he stiffens, twists and slumps to the ground. This act of stark violence brings the *nagaswaram* in its wake. (The original *Mahabharata* contains a further reason for this act of vengeance. Earlier on, Jayadratha, who is in fact Dhritarashtra's son-in-law, had attempted to seduce and abduct Draupadi.)

The invocation of Ghatotkatcha, the son of Bhima and Hidimbi, now fully grown into a shamanic demon. In the deepening shadows there follows a slow-motion battle-ballet of torches, to the accompaniment of didgeridoo and clapping sticks: the dance of *thanatos*. A triangle of torches is laid on the earth, Krishna tosses fistfuls of magnesium powder through naked flame to produce belching flashes of fire. And Ghatotkatcha materializes, his face lit from below by a single sputtering torch: garish Kathakali emerald-green make-up, red eyes, African headdress. He is thrown into battle at once, a scene that startles visually and sensually. Volleys of arrows in the half-darkness, cymbal clashes, spitting torches, tiny splashes of fire on the earth, the sharp smell of smoke. Flambeaux are slashed through the air, fizzing and flaring, by unseen hands. Stylization is simple, the mechanics unconcealed. So, for example, clouds of ochre brick dust are openly tossed by the fistful into the air from the side rungs – the dust and chaos of battle, the puffs of imagined canons, the filth churned up by invisible chariots, even sprays of blood.

The two central combatants, Karna and Ghatotatcha, narrate in the third person as they enact this episode: impersonation is distanced. As Karna cries, 'Karna exterminates them all . . .', he plunges the torch he carries into the pool, extinguishing its flickering life with a shrill hiss. The scene is structured to suggest horrendous carnage on an epic scale: a Passchendaele of mud, weapons, smoke, flames, shattered bodies strewn everywhere in the gloom. The air is full of the sounds and smells of war: the Forest of Bliss has become Shiva's Great Cemetery. To one side, Gandhari and Dhritarashtra ask a stream of fervent questions of the all-seeing Sanjaya – the boon of supernatural vision has been granted him by Vyasa, for Dhritarashtra's benefit. A repeated refrain, 'What's . . . doing?', serves to heighten the tension, as well as furnishing a rationale for multi-vocal narrative clarification in this chaotic pullulating half-light. Eventually Karna's spear (echoes of Parsifal or Arthurian legend in this gift from a god) is carried by him, slowly twisting across the space towards Ghatotkatcha, its tip lit by a hand-held torch: another instance of temporal manipulation with this missile in slow-motion flight. It moves through the space and beyond, out of sight. Once used, this divine weapon is redundant, but Ghatotkatcha lies dead. Bhima intones a haunting funeral plaint with Hidimbi, an African dirge, as they too carry out the corpse of their son. The shocking inhumanity of expediency.

Krishna dances, centre stage, in celebration of the expending of Karna's lance, and therefore by inference the inevitable demise of Karna himself. In silence, Bénichou performs an Indian folk dance of lightness and delicacy, a torch in each hand. They whisper minutely as they move through the air, the tiny sounds resonating unaccountably after the apocalyptic cacophony of the preceding scene. Then a final lingering hiss as they are thrown into the pool and extinguished. They have served their purpose of illuminating and focusing Krishna's dance, which was also an active prayer of respect and thanks to Ghatotkatcha, a monstrous sacrificial lamb.

The sudden appearance of Dhryshtadyumna (Alain Maratrat), a bizarre figure of death with iconic suggestions of sources in Chhau, Kathakali and Kalarippayatt. However these allusions are never formally specific and explicit – hybridization relativizes, creating new composite configurations. Jingling bells on his spiked mace and ankles lend him a jarring quality of frivolity, rendering him somehow more menace-laden. His tiny stamping movements possess a violent automaton quality. He floats, apparently propelled by the spring sword (*urmi*) he scythes through the air in a hissing blur above his head, a double-edged 2 metre metal ribbon integral to Kalarippayatt. Here, removed from its usual context, the blade remains an unparallelled armament, but also accrues suggestions of invisible force field, rotor blades, and unearthly vortex of wind and maleficent energy. With scarlet face, tunic and gloves, a green tongue and a hefty ceremonial sword in a stumpy black scabbard, he is a nightmarish ghostly presence: an animated blood clot hovering across our field of vision. Aswhattaman's clumsy human efforts to strike him are derisory, for Dhryshtadyumna skips and pirouettes around the warrior's thrusts in slow-motion. In Carrière's version, he remains alien, unexplained, radically otherworldly. In the original *Mahabharata*, he has been born from the flames of a sacrificial fire, like his sister Draupadi (and Sikhandin), his express destiny to kill Drona.

The confrontation of Arjuna and Drona. The arrow-firing convention, now firmly established, is here used to great comic effect. Drona 'catches' arrows in mid-flight, or plucks them from a thigh with a triumphant laugh: he is proud of his protégé. At one moment, Arjuna is impaled with an absurd number of arrows; they bristle from his torso in clumps of more than a dozen. Although on one level the scene accords closely with descriptions in the original *Mahabharata*, there is something here of the self-conscious exaggeration and mock heroism of comic strips, as well as the compositional lyricism of battle sequences in Kurosawa's Samurai films.

Another scene of comedy for the death of Aswhattaman, the elephant. Bhima's exit, wielding his cumbersome club, is immediately succeeded by the enraged trumpetings of some invisible beast off stage – a sound effect of the kind usually associated with children's animations. The scene is played for laughs, and what follows is all the more startling and horrifying in juxtaposition.

Drona's entrance is stately and dignified in his jet-black martial arts gown, in his wake the leaping Dhryshtadyumna, his nemesis. Percussion, always more than just an affective lubricant, sustains the tension, punctuating dialogue and animating silence. Yudishthira (*satyadharman*, 'having truth as his principle') confirms the death of Aswhattaman, 'the elephant' mumbled by him as a stage-whisper from the corner of his mouth directly to the audience: a half-lie for which he will later be held accountable. The Sanskrit tells us that until this point the Pandava prince's chariot wheels floated 'four fingers' above the ground. As a result of this deception, they sink back to earth.

Recognizing that he must abandon the battle, Drona acquiesces passively to death with the controlled silence and dignity of a Samurai confronting *seppuku*. He strips off his black cloak to reveal a pure white shirt, then subaquatically slowly lifts a massive earthenware water-carrier as if to wash the dust and sweat from his lips for the last time – an immense weight for a man borne down by the sense of a destiny imminently realized. Instead of drinking, he empties the vessel's contents over his bowed head, for it is full of blood. Steeped in gore, death is a merciful release. Drona/Oida is literally inundated with blood: his shirt changes colour, pools form on the earth at his feet. He slumps into a meditative position before Dhryshtadyumna slashes off his head with a blur of his giant blade. Drona's head falls forward to the floor in death, blood still dripping to the ground, seeping ever further through his white sleeves. Then a blanket is thrown over him: a headless trunk in a pool of gore. A ghastly and utterly disarming sequence.

The playing space is now littered with the debris and carnage of war: patches of mud, pools of blood, arrows and other weapons, the ashes of torches, a decapitated body. (Is this war a grotesque enactment *in extremis* of the wholesale sacrifice of animals in days gone by during the Hindu Durga Puja?) Drona now merges chromatically with his executioner Dhryshtadyumna. A stream of associations scream within: Mishima's death in 1970, the self-immolation of Buddhist monks during the Vietnam war, even Stephen King's *Carrie*.

Aswhattaman's divine weapon – Narayana, another boon from the tenebrous Shiva – is to be used in revenge for this treachery. In Avignon, this was conveyed through a terrible white light, a blinding magnesium explosion of positively nuclear dimensions. The Boulbon quarry was filled with acrid smoke, engulfing actors and spectators alike. Here Aswhattaman (Jean-Paul Denizon) carries a flaming bundle of sticks, a silent ball of fire, along the base of the back wall. 'And the angel which I saw stand upon the sea . . . lifted up his hand and swore . . . that there should be time no longer . . .' (*Revelations* X, 5). Hypnotically, time stands still, the fireball's passage ceremonially slow: ground zero at a nuclear epicentre. Another plethora of associations are released – Dresden, Hiroshima, *The War Game*.

In the original *Mahabharata*, Karna's charioteer, King Salya of Madra, has secretly promised Arjuna that he will steer Karna's chariot in a manner favourable to Arjuna. Salya scorns Karna's courage and determination in an exchange that offers a savage parody of the relationship between charioteer and warrior in the *Gita*: part of the time-honoured tradition of *parodia sacra*. Both in the *Gita* and here, the charioteers are maternal uncles to the Pandava princes – Salya is the brother of Madri, mother of the twins.

Karna prepares to commit himself fully to the battle. He washes the blade of his spear in coconut milk, a ritual cleansing accompanied by a song of preparation before a bowl of flame. The song is comprised of hard glottal consonants and buzzing sibilants, as evocative as a muezzin's call. His assumption of leadership of the Kaurava camp is signalled by a thumb-painted single red *tilak* on his forehead: a third eye. (Karna's spear tip is said to be in 'the shape of a serpent'. There is much interplay between bird and snake imagery in the original *Mahabharata*: does an ideal being reconcile both mutually exclusive aspects into a composite 'feathered serpent', like the Mayan Quetzalcoatl?)

The battle resumes, our perspectival access now transformed as a whole. Whereas formerly much had occurred in profile, a lateral or diagonal dynamic, the axis is now towards and away from us. A wall of shields set across the playing space is crushed by the Pandavas, advancing towards the audience. They burst through this barrier screen with explosive energy, emerging in the central space in a blur. Both sides of Arjuna's face are now bloodied, and his hand also drips.

The back wall is lost temporarily in a pall of dust and smoke.

Then the first appearance by Vyasa and the boy for many moons: a pause for breath.

Boy: Will the war end one day?
Vyasa: Yes, it will end.
Boy: I'm afraid. I thought I was going to die when Aswhattaman launched his weapon.
Vyasa: So did I.

Boy: But you told me, 'I am the author of this poem.' Could your poem kill you?

Figure 13.18 The disembowelment of Duhsassana by Raudra-Bhima, as performed by Kalamandalam Gopi Ashan of the Kathakali Kalamandalam, Kerala, Southern India ('The Game of Dice' at the Festival of Perth, 1989). (Photographer – Marcelo Palacios)

The creator is powerless, the lunatics have taken over the asylum. But before Vyasa can answer the boy, Bhima enters. Or rather staggers on – a horrific vision, caked in blood, grey mud matting his hair and clothes from head to foot. After sixteen days of relentless combat, he is transformed, denatured. Exhausted and wounded, he resembles a corpse preserved in a peat-marsh. The living dead. 'Is man no more than this?' He collapses onto a shield, his only remaining possession – his beloved club – as his pillow. Vyasa and the boy use two of the bamboo screens to construct a tent-like structure to cover him. Then Duhsassana, in a similar state, emerges into the space with a feral roar. Visually he is the perfect match for Bhima: he has seen and done as much; they are almost indistinguishable in this dehumanized state. (Does this scene contain a bitterly ironic echo of the traditional Christian equation of physical degradation and spiritual grace?) With sprays of fresh blood glistening on his axe-head and face, Duhsassana flattens Bhima's shelter with a crash. All of the screens now lie flat on the earth, instantly throwing open a cast and gaping empty space. A violent and sickeningly 'real' struggle ensues. The Kaurava's heavy metal axe cracks whole chunks of earth free from the beaten floor; each thud can be felt in the front rows. We flinch with every near miss.

Duhsassana's death takes place a matter of feet in front of us, the faces of both actors eminently visible. Bhima proceeds to tear open his enemy's stomach, driving his bared teeth into the exposed abdomen. He re-emerges triumphantly bloodied with a lacerated red elastic ribbon clenched taut between his teeth – a grotesquely effective use of a convention of stylized suggestion of a kind, familiar in Chinese theatre and Southern Indian dance drama, that Brook has cherished since his *Titus Andronicus* in the late 1950s. Overt artificiality and theatricality in no way diminish the charge. The muffled laughter from certain spectators operates as a safety valve, a release from horror. Bhima's vow to consume his enemy's guts and drink his blood is now fulfilled. A loathsome act, although no worse than the atrocious treatment meted out to Hector in *The Iliad*. Man as blood-bespattered carnivore, cannibalizing his own fellows; a graphic illustration of Sartre's profoundly misanthropic suggestion that mankind's greatest enemy is that 'hairless, flesh-eating creature, man himself'.

Draupadi then arrives to wash her hair in Duhsassana's blood. She washes away her longstanding sense of humiliation at his hands, for he had assaulted her during her period, dragged her unceremoniously by the hair into the gaming hall. She tosses that same head of hair back with relish, then ties it up in a bundle: she will carry his lifeblood away with her. While Bhima celebrates – giant footslapping steps to a grand percussive beat, like the bestial Raudra Bhima in Kathakali, – Dhritarashtra fumbles blindly over the corpse of his dead son. He has to feel the disembowelment with his hands. The *nagaswaram*'s brassy shriek hits us from the second balcony.

The central agon, an epic confrontation between Arjuna and Karna – the sons of Indra and Surya, the gods of storm and sun respectively – is preceded by a brief moment of much-needed silence. There is perfect symmetrical balance in this encounter, the scene as a whole a paradigm of understatement. The two archers mirror each other, aiming at each other across the space while their whip-cracking charioteers urge them on. The two actors maintain this balanced image of confrontation and equivalent strength as they walk back and out, disappearing behind the two side

Figure 13.19 'The War'. The final confrontation between Karna and Arjuna. In the foreground, from left to right: Arjuna (Vittorio Mezzogiorno), Krishna (Maurice Bénichou), Salya (Tapa Sudana), Karna (Bruce Myers). Notice the synecdochic chariot wheels. French-language production. (Photographer – Gilles Abegg)

walls. Tension is compounded by a percussive climax from the musicians. Then all is suggestion. An exchange of a cloud of arrows across the back wall takes place on the far side of the river, a rate of fire of heroic proportions from invisible sources.

Figure 13.20 'The War'. Karna's death (Jeffery Kissoon), his wheel trapped by the mud; in the background, his charioteer Salya (Tapa Sudana). (Photographer – Kay Jamieson, Perth)

When the two figures reappear with their 'chariots', Karna's wheel becomes entrapped by the mud around the pool – suddenly, inexplicably

– rendering him impotent and defenceless. The elements conjoin to affect the course of the war, the earth itself crying out to stop the bloodshed which desecrates it: the elements themselves as active protagonists in a cosmic conflict. A silent tableau as Karna forgets the *mantra* for Parashurama's divine weapon, then a further tortured moment of stasis as Krishna urges Arjuna to strike him down – before Gandiva sounds and Karna slumps across his wheel, crashing to the earth with an ear-splitting percussive boom from Toshi Tsuchitori. (Similarly in the *Rig Veda*, Indra defeats Surya by disabling one of the wheels of the sun god's chariot.) Ultimately Karna's acceptance of death possesses a quality of ceremony and sacrifice. Resigned to his fate, he embraces the earth: for in his final moments of life, he is even abandoned by the sun, his father – reminiscent of the sudden solar eclipse that marked Christ's death. Again the *nagaswaram* in the deepening gloom.

Vyasa and the boy reassume their roles as 'stage managers' to suspend a piece of chilly blue-grey material over Duryodhana, who has retreated from the carnage to sleep in the waters of a frozen lake: another convention with its source in Chinese theatre. The lights glints off the silk's silver sheen, shimmering as its surface ripples. Spectators on the ground level are able to see both material and Duryodhana curled up below, singing some gentle Polish melody. This simple image in fact comprises another polyphonous construct counterpointing and blending different moods and tastes: the stylized water convention, Seweryn's plaintive song of yearning and repose, the comic banalities of two duck hunters who stumble across this scene.

The final combat of Bhima and Duryodhana, using the unwieldy clubs, is another overtly violent sequence: in the original *Mahabharata*, the Kaurava has practised on an iron statue with the express intent of being in readiness for this. They prepare themselves quietly by ritual washing, Bhima in the pool, Duryodhana in the river: another 'imitation' of the sacred ablutions and *pujas* of Hindus. A tranquillity which is soon shattered by the exaltant bestial cries of the two warriors, then Duryodhana's screams of pain as his thighs are crushed – illegally, on the advice of Krishna;[5] another problematic instance of the god's expedient rupture of the envelope of accepted morality and ethical conduct to add to the tally of deaths thus far: Jayadratha, Bhishma, Drona, Karna. Duryodhana had menaced Draupadi with his thigh, taunting her provocatively during the dice game; so it is perhaps appropriate that finally he should be toppled – 'emasculated' – in this way, the phallus-by-association smashed.

Duryodhana is abandoned on the threshold of death, his head partially immersed in the water of the pool. Having recognized Krishna's pivotal role, he hurls his last accusations and threats, decrying Krishna as responsible for all. Even now, his bitterness and egotistical hubris blind him to his own profound nature. For the expedient Krishna, as we know, all ethical and moral structures are relative and malleable:

> *Krishna*: No good man is entirely good. No bad man is entirely bad.
> I salute you, Duryodhana. I don't find any pleasure in your suffering, but your defeat is a joy.

A crushed and broken man, the vanquished *theomachos* Duryodhana lies alone, listening with us to the distant songs of Pandava celebration. A final bitter pill to be swallowed in darkness, solitude and filth. Collective festivity is set harshly against embittered isolation and exclusion. *Sic transit gloria mundi*. Aswhattaman arrives promising revenge: momentarily an alternative *pietà* in the arms of Drona's son. Any Pandava celebration is premature, the bloodletting is not over yet.

The return of Aswhattaman – a scourge, an avenging angel, his entrance prefigured by dark disjointed sounds. The original *Mahabharata* tells us that Aswhattaman has conceived of his mode of revenge in a vision he saw while mourning his father: a huge bird of prey swoops down on a flock of sleeping crows to massacre them. Here the brahmin who has lost all qualities of 'brahminhood' stumbles blindly along the river, lost in horror. A low lateral light projects his shadow before him. His entrance through the water is profoundly disturbing: it becomes his 'multitudinous seas incarnadine', a river of blood, just as in the original epic the battlefield itself is often compared metaphorically to 'a horrible river of bloody current'. The unhinged and apparently catatonic rigidity of Denizon's expression implies experiences beyond understanding. As he emerges in the forward space beside Duryodhana, his knife a sticky mess still gripped tight, he sits, possessed and transfixed by something akin to Rilke's *grimmige Einsicht* ('terrible insight'); the *Mahabharata* suggests he has been possessed by Shiva himself.

The accusatory light slashes a narrow passage through the darkness, as he goes on to enumerate a catalogue of horrors for Duryodhana's delight. He describes unnatural cosmic events, evidence of the repercussions of his adharmic acts. He can only blink through his veil of blood, his haunted stare unnerving. The words remain largely uncoloured by Denizon; a deranged sense of calm pervades his flat dispassionate delivery. Meanwhile Duryodhana, despite his pain, revels in this account of a 'massacre of the innocents', atrocities as appalling as those in My Lai or Cambodia. Aswhattaman cradles the Kaurava warlord's head – another moral and affective inversion of the *pietà* configuration – and some of the Pandavas' blood now marks Duryodhana's own face. The episode in its entirety is conducted to a single gong accompaniment, the words so explosive and shocking they need little support. Contented, Duryodhana dies in the pool where he was born; the circle is now complete. 'Et pendant une éternité, il ne cessa de connaître et de ne pas comprendre' (Valéry). In the Sanskrit

Mahabharata, Aswhattaman is later cursed by his nemesis Krishna to wander alone and detested for 3,000 years. Unable to die in glory as a warrior, condemned to a life of pain and disgrace as an outcast, 'the eater eating is eaten'. Law and lore are indistinguishable in The Epic.

After a prolonged moment of silence, suddenly a new space and an uncomfortably bright wash of light as all of the corpses are laid out on the ground. The *nagaswaram* stabs through the air, for victory in war can only ever be Pyrrhic. The women mourn their losses, their silk saris vivid splashes of colour against the earth and back wall: burgundy, magenta, emerald, indigo, set against ubiquitous pitch-black headscarves. Then Bhishma is carried in again, still immobilized on his funeral bed by innumerable arrows. He has observed all, able to choose the precise moment of his death, when the sun is at its zenith. The uniqueness of his sanctity and purity is further heightened when contextualized in the midst of the debris of war.

Figure 13.21 'The War'. Bhishma delivers his final words from his deathbed ('the taste of honey'), the battlefield now littered with corpses. *Lacrimae mundi*: widows and mothers mourn their losses. On the far left, Krishna sits, impassive; in the background, Vyasa and the boy, located in a 'different' reality beyond the river. French-language production. (Photographer – Michel Dieuzaide)

As one of the stunned survivors in this vast blood-soaked desert, Yudishthira is consumed with useless guilt and self-loathing. Like Timon, he wants to escape, to lead a life of solitude in embittered Thoreauvian retreat. In this tormented *mea culpa*, he refuses to accept Krishna's dispassionate observance of *dharma* – truth in personal and transcendental terms. Instead he threatens to retire into extreme misanthropy, an emotional refusal of a scarred and imperfect world, plunged into absurdity. And who can blame him at this juncture? Both he and his brothers have been obliged to meet the demand to defend *dharma*, even if the fight destroys them and everything around them. Is this hideous cost a prerequisite of clarity of vision and knowledge? Can it be worth it? 'After such knowledge, what forgiveness?' (Eliot's *Gerontion*).

Bhishma's final words, an allegorical account of the human condition, are all that remains of the lengthy volumes of instruction he delivers from his deathbed in the full Sanskrit *Mahabharata* (Books 12 and 13, the *Shantiparvan* and the *Anushasanaparvan*). And in fact these are originally Vidura's words from the 11th book, the *Striparvan*. The allegory is traditionally deciphered in the following way. The forest is *samsara* (literally 'passing through') – the cycle of rebirths; its creepers and beasts are disease and old age; the well represents the human body, the snake – time; the elephant embodies a year – it had twelve feet in the original; the mice – nights and days; the bees – desires; and honey is the illusory lure of enjoyment, the fruit of desires.[6]

It is an enigmatic and quietist death – Bhishma no longer desires to live, to taste the drop of honey, although he dies with a finger on his lips. This resonant and ambivalent image suggests some lingering glimmer of hope, an indestructible impulse to persevere with life against the severest odds. At the same time his self-willed death at this point undercuts that suggestion, extinguishes the glimmer. A paradox: is there no 'honey' left? or is that 'honey' really no more than an imprisoning bond, an illusory 'sweetness'? His readiness for the liberation of death is understandable in the light of his origins – as *vasu* condemned to life in a mortal frame – and of what he has seen become of his family. In the end, *The Mahabharata* contains no easy moral – politically, ethically, psychologically – no conveniently detachable 'message' to pop into some mental doggy-bag and take home. At times it suggests a deep misanthropic pessimism (as perhaps here), although this nihilist strain of thought is in turn counterbalanced by a repeated call to action, a positive humanist appeal to embrace a contradictory plurality of experiences, to go 'to the end of oneself'. Therein lies meaning.[7]

Dhritarashtra makes a final, despairing attempt to transcend his blindness and impinge upon reality, although in effect it confirms that he is doubly blind. Now 'a man cut to th'brains' like Lear, he will avenge the killer of his progeny by throttling Bhima. However Krishna anticipates his intentions and substitutes a corpse. Cieslak wheezes and grunts with the effort of choking someone already dead, before himself being crushed utterly, his expectations dashed for the last time. Visibly he dies within, convinced of his own impotence and worthlessness: the hollow shell of a man, a 'ruin'd piece of nature', an ashen relic. Like his fellow *paterfamilias*

Lear, he will only ever be able to learn of humanity and wisdom through the tormenting madness of loss. As in Dostoevsky, suffering is located as source of knowledge. Cieslak's face empties of all emotion, a silent mask. His demise recalls Scofield's agonisingly slow backward fall out of frame after Cordelia's death in Brook's film of *King Lear*: a man toppled by the burdens of experience. All that remains is a blank white screen.

Gandhari's final condemnation of the role of Krishna. Her parting curse determines Krishna's predicament, and that of his people. Krishna accepts her accusations, but urges her that his intervention has been necessary. We catch a fleeting glimpse of Abhimanyu's pregnant widow in the distance by the back wall – the seed of hope for a future, the sole survivor bearing the human race (a son, Parikshit) in her womb – and Krishna quietly says, 'Even if you can't see it, a light has been saved'. His essential role has been to encourage each individual to pursue their own *dharma* to the very end. The blurring of a man-god differentiation embodied by Krishna seems to mark the transition from myth to history. As an avataric divinity, he has been imprisoned within his prescience, a curse in human terms: as a man, he has only ever been able to urge others tacitly to a point of self-knowledge. And this connects with a question that runs through Brook's mature work like a blood-red thread: how does one affirm and implement free choice and one's personal imperatives within the omnipresent framework of an ineluctable destiny? How can one embrace life, strive to live it abundantly, given the ineradicability of death? The poem tacitly points us towards something that Rilke expressed in the following way: 'What we call fate does not come to us from outside, it goes forth from within us . . .'[8]

An instant jump of thirty-six years to **Krishna's death** (Book 16 of the *Mahabharata*, the *Mausalaparvan*), which he has already admitted to be inevitable, 'like all life'. Once again the scene is staged by Vyasa and the boy. As Krishna slumbers in a forest (i.e. on a green cloth), an arrow is carried by a hunter called Jaras ('old age') and wedged between Bénichou's feet: a direct reversal of Krishna's own earlier agency as arrow-bearer. He dies peacefully, smiling in the calm detachment of *yoga*. Nevertheless there is no ideal, no utopia. Even the gods are destructible. The boy's unanswered questions hang in the air. A simple vanishing trick with the hand-held curtain, and Bénichou rolls off and out of sight, apparently swept away behind it (like a cinematic wipe), vanishing into thin air.

In Hindu tradition, Krishna's death marks a *yuganta*, the end of an epoch. The narrative has taken us through a pivotal juncture between a mythical heroic age – the yellow or gold *Dvaparayuga* – and the beginnings of our own historical age – the *Tretayuga*. With a further waning of *dharma* in the cycle, we move into the iron or 'black' age of Kali, within which the performance of *dharma* is almost impossible, and Time becomes a pitiless devourer: not simply an era, but also a quality of time.

The Epic seems to be located in a liminal period at the very end of the preceding age, within which all four ages of the *Mahayuga* are conflated and echoed.[9]

The final days of Gandhari and Dhritarashtra recall the simplicity and reflective solitude of the Pandavas during their forest exile. Kunti makes a circle of flowers around a candle. Grains of rice are scattered at the four corners of a square within the circle, then sprinkled with river water. A 'natural', if invented, ritual of offering and prayer for renewed growth. The forest fire that awaits them is signalled using the same scenic device as that for Pandu's funeral pyre in *The Game of Dice* – Vyasa carries a flaming twig bundle. The original *Mahabharata* records that this fire had started as a result of the negligence of some brahmins undertaking a sacrifice. So in effect they are to lose their lives in a beneficent sacrificial fire – the route to the beyond will be painless. In death, Gandhari and her blind king are to be united and illuminated at last. As they walk towards death, Gandhari has a rapturous vision of the hereafter:

> I have just seen a whole army rise out of the river. All my sons, smiling, their wounds healed, reconciled. An immense wave of men, all white, mounting into the air . . .

Wish fulfilment as well as prefiguration of the final scene in 'paradise'. Kunti joins them as they head for the flames across the wooden bridge – now a literalized point of access to another realm. She too seeks repose, and will be as unbending in death as she has been in life.

Yudishthira's admission to paradise (Svarga) – the final step in his expiative rite-of-passage, and all that remains of Books 17 and 18 of the *Mahabharata* (the *Mahaprasthanikaparvan* and the *Svargarohanaparvan*). Led by Vyasa, he is obliged to undertake an initiatory journey around the space, an Eleusinian enigma, like the final scenes of *Conference*. For the last time Vyasa enacts a role within his own fiction: is he Indra, setting up the ultimate injustice of 'the final illusion'? As the lights come up, Yudishthira's first sight is of the two Kaurava brothers – happy, calm, literally cleansed of the filth of war and earthly conflict, now smiling benignly in radiant white. Meanwhile the Pandavas are reported to be condemned to some grimy hell, which is described in lurid detail. The Pandavas' voices, Karna now amongst them, call to Yudishthira from behind the ground-level seats. He must confront the ultimate absurdity: what has been the point of his life given this eventual outcome? He curses the malevolent divinities that have stripped his actions in life of meaning.

The Mahabharata has often been interpreted by commentators as a treatise of royal initiation, the education and forging of a king, Yudishthira: an ideal being with one tragic flaw – a love of gambling. In many ways Yudishthira has shared the journeys of Colin Turnbull, the anthropologist in *The Ik*, or of Timon, into their own 'hearts of darkness'. A journey from a philanthropic position of commitment to liberal altruism, through a crisis of enforced lucidity concerning the destructive and materialistic motives of others, to metaphysical pessimism and misanthropic *contemptus mundi*. Unlike Timon and Turnbull, however, Yudishthira ultimately refuses self-annihilation in anarchic despair and confusion. Like those birds who survive the journey across the deserts and valleys to the court of their king in *Conference*, he 'goes to the end of himself', and is able to find a point of transcendent understanding by confronting and assimilating the essence of all aspects of experience, including the 'final illusion' of death: in Hinduism, a living state coextensive with life. His journey is finally a restorative reappropriation of self, the acquisition through suffering of what the Greeks called *sophrosyne*.

Vyasa calmly delivers his final third-person speech:

> Stop shouting. You have known neither paradise nor hell. Here there is no happiness, no punishment, no family, no enemies. Rise in tranquillity. Here words end, like thought. This was the last illusion.

The 'last illusion' as much for audience in this and actors as for Yudishthira, for the performance now draws to a close: the 'world' of performance, the 'world' of *maya* and the 'real world' blur.[10] Ganesha, who has reappeared with his mask, repeats Vyasa's final words as he inscribes these last words in the great book. The final stamp of authority on the performance as story to be told and heard. Ganesha hands over the finished work to the boy, 'This is your life . . .'

Conference of the Birds climaxed with the birds' arrival at the threshold of paradise. Here the culminating image presents us with what some have chosen to read as a vision of paradise, a gently place of serenity, peace and dignity, an atmosphere brimming with congenial and harmonious ease. The actors are now all in white: the blind are able to see, the wounded and dead restored, all animosity is forgotten. I would suggest that these few minutes of tranquillity perhaps best serve as a liminal *diminuendo* marking the dissolution of the fictive world, a transitional bridge affording us a shared space to catch our breaths, to look back on what has happened and to look forward. There can be no more pretence, these are simply actors who have earned this time for relaxation and enjoyment. The five musicians have positioned themselves centre stage, the other performers loll around the space in small groups. Food, wine and music are shared. All members of the company have washed and drunk from the river, once more a source of life, a meeting point. Candles on silver foil lotuses float in both pool and river, as if it were *divali*, the Hindu festival of lights. As the music grows in volume, the audience clapping along, the candles are extinguished one by one, as in the Haydn symphony. Music fills the darkness for a moment, then applause erupts.[11]

This final image is therapeutic, a gentle shared act of pre-fall, Gondwana-like reintegration and celebration at the culmination of a story told, the collective bringing into life of a resplendent *theatrum mundi*. As a coda, inevitably it eschews closure. We have come to taste directly what Hindus refer to as *lila*: the world as cosmic illusion and play, mankind's celebration of its humanity.

All theatre is written on the wind, but only rarely in a lifetime does it ride and soar on the wind in our hearts. The theatre can become our *fiesta*.

NOTES

1 The wheel replicates, in a somewhat essentialized form, any one of the twenty-four carved stone chariot wheels built into the walls of the celebrated thirteenth-century temple in Konarak, India, dedicated to Surya, the sun god. See also the bas-reliefs of Angkor Wat in Cambodia (eighth to twelfth century AD), or the winged sun-discs fo the Zoroastrian Ahura Mazda, reliefs of which Brook would have seen in Persepolis.
2 Ezra Pound, 'A Retrospect' (1918), reprinted in T. S. Eliot (ed.), *Literary Essays of Ezra Pound* (London, 1954, p. 4).
3 The book contains eighteen chapters in all, just as eighteen armies are engaged in an eighteen-day battle.
4 See Kafka's diary, 1910: 'Zeno, pressed as to whether anything is at rest, replied: Yes, the flying arrow rests' (quoted by John Peter, *Vladimir's Carrot*, London: Methuen, 1987, p. 168).
5 Incidentally this fight with Bhima forms the core of Bhasa's famous 1,800-year-old one-act Sanskrit play *Urubhanga* ('Thigh Fracture').
6 A Christian version of the same allegory was translated into a well-known bas-relief by the thirteenth-century Italian sculptor Benedetto Antelami. It can still be seen on the Porta della Vita of Parma's Battistero.
7 Cf. van Buitenen: 'The epic is a series of precisely stated problems imprecisely and therefore inconclusively resolved, every inconclusive solution raising a new problem – until the very end, when the question remains: whose is heaven and whose is hell?' (quoted in Hiltebeitel, *The Ritual of Battle*, Ithaca, NY and London: Cornell University Press, 1976, p. 127).
8 Krishna should not be seen as a 'pious hypocrite' (E. W. Hopkins, *The Great Epic of India: Its Character and Origin*, Calcutta: Punthi Pustak, 1978) or as a Machiavellian figure, despite his being the guiding hand behind almost all of the Pandava 'crimes'. He has endeavoured to engineer a reconciliation, and he has never acted for his own ends. He has performed the role of agent of resolve in a number of individual struggles, tacitly encouraging all protagonists to confront themselves and their personal *dharma*, and no destiny has been accepted passively. We have seen the gamut of responses to the impingement of destiny, from defiance, courage and faith to doubt and self-discovery. His function is fundamentally restorative, a counterbalance to the destructive roles of Shiva and Kali.

Krishna himself has been caught in a double-bind. He has tried to prevent a war he knows full well must happen. Locked within a web of contradictions, Krishna is never fatalist or nihilist. His actions offer a direct and consistent provocation to the limitations of any imposed moral framework.

What may initially surprise audiences in the west is the distance between this Krishna and the familiar 'received' image of him, the frolicking lover of *gopis* in Jayadeva's *Gita Govinda* or the *Bhagavata Purana*. As Dhritarashtra says of him in the original *Mahabharata*, just before the battle commences: 'Like the wind, difficult to seize with the hand: like the moon, hard to touch with the hand: like the earth, hard to bear on the head: Krishna is difficult to seize by force' – or indeed to pin down in any way.

See also Lao Tzu's 'Man of Tao' in the *Tao Te Ching*, XV:

He is modest, like one who is a guest.
He is yielding, like ice that is going to melt.
He is simple, like wood that is unplaned.
He is vacant, like valleys that are hollow.
He is dim, like water that is turbid.

9 Significantly the names of the four ages in the cycle (Krita, Dvapara, Treta and Kali) are also names given to the different dice throws that cause the Pandavas to lose their kingdom. Shakuni, the Kaurava gambler, is said to be an incarnation of Dvapara, the *asura* who lent his name to the third of the four ages; Duryodhana is supposed to be an incarnation of Kali. So the course of the game reflects in miniature the cosmic increase in the forces of *adharma*. And indeed the course of the world as a whole is said to be the result of an unending celestial dice game between Shiva and Parvati on Mount Kailsa.

10 David R. Kinsley quotes Mircea Eliade on a 'method of release' through *maya*: 'To tear the veil of *maya* and pierce the secret of cosmic illusion amounts primarily to understanding its character as 'play' – that is to say free spontaneous activity of the divine – and consequently to imitating the divine action and attaining liberty. The paradox of Indian thought is that the idea of liberty is so concealed by the idea of *maya* – that is, of illusion and slavery – that it takes a long detour to find it. It is enough, however, to discover the deep meaning of *maya* – divine 'play' – to be already on the way to deliverance' (*The Divine Player*, Delhi: Motilal Banarsidass, 1979, p. 18).

11 In the marathon all-night versions of Avignon, and later in Perth and Adelaide, during the world tour, the sense of renewal and rebirth was further heightened by synchronizing the performance's end with the first light of dawn colouring the stone of the quarry: a new day for a new world – an idea Brook first explored at the genesis of the Centre with *Orghast* in the tombs of Persepolis.

POSTSCRIPT: BROOK'S SCENOGRAPHY

In conclusion, I will enumerate what appear to be the primary determining strategies and characteristics of Brook's scenography here – his *poetics*, if you like. In one sense, the divisions that follow are misleading, for each of these structural elements is complementary and interdependent: parts of a whole.

MOBILITY AND ESCHEWAL OF REPRESENTATIONAL CLOSURE

In *The Mahabharata*, temporal (and spatial) dimensions are fluid, virtual, mobile, as open and free as the Elizabethan theatre's *tabula rasa*, effortlessly compressed or distended in the twinkling of an eye. Structurally, the production celebrates the free play of concentration and dispersion, settlement and diaspora: an alchemical *solve et coagula*.

As a director, Brook has assimilated a great deal formally from film language. Our perspective is multi-directional and fluid, and indeed Brook's consistently articulate manipulation of space, at the very heart of his scenography, possesses something of the mobility, economy and clarity of film montage and focal/framing techniques. Images and situations are strung together like pearls on a string of energy, established then dissolved like camera shots. Although Brook is not averse to self-citation scenographically (e.g. carpets, bare earth, sticks, etc.), there is no trace of either narcissism or closure (i.e. representational or narrative *dis-closure*). Consistently foregrounding its own theatricality,[1] the performative idiom itself evolves, erasing and rewriting itself continuously. Like the original Sanskrit text, with its mobile narrative voice, the performance oscillates tirelessly (and dialogically) between jolting savagery and cool objectivity. Analeptic and proleptic shifts, and recurrent slippage or collision between different fictive levels, resist the linearity of classical narrative structures. Yet these are changes of gear in an affective rather than an intellectual dialectic, reflecting for Brook the 'painful but inseparable' coexistence of illusion and disillusion that characterizes life itself. Nevertheless this active exploration of theatre discourses, entailing a critique of inherited codes, releases utopian and interrogative impulses in relation to individual and social life beyond the theatre.

The structural principle of discontinuity, both synchronic and diachronic, reconfigures and liberates Brook's performers. The actor *as* storyteller is free to step out of his/her role at critical moments (e.g. Bénichou as Krishna during the *Bhagavad Gita*, or the *visvarupa* theophanies), interrupting the linearity of his/her portrayal to continue the narrative in the third person. With the absolute prioritization of the imperative to meet the demands of an ongoing narrative, it is inevitable that impersonation should be repeatedly ruptured. In narrative terms, this shifting distance between actor and role proves very effective, furnishing him/her temporarily with the objectivity, lucidity and compassion of a narratorial commentator or puppeteer – 'distanced without distancing'. (In addition, in both examples cited, it neatly sidesteps the problems of embodying a god.)

Very few entrances and exits are made through the auditorium, perhaps only by Vyasa. This is a 'heroic' presentation, kept at a certain distance. Hence the magnitude and weight of gesture: there is much grand Samurai bravado, the 'outline' of emotions painted for us. Interpretation operate primarily on the levels of physical engagement and conviction, rather than of subtly nuanced sub-textual business, physical or vocal. *An epic style* – physically rooted, dynamic, immediately legible.

Representational flux is a constant on a technical level as well. So, for example, *The Mahabharata* seems to mark a turning point in Brooks's conception of the role of lighting. Gone is the glaring and all-embracing wash that had characterized his work since *King Lear* over twenty years earlier. Light has become an active participant again, used throughout to establish location, concentrate atmosphere and generate tension: a further medium on the palette. Throughout the performance, light continually repaints the flaking back wall, from deep bronze to honey, mustard or salmon. When the back wall is lit laterally, a different space (both literally and metaphorically) is conjured up, a reality further separated topographically from the central space by the river.

In addition to providing an anti-illusionist shell for the action, framing it meta-theatrically as 'play', the soaring pock-marked wall itself can lend an immense depth and majesty to images. Sometimes its literality as wall is foregrounded, sometimes it recedes and dissolves: it fluctuates between presence and absence. On one occasion, the lighting designer Jean Kalman even bounced a bluish wash on to the wall from the river, like a ripple tank: the rock appears to dematerialize into tiny waves, to liquefy. Such effects are compounded by the hypnagogic quality of images for an audience on the threshold of a different state of consciousness, particularly so for those present at an all-night marathon.

Compare this with the expressionistic use of low-level lateral light on the central area. In general, it is employed either symbolically, often to undercut a superficial harmony with sinister undertones (e.g. the casting of distended, bloated shadows), or spatially, to frame and foreground significant moments, for a sense of emotional and psychological proximity equivalent to close-up.

Indeed, even all four elements are omnipresent, active and protean in this most elemental of stories: they are mobilized as a scenographic base for the performance as a whole.[2] The beaten red earth of the egg-shaped playing space – Mother Earth, source and end of all, and the storyteller's milieu in any Indian village; the free-flowing water of the river beside the back wall – the flux of life, movement and fertility in the holy Yamuna and above all Ganga, the 'river of heaven' and the goddess ancestor of the protagonists,[3] and the enclosed water of the pool at the spectators' feet – fixed, sterile, a reflective surface to mirror the action, a place for refreshment and ritual ablution, an *omphalos*, a place to die; naked candle flame as generative transformation, invocation, purification, illumination, creativity and *gnosis*, and sputtering ball of flame as weapon, force of ignorance, threat to humanity; and finally, particularly in the open-air quarry venues used, the air that we share with the actors – *prana, pneuma, ki*, the creative and empowering spirit of inspiration, the breath of life.

SUGGESTION THROUGH ELLIPSIS

The language of Brook's actors' storytelling revolves around the use of simple metonyms and synecdoches generated through the manipulation of transformable everyday objects. These objects are semanticized through the actors' play, then abandoned and desemanticized, emptied of their referential charge and therefore available for further exploitation and redefinition. Nothing is ever fixed: all is suggested ludically with pellucid simplicity. Mallarmé's 'Suggérer, voilà le rêve' has become a battle-cry: the fluidity and indeterminacy of suggestion, rather than determinate (closed) reference, in some sense disrupts and sabotages the received signifying conventions of naturalist representation and their coercively imposed 'ways of seeing'. Actors gently invite spectators to participate interactively in their imaginations – to 'beat the other wing', as the existentialist Jaspers said – for their creativity is celebrated here too. As spectators, we come to understand how seeing need not be passive – the performance as object of a detached gaze; in relation to ellipses, it can be an *action*, engaging intellectually and socially. Brook's chosen word 'naivety', an appropriation from Brecht, conveys something of the remarkable clarity and economy of form. At times, literal representation is not only impossible but also patently undesirable (e.g. Krishna's *visvarupa*). In such contexts, special effects or pyrotechnic technology would run the risk of trivializing or blocking through over-literality. Repeatedly we are shown how suggestion, free from representational closure, can paint vivid pictures in our imaginations.

Above all, Brook's scenography is characterized by a consistent avoidance of schematization. Everything has been arrived at pragmatically, rather than analytically. Scant respect is paid to notions of aesthetic continuity or an imposed uniformity of style and means. The ultimate theatrical sanction for all popular theatre practitioners like Brook, a director wilfully operating from intuition and instinct rather than any theoretical or conceptual base, is that if something 'works' in theatrical terms in a specific context, then it is appropriate at that time, and perhaps only at that time. Of course Brook himself selects material and ultimately determines what does 'work', even indeed what constitutes 'working'. A paradox is in evidence throughout this production: the actors' creativity is repeatedly foregrounded and celebrated, yet at the same time the very fabric of the actor-based stage language(s) used visibly bears Brook's recognizable imprint. This production signals his final abdication of the directorial Olympus, and yet he is forever present in his absence: the king is dead, long live the king.

POLYPHONY AND MULTI-TEXTUALITY

'*What works, works . . .*': Brook's practice prioritizes narrative and referential clarity within formal discontinuity, while at the same time contriving to generate surprising hybrid conjunctions of complementary elements, a carefully constructed admixture of an aural, visual, affective and thematic multi-textuality. He blends colours, tastes, atmospheres, in search of a *salade juste*. A second paradox – coherence and unity here *stem from* heterogeneity: *e pluribus una*.

Each component of a polyphonous construct retains its particular savour in a heightened form, yet the sum of discursive elements present momentarily creates something fresh and texturally 'other'. The Pandavas, for example, operate as a multi-faceted supra-individual storytelling unit: they exist as a microcosm reflecting the centre group and its concerns as a whole. The fabric of the narrative is refracted through the individual cultural identities of each narrator/performer. The sum effect, perhaps best apprehended in musical terms, is of instruments of different tone/timbre/ colour, their individual connotative qualities fluid, conjoining to form a series of chords. The individual remains true to him/herself while always being subsumed, and paradoxically finding a fuller expression of individuality and difference within a collective. Conceptually, this is at the root of the company's multicultural structure. Perhaps echoes of the cultural palimpsest that India is often perceived to be (the metaphor is originally Nehru's) are to be found in the multi-textual heterogeneity of both performance language and company structure, as also in the Bouffes' blurred overlaying in simultaneity of past, present and non-specific future?

For, as has so often been the case with the Centre's productions at the Bouffes, this space is thematically coherent with the material. Here is a civilization at an indeterminate transitional point somewhere between the dissolution of crisis and a new reconstructive ordering – the perfect frame for a scenography that subverts and remakes itself endlessly. The marks of demolition and incomplete renewal are etched into the very texture of this building, an elemental atemporal bowl apparently hewn from the rock, like the caves in Ajanta or the open-air quarries for which Brook has such a strong liking. Above all, this space is a silent witness to the passage of time, bearing visible traces of its past. To borrow a phrase from one of Shakespeare's sonnets (no. 55), it is a place of 'unswep't stone besmear'd with sluttish time'.

Evidently Indian culture is present at every level in this work. However, Brook's mythopoeic sensibility implicitly embraces a Jungian sense of the existence of a common pool of human archetypes of an intercultural kind; and the non-homogenous blend of forms, styles and accents in Brook's essentialized 'realism of suggestion' serves to free the 'universal' qualities of the epic. Whether one perceives his work as that of appropriator or liberating interpreter, Brook insists scenographically that *The Mahabharata* belongs not only to India, but to the world. Hybridization decontextualizes and relativizes, i.e. universalizes: at the very outset of this re-visioning, Vyasa had acclaimed his narrative as 'the poetical history of mankind'.

NOTES

1 One remembers Barthes' cherished slogan, *Larvatus prodeo*: 'I advance pointing to my mask' (quoted in Jonathan Culler, *Barthes*, London: Fontana, 1983).

2 As Georges Banu has pointed out ('Le fleuve et la flaque' in *Alternatives Théâtrales*, no. 24, July 1985, p. 43), Brook's concrete use of the elements as scenographic base engenders what the phenomenologist Gaston Bachelard called 'material imagination', which 'can continually awaken and restore traditional images, and inform certain old mythological forms with life'. See Bachelard's *La Poétique de l'espace* (Paris: Presses Universitaires de France, 1957), and his long series concerned with the elements: *La Psychanalyse du feu* (Paris: Gallimard, 1949), *L'Eau et les rêves* (Paris: Corti, 1942), *L'Air et les songes* (Paris: Corti, 1943), *La Terre et les rêveries de la volonté* (Paris: Corti, 1948), etc.

3 Scenographically, the functionally mobile river literally bears out Heraclitus' celebrated dictum, 'you can never bathe in the same river twice'. In his *Last Will and Testament*, Nehru wrote of the Ganges: 'The Ganga is the river of India, beloved of her people, around which are intertwined her racial memories, her hopes and fears, her songs of triumph, her victories and her defeats. She has been a symbol of India's age-long culture and civilization: ever-changing, ever-flowing, and yet ever the same Ganga' (quoted in Eric Newby and Raghubir Singh, *Ganga: Sacred River of India*, Hong Kong: Perennial Press, 1974, p. 9).

Part IV

PRODUCTION – CRITICAL PERSPECTIVES

14

THE GREAT INDIAN EPIC AND PETER BROOK

Vijay Mishra

Vijay Mishra is a Senior Lecturer in Comparative Literature at the University of Murdoch, Perth, Western Australia.

It is perhaps not too much of an exaggeration to say that *The Mahabharata* is the founding text of Indian culture. The Puranas, dramatic texts (both classical and modern), medieval romance, the Indian bourgeois novel and finally the Indian film all retrieve the rules of their formation from *The Mahabharata*. There is something so dreadfully imperialistic about this text that, in a moment of wilful generalization or enthusiasm, we may indeed claim that all Indian literary, filmic and theatrical texts endlessly rewrite *The Mahabharata*.

The Epic itself reached its final form probably around the second century AD. Its *terminus ante quem* is generally placed around the seventh and sixth centuries BC, making its early versions (which are only a matter of conjecture) almost contemporary with Homer. Throughout its long history, this vast, heterogeneous text of 100,000 verses (or *shlokas*), absorbed a large number of quite divergent narratives – anecdotal and fantastic, as well as historical and theological.

Confronted with such a diversity of discourses and genres, the German Indologist Herman Oldenberg actually claimed, rather excessively, that, though *The Mahabharata* began as a simple epic narrative, 'It became, in course of centuries, the most monstrous chaos'.[1] From this 'chaos' (which existed only in Oldenberg's mind), redactors and readers distilled texts (or narrative fragments) to suit their specific needs. One of its best-known sections, the *Bhagavad Gita*, quickly became a text in its own right, and began to be seen as a self-contained poem about self and liberation, relatively independent of *The Mahabharata*. But texts undergo a very different kind of transformation in India. Since the original has no auratic status as such, a text is always what it is at a given moment in history. Consequently, the Indian hermeneutic and exegetical traditions never tried to reconstruct the original, but instead allowed the popular imagination to add to *The Mahabharata* and 'translate' it into a didactic text obviously

195

of quite bewildering complexity but with strong religious appeal or dimension.

This transformation – the 'sanctification' and consequent canonization of a text – is very Indian and must be placed in the context of what constitutes literary/religious value in Indian society. Thus *The Mahabharata* became a *smrti* text, part of an entire tradition of 'remembered' texts which collectively constitute the phylogenetic heritage of the race. This tradition of assimilation and absorption, however, hides *The Mahabharata's* radical difference from other texts, notably from its sister epic, *The Ramayana*. The Indian sees the latter as life-atoning, and recites it regularly at home. *The Mahabharata*, on the other hand, is never recited in full for fear that this would lead to disharmony and chaos in the family. Whereas *The Ramayana*, read allegorically, affirms genealogy, order and the sanctity of the family and constructs the Indian ideals of man and woman, *The Mahabharata* is about power and politics, about national disintegration and schisms: the Indian here confronts the forces of history and, in the story of Karna, the closest approximation to the genre of tragedy to be found in Indian literature. Through endless variations on the same theme, *The Mahabharata* telescopes its message of discord and strife into a ritual of battle. These two epics, originally part of a pan-Indian epic tradition, complement each other, as national epics usually do, to warn Indians of the essential precariousness of their lives and the tricks that history is wont to play. Yet the history within the text is an artificial construct, a falsification of history, in fact a narrative.

One of the great Indologists of our times, the late J. A. B. van Buitenen, called genealogy the grand design of *The Mahabharata*. In the Indian epics (and indeed in many other Indian narratives) genealogy problematizes a complex set of relationships around birth, power and ownership. The passion for genealogical purity is an Indian obsession. As if such a passion needed literary endorsement, *The Mahabharata* too is structured around genealogy. Yet at one level the seeming purity of *The Mahabharata* genealogy is completely illusory. The Epic sets aside a lot of space for its male heroes – Bhishma, Drona, the Pandava brothers, Duryodhana – but the secrets of biological descent are known only to women whose own sexuality confuses the confirmatory force of genealogy. Seen through the eyes of Satyavati, Ganga, Kunti, Gandhari, Madri as well as the lesser women figures such as Ambika, Ambalika and the 'Serving Girl', another picture emerges, a different statement about genealogical purity is made. The dynasty of Bharata, of which Santanu is in direct line of succession, is in fact rotten from the start. Santanu's lineage dies with his two sons; his dynasty moves through his wife who had borne a child from an earlier affair with Parashara, himself only remotely connected with the dynasty. Thus both Dhritarashtra and Pandu, 'fathers' of the two warring clans, the Kauravas and Pandavas, are themselves polluted; their genealogical connection with the race of Santanu is symbolic, not real. When the battle between these two warring clans is finally fought over eighteen days, Krishna, the Hindu god, must endorse order and genealogical purity and helps the Pandavas win. But in doing so he affirms not the sanctity of genealogical purity, but the superiority of gods over men. Gandhari's children, the Kaurava clan, are not born of gods (though the text does in places connect them to anti-gods such as the Asuras); Kunti's, that is the Pandavas, are. The great Indra, the wind, and Dharma himself had fathered three of Kunti's five sons. But so had the sun god when Kunti was a young girl. The product of this liaison, Karna, is superior to everyone else through his own special lineage; but, in an alarmingly contradictory fashion, he is deemed an outsider, because he was born before Kunti married Pandu. This ambiguity confuses precisely the principles of genealogical purity Krishna seemingly endorses. Since the figure of Karna is subversive of that order, he must be neutralized. In doing so, Krishna demonstrates that the battle of *The Mahabharata* is essentially between those blessed by the gods (who transcend genealogical transmission) and those who aren't. And such godly power as may come their way – Gandhari's request to see Duryodhana naked so that he might become invincible is a case in point – is neatly circumvented by the divine clown and jester, Krishna himself.

Whatever there is of Santanu's lineage (and even this concession is illusory) disappears upon the deaths of Bhishma and Duryodhana. What triumphs is matrilineal genealogy, the secrets indeed of Kunti and her godly lovers. The point I wish to make is that The Epic is ambiguous in its claims on this score, seeming to confirm, and yet subverting, age-old genealogical principles, patriarchy and purity of the race. That these ambiguities have been reduced to a perceptible order and continuity is a consequence of an Indian regime of reading not necessarily endorsed by the text, which remains conscious of the gap between the ideal and the real, and delights in constructing a 'textual world' capable of sustaining conflicting readings.

At another level, genealogy may be deemed a riddle that The Epic proposes to uncover. Thus the cause of Bhishma's death at the 'hands' of Sikhandin the transvestite has to be recovered further back in time, when the imperious Bhishma was insensitive towards Amba, then already betrothed to the young King Salva. A similar riddle is uncovered when Karna realizes that Arjuna is his half-brother. Since Arjuna's father was Indra, the conflict between Karna and Arjuna is a replay of a much larger conflict between two pre-eminent Hindu gods: Indra and the sun god. Sandwiched in between these two major heroes is their mother, who had kept this genealogical secret to herself. Genealogy as riddle finally endorses my earlier point that, since the secrets of genealogy are known only to woman, *The Mahabharata* somewhat radically advances woman as the source of real power.

Here again Krishna's role is crucial. It is he who reads the entire epic as a game that had been already played out in human history. For him, The Epic is a re-presentation of a conflict not unknown to the gods. And since the cyclical form of the game makes it essential that the 'correct' transmission of genealogy and the maintaining of order be confirmed anew in every age, Krishna must take the side of the righteous or the seeming righteous, even when the 'truth' of genealogy itself is in considerable disarray.

Krishna thus in one way endorses the importance of order in society. The first readers of the text responded to this by developing 'essentialist' readings. Two terms that continually crop up in the critical literature are *karma* and *dharma*. When applied to *The Mahabharata* these terms produce 'karmic' and 'dharmic' regimes of reading. Both these terms have an enormous semantic field. The term *karma(n)* comes from the root verb *kr* 'do', and has a range of related meanings. Its first set of meanings incorporates 'act, action, performance, business', which extends quite naturally into 'duty', 'office' and 'obligation'. As a word signifying action, it is often opposed to inactivity or rest. In religious parlance, *karma* is a religious act or rite which is undertaken with future recompense in mind. *Karma* is the first word of many compounds, chief among which are *karma-tyaga*, the abandonment of worldly duty, *karma-phala*, the consequence of actions, *karma-yoga*, the performance of one's religious duty, and *karmatman*, a person endowed with principles of action.

To read *The Mahabharata* as a karmic text implies two very different kinds of acts in itself. One part of this karmic reading requires a strong metaphysical input. *The Mahabharata* is read as a replay of a cosmic action, games that the gods and the anti-gods have already played out. There is on this level an 'action', a 'performance', which at the worldly level confirms those acts which keep the cosmos itself rolling. But the second part of this karmic reading takes us to the notion of character itself, as predicated upon prior actions, and is therefore constant. There is thus a karmic inevitability about the narrative, a fatalistic element which explains why heroes are foredoomed. It also involves a compulsion to repeat, throwing caution to the winds in the process. Given this karmic inevitability, the narrative functions in two ways. In the first instance, characters are doomed because of some earlier deed: Pandu must die, because he had killed a sage copulating with a doe; Bhishma too must die, at the 'hands' of Sikhandin, because of Amba's betrayal. In the second instance, a character is doomed because his actions are not seen as pure. Karna's nobility leads him to give his coat of arms and ear-rings (signifiers of invincibility) to Indra, who comes disguised as a brahmin mendicant; but Karna himself is nevertheless condemned because his action is not 'pure'. He must finally die because in the complex world of *The Mahabharata* only the 'compulsively tragic' can afford to live gloriously in an illusory world of purity.

Cutting right across this idea of 'fruits of action', is the concept that higher forces must control the narrative. Thus Indra's intercession ensures that Karna cannot triumph over his son Arjuna. In another instance, Drona must ask for the right thumb of the extraordinary Ekalavya, because he threatens the primacy of his favourite pupil Arjuna at archery. In this respect *karma* itself is manipulated to ensure the triumph of a particular narrative, and to create moments in the text which remain alluring and mystifying to the end.

The second regime of reading *The Mahabharata* is as a dharmic work. Most ancient and modern Indian critics (Madhava, Anandatirtha, V. S. Sukhthankar, P. V. Kane, for example) have read *The Mahabharata* as a treatise on *dharma*, a metaphysical text which is the source of ethical norms for the Indian. Like *karma*, *dharma* has a wide variety of meanings. Monier-Williams' Sanskrit dictionary has over 200 entries under this word.[2] From these entries I have taken, in summary form, three basic meanings.

(a)   that which is established or firm, steadfast; a decree, statute, ordinance, law;
(b)   usage, practice, right justice, duty;
(c)   virtue, mortality, religion, religious merit.

The word enters into compounds such as *dharmaksetre* 'law-field', the first word of blind Dhritarashtra in the *Bhagavad Gita; dharmajanman* born of *dharma*, a name used for Yudishthira; *dharmajnana*, knowledge of duty; *dharmadeva*, god of justice; *dharmanandana*, joy of *dharma; dharmanetra*, eye of *dharma; dharmapatni*, a dutiful wife; *dharmaputra*, Yudhishthira's name yet again; and *dharmashastra*, the holy text.

The ideology of *dharma* is variously manipulated by the text and complicated, furthermore, by its numerous redactors and commentators. In Rajagopalachari's translation, for instance, *The Mahabharata* is clearly presented as a dharmic text. He unabashedly appropriates this ideology for political ends to advance India's search for a national identity. His preface to the January 1952 edition, for example, is also a plea against the regionalism that had begun to hit the fledgling nation. 'But the highest literature', he writes, 'transcends regionalism.'[3] *Dharma* is seen here as spiritual strength. Yet Rajagopalachari also feels that there is a 'pure' *Mahabharata* from which all 'floating literature' may be omitted. This *Mahabharata* is the 'pure' epic, untainted by politics or government or, for that matter, philosophical or theological disputations. It represents India itself, with its many regions and languages unified by a higher order, a *dharma*. Its further association with *jaya*, victory, is meant to underline this equivalent. In Rajagopalachari's translation, then, it is the third meaning of *dharma* – virtue, morality, religion – that is used as the key to a reading of *The Mahabharata*. This is also the ideology of popular Indian cinema.

The same emphasis on *dharma* may be detected in one of the best-known film versions of *The Mahabharata* (*Mahabharata*, 1967). Since the popular Indian film industry simply endorses commonly accepted Hindu norms, filmic representations of The Epic simply expand this particular hermeneutic model of reading. One of the great successes of recent times has been the Indian *Doordarshan* (Indian TV) version of *Mahabharata*'s sister epic *The Ramayana*. The serialized verison of this epic, in a Hindi translation, brought the entire Indian nation to a standstill on Sunday mornings. Its success is directly attributable to the way in which this serial responds to Indians' own preferred reading of the text. And, quite predictably, the *Doordarshan* success of *The Ramayana* was immediately followed by the serialization of the massive *Mahabharata* itself. The latter, one suspects, will continue for many more months, if not years, to come. What the serialization loses as art it gains, I think negatively, in popular appeal and, sadly, jingoistic nationalism.

As I have said, *The Mahabharata* is a grand text, in fact the founding text of Indian culture. It is arguably the grandest text of world literature, not simply because of its length but because of its uncompromising artistic integrity and moral force. It is the 'post-modern' text towards which all literatures aspire. It knows its worth and proclaims as much quite early on:

> dharme ca arthe ca kame ca
> mokse ca bharata rsabha
> yad iha asti tad anyatra
> yad na iha asti na tat kvacit
> (I, 56, 34)

> [Giant among Bharatas, whatever is here on Law,
> on Commerce, on Sex, on Liberation is found else-
> where; but what is not here is nowhere.][4]

Yet precisely because of its 'expansiveness', its encylopaedic design and claims, in its 'received' forms (and I use 'received' in a much wider cultural sense here), *The Mahabharata* is a number of texts. There is, of course, the text as edited, the text which is a result of a labour of scholarship, probably alien to Indian editorial practices. The monumental Poona Critical Edition[5] gives us variant readings, and a thorough-going collation of all the known manuscript recensions. But there are at least three other very important texts of *The Mahabharata*. The first one of these comes closest to the Indian's heart because it is passed on from mother to child.

Initially told in fragments, over the years a complete *Mahabharata* text is handed down. Every Hindu child receives it, and knows it genealogy off by heart. Second there is the *Mahabharata* text as it exists through folk, theatrical and filmic representations. Since these forms permeate Indian society at every level, *The Mahabharata*, for the Indian, is mediated through these cultural practices or forms. Finally, there is the *The Mahabharata*-in-translation, both in Indian vernaculars and in major world languages. Here, depending upon the culture of the receptor language, *The Mahabharata* becomes an extraordinarily varied and unstable text.

I have used this lengthy preamble to introduce what I consider is both a continuation and a radical reinterpretation of the textual and critical traditions of *The Mahabharata* outlined so far. This is Peter Brook's *Mahabharata*, arguably the theatrical spectacle of the century, nine hours of sheer theatre unsurpassed in the known history of *The Mahabharata*. It is a theatrical event of such epic proportions that it will change the *Mahabharata*-as-world-text forever. Yet in Australia, at any rate, the publicity it has received, though generous, has on the whole failed to relate *The Mahabharata* to the known history of The Epic or to that essential difference which is the hallmark of Peter Brook's *Mahabharata*. A quick look at media coverage indicates that the public utterances of Brook and his somewhat universalistic interpretation of the text have been accepted at face value and not recontextualized into the actual performance. Indeed, the ease with which journalistic criticism especially (and most criticism of *The Mahabharata* has been journalistic in Australia) has dictated the terms in which The Epic may be read raises some serious questions about how a non-western text is received in the west. The criticism, furthermore, implies that at best non-western art requires no labour of knowledge, and at worst that orientalist modes of thinking are still alive and well. To probe this further let me be the priestly inquisitor and suggest that Peter Brook himself seems to invite this manner of thinking. In other words, if it is true that the source culture alone can represent itself, then by what right can Peter Brook represent the Indian? Whilst conceding that ' The *Mahabharata* remains to this day, the very basis of cultural life in India', Peter Brook nevertheless succumbs to the power of the seductive extension of the Sanskrit words *maha* and *bharata* to mean 'The Great History of Mankind'.[6] Some Australian reviewers ill-advisedly reproduced Peter Brook's own ruminations as they appeared in the *Mahabharata* programme brochure. Yet a closer reading of his words indicates that, even with the desire to keep universalistic principles and humanism intact, Peter Brook was conscious of The Epic's propensity to destabilize, distort and confuse the basic categories of good and evil, fate and free will. Brook, however, maintains that, in 'jumbling' these terms, The Epic finally releases them from their historical accretions so that the words, bare, precise, pristine – as a dictionary entry so to speak – look back at us.

This is the strongest part of Brook's interpretation because it is so very post-modern. The weaker sections relate to Brooks' nagging belief in mythic correspondence and an almost Gandhi-like insistence that *The Mahabharata* is really about truth, but truth presented through sets of contradictions which necessitate an extremely high (indeed rare) degree of self-questioning and analysis. I raise this because the night we saw the nine-hour performance at the Boya Quarry, Perth, these philosophical questions were completely subsumed by the form, by the 'theatre' itself. Indeed, the reason why both the orientalist argument (self-representation versus other) and the universalist tendencies (the text of mankind) do not distract us from the essential achievement of Brook's version is that Brook in fact used *The Mahabharata* to revolutionize theatre itself, and to reassert it as spectacle, a role so dramatically wrenched from it by film, that alarmingly anti-auratic product of mechanical reproduction. Yet precisely because of its down-playing of aura and the sanctity of the original text, film becomes an important force in the production. It is film (and filmic techniques of representation, though without the camera) that is the mediating principle in Peter Brook's version of *The Mahabharata*. Vyasa, the principle interlocutor of *The Mahabharata*, in fact historicizes himself – he is the here and now as well as the there and then. With the use of a viewer or viewers, (the child, Krishna/Ganesha), this self-historicization acts as a 'montage', juxtaposing one event and another, one image and another. The parallels are not complete but, in the Boya Quarry performance at any rate, one got a very strong feeling that the audience was in fact beginning to see Brook's *The Mahabharata* as film. This is in fact how the Indian views *The Mahabharata* anyway, though the mediations in his case are the various filmic representations of the text in Indian vernacular languages.

Brook therefore emphasizes *The Mahabharata*'s own theatricality, its gripping narrative, at the expense of its Indian roots. Indeed he can't do otherwise, because to return *Mahabharata* to its Indian roots would require skills of such bewildering complexity that no one, not even the Indians themselves, can ever hope to stage it adequately. Yet Brook's insistence upon *The Mahabharata*'s universality, as the world text, leads to a basic conflict between the text as performed and the humanistic interpretations advanced in its favour. The performance, in other words, presents a text at odds with its prior commentary. And in this respect it is the presentation which comes closer, ironically enough, to the spirit of *The Mahabharata*, a text that, like a palimpsest, always betrays its origins. For *The Mahabharata* is a political text imbricated within history as eschatology: *The Mahabharata* claims that it is a history (*itihasa*), not an epic (*mahakavya*). But, apart from Krishna, no one knows history or the nature of ends. This lack of knowledge has led, as we have seen, to readings that attempt to slot its political impetus into the metaphysical categories of *karma* and *dharma*. So, instead of endorsing history (or negotiating it with a view to blasting open the implied continuum of history), the Indian regimes of reading highlight moments of tension within *dharma* rather than mere political bungling on the part of its crucial characters. Central to this dilemma is Yudishthira, who lies so as to secure Drona's downfall but also becomes a compulsive gambler. Since the lie is a threat to *dharma*, which Yudishthira symbolizes, it is highlighted at the expense of a much more important flaw (the king as gambler) which is at the centre of a political history within *The Mahabharata*.

Peter Brook's production – the play as performed – transcends the limitations of these prior readings in which Brook as commentator is himself occasionally trapped. It recognizes that the text is outrageously open-ended. Reading it, one gets the distinct impression that it is a collection of voices, each trying to assert its own utterance as logos; yet none gets authorial endorsement. In a proto-deconstructive vein the text keeps all these voices in abeyance, and releases them like the primal sounds of the unconscious. Not surprisingly, the text is replete with 'Vaishpayana uvaca' ('Vaishpayana said'), 'Bhishma uvaca' ('Bhishma said'), 'Janamejaya uvaca' ('Janamejaya said') and so on. They're all saying things without anyone ever gaining ascendancy. The text in fact becomes polyphonic.

To retrieve (or reinforce) this sense of polyphony, Peter Brook brought to his *Mahabharata* a large number of actors who were not native speakers of English: an African/Black Bhishma/Parashurama, Karna, Bhima, Kunti and Madri; Middle Eastern Gandhari and Shakuni; Vietnamese Amba/Sikhandin; Italian Arjuna; Polish Yudhishthira and Dhritarashtra; Greek/French Duryodhana; Indian Satyavati/Draupadi; Japanese Drona; Indonesian Pandu. Apart from the Trinidadian Jeffery Kissoon, who plays Karna, the only major actors who are native speakers of English, whose voice and consciousness are one, are those who play the roles of Vyasa and Krishna/Ganesha. The first group of essentially non-native speakers bring to English a multiplicity of other voices, traces that supplement and add a discordance to the presumed univocality of the theatrical language, English, which is left with the narrator Vyasa, and the divine hero Krishna, who keeps history in check so that it does not spill over into chaos. There is a third 'voice' (beyond the multiplicity of native languages and the language of transmission) belonging to Satyavati/Draupadi, the only role given to an Indian. Through her we get the voice of the 'original', not with the immediacy of the Sanskrit original, but at least a voice which could be traced back to it.

This use of many races and accents, this 'cacophony', may be read either as a sign of *Mahabharata*'s universality or, more accurately, as an addition to the text. The multiplicity of voices adds both a new *Mahabharata* text to the canon, as well as extending the sense of 'sounds' and 'voices' which make up any open-air theatre in India. A western audience sits in silence;

an Indian audience adds its own voice to the performance, confusing, 'jumbling up' what is being performed. Peter Brook gave his theatre both these roles, the voices of the performers as well as the chaos of the Indian audience. Incorporating dance and theatrical forms borrowed from Greek, Indian, Balinese and Japanese theatres (here both the Noh tradition and Kurosawa are important) as well as the Australian Aborigines, Brook transformed and refined the 'chaos' that Oldenberg referred to so many years before.

Peter Brook's *Mahabharata* (even for an Indian who may wish to demur on narrow cultural grounds) is thus a bold attempt to give theatre life again, to reinforce what has been so rudely prised out of its grips. The Epic becomes a vehicle through which an extremely important statement about theatre and drama is made. Many years ago, Georg Lukács in his brilliant essay *The Theory of the Novel* read the epic as a product of a total, self-enclosed, economically unfractured society.[7] While ancient Indian society was alarmingly feudal and probably despotic, the epic nevertheless projects a society that did not suffer the social and economic disjunctions which lead to a morbid, ironic world-view and to the novel form. Where the novel (as well as tragedy) asked the question, 'How can essence come alive?' the epic, more philosophically, and with a much greater sense of self-assurance, asked, 'How can life become essential?' The epic was therefore produced by civilizations that were certain of themselves and knew, or believed in, the 'correctness' of their social and political institutions. In a post-modernist situation, it is really this self-assurance of the epic (its relevance to us now) which must be reread. As the history of *The Mahabharata* indicates, each age read it in terms of its own needs. In Peter Brook's version we return to a *Mahabharata* as spectacle, as performance, which remains deeply ambivalent about its political implications and about the possibility of order. If this reading leads to a conflict between Brook's pronouncements on *The Mahabharata* and his art, then it is art rather than philosophy which must be given the benefit of the doubt. Peter Brook not only makes a statement about the place of theatre in post-modern life, but also adds a fifth text to *The Mahabharata*. This text will inevitably modify the text as received so far, and radically challenge (if not alter) the Indian regimes of reading.

NOTES

Originally published in *Meanjin*, 47 (2), Winter 1988, pp. 343–52.

1 Quoted in C. R. Deshpande, *Transmission of the Mahabharata Tradition* (Simla: Indian Institute of Advanced Study, 1978), p. 6.
2 M. Monier-Williams, *Sanskrit-English Dictionary* (Delhi: Munshiram Manoharlal, 1976).

3 *The Mahabharata*, English version by C. Rajagopalachari (Bombay: Bharatiya Vidya Bhavan, 1951), p. 5.
4 *Mahabharata*, 'The Critical Edition', edited by Vishnu S. Sukthankar *et al.* (Poona: Bhandarkar Oriental Research Institute, 1959).
5 ibid.
6 Peter Brook, The *Mahabharata* (programme brochure for the Boya Quarry performance, 1988).
7 Georg Lukács, *The Theory of the Novel* (London: Merlin Press, 1976, translated by Anna Bostock).

15

INTERACTION-
INTERPRETATION

The Mahabharata from a Socio-Cultural Perspective

Maria Shevtsova

Dr Maria Shevtsova is a Reader in the Department of French Studies at the University of Sydney, Australia.

The Mahabharata has sustained the everyday life of countless millions of people across the whole social spectrum of India. Its cultural importance, past and present, is beyond dispute. What has caused some controversy, above all in India, is its actual status. Is this extraordinarily multi-layered work essentially a sacred text to be preserved in all its sanctity; a 'true' record of historical events, a compilation of myths, fables and folktales with little relation to historical reality, or an epic and so primarily a literary, erudite creation, as distinct from an oral and folk one?[1] And are these 100,000 verses in Sanskrit constituting eighteen books (*parvans*) so fundamentally Indian that foreign incursions into them are a transgression of Indian religious as well as secular culture? This question has been raised about Peter Brook's production mounted by actors, musicians and other collaborators drawn from around the world, but of whom one, Mallika Sarabhai, is Indian. Since it stems from a point of view on what *The Mahabharata* is, we might be in a better position to assess this particular question after looking briefly at the work's genesis and evolution.[2]

Scholars generally agree that *The Mahabharata* grew in stages over at least 3,000 years, starting from its earliest form in the first millenium BC, when it was known as the *Jaya* (victory). Verses were then added which gave the work the name of *Bharata*. It then acquired the expanded form we have today. The title is said to mean great (*maha*) race (*bharata*), the latter term referring to the martial race holding sway over the region lying between the Ganges and the Yamuna rivers.

Bharata is also said to mean any descendant of this race or anything about it, as, for example, the story of, or narrative about, the Bharatas.[3] In so far as the core of the tale is the feud between cousins, the Kauravas and the Pandavas, which leads to a devastating war on the Kurukshetra plain between them and their respective allies, the title could mean 'the great narrative of the battle of the Bharatas'.[4] Since *Bharata* also means India, the title could be interpreted as 'great India'. Because India has been thought to be the cradle of humanity, the word may be understood to say 'the story of all human beings'. This very idea appears in the Sanskrit text and is retained by Jean-Claude Carrière for Peter Brook's production. Here Vyasa the sage announces that his narrative/creation is 'the poetical history of mankind'. Vyasa fathered Dhritarashtra and Pandu, the fathers of the warring cousins, and, besides being the main storyteller among many of *The Mahabharata*, is also its attributed author.

The Mahabharata is believed to have been largely composed, preserved and sung by *sutas* who were counsellors, friends, charioteers and bards of the *kshatryas*, and usually their illegitimate progeny.[5] The *kshatryas* – kings, princes, free warriors and their wives and daughters – incarnated the power of the state. At the time it was known as the *Jaya*, it was a poem of triumph, its narration of the victory of one king over his kinsmen no doubt also serving political purposes. Then, as afterwards, it was recited in courts during great festivals and sacrifices honouring a ruler, embellishments suitable to the occasion woven into it. But it was also carried beyond the high caste by bards who travelled from region to region and village to village and added details, explanations and commentaries in response to listeners whose social experiences and expectations would hardly have corresponded exactly with those of the ruling dynasties.

An assertion to be found in *The Mahabharata* that it is a history (*itihasa*; literally 'it is what actually was') most likely refers to the events that constitute its central epic.[6] The sequence may be summarized briefly as follows: the return of the Pandavas from their dwelling in the forest to Hastinapura and the court of the Kauravas; the rivalry between the cousins, which eventually leads to the game of dice when the Pandavas lose Khandavasprastha, the kingdom given them by Dhritarashtra (and lose everything else, besides); the Pandavas' twelve-year exile in the Khandava forest and one year incognito at the court of King Virata; their return from exile, when they demand the return of their kingdom; the Bharata battle, when the Kauravas are virtually wiped out and the surviving Pandavas win the entire empire.

A mythologized genealogy of the Bharatas introduces the core epic, explaining why its characters, when not gods, are demigods or demons. It covers Pandu's marriage to Kunti and Madri, the birth of their five demigod sons, the birth of the hundred Kaurava brothers and one sister, and other details related to the clan's origins and fortunes. The chronicle may be called a history in so far as the events recounted appear to have actually taken place. It is certainly a story, the concept itself embedded in the notion of history. Its heroic exploits, although first transmitted orally, were written down, also making it epic literature. It was copied and recopied by scribes who most probably added something of their own to whatever was handed down to them. These anonymous compilers were called *vyasas* – perhaps the reason why Vyasa is said to be the author of a truly collective work.

At some point in its evolution *The Mahabharata* went into the keeping of the brahmins, who added religious meditations, didactic sections, brahminical legends and moral tales. *The Bhagavad Gita*, which is considered to be the embodiment of brahminical religious teachings and, from these, of Hindu sacred lore, is thought to have come from this time. Many of the scribes referred to are thought to have been brahmins or closely associated with them. In its passage through the centuries and through different social situations, it assimilated traces of the ancient Vedic scriptures, religious, philosophical and ethical digressions, customary law, legends, myths, fables and folktales. What is especially important from a socio-cultural point of view is that its numerous interpolations and accretions (some clustered around its main story, others shooting out in seemingly unrelated directions) show it was appropriated and adapted by different castes and, later, classes according to their world outlook, ideologies, values and needs. The purpose of these accretions, it has been argued, was 'to bring the epic up-to-date with contemporary changes as well as to use it as a channel for new ideas and new ethics'.[7] Consequently, by being used meaningfully in different historical circumstances, the book stayed alive. Although the Hindu book of life, it was used by Jains and Buddhists in their non-canonical literature.[8] And although it may have started out as the cultural expression of a ruling élite (notwithstanding the ambiguous position of the *sutas* in relation to the *kshatryas*), it was quickly absorbed in the secular popular culture, absorbing in turn definable aspects of that culture such as the folktales mentioned. Since folktales have a collective genesis, their incorporation into the book reinforces its collective character.

The Mahabharata did not remain an exclusively Sanskrit work. It was translated and paraphrased into other Indian languages within a few centuries of its composition. Nor did it remain an exclusively Indian work. As the Indian empire expanded from the first years of the Christian era onwards, it followed the trade routes of the Indian subcontinent and South East Asia, going to Burma, Thailand, Indo-China and even to the spice islands of the Pacific. Wherever it went, it was 'reworked, rewritten, condensed and phrased in contemporary terminology and in terms of the adopting culture'.[9] Here, too, the issue of what local versions made of it and the diverse functions they served for priests, princes, newly emerging élites and the common people of the receiving countries is relevant.[10]

The Mahabharata's journey, then, both inside and outside India, shows why so many questions have been asked about what it is *essentially*. What it might be today depends to a large extent, as in the past, on who interacts with it, interaction necessarily involving interpretation, which takes place in some kind of cultural environment. The latter, in either a diffused or clearly guided way, filters through the perceptions, sensations and actions of interpreters; and this helps to explain why certain aspects of any received 'classic', even when it is identified as a holy book, suddenly seem to surface, whereas they were more or less hidden in another historical time and place.

The Mahabharata in contemporary India does not give rise to a single, uniform interpretation. How could it in such a vastly heterogeneous society where, to boot, the cultural heritage is constantly up against the demands of a modern, industrialized society and all the inroads it has made on the habits, customs and values bequeathed by tradition? The linguistic richness of the Republic of India, with its fourteen major languages recognized by the constitution and some 220 dialects, alone suggests that multiple cultures have forged the national culture and continue to ferment in the country, destabilizing what in fact is not one but many traditions and providing not one but many encounters with a market economy. Social reality is the link between *The Mahabharata*'s encyclopaedic scope and its plural meaning. Recognizing how social reality intervenes in interpretation should not cause offence to those for whom *The Mahabharata* is, above all else, a sacred book.

All of this is just as important when interpreters from non-Indian civilizations, in our case members of the CICT, open the same book. To argue that the book does not belong to them and, consequently, leads to misunderstanding as to its real content raises a whole host of problems about how ethnic identities are both expressed and invested in cultural creations and why these identities are defended when they are perceived to be under threat from outside forces.[11] These can be experienced as the forces of domination by a majority culture over minority cultures, by an imperial power over a colonial or neo-colonial situation, or by western society, broadly speaking, over eastern society conceived just as broadly (although what is usually implied here is the distinction between 'industrial' or 'consumer' society for the first and 'non-industrial', 'archaic', or 'traditional' society for the second). Yet although the problems entailed cannot be handled easily, argument in terms of cultural 'property' is simply inadequate. This holds for our age as well, where national-cultural autonomy and minority marginalization within one society, let alone within the 'world community', are among the most pressing issues. Argument in terms of interaction-interpretation, why it occurs and where, is far more to the point. The very history of *The Mahabharata*'s passage from social group to group within a myriad of cultures, national and foreign, indicates that the terms mentioned are just as pertinent today, even though the social conditions for cultural dissemination have changed enormously since ancient times.

There is no reason to doubt that Carrière and Brook wished to make known a work they understood was alive and not dead (as are museum artefacts) to societies (indeed, to so-called western societies) that may otherwise not have had contact with it. The care, time and energy over ten years of preparation, as well as the monumental task of putting the production together, speak for a commitment that goes beyond petty self-interest. Now, while it would be reasonable to believe that some fifteen years of research with the CICT went into the production (probably making it the apotheosis of that research), it would be unreasonable to assume that the production's exploration of what theatre can do, could be and could convey to diverse audiences denotes purely aesthetic objectives. There is ample evidence in Brook's past work with the CICT, in interviews with him and in his writings that his theatrical quest is interconnected with a search for maximum communication with audiences about something touching their everyday life, however that 'something' may be defined by them. At the same time, he has a vision of his own to offer, which envelops the presumed total sum of human experience rather than focuses on particular, socially bounded experiences. How Brook's reliance on a multiracial group of performers for *The Mahabharata* is integral to that vision and how it might be oriented towards a universal rather than culturally specific type of theatre will concern us shortly. The point to be noted right now is that interpreting *The Mahabharata* through the theatre and also making a theatre work commensurate with its own creative principles (Brook and Carrière's 'dramatic truth') is not solely a matter of theatre.[12] For a start, work involving numerous collaborators and hundreds more spectators is a communal, and therefore social, event. And while we might be hard-pressed to define the production in precise social terms, it has social resonance and seeks social impact through the artistic means at its disposal.

Storytelling through the ways of the theatre is characteristic of Brook's work with the CICT. Storytelling in this particular case is crucial, for, by following the main narrative, which is intricate enough on its own account, Carrière and Brook gain access to what can only be described as a massive, rambling construction. As is well known, selected parts of *The Mahabharata* have appeared and reappeared in classical performative forms such as Odissi dance and Kathakali. Where modern forms are concerned, the 1989–90 Indian television series is the only attempt, besides Brook's, to deal with the entire work in a cohesive fashion.

The dialogue given to Vyasa at the outset ('poetical history of mankind') is an interpretative choice, indicating that the tale's imputed universal significance is given precedence over its specifically Indian, or specifically Hindu, content and context. Since the playscript was developed with staging in mind – Brook and performers trying out pieces for a conceivable production along the way – it would be futile to separate the text from the production that finally took shape. The organic relationship between the two means that Vyasa's declaration can be taken to be the guiding line of the production as a whole. In other words, the idea stated not only underpins the narrative as such, but, as we shall see, is refracted through all the non-verbal processes – gestural, musical and so on – that make the production a much larger entity than the script devised for it.

Storytelling serves other fundamental purposes. It allows author and director to pull together a number of structural elements, dramatic qualities and philosophical-moral threads of *The Mahabharata* as it exists on paper today. By doing so, they are able to keep the 'original' in sight and, at the same time, transform it. Consequently, although the production is no longer an Indian work, it is not completely removed from its source. India is present, but not reproduced.

The Indian epic, for instance, is relayed through a network of interchangeable roles: tellers are protagonists, and speakers are listeners. The production highlights this feature while introducing a new one integral to a *play* dynamic, the movement from one genre (literature) to another (theatre) being part and parcel of the transformative process referred to above. Here protagonists, tellers and listeners also become spectators of themselves and each other. They 'frame' a sequence in the narrative by standing to one side of the action taking place. Or they 'freeze' part of their own action, watching it and explaining to onlookers, on stage and off, what it is about. Besides Vyasa, the salient examples are Krishna, Arjuna and Dhritarashtra, who step in and out of their multiple roles at the very moment they carry the narrative forward. *The War* (the third part of the production) has a composite series of such displacements when blind Dhritarashtra anxiously asks about the turn of events. Scenes of the battle, similar to shots from a film, are related to him and to his wife Gandhari in a recitative-like way by Sanjaya, the 'king's eye' (by Vyasa's decree). Arjuna and Krishna narrate what they are doing, other spectator-participants meanwhile confirming, by either questions, declarations or deeds, what has taken or is about to take place. The shifting roles provide the voices of a contrapuntal structure where each voice, Dhritarashtra's included, takes the lead or becomes an accompaniment according to which particular aspect of the rapidly evolving scenes is foregrounded against the rest.[13]

Since protagonists perform and tell the tale in one and the same instant right through the production, action belonging to the past has all the immediacy of action in the present. The channels used for merging different orders of time certainly generate theatrical excitement, as well as a good deal of the fun rippling through the performance from beginning to end. But the temporal fusion also reinforces Vyasa's claim that the action occurring embraces all human beings, irrespective of their historical and cultural context. The 'history of mankind' is, after all, an absolute and an abstraction. Vyasa gives it a concrete dimension by speaking directly to a young boy on stage who – figure of the past – is the direct descendant of Arjuna and who – figure of the present – metonymically stands for the the audience.

The moral implications of the philosophy at hand, as of related threads taken from *The Mahabharata*, are not quite unequivocal. Numerous difficulties here converge. The production, like others by Brook with the CICT, is a theatre not of statement or 'message', but of suggestion. For this reason, Vyasa's 'poetical' for his creation is apposite to the production itself. Yet this work of allusions, verbal, musical and visual collocations, and accumulated implicit meanings must also convey the sense of *dharma* (one of the threads referred to), which cannot be transferred across cultures without significant loss. The production attempts to resolve the problems of cross-cultural interpretation posed by it by blending it into the entire action instead of drawing attention to it explicitly. Krishna's lesson on *dharma* to Arjuna, when Arjuna hesitates about going into battle, is especially problematical. The lesson constitutes *The Bhagavad Gita*, which, as we have already noted, is of vital religious and moral importance to Hindus. Brook's solution to this particular problem is to suggest the grave importance of Krishna's words by having them whispered to Arjuna. Arjuna, by contrast, voices his horror at the oncoming destruction.

The actual moment of Krishna's intervention is indispensable to the narrative. It is, moreover, the turning point of the universal 'history' being unfolded on stage. For at least these two reasons, Brook could not have left the moment out. However, since from a Hindu perspective the whole thrust of *The Mahabharata* is thought to be *The Bhagavad Gita*, Brook's elliptical treatment of the sequence has elicited a strong critical response.[14] The criticism for the standpoint mentioned may be justified. On the other hand, it presupposes that the teachings on right conduct with regard to self, others and the world (one legitimate interpretation of *dharma*) and which are not confined to *The Bhagavad Gita*, must necessarily be rooted in theological exposition and religious practice. The fact that the ethical principles to be found in *The Mahabharata* have also been and continue to be used in India for secular purposes suggests the contrary.

The production, in any event, seeks neither to illustrate moral points nor to draw moral conclusions. Whatever moral dimension can be attributed to it comes from how it knits together images of human action. Everything, as the story makes plain, leads to the war. The enactment of the war releases a phenomenal array of impressions, sensations and images that appeal to all the senses at once. They are brutal, subtle, gentle, horrifying, some sharp and succinct as only poetry can be, while others flow on, extending their reach and gaining momentum as they go. Vertical, horizontal and diagonal lines are marked out by the performers and the few props they manipulate. All spatial zones are used: the earth, the walls, the deepest recesses of the quarry as well as its upper edges, where earth and sky meet. Horns blow upwards towards the sky from the highest platforms of the space filled by the audience. The design seems to trace the circumference of the globe, the audience also circumscribed by it.

Theatrically it is stunning. Yet the great power of Brook's theatre lies in its capacity to interact with contemporary audiences at all levels of their inner experience of the outer world. This is why it is never gratuitous or anachronistic. The war of the Bharatas is no exception. Thus when *pasupata*, the 'ultimate weapon', explodes in a blinding magnesium flare, the image can only be understood, in our time, by reference to the nuclear holocaust. The production provides a commentary on the destruction of humanity. Mud grips the wheel of Karna's chariot, as if the earth itself were rising up in protest. After the lethal weapon has been unleashed, Draupadi confronts Krishna over his doings, asking what can be the sense and purpose of all his actions when they have come to this: carnage, grief, abjection and the virtual annihilation of the human race. Do all human actions inevitably lead to the same conclusion? Her questions are of immense importance to the spectators who have just witnessed scene upon scene of devastation.

And this brings us to the difficulty of understanding what, exactly, can be concluded from the production's principles of suggestion and the whole host of moral implications they conjure up from a social, secular and not religious, point of view. The young boy on stage is a symbol of the future, and, therefore, of the hope of survival. The dust thrown up by the war settles. The performers wash themselves in the water where blood and fire ran. The river and the pool, which were two sides of the same metaphor for life-death (the river also evoking the Ganges, mother of all life), are now graced with the light of floating candles. The performers dress in white robes and sit beside playing musicians in the circle of community and communion. Harmony and order are restored. It is profoundly beautiful although, for this particular spectator, profoundly disturbing. The nuclear blast does not promise such a beatific version of the end; and cannot guarantee that life of any kind will come after it.

The last, framing image is the coda of both tale and performance. The tale itself ends when Yudishthira approaches the gate of paradise with his dog. As he steps over the threshold he discovers his foes. Renouncing paradise, he is led by Vyasa to his brothers and Draupadi in hell. 'Right', which appears to have been on the side of the Pandavas, since they were initially 'wronged' by the Kauravas, here, in a zone beyond the earth, seems to have had no bearing on the ultimate outcome of human action. The vision before Yudishthira is, as Vyasa puts it, the 'last illusion'. Vyasa is quoting the keeper of the 'last dwelling'. He relates these words to

213

Ganesha who has been writing the story and who repeats them – the last uttered in the performance.

What is this 'last illusion'? On the most immediate level it refers to the powers of make-believe, in this case, of a performance that is enthralling, like magic. On a deeper level of meaning it refers to the brahminical world-view built into *The Mahabharata*, where 'illusion' fundamentally means 'the vanity of all human action'. And if this, finally metaphysical conclusion, is what we must take away with us from the production, then surely our hearts, minds and, yes, actions must rise up in protest against the last action, which precedes the 'last dwelling', and which is the destruction of the universe. At which point metaphysics must be abandoned for concrete, social protest. Saying this may well amount to asking for another conclusion to the production, one that is not quite so equivocal or quite so delicately understated.

Understatement, though, is the hallmark of Brook's craft and requires a few more brief remarks. It is articulated through ellipses common to folk theatre where a detail of dress, expression, movement, or physical or moral behaviour outlines a particular character, leaving the rest of the portrait to the imagination of spectators. Similar elliptical, emblematic and metonymic procedures are at work in folk theatre when, for instance, a gesture, object, sound or light signals a change of time or location, or a change of direction in the action performed. These are simple cues to audiences which, because they are bounced back through the spectators' reactions, establish an intimate relationship between them, performers and performance. Intimacy is secured, at the same time, because the communication taking place in the strongest sense of the word stems from shared, rather than disparate, cultural assumptions. This is principally why folk theatre has always been the expression of a community – historically, of a rural village community – and not the expression of the personality of one or several individuals.

Brook's production cannot hope to reproduce, in the industrialized societies from which it draws its public, the conditions that generate folk culture as such. However, it does succeed in creating the close contact necessary for a sense of community of some sort. This is brought about through devices which, as in folk theatre (or, for that matter, as in child's play) rely on the capacity of audiences to seize quickly what has been offered them and accurately fill in the gaps. Thus a simple detail is joined, in the make-believe reciprocated by spectators, to a number of points simultaneously – character, narrative, sense of action, cultural meaning and so on – which the spectators must expand upon imaginatively. A piece of cloth around a stick marks Pandu's regal office. Saffron and white scarves belonging to Yudishthira and his brothers are snatched from them when Yudishthira loses the game of dice. These scarves signify their lost kingdom. White cloth is placed around Karna's neck when he is made king. It replaces the sumptuous paraphernalia that is, nevertheless, implied. Tassled parasols high in the air give a majestic procession, invisible elephants and all, for the arrival of Gandhari, who is to become the wife of Dhritarashtra; and the brilliant light calls to mind the bustle and festivity which are sketched in physically and musically but not portrayed in full.

Carpets and cushions are arranged on the earthen floor to designate Virata's court. Hand-held curtains and rush mats held vertically anticipate a turn of events, or reveal essential information, as happens when Krishna is shown sleeping peacefully, his divinity as well as human identity conjured up by his tranquil pose. The saffron curtain used here alludes, through its colour, to Krishna and opens in a completely literal manner on to a scene of Krishna's life when Ganesha relates episodes of that life to the young boy accompanying him and Vyasa. Krishna's pose recalls classical Indian iconography and, by doing so, builds into the production a reference to the culture that produced *The Mahabharata*. The parasols, imaginary elephants and Ganesha's red elephant-head, which the performer wears or carries under his arm, have the same referential quality. Red is the colour of Ganesha, his head part of his mythological as well as divine origins. Both his colour and form summon up Indian representations of him.

Mats and curtains, besides being typical props of folk theatre, evoke a village setting, so that even in Virata's court they suggest that village life exists beyond the royal enclave. Mats, twigs, sticks, pottery and other artisanal utensils in *Exile in the Forest* – all indices of a rudimentary, hunting or peasant society – denote geographic location, the changed fortune of the Pandavas, the trials imposed upon them and the ascetic life of hermits who withdraw into the forest in search of spiritual salvation. The ochre-red earth, which is right there throughout the production, is all the more noticeable in the second part because the performers are consistently close to it in their kneeling, bending, sitting or recumbent positions. The earth is not a mere backdrop for the human drama played out upon it, any more than the river when it runs with fire and blood. These natural elements are caught up in the destruction wrought by human hands and, in this respect, stand for the very universe which *pasupata* threatens to blow into extinction.

Just these examples among many more show how the production builds up and maintains an intimate atmosphere, irrespective of its grandiose proportions, grand themes and spectacular effects. Even the dense, intense activity of *The War*, with its jostling bodies, whirl of sticks, whips and wheels, mobile bamboo screens, torchlit battle and marked contrasts between light and darkness (indicating the passing of days into nights), does not drive that intimacy out. What we have here, over and above the eloquence of folk theatre, is the intimacy of epics which, for all their majestic sweep – and this is especially true of *The Mahabharata* – contain the warmth of voices that *speak*.

The vast scope of *The Mahabharata* allows everybody to find in it whatever is particularly meaningful to them. While Brook has found a great deal in it for a production that, as has already been stressed, by no means intends to duplicate the work, he appears to have been particularly sensitive to its oral quality. It is as if, in listening acutely to the voices speaking in *The Mahabharata*, Brook has picked up the tones of those wandering bards who, in time immemorial, sang The Epic in its earliest form to the common people. These tones have led him to what, for him, is the essence of the great poem: its oral, popular storytelling in recital which, in itself, is a performance uniting the performer, the content of the performance and its listeners/spectators. The production is a crystallization of this process.

Now is the appropriate moment to return to the question, based on what emerges from his productions, of Brook's search for a universal theatre. The idea makes sense when we take into account the triple goal embedded in them all, but which is realized on an unprecedented scale in his *Mahabharata*:

(1) generate maximum communicability through stage processes working to the full simultaneously (so that, for instance, music reinforces gestural meaning, or develops, reinterprets or counterpoints it, as the case may be):

(2) extend far enough outwards to have universal reach, that is, interact with extremely heterogeneous audiences and convey meaning to them, irrespective of the national or social contexts of spectators in them, or of the cultural baggage they have acquired;

(3) concentrate on these spectators in unison, as if they formed a unified whole.

The last two goals are contradictory (heterogeneity versus homogeneity), but we could say that the purpose, at least for the *duration* of the performance, is to galvanize spectators as one.

Brook's *Mahabharata* is all the more likely to spark off a feeling of unity among spectators because it totalizes its own heterogeneous elements. Furthermore, the chances of achieving its triple goal are higher because India's *Mahabharata*, the production's inalienable starting point, is universal. By 'universal' here is meant that *The Mahabharata*'s tremendous scope referred to above allows virtually everybody to take from it what they need in given circumstances. It can be turned to for personal inspiration and edification, spiritual or secular. It can be used for the great public issues of our time. Draupadi's questions to Krishna on the consequences of war concern the entire globe, and in this respect alone have truly universal significance. The same dialogue crystallizes other subjects of public importance (freedom and constraint, volition and the limits to action, and so on), which also find their place in Brook's production.

In short, whatever may have caused Brook to discover *The Mahabharata* initially, his encounter with it was not fortuitous. Its universality could be nothing but compelling for a director who believes that theatre fulfils its potential when it brings together and blends all the imaginable contours of human experience – this giving theatre its social character and, at the same time, its artistic justification, beauty and pleasure. Nor does Brook come to the work with a clean slate. He brings to India's *Mahabharata* a world-view steeped in the European humanist tradition winding its way down to the present from the Renaissance. The perspective of his production is humanist in so far as it accentuates transcendent values – universal, 'human' values – rather than sociologically differentiated ones which coterminously define a culture in the broadest and strongest sense of the word.

Here we must inevitably look to Shakespeare who, far more than Homer's and Virgil's epics, with which scholars have compared *The Mahabharata*, leaves his imprint on Brook's production. *The War* is finely overlaid by motifs appearing in Shakespeare's history plays and tragedies, the section highlighting the intimate connection between social order and cosmic order, which, as in Shakespeare, entails nature's protest against the deeds of men. We have already mentioned the image of Karna's wheel trapped in the mud where literal and figurative meaning are conjoined, implying nature's judgement. Instrumental sounds of varying pitch and intensity articulate the combined chaos on earth and in the spheres. The montage of scenes, their rhythm, pace and orchestrated exists and entrances, are in a Shakespearean vein, as is their resolution, Vyasa and Krishna meanwhile performing roles similar to those played by Shakespeare's wise fools. Comic interjections – primarily verbal, musical and facial – are juxtaposed against sequences carrying enormous dramatic weight. The visual coda or epilogue cited earlier (order restored) closes and comments on the ensemble of actions, themes, episodes and emotions building up from the beginning of *The Game of Dice* until they spill over at the very end.

Shakespeare's histories and tragedies, although redolent with universals couched in metaphysical terms, are anchored in concerns specific to Elizabethan England. Among them is the politics of state, which involves the problem vital to the epoch of legitimate monarchy and illegitimate usurpation of power. The politics of state, albeit in a totally different timeframe and having quite different implications, is a theme of *The Mahabharata*. Yet the theme as such is not underscored in Brook's production, despite the narrative line which actually contains it. This of itself suggests that the metaphysics rather than historical precision in Shakespeare provides his main frame of reference. In other words, the Shakespeare who offers Brook a key to *The Mahabharata* also corresponds with the perspective Brook brings to bear on it. In addition, this Shakespeare is cast in the storytelling form endemic in popular culture, his epic dimension taking on the more modest proportions of a tale related through intimate speech.

What Brook seems to be saying through this overlap is that Shakespeare configures the nearest 'equivalent' in European civilization to the Indian work, but that even he does not equal it. If so, then dismissive reactions to his interpretation via Shakespeare are misplaced. *The Mahabharata*'s voyage far and wide over the centuries shows it has been interpreted through innumerable channels. Can Brook really be an exception, especially as we cannot avoid bringing what we have to what we do not have in order to understand and share it? The idea that we come with nothing, in some sort of pure, 'virgin' state, to art (conceived equally as 'virgin' territory) as well as to our relations in society may be appealing, but is sheer myth.[15]

Apart from the aspects already outlined, how Indian and non-Indian signs coalesce in it is just as necessary for the production's universal thrust. The most obvious point to make in this regard concerns the performers themselves. India, Japan, Vietnam, Iran, Turkey, Trinidad, Senegal, Poland, Italy, France and Britain do not exhaust their combined national origins. National identification does not deprive them of their individuality. Nevertheless, the individual qualities they bring to the performance as a whole are traced over by cultural markers. The colour of skin, physique, gait, mannerisms, accent, intonation and cadence of speech and, above all, a way of seeing and doing, which are also acts of interpretation and affect how a role is performed, are markers in their own right. They are distinctive enough in the production to give the impression that delineated cultures, and not solely a mixture of individual traits, converge to produce a pluricultural composition. At the same time, because they are sufficiently distinctive, the cultures they evoke do not blur into indiscriminate, amorphous mass. The upshot of this is that plurality does not destroy singularity, even though the universal rather than the particular is sought from their conjunction.

It would be extremely difficult to show precisely how the national background as well as defined culture pertinent to it informs the work of each CICT performer. ('Defined' because every nation engenders a variety of cultures according to its social stratification – giving élite, official, peasant, working-class, subordinate, alternative or whatever cultures, which nurture performers and spectators alike, albeit to different degrees of receptivity and depending on where they are in the social spectrum and where they wish to be.) A study of, say, Vittorio Mezzogiorno as Arjuna in the light of his Italian and specifically Neapolitan background would require detailed analysis in almost laboratory-like, controlled conditions.

The fact that these conditions do not prevail in a performance situation is only one of several obstacles to precision. Reliance on the kind of generalizations we normally call stereotypes is another (although eliminating them altogether is probably impossible at the best of times, 'laboratory' situation included).

The onerous task would be compounded by a number of additional factors. First, Mezzogiorno's performance cannot be isolated from all the performances which criss-cross each other and give the production its internal dynamic. No unit, even when rehearsed separately or carved out for analytical purposes, is self-contained: it looks back to, intercepts or anticipates another moment, fragment, scene or sequence. A scene from *The Game of Dice* can serve as an example. It concerns Mezzogiorno/Arjuna who kneels blindfolded facing the audience, his arrow pointed upwards to shoot a bird in the sky. The arrow is not released. His prowess as an archer is translated visually when another arrow pierced through a bird falls with a thud to the ground. Everything about the scene anticipates a moment in *The War* when Arjuna fires at Bhishma. Once again Mezzogiorno holds the arrow firm. It is taken and carried by Krishna, who twists it slowly through the air and, seconds later, plants it into Bhishma's heart. In both cases the events are carried out in silence, the second in accentuated slow-motion. Arjuna's taut body and concentrated attention focus both scenes, the suspense of one echoed in the other.

Second, Mezzogiorno, like most of the performers, does not use his native tongue, whether the language used is French or English (English being the language of the production on its international tour). The gestures that usually accompany a prescribed language and physically extend or translate verbal meaning change according to the linguistic change. Thus what might be a series of Neapolitan gestures coming to Mezzogiorno's aid if he were performing in Italian necessarily undergo a metamorphosis when he must think, feel and act in French and, again, when all must be done through English. Cultural interference twice over mitigates the initial impact of Mezzogiorno's primary culture on his play.[16]

Third, the accretions from former or contiguous artistic experiences, which are not necessarily nationally based, need to be taken into account. How much does Mezzogiorno bring from his film-acting, moreover in international cinema, to the stage? And how much of it is useful for Brook, who draws on a considerable range of cinematographic techniques for the production? A similar line of enquiry is relevant for Mallika Sarabhai in the role of Draupadi, among others. In the case of Ryszard Cieslak it is worth asking how much is due to his formative years in Poland, where his work with Grotowski looms large. An assessment of Cieslak's professional background would need to cover the issue of whether the Laboratory Theatre's psycho-biological experiments, which concentrated on inward-bound experience as distinct from outward-bound discovery, capture a social tendency, or perhaps only a general mood, prevalent in Poland at the time (supposing satisfactory answers can be given). Just the same, we would still have to address the question of the contribution made to his present performance by the new demands placed upon him.

Performing in foreign tongues imposes heavy demands, especially as they are resonant with cultural peculiarities, body language included. These demands are then complicated by the paradoxes of a situation that is unique because, despite its having a common language of performance (French or English), no one set of cultural parameters binds the whole. Even the relative binding provided by a common spoken language is not available in so far as the group's *lingua franca* is spun out of the occasion. The performers acquire a second or third language (in some cases, a fourth or fifth) expressly for the production. Or, if they have mastered it beforehand, for ordinary transactions, they still have to rework it for performance purposes as well as for the specific purposes of the production at hand. This means that the linguistic cohesiveness, which in monolingual companies involves a monocultural orientation, irrespective of its individual members' linguistic abilities in private circumstances, gives way to a linguistic porosity especially noticeable in accents, tones and timbres and the overall shape of utterances. The profusion of accents in Brook's *Mahabharata* in English has been remarked upon negatively – by critics in New York, no less, where every variety of English imaginable fills the streets![17] Whatever else this curious reaction harbours, it protects a puristic notion of language. Social life, on which the very stuff of language depends, can hardly secrete linguistic purity, least of all in a century of unprecedented migration. Brook's conscious appropriation of impure accents for his production is a way of acknowledging contemporary realities. Furthermore, although these impurities are restrained for the sake of clear diction and, therefore, for adequate communication, the fact that they are not systematically wiped out demonstrates that they are intended to be an indelible component of the production in its totality. They help project its global view – the 'poetical history of mankind' and the goal of universal theatre here in concert – and link up with the spectators who, the world over, speak with impure tongues.

Fourth, though not conclusively, sifting out the Italian-Neapolitan and even social class signs backing Mezzogiorno's performance would perhaps help grasp the nuances of his performance – not insignificant, assuming that the sifting out can be done reasonably accurately. Even so, gauging these signs would have restricted value because the production does not take its cue from individual performances as such. Individual performances are harnessed for the ends of ensemble playing so that the whole can, in fact, be greater than the sum of its parts. Emphasis on the collective character of performance in Brook's *Mahabharata* is in line with the principles of folk theatre explored by it. Since the goal is ensemble playing, the value, say, of an individual's accent lies in how it tunes into the range of accents going at once. The same applies to something far more elusive like temperament or, again, sensibility.

Much has been made of Brook's experiments in *Orghast* at Persepolis (1971). However, more could be made of why *Orghast* had lasting importance for the directions he was to take in the future. The artificial sound-system devised for the event, which was to have the semantic, syntactical and expressive capabilities of a natural language, compelled the actors, in the absence of received sense and meaning, to develop the communicative powers of their bodies. Unknown syllabic groupings were given meaning on their own account by sounds surging from deep within the body and from all the emotions and memories stored in it. (Sounds, after all, are produced by the whole body and mind combined and not merely by vocal organs.) Inflection, pitch, rhythm and all other vocal attributes including paralinguistics (shrieks, howls, groans, and the like) were paraphrased by gestures, mimicry and movement, this coordinated articulation producing a composite 'language' where language in the customary sense of the word was not so much superseded as made relative. The open spaces and the monolithic ruins of Persepolis, neither of which could provide a support for the performers, left them to rely solely on their own resources.

Brook's research into physicality and plasticity through *Orghast* was continued in the outdoor carpet shows in Africa, albeit now on a more intimate scale, the abstractions of *Orghast* converted into delimited, concrete tasks for the cause of immediate communication. It was carried through in one form or another in CICT productions preceding *The Mahabharata*. It is fundamental to *The Mahabharata* in that the multiracial performers (musicians not excluded, who are here actors in their own right) each represent a micro-*Orghast* to be welded into a macro-structure where the composite 'language' just described can reign supreme, only this time in the realm of a *natural* language, French or English.

The socio-cultural implications of such an enterprise are commensurate with the universal theatre represented as never before by Brook's *Mahabharata*, India's *Mahabharata* perhaps providing the only possible correlative for the undertaking. The production is neither logocentric nor does it base its aesthetic organization on any other hierarchical order (precedence given to corporeal expression, costumes or whatever other process making a stage work). Its aesthetic is driven by a vision set on eroding hierarchies between nationals, races, castes or classes, or any other socially determined privileges. In this respect, too, Brook creates in *The Mahabharata* a totally new theatrical genre for which existing names are inadequate. By modelling its own features, this genre both anticipates coeval audiences and presupposes it can help create them. Once again, as always in Brook's

CICT work, theatrical and societal motives, although by no means indistinguishable, are mutually dependent.

Brook has justly denied that the CICT is a theatrical version of UNESCO. For a start, it is not an international agency, institutionalizing and serving defined political-cultural-bureaucratic ends. Nor does the dignity of diverse peoples, which is upheld by his *Mahabharata*, constitute proselytism of any kind on Brook's part. Nor yet is it appropriate to cite either Brook's initiative in forming a plurinational research/performance group or this particular production as prime examples of an interculturalism spread by the 'global village'. His *Mahabharata* is intercultural and, in respect of its universal aims, is also transcultural. But it does not presume that everywhere is the same place and every ethnic group a replica of the next, all societal and cultural differences – the very differences that constitute dignity – eradicated through their contact.[18] This syncretism, which is inherent in the 'global village' syndrome, is neither the objective nor the outcome of a production that *synthesizes* disparate elements, not least those provided by a multiracial cast. Syncretism and synthesis are vastly different projects: the first evens out peculiarities in the search for a union foregrounding resemblances, while the second pulls them together, allowing each one to hold its own strength, and maintain its distinctive profile. Furthermore, the notion of 'world community' underpinning Brook's work is much closer to the spirit of synthesis and, for that matter, to the humanist perspective noted, not to mention its humanitarian and even utopian impulse.[19]

The production deliberately multiplies its disparate elements, which is precisely what prevents them from masking differences. The composition alone of the large group of performers highlights the meeting of contrasts. By the same token, it facilitates the use of disparate elements in one frame, each element associated with the next (Italian with Japanese with Indian, and so on). Perhaps it is their associate pull in relation to each other that succeeds in giving these elements a *gestalt*-like energy.

Whatever the best description for the procedure may be, the continuum of associations allows the Shakespearean interpretive and structural aspects of *The War* to sit beside the Indian, Persian, Chinese and Japanese features introduced through the martial skirts worn by the warriors, the martial-arts postures and sounds of these scenes, as well as the sticks wielded in them. Yoshi Oida's litheness which, although emanating from his training, is also connected with his physique, throws into relief a variety of agile displays, all of them reflecting in some way the physical constitution of their makers. Oida's black kimono throughout is the insignia of Drona, the great master of arms who teaches both the Kauravas and the Pandavas, Arjuna becoming his unparalleled pupil. At the same time, it recalls Oida's native Japan, which he recalls, now through his movements, when playing Kitchaka in *Exile in the Forest*. In these sequences, Oida's movements, especially through his head, eyes, hands and feet, suggest the gesticulation of Kabuki. Elsewhere, in the role of Drona, hieratic positions held by him have the concentrated restraint typical of Noh.

Karna's roughly-hewn chariot wheel in *The War* could well have come from an Indian or Assyrian frieze; Arjuna and Krishna's coupling of warrior and charioteer largely from Asian or European mime or dance. The choreographic organization of movement throughout the third part is striking, and reinforces the dance motifs which not only run right through the production, but are spotlighted at strategic moments in order to heighten this or that dance detail. When, for example, Arjuna is disguised as a woman at Virata's court, the shake of his smiling head, his finger to chin, quotes the configuration made by men in the part of women so often visible in Indian classical dance. The image also evokes certain European peasant dances (in Russia, for instance). A few stamps of Mezzogiorno's feet suddenly conjure up, through the power of association, Indian classical dance on one hand, and the tarantella, on the other. His swaying body instantaneously outlines a belly-dance or a disco-dance, spectators here as elsewhere free to fill out the picture of their imaginative intervention according to what is evoked in them. At another point Krishna, when in full verbal flight, suddenly holds a position characteristic of Kathakali, his upturned fingers and toes preventing any confusion between this and any other dance image. Bruce Myers in the role of Krishna gives the image a humorous touch, here recalling that Indian gods have all the attributes of ordinary human beings. At another point again his feet, ankles and wrists sketch a rather playful Indian folk dance.

The flow of dance is carried through by the women, taking its most expressive form in the arms and torso of Kunti (Miriam Goldschmidt) during the scene of Karna's death in *The War*. Billowing saris and drapes accentuate the rhythms of movement, body and costume united in each phrase. Draupadi's unending sari in *The Game of Dice* shapes a dance of its own, India meanwhile focalized in her garment. Nowhere in Brook's work, not even in *The Conference of the Birds*, his most dance-like piece until *The Mahabharata*, do physicality and plasticity so easily and inexorably lead to dance, their very essence. The dance of *The Mahabharata*, its words used to stretch the art of dance itself, is part and parcel of the new theatrical genre in embryo in *Orghast*, and which grew stage by stage with the CICT until it opened out in all its radiance in this production.

The synthesis at work in *The War*, which, of course, coincides with the end-point of the tale of humanity announced at the very beginning, encompasses India. When *The Game of Dice* is compared in retrospect with the third part, it appears to be more closely allied to India, her light diffused throughout the third part as the darkness of the tale's end encroaches upon the world. At this stage the costumes' sombre tones, black predominating, overshadow Dhritarashtra and Bhishma's white robes (stark against Sotigui Kouyate's black body) as well as the women's colours, the palette interpreting visually the content of dialogue and action. Raised voices, urgent cadences and strained pitch accompanied by an array of percussive instruments provide contrast, India possibly most forcibly present in the brass horns and notes of the *nagaswaram*. The characters cited do not, in any case, command the spectators' gaze, the most notable exceptions being Bhishma's entry into battle and death (through the tens of arrows suggested by sticks, India's immortal hero and Saint Sebastian contiguous in the one image), Kunti telling Karna she is his mother and then grieving over his body and, when the battle is done, Draupadi's exchange with Krishna.

Whatever the final thrust of the concluding part, India is the production's starting point. The opening sets in place, as if on a metaphorical chess-board, the elements marking out India. Apart from those in *The Game of Dice* noted in the discussion on metonymic procedures, they are the white, red and saffron colours of India, the last two worn to the greatest advantage by the women. Garlands of flowers, rice, powders (suggesting spices), fruit, juices and leaves connote Indian royal, agricultural, religious and marriage ceremonies. Floating candles, which are refigured in the coda, allude to *divali*, the Hindu festival of lights. Krishna's disc is taken straight from Indian iconography. It is not actually thrown in the production, as depicted in Indian comic strips of *The Mahabharata*. Its flight through the air in the performance is signalled by a whistle from the musicians in what amounts to a technique borrowed from animated cartoons. The Indian folk songs sung by Ganesha at the end of *The Game of Dice* reassert the Indian motifs permeating the whole.

India emerges strongly in order to identify a character without ambiguity, as occurs when Shiva appears with his trident in *Exile in the Forest*. Arjuna, who has called upon Shiva for possession of *pasupata*, presses his hands together above his head in a characteristic (for India) position of devotion. Conch shells, which are associated with Vishnu and Arjuna, blow in *The War*. The masks of the demons who appear in the forest recall the apparel worn for such figures in numerous Indian performative forms, Africa meanwhile also shaded into the apparition.

India is also clearly marked out by instrumental sounds in moments of great narrative importance. The nasal notes of Southern India's *nagaswaram* lament the fatal arrow's entrance into Bhishma's heart. They underscore the slaying of Duhsassana when Dhritarashtra fumbles over the corpse of his son. They have a similar air of mourning and finality for Karna, after his fall from his wheel to a percussive crash. Death, earth and the *nagaswaram* are united. The *nagaswaram*'s blasts at the height of battle have a similar narrative as well as affective and evaluative function. Of the many instruments used throughout the production, the *nagaswa-*

ram requires the greatest physical effort welling up from within the human body to produce sound, as is the case with the didgeridoo of the indigenous peoples of Australia which pulsates in *Exile in the Forest*. In this respect they may be said to most resemble those human instruments whose breath and muscles work in concert for the tale of *The Mahabharata*. The musicians, too, belong to the ensemble of instruments. They take part fully in the performance, as happens in theatre in the Indian subcontinent, as well as further east and in folk dances throughout the world. When the musicians take centre-stage as the performance draws to a close, the strings playing among them recall the sitar.

The gentle strains of music to the light of floating candles evoking *divali* give the production's end-point in India, although India was also its starting point and its associative reference all along. The production's close is not, however, a closure. Its elliptical approach and powers of suggestion pre-empt an open-ended rather than definite conclusion, as is appropriate for a work seeking wholeness of totality not through a tight grip, but through a free-flowing embrace that enfolds whatever it can into its movement, while leaving spaces for whatever it cannot envelop to ebb out.

NOTES

1 Allusion is here made to the periodic debates in India which go well beyond scholarly circles and enter the vast public domain of media coverage. The most recent debate on such a large scale took place in the early to mid–1970s. See, for reference to this, the foreword by Niharranjan Ray to *Mahabharata: Myth and Reality, Differing Views* (ed. S. P. Gupta and K. S. Ramachandran, Delhi: Agam Prakashan, 1976), pp. v–xiv. The volume, consisting of scholarly articles, is a contribution to some of the major issues involved in the long-term controversy and, to a certain extent, is a reply to a number of proposals that appear to have been put forward in this and preceding rounds of the debate.
2 See, for example, Gautam Dasgupta, 'Rites and Wrongs', *The Village Voice*, 27 October 1987, and Rustom Bharucha, 'Peter Brook's Mahabharata, A View From India', *Economic and Political Weekly*, 23(32), August 1988, pp. 1642–7 (also in *Theater*, 19(2), Spring 1988, pp. 6–20; reproduced in this volume as Chapter 18).
3 Iravati Karve, *Yuganta: The End of an Epoch* (Poona: Deshmukh Prakashan, 1969), p. 3.
4 Introduction by S. P. Gupta to *Mahabharata: Myth and Reality*, op. cit. (n1), p. 1.
5 Karve, op. cit. (n3), pp. 93–4.
6 *Mahabharata: Myth and Reality*, op. cit. (n1), p. vi.
7 Romila Thapar, untitled article in *Mahabharata: Myth and Reality*, op. cit. (n1), p. 172.
8 Introduction by B. A. van Nooten to William Buck, *Mahabharata* (Berkeley and Los Angeles: University of California Press, 1973), p. xxi.
9 ibid.
10 Romila Thapar (op. cit., n7, p. 175) argues that not enough necessary groundwork on the epic tradition has been covered to deal adequately with the 'strata

and "skins" ' of *The Mahabharata* (and *The Ramayana*), let alone with the fundamental question (to her mind) of how the function and purpose of these epics changed from age to age. Thapar believes that interest in the recent controversy (cf. note 1 above) has largely to do with 'fear of attack on the bastion of tradition as well as the desire to prove it right'. As should be clear, Thapar's pointed remarks on this score are appropriate for the argument of the present essay that the notion of transgression (which also refers to one of tradition) should be redefined in terms of purposeful interpretation.

11 Some of these problems are raised in the course of Rustom Bharucha's scathing critique (Chapter 16), where the concept of appropriation is equivalent to that of exploitation and thus unlike my own use of it in this text. Bharucha does open out the crucial issue of interpretation, arguing that, when *The Mahabharata* is interpreted from another cultural framework, the interpretation must first confront the meanings the work has been given in its own cultural context. Bharucha's explanation of *itihasa* in terms of 'history' as defined succinctly by him is very relevant to the issues involved in the controversy mentioned in my opening pages.

12 The quotation is from Jean-Claude Carrière's introduction to his *The Mahabharata: A Play Based upon the Indian Classic Epic* (New York: Harper & Row, 1987; trans. from the French by Peter Brook), p. xi.

13 All references are to the performances at the Adelaide quarry, February 1988, as part of the Adelaide Festival. The reader may find my extended analysis of Brook's storytelling useful for this particular discussion ('Peter Brook Adapts the Tragedy of Carmen', *Theatre International*, 10(2), 1983, pp. 38–55, whose pre-editorial, manuscript title of 'Narrative in the Theatre: Peter Brook's *Tragedy of Carmen*' accurately conveys the intentions and content of this article).

14 Gautam Dasgupta, op. cit. (n2), takes particular exception to this treatment.

15 In *The Shifting Point* (New York: Harper & Row, 1987), Brook states that neither actor nor director can 'jump out of his skin'. The greatest difficulty is stepping back from one's own culture 'and, above all, from its stereotypes' (p. 6 and p. 106 respectively). Stereotypes appear to be uppermost in Brook's mind when he suggests that culture is a constraining force (or so it comes across in many of the interviews held with him). If my interpretation is correct, the idea then would be to get rid of the clichés that are attached to a given culture, both from within and outside it, in order to make it a liberating force. And this seems to be one of the main objectives of Brook's *Mahabharata* in that it obliges performers and spectators alike to review routine assumptions about their own culture through its prism of cultures. Of importance to the discussion here and in the pages to follow in this essay is Brook's belief that 'each culture expresses a different portion of the inner atlas: the complete human truth is global, and the theatre is the place in which the jigsaw can be pieced together' (*The Shifting Point*, p. 129). It is also worth noting in respect of Brook's 'inner atlas', where Shakespeare is charted, that P. Lal's brief introductions to his fascicule translations into English from Sanskrit of *The Mahabharata* (a twenty-year project described as a 'transcreation' of the work) refer quite frequently to Shakespeare for comparison. Which suggests that the cultural atlas of the globe allows reciprocal cross-referencing. Lal's fascicules are published in Calcutta by the Writers' Workshop, the first dated December 1968.

16 See, in relation to these remarks, the interview with Mezzogiorno in this

volume (Chapter 12). My focus is on Mezzogiorno because I was fortunate to have been able to ask him questions pertinent to my essay.

17 Take, for example, Michael Feingold, who speaks somewhat disparagingly about the production's 'jumble of accents' *inter alia* in 'Brook of Life', *The Village Voice*, 27 October 1987. A similar unease with regard to the French of foreign performers, who were working side by side with a few native speakers, was expressed, often on a more aggressive note, in press reviews in Paris during the period of *Timon of Athens* (1974) and *The Ik* (1975), the first CICT productions.

18 These sentences especially have in mind Richard Schechner's brief paragraphs on Brook's *Mahabharata* and on his theatre research in general which are set in Schechner's overall exposition of interculturalism and syncretism, the two ideas so strongly reinforcing each other as to be virtually interchangeable (*Between Theater and Anthropology*, Philadelphia: University of Pennsylvania Press, 1985). Both stem from assumptions, as argued throughout my text, with Brook's goal of universal theatre or with the concept of 'world community' as I interpret it in respect of Brook's work. See also Richard Schechner, 'Intercultural Performance', *The Drama Review*, 26(2), Summer 1982, pp. 3–4.

19 'Utopian' is by no means used here as a pejorative. Ideals, even those commonly thought to be unrealizable (the 'utopian' of received wisdom), are necessary because they motivate social change. In the light of this, what I have called Brook's 'utopian impulse' does not in itself pose any problems. There is, however, an empirical problem which lies in existing social structures and in the very real inequalities pervading them. How can a universal theatre become accessible to everyone financially? The cost of preparing, mounting and touring *The Mahabharata* can only be exorbitant, and is partially reflected in the price of tickets wherever performances of it have been held. What this effectively entails is the exclusion of a whole range of social groups, and of a wider range still of individuals in them, from a production whose themes, mode of presentation and aims are nevertheless directed to them. Which is to say that the universality of a theatre work does not automatically bring into existence universal representation among its spectators. This, alas, shows the limits of theatre, even of Brook's theatre.

16

A VIEW FROM INDIA

Rustom Bharucha

A theatre practitioner and scholar, Rustom Bharucha is based in Calcutta.

THE MAESTRO IS TIRED. HE'S MILDLY ANNOYED that
there's no air-conditioner in the car, but his Indian friends don't seem
to notice. They are used to the heat.

They take him to a remote village, but the maestro is not impressed
by the dances performed specially for him by the villagers. 'Not
enough flair,' he comments. Then he buys a mask after checking the
price with his guide: 'Is that what you would pay for it?' Reassured,
he asks his favourite question: 'What else are you going to show me?'

It is getting dark and everyone is tired – the maestro, his Indian
hosts, and the driver who has spent eight hours at the wheel. When
they reach another village, the maestro is guided to a rest house,
which is actually no more than a room. He says, 'Thank you very
much,' and shuts the door behind him.

The Indians are left staring at the door, wondering where they will
sleep that night.

Not much of a story, but it does reveal to me how much we in India
have to learn about dealing with characters like the maestro. What is it that
prevents us from asserting our own territory? Playing the host, without
submitting to deference and exploitation?

At one level, perhaps, we all have something to gain from affiliating
ourselves to the maestro. Who knows? He may even arrange a trip abroad
for us, especially if we transport a couple of tribal performers (truly
'indigenous' material). Of course, the maestro may forget his promise, but
an invitation abroad is always worth hoping for – apart from making
connections, we could always buy a video for the family.

Let us not also forget that the maestro has important connections within
India itself, people who embody power in the highest cultural and political
offices. The maestro is a guest of the government. Not only is he
supremely established in 'the west', he has even shown the deepest 'human'

feelings for the so-called Third World (which he views synonymously with the Orient).

He loves the Orient not for its poverty (which he excludes from his consciousness), or for the despotism of its leading families (whose 'excesses' have nothing to do with his art). Rather, he is drawn to the Orient for its secrets, its ineffable truths that are so sadly absent (so he feels) in his own culture.

Now he could admire the Orient at a safe distance, like Gordon Craig, and still earlier, the Schlegels, for whom the Orient was a text. But this is difficult at a time when one has direct access to the artefacts of the Orient – rituals, ceremonies, performance techniques, costumes, masks, folk dances, poems, epics. Instead of viewing these artefacts within their own contexts, the maestro is more concerned with using them for his own purpose. He does this not by imitating them, but by converting them into raw material for his own intercultural experiments.

It doesn't matter to his friends in India what he does to this material, so long as he comes up with something that the western press can describe as 'the greatest cultural event of the century'. Through his intervention, India has once again asserted its position in the international world of culture (Attenborough's *Gandhi* being one of the biggest breakthroughs). The maestro's representation becomes the authorized model of 'professionalism', 'perfection', and even 'magic', qualities in short supply back in India.

What is it that perpetuates this appropriation of our culture? Why do we invite this usurpation of our territory? When the maestro shuts the door in our face, why do we accept it? Why can't we knock on the door and ask him to share the roof (if we happen to have some faith in intercultural exchange), or else get him to leave?

Peter Brook's *Mahabharata* exemplifies one of the most blatant (and accomplished) appropriations of Indian culture in recent years. Very different in tone from the Raj revivals, it none the less suggests the bad old days of the British Raj, not in its direct allusions to colonial history – *The Mahabharata*, after all, deals with our 'ancient' past, our 'authentic' record of traditional Hindu culture. For Brook's Vyasa, it is nothing less than 'the poetical history of mankind'.[1] Within such a grandiose span of time, where does the Raj fit? Not thematically or chronologically, I would argue, but through the very enterprise of the work itself; its appropriation and reordering of non-western material within an orientalist framework of thought and action, which has been specifically designed for the international market.

It was the British who first made us aware in India of economic appropriation on a global scale. They took our raw materials from us, transported them to factories in Manchester and Lancashire, where they were transformed into commodities, which were then forcibly sold to us in

India. Brook deals in a different kind of appropriation: he does not merely take our commodities and textiles and transform them into costumes and props. He has taken one of our most significant texts and decontextualized it from its history in order to 'sell' it to audiences in the west.

Though we may not be aware of it, our government has 'bought' this appropriation of our culture through its official support of the production in Europe and America. It will continue to support the production in Japan as part of its promotion of 'festival culture' throughout the world. Eventually, we may even see the production in India itself – where else but on the banks of the Ganges? If this materializes, I hope some concessions will be made for the tickets, which cost over $90 in New York (a sum of money that could support the average Indian family for an entire month, if not more).

One could dismiss this appropriation were it not for the scale of its operation and magnitude of its effect. It has been hailed as 'one of the theatrical events of this century' (*Sunday Times*, London) by a reviewer who, I assume, is both very old and omniscient. 'Enthralled audiences' have watched the 'landmark of our times', imagining it to be a truthful adaptation of 'a classical Indian epic'. Actually, the very association of *The Mahabharata* with western assumptions of the 'epic' minimizes its importance. *The Mahabharata* is not merely a great narrative poem; it is our *itihasa*, the fundamental source of knowledge for our literature, dance, painting, sculpture, theology, statecraft, sociology, ecology – in short, our *history* in all its detail and density.

Instead of confronting this history with his international group of actors in Paris (of whom Mallika Sarabhai is the only Indian participant), Brook has created a so-called 'story' of *The Mahabharata* in association with Jean-Claude Carrière. This 'story' reads, in my view, like a rather contrived and overblown fairytale, not unlike their trite adaptation of a twelfth-century Sufi poem by Farid ud-din Attar in *The Conference of the Birds*. The significant difference in the adaptations is one of scale: if *Conference* resembled an oriental version of *Jonathan Livingston Seagull* in its hour-long summary of 5,000 philosophical verses, the *Mahabharata* is nothing less than *The Ten Commandments* of contemporary western theatre.

At one level, there is not much one can do about stopping such productions. After all, there is no copyright on *The Mahabharata*. (Does it belong to India alone? or is it an Indian text that belongs to the world?) I am not for a moment suggesting that westerners should be banned from touching our sacred texts. I am neither a fundamentalist nor an enthusiast of our own Ramanand Sagar's serialization of *The Ramayana* on Doordarshan every Sunday morning. Certainly, we are capable of misrepresenting the epics ourselves. All I wish to assert is that *The Mahabharata* must be seen on as many levels as possible within the Indian context, so that its meaning (or rather, multiple levels of meaning) can have some bearing on the lives of the Indian people for whom *The Mahabharata* was written, and who continue to derive their strength from it.

If Brook truly believes that The Epic is universal, then his representation should not exclude or trivialize Indian culture, as I believe it does. One cannot agree with the premise that '*The Mahabharata* is Indian but it is universal'. The 'but' is misleading. *The Mahabharata*, I would counter, is universal *because* it is Indian. One cannot separate the culture from the text.

Having emphasized the contextual necessity for any representation of *The Mahabharata*, I should stress that I am not against Brook's production because it is 'western'. What disturbs me is that it exemplifies a particular *kind* of western representation that negates the non-western context of its borrowing. Of course, one has to accept that Brook has not grown up with The Epic in his childhood, unlike most Indians, who have internalized *The Mahabharata* through a torrent of feelings, emotions, thoughts, taboos, concepts, and fantasies. It is this internalization of 'epic reality' that enables millions of Indians to watch a television serial of *The Ramayana* – synthetic, tacky, sticky in the worst tradition of Hindi films – and transform this representation into a deeply spiritual experience.

I do not expect such a transformation to take place either in Brook or in his audience, who have not grown up with Hindu faith, strengthened through a knowledge (often unconscious) of *dharma, karma, moksha*, and other spiritual concepts and values. Inevitably, any western director of *The Mahabharata* needs to define his own attitude or configuration of attitudes to The Epic. He needs to ask: What does this epic mean to me? But this question, I believe, can be responsibly addressed only after the meaning (or meanings) of *The Mahabharata* have been confronted within their own cultural context.

If this is not possible, if the context remains elusive or bizarre, then the director should not dramatize the epic. Rather, he should focus his attention on his own cultural artefacts, the epics of western civilization like the *Iliad* or the *Odyssey*, which he is more likely to understand. I should also add that if he represented the epics to audiences in the west, he would also be more accountable for his actions and interpretations. He would not be able to get away as he is likely to with his misrepresentation of 'other' cultures.

Brook, however, never once admits in his numerous interviews and comments on *The Mahabharata*, that the Indian context of the epic posed a problem. In fact, the context is never an issue for him. What matters is the 'flavour of India'[2] that is suggested through the *mise-en-scène*. Now at one level, this might seem appropriately modest: a 'flavour', after all, does not seem as important as the 'substance'. But in actuality, nothing could be harder in the theatre than to represent the 'flavour' of another culture. If Brook had been sufficiently aware of the numerous metaphors of cooking that have been used in the *Natyasastra* and other aesthetic commentaries on the *rasa* (literally 'taste') of a performance, he might have used the word with more caution. 'Flavour' is not some mystical aura that emanates from a culture. It is the outcome of a process wherein specific ingredients have been seasoned and blended with spices in particular combinations. The 'flavour' of Indian culture has a definite context. It is what differentiates a curry from a stew, and I am referring not just to the taste, but to the entire history of a people that shapes taste in particular ways.

When Brook says in the foreword to his play that 'we have tried to suggest the flavour of India without pretending to be what we are not', he is gracefully evading a confrontation of the historical context of Indian culture. No one wants Brook to resort to antiquarianism. When he claims that 'we are not attempting a reconstruction of Dravidian and Aryan India of three thousand years ago',[3] we can accept that position. But when, in the next line, he says, 'We are not presuming to present the symbolism of Hindu philosophy,'[4] this qualification is more questionable.

What is *The Mahabharata* without Hindu philosophy? Apart from Krishna (whose pedestrian representation I will deal with later), Brook gives us vignettes of Ganesha, Shiva, Hanuman; some bleak predictions about the end of the world; a scattering of references to *dharma*; and a five-minute encapsulation of the *Bhagavad Gita*. It did not come as a surprise to me when the audience laughed on hearing Krishna's famous advice to Arjuna: 'Act, but don't reflect on the fruits of the action.'[5] If the New York audience laughed, it is not because their own ideology of capitalism and self-interest has been called into question. Krishna's statement came out of the blue without any depth of meaning or resonance. What could have been a moment of revelation was reduced to banality.

The problem is that there is no framework of reference in Brook's production that provides a Hindu perspective of *action* in the larger, cosmic context. No wonder all the characters seem to act arbitrarily, or else under the instigation of Krishna. There is no clear sense of what the characters are compelled to do by virtue of their *swadharma*, or life task. *Dharma* remains an abstraction in the production, evoking neither 'law on which rests the order of the world', nor the 'personal and secret order each human being recognizes as his own'.[6] Even these generalities of *dharma* (as defined by Carrière in his introduction to the play) would be acceptable, though a more rigorous adaptation of *The Mahabharata* would need to represent a character's *swadharma* according to:

desa – the culture in which a person is born;
kala – the period of historic time in which he lives;
srama – the efforts required of him at different stages of his life;

gunas – the innate psycho-biological traits which are the heritage of an individual's previous lives.

All these 'co-ordinates of action' as defined by Sudhir Kakar in *The Inner World*[7] are conspicuous by their absence in Brook's conception of character. Or else, they are travestied through:

a mish-mash of cultures with an overriding aura of 'Indianness';
a total avoidance of historicity, of the social transformation underlying *The Mahabharata* from a tribal to a brahmin-dominated caste society;
a monochromatic presentation of characters with no sense of their evolution through different stages in life;
a failure to suggest that this life is just part of a series of rebirths, relivings of past transgressions, that can cease only through *moksha*.

Not once in the production does one sense that these characters could have lived previous lives (with the exception of Sikhandin, whose tranformation is all too obvious). Nor is there a strong sense of what lies beyond this life; the pyrotechnics on stage and the religiosity of the theatrical atmosphere (particularly when Kunti evokes the three gods to give birth to her sons) convey, at best, a sense of the supernatural. In the absence of any defined religious framework, it is only inevitable that the characters seem to share the Christian universe of their audience – a lapsed Christianity, perhaps, neither fervent nor cynical, but one which nevertheless continues to assume that there is a definite beginning and end to life, a Heaven and a Hell. When the fire burns on stage and there is an aura of incense and marigolds, these are merely oriental touches.

Perhaps another reason for the conceptual fuzziness of the production has to do with the absence of caste distinctions, without which the actions of the characters cannot be fully clarified. Indian characters do not merely act according to their feelings (which is what Brook's characters appear to do), but in accordance to how they are expected to act by virtue of their *dharma*, which in turn is determined by caste. We hear of *kshatryas* in Brook's production, and we see them fight, but we do not learn much about the ethos of their caste. For Brook, the action of fighting is predominantly external; it does not resonate an inner code of values, unlike the *samurai* in Kurosawa's films, who register a total way of living and being through their gestures and stillness. Carrière needs to do much more than to retain the Indian word *kshatrya* to withstand the 'colonization by vocabulary'.[8] He needs to evoke *kshatrya-dharma* through language, gestures and sentiment in a way that transcends the image of the Pandavas and Kauravas as 'warriors'.

As for brahmins, we learn only through inference that the irascible Parashurama is one, even though he is described vaguely as an 'extraordinary hermit' who 'felled twenty-one generations of kshatryas with his

axe'.[9] Why? One never knows. And, then, there is Drona, whose brahminical status is known only before he dies, when Dhryshthadyumna confronts Aswhattaman. How Drona's ritual status contradicted his early
poverty, and how he was rejected by his *kshatrya* friend, King Drupada,
is never touched on in the production. In fact, Drupada is never mentioned
even by name, and Dhryshthadyumna appears only at the end as an
apparition, whose relationship to Draupadi is never acknowledged.

If the caste distinctions had been retained in the production, they would
surely have enhanced the relationships that exist between friends. Krishna
and Arjuna, who belong to the same caste, share an intimacy (not explored
in the production) that Duryodhana and Karna can never hope to share.
As a *suta*, the adopted son of a charioteer, Karna will always be dependent
on Duryodhana's magnanimity. His friendship will always be conditioned
by servility. I don't think that Brook's audience had a clue about the
intensity of Karna's humiliation as a *suta*, because he was never differentiated from the Pandavas or the Kauravas on the level of caste. True, he
does refer to himself as the 'son of a driver',[10] but the rupture in his ritual
status, and his consequent rejection of this status, have no resonance
beyond the obvious fact that he has been wronged. Karna's dilemma seems
entirely personal; it is not situated within the social and ritual structure
of Hindu society, with its accompanying tensions and constraints.

My focus on caste distinctions may appear to be pedantic to the western
spectators of Brook's production. But how does one react to their laughter
when Yudishthira is prevented from entering Heaven because of his com-
panion – a dog?[11] It is not associated with pollution. Its presence is not
likely to desecrate a sacrificial offering of *puja*. But, to the average Hindu,
the significance of Yudishthira's insistence on entering the Kingdom of
Heaven with a dog is profound. His humanity is totally lost in Brook's
production, because there is no context in which to place his seemingly
sacrilegious demand.

At this point, I should stress that it is not impossible for Brook to
suggest the Hindu context of significant gestures and relationships. There
is at least one relationship in the production that is rooted in the Indian
context: the *guru-shishya parampara*. After demonstrating Arjuna's
allegiance to Drona, Brook inserts a masterful scene, barely ten minutes
long, in which a 'minor' character called Ekalavya offers himself to Drona
as a *shishya*.[12] The *guru* rejects him. Undaunted, Ekalavya retreats to the
forest where he worships an idol of Drona (played by Drona himself),
and perfects his archery so that he can pierce 'seven arrows in the jaws
of a dog in the span of a single bark'.[13] Drona discovers his skills and
demands his *gurudakshina* – nothing less than Ekalavya's thumb on his
right hand. The *shishya* obliges and leaves, his skills destroyed forever. Is
this 'cruelty' or 'foresight'?

The representation of this scene indicates that it is possible for Brook to illuminate the Indian context of a particular relationship. He achieves this by juxtaposing the attitudes of Arjuna and Ekalavya to Drona, so that we can sense the interplay of authority and obedience in the traditional teacher-student relationship. The scene 'works' because of the thought contained within it, at once deftly dramatized and sharply punctuated within the mainstream of the narrative. It interrupts the relentless flow of action, where there is almost no lingering on details and episodes. In Ekalavya's absence, the 'story' could have gone on, but this presence is what provides the play with one of its few moments of meaningful exchange.

So much has been made of the fact by westerners that Brook's production is nine hours long. For an epic that is fifteen times longer than the Bible, nine hours is really not that long; in fact, it is pitifully short. To attempt an encapsulation of *The Mahabharata* in its entirety is a *hubris* of sorts, but to limit that encapsulation to nine hours is the *reductio ad absurdum* of theatrical adaptation. It would have been better for Brook to focus on a few scenes.

In India, a Kathakali or Koodiyattam performance would need approximately nine hours to dramatize a single episode from the text, perhaps one of the anecdotes in Brook's production in which we learn, for instance, about how Ganesha got an elephant head.[14] The purpose of traditional performances is not to tell a story from beginning to end, but to dwell on specific moments in the story, so that its minutest details can evoke a world of sensations and truth.

At this point, I should emphasize that I am not advocating Brook should have imitated our traditional performances, whose disciplines require years of training and total dedication. I respect his decision to create his own idiom of theatre and acting, but I regret that it has not absorbed some of the fundamental *principles* underlying traditional narratives in India. Without an understanding of these principles, I don't believe that the narratives make much sense.

Unlike the 'west', where there is no performance tradition that has come down to us from antiquity, where the most definitive treatise on Greek theatre, the *Poetics*, has little to say about performance, we in India have a living history of traditional performances and a body of critical writing on acting and aesthetics, where the most intricate iconography of performance has been schematized. Unlike contemporary directors of Greek plays, who inevitably run up against problems of representation, a director of any traditional literature related to India has both the advantage *and the responsibility* to confront traditional performances within their own aesthetic contexts.

Once again, I emphasize that the purpose of the confrontation is not to imitate, but to imbibe principles of narration and performance that can inspire significant points of departure for the contemporary artist. This confrontation is necessary for both Peter Brook and the contemporary directors of the Indian theatre, whose attempts to 'imitate' tradition have frequently resulted in exotic, proscenium-bound, 'folk' spectacles. I am aware that the confrontation is not without pain for many of our artists, who are at once close to tradition, and yet removed from it. I also realize why some of them may feel the need to reject tradition altogether, but this rejection, I believe, can be meaningful only after confronting it, almost 'fighting' with it in the tradition of *The Mahabharata*. If we have to 'kill' our tradition today, we must be in a position to do so *respectfully*. Yudishthira had to touch Bhishma's feet before receiving the right to kill him.

Whether Brook has considered if he has earned the right to 'kill' tradition, I do not know. Perhaps this consideration comes from my own sense of history, which is different from Brook's. Certainly, one does not sense any struggle in his representation of the text; the 'gigantic undertaking' is supremely controlled like any big production on Broadway, the material always kept at a safe distance, so that its tensions never ignite. For all the years of work that Brook and Carrière have spent on their *chef d'oeuvre*, it seems to me that their impulse has been not to get closer to India, but to distance themselves from it altogether.

Significantly, when Brook encountered *The Mahabharata* for the first time in Kathakali performance, he admits that after the 'unforgettable shock' of the dancer's first appearance, he found himself moving away from the performance. The story being told was 'something mythical and remote, from another culture, nothng to do with my life'.[15] While appreciating the honesty of this response, I wish that Brook could have devoted more time to understanding the 'hieratic gestures' of the performance, instead of settling for a more 'ordinary' and 'accessible' repetition of the same performance.

Brook's inadequate confrontation of Indian tradition is characterized by short cuts. Instead of opening himself to the discomfort and vulnerability of learning the gestures of a tradition (which could have resulted in failure), Brook arranges for the tradition to be represented in such a way that he can understand it. He does not enter the 'jungle' of the text with its labyrinthine paths and dense growth: rather, he listens to versions of the text, from which he creates his own paraphrase. Despite the much-publicized 'research' for the project (which Carrière claims received the 'benediction of saints', though P. Lal is the only living Indian scholar mentioned by name[16]), it seems to me that very few risks have been taken in preparing the script for the production.

Accessibility is the determining principle of this adaptation. So dominant is the directorial impulse to engage the western audience's attention that a dramaturgy is created which makes no demands whatsoever on the very act of seeing an epic on stage. For Carrière, the 'inexhaustible richness' of The Epic 'defies all structural, thematic, historic or psychological analysis'.[17] Perhaps it is with this premise in mind that he has reduced The Epic to a chronological sequence of episodes that are structurally linked to the well-made play tradition of Scribe and Sardou and the historical chronicles of nineteenth-century theater. Vyasa's epic has been systematized into three parts: *The Game of Dice, Exile in the Forest, The War,* his intricate structure of storytelling reduced to a line of action.

If Brook had given some importance to the cyclical nature of time that pervades *The Mahabharata*, he would have rejected the validity of dramatizing The Epic in a predominantly linear narrative. Nothing could be more foreign to *The Mahabharata* than linearity. This 'foreignness' is not just a formal blunder, it distorts the very meaning of the narrative. Only at rare moments in the production (which are also memorable) does the past coalesce with the present, such as the time when Kunti is visited by the Sun – a flashback that interrupts the sequence where Karna first appears in the tournament.[18] A more intricate dispersal of time occurs during Arjuna's encounter with Shiva, which is observed by four other characters in a different time-space, who all kneel when the god reveals his identity.[19] In this scene, there are sharp transitions between dialogues with Karna and Arjuna, then Karna and Duryodhana, and finally Arjuna and Urvasi. What is missing from the dramaturgy is a simultaneity of action; the differing sets of time and space do not dissolve in a continuum.

Nowhere in the production is there a recurrence of a particular image that gains in depth through its repetition. The blood that steadily reddens the pool of water on stage in *The War* is merely a visual effect. What one misses is a sense of time that transcends chronology, time concretized through gestures and echoes, time that stretches into infinity. In his introduction to the play, Carrière pays tribute to this 'immense poem, which flows with the majesty of a great river'.[20] And yet his own flow of words is more like a sputter, the rhythm chopped with mechanical precision. Time is truncated into blocks of action, acts and scenes that have definite beginnings and ends.

When Brook's Krishna says that 'He spoke for a long time, a very long time'[21] in his discourse to Arjuna on the battlefield, we should *feel* this 'long time'. In addition, at different points in the production, we should sense the interpenetration of past, present and future, through either imagery or language. In the original text, after Draupadi has been humiliated, the blind Dhritarashtra says: 'I see the scene right before me now: long-armed Satyaki dragging and molesting the entire Kaurava army as if it were a weak, helpless woman'. He is seeing the future on the battlefield, while unconsciously remembering the immediate past (in which Draupadi has been dragged by the hair and molested), and he is registering both these events in the present moment.

Needless to say, there are no such encapsulations of time in Brook's production. The narrative always moves forward with predictable briskness, especially towards the end where the death of Abhimanyu is followed by the deaths of Ghatotkatcha, Drona, Duhsassana, Karna and Duryodhana in quick succession, one scene for each death, all over in less than three hours. What is the point? I asked myself while watching this saga of action. Kurukshetra is not the fifth act of *Macbeth*. There are sentiments, lulls in the action, and the deepest tragic moments that need to be lingered over for the action to make any sense. Without pause, intensifications of detail and patterns of return, this *Mahabharata* means nothing. It is 'a tale told by an idiot, full of sound and fury, signifying nothing'.

After seeing the production, I was compelled to question whether the 'story' of *The Mahabharata* makes much sense outside of the conventions of storytelling to which it belongs. Can a story be separated from the ways in which it is told to its own people? We Indians are known for our circumlocutions. Whether we are describing a family quarrel or the plot of a Hindi film, we never seem to get to the point. Always, the elaboration is more important than the thrust of the narrative. There is no steady progression in our narratives from exposition to complication to climax to denouement, as in the well-made play. For us, the climaxes are at the very beginning, while the complications invariably stimulate new beginnings. Time never seems to matter – a story lasts for as long as there is a need for it. In this regard, the teller of the story is totally dependent on the participation of the listener, who is invariably vocal and deeply involved in the labyrinthine process of the story which he may already know.

Of course, the situation is different for Brook, who is telling the 'story' of *The Mahabharata* to a western audience *for the first time*. Consequently, one cannot expect any 'shared experience' (to use Walter Benjamin's phrase) that unites the actors and spectators within the world of the story. Perhaps, to counter this problem, Brook introduces the character of the Boy, who listens to the story as told by Vyasa from beginning till the end. Unfortunately, this child does not participate in the action at all – he merely asks questions in a rather uninflected, disinterested way: 'Who are you? What's that? Where have you been?' Sometimes he is permitted a little levity, for instance when he asks Ganesha how his mother managed to 'do it alone'. More clumsily, he is given the privilege to ask the final questions of the dying Krishna: 'Why all your tricks? And your bad directions?'[22] (Imagine a child saying that to a god!)

None the less, the child survives Krishna and becomes the contemporary descendant of the Bharatas, 'one of us'. More than as an emblem of survival, however, the Boy serves as Brook's central narrative device by linking the various episodes through his questions. Brook uses the Boy to control the receptivity of the audience. By lulling us with his innocent questions, to which he always receives paternalistic responses from Vyasa (Brook's surrogate), the Boy disarms criticism and compels us to watch the play with naive wonder.

With such a strategic use of the Boy, it is not surprising that he has no life as a character. But how can one accept a lacklustre, two-dimensional portraiture of Krishna, who comes across as an elder statesman, doctrinaire and avuncular? We know that the Krishna of *The Mahabharata* does not belong to the *bhakti* tradition, but is it possible to imagine any Krishna without charisma, without flashes of divinity and danger?

In Carrière's text, almost all of Krishna's 'misdeeds' are summarized – how he got the sun to set so that Jayadratha could be killed, how he instigated Karna to use his sacred weapon against Ghatotkatcha, how he organized Aswhattaman's false death. The audience gets to know all these facts systematically as the scenes are presented in a precise chronology, but we never really *see* Krishna in action, attacking Bhishma 'like a destructive comet'. When Sisupala insults him, he merely raises his voice, but his presence does not change. In fact, as played by Bruce Myers, there is little or no transformation in this most elusive of characters.

This is particularly evident in the scene depicting Krishna's death, where there is no evocation of the massacre of his clan, which he has willed himself. Without the massacre, there is no context in which to situate Krishna's choice to end his life. In his final moments, we should no longer see a 'god embellished in glory', but, as Buddhadeva Bose says, 'a life-weary being ... who has assumed an explicit mortality as proof of his divine power'.[23] The triviality of Krishna's death (suicide?), caused by a stray arrow, has no poignance in Brook's production, because we never feel anything for his Krishna. Myers illuminates neither the divinity nor the intense mortality of his character, leave alone their interpenetration. An actor playing Krishna should be more human than any other actor on stage, and yet evoke a spiritual order of being; he should fill the stage with his energy, and yet remain curiously detached. These contradictions, however, would need a more textured, multi-levelled text than the one provided by Carrière.

Almost all of the characters in Brook's *Mahabharata* are presented in outline, with their inner energies and fire missing. Brook seems to use the characters to tell *his* story, so that they rarely ignite and acquire lives of their own. Most of the characters are so undifferentiated that they almost blend into each other. The ones who stand out are those who assert energies in solitary splendour. Amba, for instance, is given a thoroughly convincing performance by Hélène Patarot in a characterization driven by hate. In her own way, this French actress has delved into the *sthaibhava* of the role to create a revengeful state of being. 'Hate keeps me young'[24]: we see the very drive of this emotion in Amba's second exit, as she sloshes her way through the river on stage, her heavy skirt dragging along, in pursuit of Bhishma.

Like Amba, the other characters who make a strong impression – Bhima, Karna and the Sun – are played by actors whose energies cut through the triteness of the text. Bhima, in particular, played by the robust Senegalese actor Mamadou Dioume, conveys dimensions of anger. In his outraged response to Duryodhana's insulting offer of 'stinking bogs',[25] the actor is able to suggest a raw, yet potent awareness of land as property. When he tickles Kitchaka to death, his wrath activates and ultimately overwhelms the farcical situation. And finally, on removing Duhsassana's guts (picturesquely concretized through a ribbon), he builds his rage to a truly rousing dance of vengeance, before subsiding into silence: 'We weren't born to be happy. Farewell.'

Indeed, a great deal of Bhima's theatricality is somewhat contrived, especially when he relishes his enemy's blood, 'more delicious than mother's milk'.[26] Despite this broad bravura that caricatures the 'noble savage', Bhima does hold one's attention in an undeniably vibrant performance. Equally winning is the Sun, played expansively by Mavuso Mavuso, an actor of Swazi origins, who exudes lust without trivializing the status of the role. Most riveting of all is Karna, played by Jeffery Kissoon (yet another actor partly of African origin), who expresses the rejection of his character with smouldering fire and dignity. I admired the intensity of the performance, but found it constrained and falsely coloured by the traps of 'psychological realism'. Particularly in the scene with Kunti, where Karna promises to kill Arjuna, I realized how inappropriate it is for actors to play an 'epic moment' by surrendering to emotions and clutching on to each other in mutual pain. The grief of Vyasa's characters cannot be physicalized in so literal a manner. It is both part of our world, and yet goes beyond it.

Brook has failed to provide his actors with modes of representing emotion that belong to the 'epic'. Apart from some attempts to 'distance' the characters through third-person narratives, he settles for a heroic mode of acting that passes off as Shakespearean in the 'deadly' tradition of British theatre. Most of *The Mahabharata* actors could have been playing Shakespearean roles: Abhimanyu is startlingly similar to Young Siward in his youthful courage; Duryodhana fights like Macbeth, ranting and raving, but he also evokes Richard III in his Machiavellian strategies and self-destruction ('I want to be discontented')[27]; even Arjuna has a moment when he suggests Macduff's grief on losing his son. Apart from 'Shakespeareana', Brook uses the colourful and extravagant pantomime tradition for 'oriental characters' like Virata, Gudeshna and Kitchaka; as for Satyavati's father, he is straight from the *Pirates of Penzance*.

Apart from simplifying the epic characters within these modes of acting,

240

reducing them at times to the level of cartoons, Brook erases some characters altogether. The contemplative Vidura is cut, because, as Carrière
claims, 'his effect on the plot is minor'.[28] 'Plot': that's just the problem.
An epic doesn't have a plot; it has levels of action that merge and separate,
creating a multitude of circles, eddying and blending into one another. If
one wants to adapt an epic for the stage, one must be aware of these
levels of action. Carrière's workmanlike affinities to the plot would be
more appropriate for a Hollywood scenario of *The Mahabharata*.

In fact, it is odd how closely the text resembles the screenplay of
Attenborough's *Gandhi* in its organized, steadily paced linearity, all the
actions thudding along with predictable clarity. Both works are reductive
encapsulations of epic material, big-budget enterprises that are part of the
dominant productive systems in the west. Both represent images of India
that are essentially removed from our historical reality, though Brook's
orientalism is more apparent in colour and spectacle than Attenborough's
more muted representation of the Raj. Perhaps the crucial difference is
that Brook is something of a nihilist, who seems to accept the end of the
world with equanimity – Kenneth Tynan was the first to emphasize his
'shallow and factitious pessimism' and 'moral neutrality' in his representation of *The Ik*.[29] Attenborough, on the other hand, is more of an
optimist, who propagates by his own admission a Mary Poppins brand of
old-fashioned humanism.

Now to return to the problem of erasure in the representation of
The Mahabharata's characters. Very often, a character appears with no
background whatsoever, and disappears in a few minutes without providing anything beyond 'plot development'. One of the most enigmatic of
such presences (or, rather, absences) is Maya, who introduces himself as
the 'supreme architect', who wishes to build a palace for the Pandavas –
a 'magic palace . . . where thoughts become real'.[30] Instead of indulging
these pretty phrases, Carrière should have given us some clue as to why
Maya wants to favour the Pandavas with his skills.

The truth is that he is obliged to do so. Maya, an *asura* or demon, is
one of the seven characters who escaped from the Khandava forest, after
it was burned down by Agni with the active assistance of Arjuna and
Krishna. Obliged to satisfy Agni's 'hunger', these two heroes guard the
forest on all sides, preventing every bird, animal and Naga from escaping.
Mayasabha, the 'magic palace', is built on the ashes of their unpardonable
genocide.

Even if one accepts that it would have been difficult for Brook to stage
the burning of the forest, though a narration of the event would have
been chilling in its own right, how can one accept the erasure of context
from Maya's representation? More critically, how can we begin to understand a major character like Kunti if we don't know anything of her past
oppression – the cursory way in which she is handed over by her own

father to Kuntibhoja, so that she can look after the irascible sage Durvasa like a good hostess? And then, of course, she is married off to Pandu, who is doomed to be impotent. Instead of reflecting some attitude to the circumstances of her life, Brook seems to accept her lot with equanimity. I am not advocating an explicitly feminist reading of Kunti, though many women (both Indian and western) would legitimately demand one. I call into question the seeming neutrality of the entire representation that prevents Brook and Carrière from taking a position in relation to the problem of the text.

In the opening sequence of the production, Vyasa claims that his 'poetical history of mankind' is as 'pure as glass, yet nothing is omitted'.[31] His rhetoric reveals the aura of completion that pervades Brook's production, an aura that gives the illusion of The Epic speaking itself with minimal interventions. This view is substantiated by Carrière himself in his introduction to the play, when he emphasizes the necessity of entering the 'deepest places' of the characters 'without interposing our concepts, our judgements or our twentieth-century analysis, in so far as that is possible'.[32] What seems like a very graceful concern for the integrity of The Epic is also an evasion of responsibility. Carrière assumes that a perception of the 'deepest places' is possible without a critical consciousness. It is almost as if *The Mahabharata* lies beyond questioning, and that its 'story' can be told only through some mystical communion with the work itself.

Nothing could be more removed from the truth. If *The Mahabharata* is very much alive in India today, it is because it has always invited the most turbulent questions from its most ardent supporters. When I stress how the work should be situated in its context, I do not for a moment assume that this context cannot be questioned in relation to our own consciousness today. Take Irawati Karve, one of the most respected interpreters of the text, who is not reluctant to state categorically that 'the sole aim of the burning of the Khandava forest was the acquisition of land and the liquidation of the Nagas'.[33] She goes on to judge the event: 'But the cruel objective was defeated. Just as Hitler found it impossible to wipe out a whole people, so did the Pandavas. All they gained through this cruelty were the curses of hundreds of victims and three generations of enmity.'[34]

If Carrière had been truly inspired by Karve's *Yuganta* (which he acknowledges in his introduction), he would not have 'purified' *The Mahabharata* of 'concepts', 'judgements' and 'analysis'. Actually his very attempt to dramatize *The Mahabharata* without contemporary interventions is disingenuous, because the production does have a dominant theme. 'That theme is threat', says Carrière, 'we live in a time of destruction.'[35] There are countless references to this theme (Brook's all-time favourite) in *The Mahabharata*, particularly towards the end as the play draws to a bloody close. At one point, a nuclear calm descends on the earth after Aswhattaman's 'sacred missile' infiltrates space and is countered through non-resistance. 'Quick, lie on the ground, don't move,' Krishna advises the Pandavas, 'empty your minds, make a void. One mustn't resist this weapon, not even in thought.'[36]

It is unlikely that this attitude would receive the support of anti-nuclear activists, but at least there is an attitude here that directs the text in a particular way. Unfortunately, there are no clearly discernible attitudes in Brook's approach to Kunti, who merely suffers with a stoic calm. So does Gandhari, a monolith of endurance, whose passivity is rarely disturbed by flashes of inner resentment. How does a woman who is married off to a blind husband accept her lot? What is the significance of her self-enforced blindness? When Brook's Gandhari ties a band around her eyes for the first time, she declares: 'Now I can never reproach my husband his misfortune.'[37]

Immediately after this noble statement, an apotheosis of resignation, she is joined by Dhritarashtra. 'Deeply moved,' so the stage direction goes, 'he takes her in his arms'.[38] Now this is just too touching even by Hindi film standards. If Brook had wanted to show this image of total fidelity and mutual acceptance, and later counterpoint it with expressions of Gandhari's resentment, the strategy could have been effective. But his Gandhari remains the same from beginning till the end. Not once do we suspect that she conceals a deep anger, or that her wedding night (so tellingly emphasized by Karve)[39] was a torture for Dhritarashtra. Only at the end, when they retreat to the forest, does Brook's Dhritarashtra acknowledge, 'I felt your anger. I always felt it close to me'.[40] If only we in the audience had felt it. Mireille Maalouf's stately Gandhari would have been memorable. But unfortunately she remains dutiful to her director, who does not permit her to take off her blindfold, even though her husband orders her to.

Unlike Gandhari, Draupadi is permitted more anger by Brook, but once again it is not sufficiently contextualized. The status of Draupadi, her birth through *yajna*-fire, her family and political affiliations, are never clarified in the production. She merely appears early in the play and is promptly shared by the five brothers, because Kunti 'can't take back her word'.[41] Draupadi, 'the paragon of women', accepts her situation in silence.

Contrary to what some spectators in the west may believe, polyandry is not a common practice in India. Draupadi's marriage poses problems even in the Indian context. Commenting on the problem, Buddhadeva Bose says that 'Kunti was mortified about *adharma* when she saw Draupadi', after giving her word.[42] Yudishthira, too, encouraged Arjuna to marry her, though this would have resulted in another form of *adharma* (a younger brother cannot marry first). In addition, Bose emphasizes that Draupadi's marriage was strongly resisted by her own father, Drupada, who asserts that, 'The *sastras* may approve of one man having many wives, but we have never heard of one woman having many husbands'. All these oppositions and doubts are erased in Brook's production. His Draupadi accepts her lot because of the mother-in-law's word.

'*Nathyavati anathavat*': married, but like a widow. This terrible paradox in Draupadi's life is a source of pain, but it also elicits the deepest questions. What is stirring is that these questions come from Draupadi herself. She argues her own case, rejecting a woman's traditional silence, and acquires in the process the reputation of a 'lady pundit'. Draupadi does not allow her anger to simmer within herself. It explodes in the scene where she is dragged to the assembly, after her first husband has presumed to lose her in a game of dice after losing himself.

To whom does she belong? Her husband or to herself? To what extent is a wife the slave of her husband? What are the rights of slaves? Does Yudishthira have more rights over Draupadi than her other husbands? Can the four brothers collectively disown Yudishthira? Only some of these questions are raised in Brook's production without enhancing the intense humiliation of Draupadi. When she entreats Bhishma, 'Can one belong to someone who has lost himself?', he responds quizzically, 'I am troubled. The question is obscure.'[43] This line gains a tremendous laugh, because not once are we made to feel that Draupadi has been seriously wronged.

Brook directs the scene with a fast pace, his eye on the 'miracle', when yards of cloth unfold from Draupadi's robe in the tradition of stage tricks from pantomime, the sea of tears in *Alice in Wonderland* created through cloth. One never really senses the threat of rape in Duhsassana's handling of Draupadi, and, consequently, Krishna's intervention seems merely obligatory. In the original text, the nakedness of Draupadi is heightened through her dress, a single garment tied around the waist, which is the traditional garb of a woman in her period, a state of ritual pollution. Instead of heightening the outrage inflicted on her, Brook covers it up with facile theatricality. Like the actors on stage, we watch the scene without feeling any need to judge the action. When Draupadi wails, 'Where is dharma?', it seems like pointless hysteria, a case of a woman not being able to shut up on time.

Draupadi's lines do not resonate because of Mallika Sarabhai's monotonous delivery. Though she obviously knows English better than many of the other actors, who are speaking it for the first time on stage in a bewildering range of accents, her own voice never comes through. She speaks as she has been directed to speak, unlike some of the African actors, whose rhythms resist the 'simple, precise, restrained language' created by Carrière and translated by Brook. Sarabhai's energy is somewhat muted, even though she is obviously the only 'authentic' Indian presence on stage, with black hair, brown skin and expressive eyes. Unfortunately, her gestures are constrained within a realistic structure of acting, which does not permit any suggestion of Draupadi's sensuality in the original text.

When she approaches Bhima before the killing of Kitchaka, she does not merely wake him up in an agitated state, as in Brook's production. She is subtlety itself in her movement: 'Like a white-winged female crane or a three-year old forest cow, the bathed and cleansed Draupadi appeared in the kitchen before Bhima, who was like a bull in strength and size. As a creeper climbs and clings around a giant sal tree on the banks of the Gomati, so did she embrace the middle Pandav. . . . Like a female elephant, she pressed herself upon Bhima, the great elephant, and said in a voice melodious as the *veena* of a *gandhar*, "Wake up, Bhimsen, wake up . . .".[44] I quote this passage at length to convey the possibilities of texture in the gestures and movements of Draupadi, so sadly absent in Sarabhai's performance. Brook does not give her the freedom to dance, the primary constituent of *abhinaya*. Now if she could have expressed herself through dance even for a few moments, her culture would have been embodied in the performance. But that's obviously what Brook didn't want; it would have become 'too Indian', destroying the balance of his intrinsically western order and taste.

What is the point of assembling an international group of actors if the expressive possibilities of their cultures are negated in the production? The cast includes actors from England, France, Turkey, Japan, Iran, Poland, Italy, South Africa, Senegal, Indonesia and India – an impressive representation, no doubt; the United Nations of Theatre. But what is the point if most of the actors' voices, rhythms and performance traditions have been homogenized within a western structure of action, where they have to speak a language unknown to most of them? Of course, this language has to be either English or French – how could one possibly imagine this *Mahabharata* in Sanskrit, or, for that matter, in any non-western language?

What would be harder to question is Brook's use of *one* language for the entire production. He has obviously learned from his early experiment on *Orghast* in Persepolis, for which Ted Hughes created a 'universal' language from the sounds and syllables of Greek, Latin and the ritual language of the Zend-Avesta. This 'pretentious gibberish' (as Ossia Trilling described Hughes' 'adapted language'[45]) is far removed from the chaste English used in the American production of *The Mahabharata*. In fact, I would be tempted to describe it as the 'Queen's English', it is so proper and grammatically precise.

Undeniably, when Yoshi Oida speaks this language, he brings a very appealing humour to the intonations of Drona. He is also able to separate himself from the language – his voice does one thing, his body another, which creates a very interesting tension. But for many other actors, who have had much less experience with Brook's interculturalism, the enforced use of the English language is unfortunate. Their voices are reduced to accents, almost incomprehensible at times, which distract attention from their presence on stage. It was particularly sad to see (or rather, hear) the great Cieslak hindered by his muffled diction in an otherwise regal performance as Dhritarashtra. But what is the point of a 'real performance' from an actor who has probably crossed more psycho-physical barriers than any other performer in the western theatre? This Dhritarashtra is a regression for Grotowski's foremost disciple – it is like watching a great artist play Blind Man's Bluff in a charade.

Many critics in New York complained about the unintelligibility of some of the actors. Brook associated their comments with a 'form of conservatism' that 'jealously protects values, *European* values, which in Europe are much freer'.[45] Though there is some truth in this statement, I believe that it is Brook himself who is more seriously Eurocentric in his advocacy of a theatre where the cultures of the world can be subsumed within his European structure and framework of values.

As much as he dislikes the term, Brook's *Mahabharata* is a 'cultural salad' of which he is the unacknowledged chef. The materials of this 'salad' have come from all parts of the world, but it is Brook's 'house dressing' which gives the 'salad' its distinct taste. Occasionally, we do get some faint 'tastes' of other cultures that manage to retain their identity; there are also eruptions of energy that break through the *mise-en-scène*. But, invariably, these energies are constrained by the limits set on them, or else they are permitted to indulge in what becomes a parody of otherness (for example, the tribal tomfoolery of Hidimbi and Ghatotkatcha that exudes 'Africanness').

What cannot be denied is that Brook controls his disparate materials with total authority. He puts his stamp on all of them, whether it is a mask or a prop or an instrument. His eclecticism is perfectly disciplined, there is never an element out of place. He knows exactly what he wants, and he gets it. Once he places his mark on his materials, they no longer belong to their cultures. They become part of his world.

While I would situate this directorial method within the context of appropriation, there are many other scholars and artists who would view his work in a more harmonious and universal context. Richard Schechner, for instance, in an interview with Brook himself, has claimed that, 'Of the intentionally intercultural productions I've seen, your *Mahabharata* is the finest example of something genuinely syncretic'.[47] During a particular moment in the production, when Australian Aborigine didgeridoos (long flutes) were played, Schechner states that, 'The performance actualised (for him) the cultural layerings of India herself: Melanesian, Harappan, Vedic, Sanskritic, Hindu, Muslim, English, Contemporary'.[48] If only such insights were available to us in India, we would not need to worry about the dissensions in our culture. All we would need to do is listen to flutes – not Krishna's but the Australian Aborigine's – to realize our total heritage.

For me, the didgeridoo was one more eclectic element in an orchestra that included a range of exotic instruments. From the programme, we learn of the use of *ney, shanaj, launeddas, fujara, kamantche, analapos,* and of course – for some 'authentic' Indian sound – the *nagaswaram.* Predictably, Brook was happy with Toshi Tsuchitori's score which 'wasn't quite Indian, nor non-Indian, a kind of music that has the "taste" of India'.[49] Though I would not expect to hear *ragas* in Brook's production, I was irritated by the synthetic 'Indianness' of the score – the amateur atmospherics on the *tabla* and obligatory *nagaswaram*, of which we are told that it took three months before Kim Menzer could get a sound out of it.

The music epitomizes the general confusion of the production: it doesn't want to be Indian, and yet it tries to be Indian in its own way. In his interview with Georges Banu, Brook himself clarifies the problem: 'To tell the story we had to avoid evoking India too strongly *so as not to lead us away from human identification*, but also we had to nevertheless tell it as a story rooted in Indian earth' (my italics).[50] This balance is definitely not found in the production. By avoiding a strong evocation of India to ensure 'human [read western] identification', Brook's 'story' could not be 'rooted in Indian earth'. It had to float in some kind of make-believe India, somewhere between imagination and reality, neither here nor there.

The space of the production provides an ideal site for Brook's ambivalences. Once again, there is an 'empty space' (his eternal signature) – a patch of brown earth with a pond and small river, set against a large, dilapidated wall, almost Pompeii-like in its aura of antiquity. This 'natural' vista is framed within the elaborate proscenium of the Majestic Theatre, an 84-year-old vaudeville and opera house, which was abandoned many years ago and then remodelled for *The Mahabharata* production. Millions of dollars were spent not just to renovate the theatre, but to retain its omnipresence of decay. Chloé Obolensky's ambitious design extends to the entire auditorium, where artistically preserved disfigurements and patches of brick on the wall enhance the antique aura on stage.

Only 'the west' could afford to renovate a theatre and then spend more money to make it look old again. This 'aesthetics of waste', as I am tempted to describe the multi-million dollar reconstruction, is symptomatic of post-modern experiments in architecture, where traditional elements are superimposed on contemporary sites. But there is a self-consciousness that guides the best of these experiments, providing irony and wit, tensions that stimulate self-reflexivity and thought. In contrast, Brook's space is predominantly atmospheric. It provides a mystique to the very act of going to the theatre. It makes an occasion out of our attendance.

Where does India fit into this scenario of remote landscapes and evocations of the past? Once again, it exists as a construct, a cluster of oriental images suggesting timelessness, mystery and eternal wisdom. Brook may oppose cultural exoticism in theory, but his own work is exotic in its own right. From a press release of *The Mahabharata*, the selling of the Orient is apparent: 'It unfolds in a swirl of colour – saris, gowns, and garments of saffron, crimson and gold, umbrellas of rippling blue silk, red banners and snow white robes. Heroes lose kingdoms, virgin princesses elope with gods.' Even making allowances for the rhetoric of publicity, I believe that the production does live up to its expectations. It is not a victim, but the apotheosis of hype.

What do people remember of *The Mahabharata*, I wonder? Certainly not the *Bhagavad Gita* (which is over before one is even aware of it), or the characters (who tend to blend into one another after a while). Let us forget more profound matters like the meaning of the 'story' and the context to which it belongs. I believe that what keeps the production going are visual effects, sometimes blatantly magical, like the totally redundant levitation act in Virata's court, and, more pertinently, the disappearance of Kitchaka into a sack after he has been dismembered. There are more sensational effects like Drona pouring a pot of blood over his head, and the serpentine ring of fire that springs out of the earth. Sometimes, the visuals are surprising in their very literalness – for example, the iron ball that emerges from Gandhari's costume and then rolls into the pond, and Bhishma lying on a bed of arrows. Decorating the entire *mise-en-scène*, of course, are explicit icons of Indian culture, now popularized through our cottage industries, like carpets, durries, mats, thalis, marigolds, divas, incense.

In this visual feast of the Orient, India retains its 'glamour' and 'novelty'. For how long, one doesn't know. Already the lure of the Raj is beginning to pall; it is no longer as lucrative for producers to finance another *Far Pavilions*. Interculturalists, who are always on the hunt for materials from the east, are beginning to turn away from India to discover new sources to feed their theories and visions. This *Mahabharata*, now hailed as 'the theatrical event of the century', will be remembered as yet another landmark in Brook's career. But how many people will remember *the Mahabharata* itself? Has this glorious trivialization of our epic brought western people closer to an understanding of India? Or has it merely enhanced the distance that exists between us? Unavoidably, the production raises the question of ethics, not just the ethics of representation, which concerns the decontextualization of an epic from its history and culture, but the ethics of dealing with people (notably Indians) in the process of creating the work itself. For me, the process of Brook's intercultural method of research cannot be separated from the production, even though their links may not be immediately apparent.

Among the numerous directors, writers and artists who have visited India in recent years, either in connection with films on the Raj or for their personal research, Peter Brook has probably left one of the most bitter memories among many of his Indian hosts and benefactors. Of course, he continues to have 'friends' (connections) in the highest places, many of whom have gushed about the French production of *The Mahabharata* (though their knowledge of the language, I suspect, was questionable). But among the many Indians who helped Brook to see traditional performances, meet with gurus, arrange workshops with actors – none of whom received an invitation to Paris – there is a sad consensus of having been used by Brook, of being 'ripped off' as the Americans would say.

There are many stories which have circulated in Indian theatrical circles about how Brook promised to invite a 16-year-old Chhau dancer to Paris, and then forgot about him; how he and his actors invariably failed to respect the ritualistic context of performances; how they were so concerned with their own schedules that they rarely found the time to interact with Indian people; and perhaps, most ignominiously, how they handled money in their deals with Indian artists.[51]

Now there is nothing more powerful than money in the creation (or destruction) of relationships in the Indian theatre, especially at a time when traditional sources of patronage are disappearing and the government support of the arts is both meagre and dependent on official whims. Money has a very different value for an Indian theatre person than for Peter Brook and his company, whose production has been sponsored by numerous foundations (including Ford, Rockefeller and Hinduja), corporations (like AT & T and Yves Saint Laurent International), charitable trusts (the Eleanor Naylor Dana Charitable Trust), industries (Coca-Cola), television channels (Channel 4 – London), and numerous government organizations, notably the French Ministry of Culture and the Indian Council for Cultural Relations. Other official Indian support came from Air India and the Handicrafts and Handlooms Exports Corporation.

In the context of this liberal funding, how can one possibly justify the incident in Kerala where a member of Brook's company refused to pay a petty sum of money that had been agreed upon for a Theyyam performance? It appears that it did not meet the expectations of Brook's group. For another performance organized by Probir Guha, the fee of Rs.900 for three days' work was regarded with suspicion: 'What is the *real* charge: why is he demanding so much?' Nine hundred rupees was cheap for the work involved, but the attitude of Brook's actor was even cheaper.

Most of these insults have been borne in silence. People talk about it only among themselves. There has been no formal protest against this kind of behaviour. One gets used to it after a while. And yet, when I heard a very intelligent, Marxist critic tell me about how he had been personally humiliated by Brook – he was shaking with rage as he told me his story – I was compelled to ask: 'What did you do?' He replied: 'Nothing. What to do? He's our guest'. The old values, I fear, perpetuate our colonialism.

One must sympathize with Guha's discomfort when Brook failed to follow up on an invitation for a Chhau dancer, who is represented by Guha himself. One senses Guha's loss of credibility in relation both to the boy and to the villagers. But for all his legitimate anger ('We don't want to be guinea pigs for experiments') and the hurt that comes through receiving discarded 'gifts' like a sweater ('It was just an extra for them . . . they don't know how to give'), one is ultimately left with the sense of Guha's deprivation, of feeling left out: 'I really expected at least one invitation to the *Mahabharata*. It's nothing, I wouldn't go because I don't have the money. But I would feel honoured that he remembers me.'

'Honoured': there is true poignance in this word given the context of the relationship. At one level, it is part of our colonial residue, our hankering for some sanction from the west, even after being exploited by it. But what is it that perpetuates this hankering for the west in India today? Perhaps, it is an absence of recognition and economic support that gives Indian artists like Guha the false hope that they can improve their lot by affiliating themselves to Festival India and ventures like *The Mahabharata*.

Why did Guha continue to crave an invitation from Brook, even after being hurt and losing his credibility at home? Awanthi Meduri answers the question boldly: 'He needs the big fish, as much as the big fish need the small fish.' In our existing system of power, Meduri believes that the myth of intercultural exchange, based on premises of trust and friendship, should be associated more categorically with 'transaction'. One should not seek the friendship of big fish; rather, one should 'negotiate a professional relationship' with them.

Though this is by no means an easy task – the big fish are always likely to swallow the little ones, or else co-opt them into their way of thinking – one can begin this 'negotiation' by asserting one's territory. And by territory, I do not merely mean land, or technique or knowledge, but *what is part of us*. There is no need to invite appropriations of this culture: they are neither uplifting for our morale nor particularly lucrative in the long run. Appropriations may not disappear overnight, but we can be more vigilant about them. If there is a need to exchange our culture for insights into another, then the door can be left open for negotiations based on mutual needs and respect. But if someone like the maestro is going to take our culture and, in the bargain, shut the door in our face, we must not be silent any longer.

There is a *Mahabharata* to be fought in India today, not just against cultural appropriations like Brook's production, but against systems of power that make such appropriations possible. We can begin by fighting this battle on our own soil, for our own territory.

NOTES

Originally published in *Theater*, Spring 1988, pp. 6–20; reprinted in Bharucha's *Theatre and the World: Essays on Performance and the Politics of Culture* (New Delhi: Manohar Publishers, 1990).

1 Jean-Claude Carrière, *The Mahabharata* (London: Methuen, 1988), p. 3.
2 Peter Brook's foreword to *The Mahabharata*, op. cit., p. xvi (included in this volume as Chapter 3).
3 ibid.
4 ibid.
5 *The Mahabharata*, op. cit., p. 159.
6 Carrière's introduction to *The Mahabharata*, op. cit., p. xii (included in this volume as Chapter 6).
7 Sudhir Kakar, *The Inner World*, New Delhi, Oxford University Press.
8 Carrière's introduction to *The Mahabharata*, op. cit.
9 *The Mahabharata*, op. cit., p. 109.
10 ibid., p. 36. [The 'mocking' description is Bhima's – ed.]
11 ibid., p. 235.
12 ibid., pp. 30–2.
13 ibid., p. 31.
14 ibid., pp. 4–5.
15 Brook's foreword to *The Mahabharata*, op. cit., p. xiii.
16 Carrière's introduction to *The Mahabharata*, op. cit., p. viii.
17 ibid., p. ix.
18 *The Mahabharata*, op. cit., pp. 34–5.
19 ibid., pp. 98–9.
20 Carrière's introduction to *The Mahabharata*, op. cit., p. ix.
21 *The Mahabharata*, op. cit., p. 160.
22 ibid., p. 231.
23 Buddhadeva Bose, *The Book of Yudhishthir*, translated by Sujit Mukherjee (Hyderabad: Sangam Books, 1986).
24 *The Mahabharata*, op. cit., p. 81.
25 ibid., p. 22.
26 ibid., p. 212.
27 ibid., p. 59.
28 Carrière's introduction to *The Mahabharata*, op. cit., p. x.
29 Kenneth Tynan, 'Director as Misanthropist: On the Moral Neutrality of Peter Brook', *Theatre Quarterly*, 7(25), Spring 1977.
30 *The Mahabharata*, op. cit., p. 46.
31 ibid., p. 3.
32 Carrière's introduction to *The Mahabharata*, op. cit., p. xi.
33 Irawati Karve, *Yuganta: The End of an Epoch* (Poona: Deshmukh Prakashan, 1969), p. 146.
34 ibid.
35 Carrière's introduction to *The Mahabharata*, op. cit., p. ix.
36 *The Mahabharata*, op. cit., p. 200.
37 ibid., p. 21.
38 ibid., p. 22.

39 Karve, *Yuganta*, op. cit., (n31), p. 60.
40 *The Mahabharata*, op. cit., p. 233.
41 ibid., p. 38.
42 Bose, *The Book of Yudhishthir*, op. cit.
43 *The Mahabharata*, op. cit., p. 66.
44 Quoted by Buddhadeva Bose in *The Book of Yudhishthir*, op. cit., Ch. 16.
45 Ossia Trilling, 'Playing with Words in Persepolis', *Theatre Quarterly*, 2(5), January/March 1972.
46 Glenn Loney, 'Myth and Music: Resonances across the Continents and Centuries', *Theater*, 19(2), Spring 1988.
47 *The Drama Review*, 30(1), Spring 1986, p. 57.
48 ibid., p. 55.
49 Interview with Georges Banu, *Alternatives Théâtrales*, no. 24, July 1985, p. 8; translation into English by Rustom Bharucha (included in this volume as Chapter 4).
50 ibid., p. 6.
51 See e.g. Phillip Zarrilli (ed.), 'The Aftermath: when Peter Brook came to town' (an interview with Probir Guha and Deborah Neff), *The Drama Review*, 30(1), Spring 1986; also 'More Aftermath after Peter Brook', *The Drama Review*, 32(2), Summer 1988.

17

SOMETHING MORE VOLCANIC

Michael Kustow

Since collaborating with Brook on *US* in 1966, Michael Kustow has worked as literary adviser at the National Theatre (he was an NT Associate, 1973–80) and as director of the Institute of Contemporary Arts in London. At present he is the Commissioning Editor (Arts) for Channel 4 Television. With Lord Michael Birkett and Harvey Lichtenstein of the Brooklyn Academy of Music in New York, he was executive producer of the *Mahabharata* film.

An egg-shaped space, one half-shell a bank of raked seating, the other a high wall of splintered striated rock, roofed by the sky and stars that Van Gogh saw haloed from Arles. You look down into a bowl of sand dented by a strip of water and a shallow pool. On a boulder behind you a robed musician raises a twisted horn and sounds an earthy fanfare, like an elephant cry. At nightfall in this quarry a few kilometres outside Avignon, Peter Brook's staging of Jean-Claude Carrière's adaptation of *The Mahabharata* begins.

Wisdom-book and story-repository, fifteen times the size of the Bible, *The Mahabharata* was written in Sanskrit, but the words you hear are French, spoken with a piquant diversity of accents matching each actor's distinctive shape, skin and race. A diminutive North African Jew as elephant-headed Ganesha, then as Krishna. Vyasa, the bard of the poem, a ginger-haired Gascon. Tiny, tightbound Japanese, long-limbed loping Senegalese, pale-skinned Germans and Poles, a wide-lipped Lebanese, a princess with streaming black hair and etched eyes – the one Indian in this constellation of colours and silhouettes. A multicultural congregation of actors plays out an ancient accumulation of fantastic fables, wisdom parables and fierce physical confrontations over three nights in an arena of rock, sand, water and fire. You think: this is theatre and not theatre, a play and an encounter that is more than a play, as the stories start to unspool, recounted by the poet-author who is also a figure in his own tapestry of tales.

Peter Brook's *Mahabharata* is not just the reinsertion into the European

253

mind of a saga like the *Iliad*, a compendium of the marvellous like *The Arabian Nights*, a collage of earthly action and transcendental insight like the Bible – and a bumper storybook as gripping as *Star Wars* or the comic-strips through which the adventures of Arjuna and Krishna are purveyed to millions of Indian children today. It is also the culmination of Peter Brook's 15-year-old Centre International de Créations Théâtrales. Brook and Carrière have adapted *The Mahabharata* into three plays: *The Game of Dice*, *The Exile in the Forest* and *The War*. The titles describe the key scenes and actions in the combat between two related clans which forms the heart of *The Mahabharata*: the dice-game in which Yudishthira gambles away his kingdom, his family and himself; the wounding and healing exile in which he, his four brothers and their shared wife learn from loss; and the culminating battle in which multitudes die and yet the world and its inhabitants are restored to a better order, a truer *dharma*.

But *The Mahabharata* is much more than linear narrative. Brook and his company continually come up with kaleidoscopic theatrical actions which embody what is perhaps the deepest attitude of *The Mahabharata*, and of Brook's idea of theatre: that reality is deliquescent, so that there is no single way, political, psychological or moral, to seize it; that we live in a superimposed plurality of worlds and that the truest wisdom – which live theatre is uniquely placed to explore – is never to lose touch with alternative and contradictory universes, while devoting yourself completely to the demands of the world you inhabit.

It is the multi-dimensional, almost sculptural quality in this theatrical event that puts flesh on this philosophy. By framing the action (as the original poem does) with an author who is also a character, Brook and Carrière can constantly vary the conventions of *le récit*; digressing, back-tracking, inserting, speeding up to summarise twenty years in a sentence, slowing down to capture each charged second of the encounter between the warrior Arjuna and the god Krishna on the eve of battle, weaving sub-stories and perspective-shifts into the main flow just as natural and emblematic decoration twines its way into Indian illustration and sculpture, where a god's nose and forehead can be studded with an infinity of tiny figures. This *Mahabharata* is a masterly instance of the surreal plasticity of storytelling, in a theatrical form modelled on the village square.

One scene must stand as an example. Carpets are unrolled and cushions piled high on the stone and sand of the quarry to create a luxurious court. A king and his entourage loll back, enjoying a witty puppet-show produced from behind a multi-coloured cloth. The puppet seems to run amok, stealing kisses from the ladies. It's all very relaxed, recalling the convivial atmosphere of the court entertainment in *A Midsummer Night's Dream*, Brook's climactic Shakespeare production in 1970, before he moved to Paris. The exiled King Yudishthira and his family appear at court, disguised as beggars, servants and eunuchs. They are ordered to tell a story. They begin the tale of Hanuman, the monkey god, and how he prevented Bhima from following the path to Heaven by barring the way with his thick, heavy tail. The disguised Bhima does a clown-show miming the difficulty of the obstacle. Three speeches later, Yudishthira is spellbinding the audience on stage and in the quarry with a fierce description of our dark era of destruction, a foretaste of cataclysmic conflicts and a fable which assumes that the world is already destroyed.

This characteristic scene is a tangible stage-picture – a disguised story-teller in a safe court – of the multiplicity of worlds: a tremor of terror can cross our minds even as we enjoy a show of comfort and pleasure. Throughout Brook's *mise-en-scène*, emblems and images conjured up in the quarry give a flickering apprehension of reality. The stage lighting of Jean Kalman shrinks, shifts and expands the space; the cracked rockface and standing sheets of water are illuminated by a galaxy of candles and torches, until they tremble insubstantially in your mind's eye. Chloé Obolensky's costumes – rich silks, expansive embroidered dresses, vivid Kathakali colours and dried-out sacking, cuirasses and boots suggesting feudal Tudors and Japanese *samurais*, saffron and white robes against glittering sand – open out the harmonics of the story and the national variety of the actors, while Brook makes her bamboo screens, bows and arrows and chariot wheels into both literal story elements and symbolic emblems of the mastery of life or the imminence of death. Rivulets of flame snake across the arena as Arjuna climbs the Himalayas to meet the god Shiva and gain knowledge of the decisive 'divine weapon'. This kind of theatre almost transcends the stubborn materiality of bodies and things on a stage.

Brook has succeeded in drawing from his company – who are truly a company, in that they have committed to stay with *The Mahabharata* through all its peregrinations until 1987 – a series of performances which, while respecting the ethnic particularities of each actor, focus a penetrating light on the characters of *The Mahabharata*. Vittorio Mezzogiorno brings to Arjuna fine-drawn attentiveness, a gentle virility which recalls the delicate strength of figures in Raphael; Mireille Maalouf, binding her eyes to share her blind husband's disability and transfixed by every fresh disclosure of the war, gives Gandhari a dignity and tragic acceptance which owe much to bitter experience of the war in her native Lebanon; Matthias Habich as Yudishthira is a flaxen-haired Dürer knight searching for the true path; Maurice Bénichou, who is French but of a North African Jewish family, has Mediterranean ease and a childlike gravity as Krishna; Alain Maratrat as Vyasa the poet has the Ancient Mariner authority of a Breton or Welsh bard; the British actor Bruce Myers as Karna, the blighted orphan warrior, is a troubled, Dickensian lost child in a man's body; the angular Sotigui Kouyate as the saintly self-denying Bhishma has the sad

255

grace of an elongated sculpture from Nigeria or New Guinea, and something of the tragedy of a calcinated Giacometti figure.

Just as we have recently learned to see 'Modernist Primitivism' in painting and sculpture as a complex incorporation of tribal languages from
Africa and Asia, so we might see Brook's *Mahabharata* as the theatre's
first assimilation of the performance culture of Asia and the east not
simply as entertainment exoticism or a source of styles and techniques for
European ideas, but as an equal embodiment in a cross-cultural actors'
group telling a far-reaching tale.

One thread guides you through *The Mahabharata*'s luxuriant forest: the
entire journey aims at one destination, the making of a good king. Like
Shakespeare's history-play cycle, this story centres on a man passing
through trials and tribulations in order to become a better monarch, of
his kingdom and of himself. The personal development of Yudishthira,
from weak goodness to a strength greater for having been wrecked and
remade, is like the journey of many apprentice rulers in Shakespeare –
Henry IV, Prince Hal becoming Henry V, Richard II in his fruitful
desolation. But here the personal is inseparable from the public, and from
the cosmic; in *The Mahabharata*, the Great Chain of Being has the
limitless reverberations which Shakespeare fully attained only in his later
tragedies and romances. And if *The Mahabharata* is about the many-
faceted making of a king, then Peter Brook's journey to *The Mahabharata*
– which began more than ten years ago and is studded with apparent
digressions and indirections – is about the forging of a theatre-maker, and
the redefinition of what theatre is. And just as *The Mahabharata* is
presided over by gods and superhuman presences – Brahma, Shiva, Vishnu/
Krishna – so Brook has been led by mentors – Shakespeare, Jerzy Grotowski, Antonin Artaud.

The Shakespearean resonances are immediately evident, and get deeper
as the story proceeds, culminating in *Lear*-like echoes of blind deposed
monarchs seeing through the veil of illusory reality into the mystery of
things. The uncompromising search for wholeness and the use of oriental
religious and theatrical disciplines, which the Polish theatre pioneer Grotowski taught Brook, are acknowledged in the poise and intensity of the
entire *Mahabharata* cast, and underlined by the tormented presence of
Ryszard Cieslak as the blind king. Grotowski's irruption into Brook's life
and work in the 1960s sharpened his spiritual search and gave him working
practices and disciplines. But perhaps the most telling of the ancestors of
this *Mahabharata* is Antonin Artaud. It was his work and example, his
fretting at limits, that was the pivot twenty years ago for Brook's transformation from a brilliant theatre-director into a seeker. In the mid–1960s
prompted by Artaud's hunt for theatre that should be as keen as hunger,
for actors who would signal fiercely through the flames of a social and

metaphysical conflagration, he turned away from the theatre of display and dazzle, from his effervescent production of *Love's Labour's Lost*, *Ring round the Moon* and *Irma la Douce*, and set off into a territory darker and wilder, although one prefigured in his work by the blatant horrors of *Titus Andronicus* and the implacable justice-machine of *Measure for Measure*. Artaud is a presiding deity (or demon) of *The Mahabharata* because Brook has, in one sense, retraced his path to that seminal encounter in 1933 when Artaud saw the Balinese dance-troupe at the Paris world fair: 'The actors with their costumes constitute veritable living, moving hieroglyphs,' he wrote, 'brocaded with a certain number of gestures – mysterious signs which correspond to some unknown, fabulous and obscure reality which we here in the Occident have completely repressed.'

How appropriate it is that, fifty years later in Provence, Yoshi Oida, a trim, hieroglyphic Japanese actor, should shape clear-cut gestures through the night air, giving pitiless archery instruction as the warrior Drona to his disciples – archery here is not just a military attainment but one of the soul's skills. For, whatever France's political racism (and this play happens an hour's drive from Marseilles, where Le Pen's National Front seized power this year by tapping prejudice against North African *travailleurs immigrés*), French culture has rarely been confined by xenophobia. Artaud is one of many French artists – Paul Claudel, Victor Segalen, Henry Michaux, René Daumal – who have opened themselves to and been transformed by India and Asia. And the anthropological riches of the Musée de l'Homme and Musée Guimet have nourished modern artists as nowhere else. All colonization may be barbaric, but some ends of empire are more civilized than others.

As you watch Yoshi Oida barking and grunting at his archery disciples with wonderful contained authority, you are reminded not only of a Zen master test but also of a Keystone Cops routine. One of Brook's continuing qualities has been to yoke the spiritual insights which Artaud and Grotowski sought in pathos or terror to a cheerful, childlike playfulness. He comes from a Shakespearean theatre of holy fools, utterly serious clowns. This duality of tone – light and weighty, deft and deep – characterizes everything in *The Mahabharata*. It is as if something so important were at stake that only the total concentration a child gives to a game could come to grips with it.

'It's the age of Kali, the dark-time, the fields turned to desert, crime stalks the city, blood-eating animals sleep in the main streets, drought, famine, the sky swallows up all the water, dead hot earth, then fire swells, swept by the wind, fire pierces the earth, destroys the underworld, wind and fire turn the world to a crust, huge clouds appear, blue, yellow, red, clouds like sea-monsters, like shattered cities with garlands of lightning, water falls, water pours down and drowns the earth, twelve years of storms, mountains tear the water, I can't see the world anymore, and then, when nothing is left but a grey sea without man, without beast, without tree, the first god, the creator drinks up the terrible wind and falls asleep.'[1] As Yudishthira speaks these words (part of a tale begun as entertainment and which has turned apocalyptic) the silence is almost unbearable. A vision of destruction imagined two thousand years ago dredges up our worst nightmares now.

Not that *The Mahabharata* tries to plug into our fears of nuclear destruction, of man-made dismemberment of the universal fabric: as a work whose vision is multiple, layered and protean, it naturally extends its story of fratricidal war on to every possible plane. Those intimations of an offence against the architecture of things which sound so movingly through the Shakespearean chronicle-plays – those descriptions of deformity in the bud, miscarriage and mutation in birthbed and manger, the very order of nature mockingly inverted – seem after-echoes of *The Mahabharata* catastrophe let loose.

When, on the third evening of this *Mahabharata*, the war between Pandavas and Kauravas breaks outs and runs its bitter course, it does so on every level. The physical: tournament skills of swirling swords and clubs, straining bows and whizzing arrows, panoply of martial arts, dervish warriors leaping, wheel formations slowly turning in a choreography of carnage, all the combat display we thrill to in tattoos or sci-fi blitzes in outer space. The magical-mystical: Krishna's devastating war-disc, and the unbeatable divine weapon Shiva bestows or whose secret mantra some strange hermit whispers in your ear. And the cosmic: war of the worlds, ultimate firestorm, everything consumed, as *dharma* pursues its path, as destiny demands.

As Brook sets his amphitheatre ablaze with torches and flares – geysers of flame splintered in pools of water strewn with bodies, stage lighting extinguished; as you sit in a rocky quarry gripped by the fear men have felt on night-time battlefields since time began, you are also suddenly aware that our contemporary traumas – Beirut, Iraqis and Iranians in desert sand, fireballs of napalm and napalm's nuclear big brother – stammer on the threshold of horror like a stuck needle. We can only envisage the end of things, again and again. The poet of *The Mahabharata*, believing that we come to see as illusion what we have spent our lives calling reality, looks through that end to new beginnings. That is the gulf between our fears and their beliefs.

Our European incredulity at the ruses of the god Krishna in the battle is a measure of this gulf. However much we know about the miracles of the Old Testament God, or the interventions of the Greek pantheon, we are still alarmed that a god stoops to such 'dirty tricks' as eclipsing the sun so that Arjuna, a marksman in the dark, can transfix his enemy with a fatal arrow. Our stubborn rigidities stumble against this childlike god, whom we often encounter horizontal and asleep, as if dreaming our world and all its (to us) consuming concerns and principles. We rebel against such apparent wiliness, we expect a 'reliable' code of behaviour. What we get instead is a deeper coherence, one that goes beyond conventional moral precept and takes on board more destruction and disaster than we are prepared to accept.

On the eve of battle, ringed by a circle of hard-breathing soldiers weaponed to the hilt, Krishna deepens his lesson. *The Bhagavad Gita*, separated from its story, has become the moral distillation of *The Mahabharata* for the west, its acceptable digest version. Reintegrated here into the plot of an immense saga, with dogs of war straining at the leash, Krishna's message to Arjuna, appalled at the massacre he will perpetrate, becomes an urgent parable, not a set of precepts.

> *Arjuna*: All men are born into illusion. How do you reach an absolute, if you're born into an illusion?
>
> *Krishna*: Slowly, Krishna led Arjuna into all the regions of the spirit. He showed him the deep movements of his being and his true battlefield, where neither arrows nor warriors are needed, where you fight alone.
>
> *Arjuna*: Tell me who you are. I am shaken to my depths, and I'm afraid.
>
> *Krishna*: Matter is changeable, but I am all that you say, all that you think. Everything rests upon me, like pearls on a thread. I am the sweet smell of the earth and I am the heat of fire, I am appearance and disappearance. I am the trickery of tricksters, I am the gleam of whatever shines. All creatures fall into the night, and all are restored to the day. I have already defeated all these warriors; he who thinks he can kill, and he who thinks he can be killed are equally mistaken. Weapons cannot pierce this life that animates you, nor fire burn it, nor water dampen it, nor wind dry it out. Have no fear, and stand up, for I love you.[2]

Then the two armies tear each other limb from limb. War as metaphor; war as brutal reality. Brook says his engagement with *The Mahabharata* began in 1966, when a young Indian came into the rehearsal room for *US*, Brook's show about the war in Vietnam, and recounted to the company this scene of *The Bhagavad Gita*. *US* was threaded through with self-immolating Buddhist monks and their Arjuna-like western emulators.

'We've always thought of a theatre group as a storyteller with multiple faces,' writes Brook in his preliminary notes to *The Mahabharata*, and the flourish of interlocking stories with which his first evening opens is an exhilarating signal of the freedom of narration to come. The beginning of the play is also the origin of written literature, as the poet Vyasa seeks a scribe for his immense epic poem about the *Bharata* (Hindus, but also humankind) which he wants to pass on to a child. Elephant-headed Ganesha, 'he who calms quarrels', appears and obliges. The bard, the child and the man-animal make up a storytelling band, protean, questioning and quizzical. Within minutes, starting with the ancestry of Ganesha and Vyasa, we have been drawn into a skein of stories involving Shiva, sperm, the goddess of the Ganges, fish and fisher-kings, sexual renunciation, gazelles, interdictions on pain of sudden death, multiple couplings (including sleeping with the Sun), a blind child and his pale-skinned brother, a mother pregnant for two years who gives birth to a football of flesh which, cut into a hundred pieces and soaked in a hundred jars, becomes the hundred sons of one of the tribes of the story.

The narrator himself is hauled into the story to couple with three princesses and supply his tale with new characters. This baroquely comic scene (the women comply, but with some disgust, for Vyasa is rough and uncomely) yokes sexual and literary conception in a way that would delight today's literary theorists, while reminding mere readers that – as Calvino has noted – the pleasure of deciphering a story is analogous to that of exploring a lover's body. Anyone who has ever fallen under the narrative spell of Borges, Marquez, Calvino or Grass, will recognize these superimposed criss-crossing stories of a 3,000-year-old epic. Brook's search into the sagas and parables of Africa and the east, his expeditions into their village cultures in search of bards and storytellers, his staging of *The Conference of the Birds, The Ik*, and the African farce *The Bone* and his film about Gurdjieff (each a stepping-stone to *The Mahabharata*) have been prompted by his dissatisfaction with the ideological, moralizing or psychological plays which inhabit most western stages today. 'I am looking for something more volcanic,' he said, some years back.

Offstage, Death's voice asks: 'What is the greatest marvel?' Yudishthira replies: 'Each day death strikes around us and we live as if we were immortal beings.' A weightless black girl ecstatically arches herself as a gazelle, like some figure from an erotic temple-frieze. A wheel whipped along by an actor to signify a chariot later becomes the wheel of life on which its rider dies. Sounds echo around the natural amphitheatre – blare of horn and trombone, wail of reeds, reverberations of sitar – as transparent cloths are stretched up to shield us from manifestations of divine glory. Scenes reminiscent of Jacobean horror, of Chekhovian tenderness, above all of those Shakespeare parables in which the cloud-capped towers dissolve and a life becomes a scene in a play, to be replaced by another but not lost. All these recapitulations of a progress in and through the theatre are there in Brook's *Mahabharata*.

At 60, Brook has reached nothing so comfortable as a resting-place. For the past fifteen years, since he set up in Paris with his international theatre research group, and began to scour the world in search of clues and traces, he has been a paradoxical presence: an institution, yet constitutionally fluid; fixed and nomadic; rooted and transitory. He has taken the enduring ephemerality of theatre to its limits. Now his current company will travel the world with *The Mahabharata*, trying and testing its reverberations each night afresh.

Of all the theatre groups which have sustained a fruitful continuity within the past twenty years, Brook's is the most ample and open. Julian Beck and Judith Malina's Living Theatre floundered in the counter-cultural pieties of *Paradise Now*, Ariane Mnouchkine's Théâtre du Soleil shows signs of an etiolated aestheticism in its recent orientalized Shakespeare – there is absolutely no *Indiennerie* in Brook's *Mahabharata*. Peter Stein has abdicated from the Schaubühne, Berlin's highly subsidized Marxist theatrical collective. And Bill Bryden's Cottesloe company, having perfected a sophisticated people's theatre in its staging of Medieval Mystery plays, looks set to follow Joan Littlewood's Theatre Workshop into commercial theatre acclaim and subsequent dispersal.

By setting his sights on a truly grand goal – the exploration of what theatre can do that communicates globally, across cultural boundaries – and by pursuing this goal with tenacity and selflessness, Brook has reached what he would call some provisional certainties. *The Mahabharata*, with its sprouting perspectives and liquid structures, is a vessel which might have been destined for his passionate detachment and for the theatre's intrinsic 'lies like truth'. In Brook's *gran teatro del mundo*, the play's the thing, and playing is the root of all.

> *Shakuni*: For the deep player, he who knows the game and weighs things up calmly, cheating is no problem. There's no crime here but simply the game, the entire game. A wise man debates with fools: do you call that cheating? A seasoned warrior fights beginners: do you call that cheating? Knowing how things are isn't cheating. You always go in with a will to win. That's how life is. Withdraw from the game if you're afraid.[3]

NOTES

Originally published in *London Review of Books*, 3 October 1985.

1 *Le Mahabharata* (theatre adaptation by J. -C. Carrière; Paris: CICT, 1985); 'L'Exil dans la Forêt', pp. 70–1 (all translations into English here by Michael Kustow).
2 *ibid.*, 'La Guerre', pp. 11–13.
3 *ibid.*, 'La Partie de Dés', p. 113.

18

PETER BROOK'S 'ORIENTALISM'

Gautam Dasgupta

Gautam Dasgupta is co-publisher of Performing Arts Publications, New York.

July 16, Jornadz del Muerto, near Alamogordon' New Mexico. Indra was not yet fully awake from his night of lengthy repose under the eastern skies. Yet the horizons were ablaze, irradiated by the lethal rays of 'a thousand suns in the sky'. With these words from *The Bhagavad Gita*, J. Robert Oppenheimer, one of the architects of this conflagration, anointed the birth of the *Kaliyuga*, our nuclear age. How fitting, indeed, that when the sun rose from the east to gaze upon the charred and stillborn sandy plain of a New Mexico desert, it brought in its wake a wisdom from the ancient land of the Bharatas.

Now, forty-three years later, when the life-sustaining light of Indra is no match for the thousands of genocidal suns we possess, comes yet another warning from the land of Shiva and Kali. The howls of doom and terror cry out from within the cavernous walls of the BAM Majestic Theatre as the Pandavas and the Kauravas line up under Peter Brook's direction on the battlefield of Kurukshetra. *The Mahabharata*, an Indian epic of immense prolixity, adapted for the stage by Jean-Claude Carrière, draws to a close after nine hours, its climactic image one of bloody carnage and tragic desolation.

The Mahabharata is a compilation, in 100,000 stanzas, of vast Brahmanic lore. The dates of its composition cannot be fixed with certainty, but scholars generally agree to place it somewhere between 400 BC and AD 200. Although tradition has it that the creator of this vast poem was the sage Vyasa, it betrays the handiwork of a succession of priests who, during the course of their storytelling sessions, interpolated sections on morality, ethics, theology and statecraft into what may have been, essentially and originally, a secular tale of war and strife. In any case, The Epic in our time has come to symbolize, through interconnected tales and legends and the morals attached to each, a virtual exegesis on the Hindu way of life. *The Mahabharata* I grew up with in India is a vital source of nourishment,

262

a measure of one's thoughts and deeds. It is not mere epic constrained by literary and narrative stragegies, but a revelatory injunction, ethical and theological in purpose, that determines and defines the social and personal interactions of millions of Indians.

Given the scope of The Epic, it goes without saying that any attempt to dramatize *The Mahabharata* is a task worthy of admiration. It is also a far more ambitous undertaking than Brook's earlier intercultural adaptations – *Orghast, Conference of the Birds, The Ik*, and *Ubu*. In all instances, he has drawn upon an international cast of actors, employed diverse acting styles and a variety of theatrical modes of representation. Underlying all this experimentation is, I suspect, a belief in a syncretic cultural universe, where the stage is all the world. A grand and perhaps even a noble vision, granted, but one that inevitably raises the problematic spectre of what Edward Said has termed 'orientalism'.

It is from this perspective that the Brook *Mahabharata* assumes an air of equivocation I find hard to dismiss. Obviously, all cross-cultural work would have to confront the idea of representing the other. But, as Said had argued in his book *Orientalism*, interest in the Orient and the field of study labelled 'oreintalist' discourse was generated by occidental schol-ars in the eighteenth and nineteenth centuries to acompany ongoing politi-cal incursions into the Orient. The Orient, according to Said's study, was not allowed to represent itself, but had to be represented by the Occident. In other words, it had to be re-presented in a manner so as to align itself within the prevailing hierarchy, with the imperial powers on top, the Orient at the bottom, of the political, social and cultural scale. Although such political hegemonic divisions do not prevail in our time, the question to be posed is whether the thematics of 'orientalism' none the less still continue to haunt us.

On the political level, it cannot be denied that such thinking continues to play a role in international affairs. Even in terms of social intercourse, 'orientalist' prejudices have not ceased to exist. Generalities about cultures abound, and this of course is by no means the sole prerogative of the occidental mind. But the question that concerns me is why so many artists in the west, particularly in the past few decades, have drawn upon oriental themes and myths to spur their own creativity? Is this because, in all honesty, they do see the world as an organic whole, or is there implicit in their cross-fertilizing instinct a recognition of their own paucity of ideas? And, at worst, does the exoticism of the Orient, its different values and norms, somehow permit them to evade criticism of their cultures, supplanting what ought to be a vital discourse on issues generated by their own society by a surrogate other-world picture? These are by no means easy questions to answer, and nor am I suggesting that we do away with all cross-cultural artistic endeavours. What concerns me is that the representations of another culture's artistic product address the lived, sensate fabric of that borrowed cloth. And more, that such expressions of culture give-and-take not decend to banal generalities about the foreign culture, but seek to uncover its specificities, its actual, and not merely perceived, links with its own society. What is it that makes *The Mahabharata*, for instance, of such paramount significance, first for its own people, and then for the rest of the world?

It should be clear that I am not remotely suggesting that representations of the east be the sole prerogative of non-western artists. Nor am I naïve enough to argue that any and all representations of this grand epic staged in India – the episodes of *The Mahabharata* are performed throughout India in theatrical forms that range from the classical Kathakali to the rural Jatra – lie any closer to the original intent of the poem. But what is indisputably true is that such stagings do address, implicitly or explicitly, a deeply ingrained structure of ritual beliefs and ethical codes of conduct intrinsic to its audience. *The Mahabharata* is nothing, an empty shell, if it is read merely as a compendium of martial legends, of revenge, valour and bravura.

And that, precisely, is the reading attributed to *The Mahabharata* by Carrière and Brook. How else can one explain the shockingly truncated *Bhagavad Gita* sequence, the epicentre of the poem, the fulcrum on which rests the entire thrust of this monumental drama of humanity, here rendered into whispered words never revealed to the audience? It is as if one were to stage the Bible without the least mention of the sermon on the Mount. I admit that there are ponderous speeches in The Epic, and many cuts implemented by the creators of this *Mahabharata* are judicious, but *The Bhagavad Gita* is, most assuredly, not one of them. Aside from its paramount thematic and contextual placement of the body of the work, it is also one of the supreme achievements of classical Sanskrit verse. Its eloquence and majesty of thought surely deserve a more prominent place, than that given to it in this staging.

It could perhaps be argued, as Brook and Carrière have intimated in the published text of the play, that they chose to stage an earlier, and perhaps a vulgate, version of *The Mahabharata*. Although such a claim cannot be substantiated with any degree of accuracy – historical philological or theological – it does raise important and problematic questions about the 'orientalist' bias of their readings. Foremost among these is their impacting a Homeric idea of The Epic on to the apocalyptic skeins of an Indian legend. There are obvious parallels to be drawn between the warrior heroes of *The Mahabharata* and *The Iliad*: the rivalry between Karna and Arjuna is sure to evoke that other long-standing feud between Hector and Achilles, as will the saga of heroes born out of union between gods and mortals.

Where these paths diverge, however, is of the utmost significance. Karna and Arjuna, by virtue of their unique and personal relationships to deities of the Hindu pantheon who continue to be worshipped to this very day, are viewed in much the same way as the gods themselves. This is to a large extent true of all the characters in *The Mahabharata*, be they men, women, children, *rakshasas* or *apsaras*. The hero of a Greek (or, for that matter, a western) epic, on the other hand, remains a mortal who may on occasion, licensed by the gods, engage in superhuman feats. In India, the heroes of this epic are perceived as some variant incarnation of a deity or as a member of a lower spiritual hierarchy. The feats performed by the characters in *The Mahabharata* are always, and invariably, seen within the context of religious framework. There is no dramatic or epic kernel to *The Mahabharata* outside of its theological value system. When Carrière says in the introduction to his version that 'Any historical or theological truth, contoversial by its very nature, is closed to us – our aim is a certain dramatic truth,' he misses the point. The 'dramatic truth' of this epic resides not in the aesthetic or narrative pull of the story, but in a very human exchange of beliefs that grounds, for the average Indian, even the most elementary reading of the many tales woven throughout *The Mahabharata*.

This Homeric compaction is felt most poignantly in the characterization of Krishna, who comes across more as a Ulysses than as a personification of the god Vishnu. Within the confines of *The Mahabharata*'s grandiose themes, the recklessness of Brook's Krishna is oddly out of place. That ungodlike aspect of Krishna remains reserved for the *Ras-Lila*, and I can find no justification for transferring the Krishna of that legend to *The Mahabharata*. True, the Krishna of *The Bhagavad Gita* attains a more radiant visage, but at all instances of this colossal poem, he is beheld as nothing less than the Krishna of divine inspiration.

Interestingly enough, one can also pose the question of whether Brook's adaptation is a prime example of an inter-textual reading, or an illustration of the west misreading the literature of the east? That Brook and Carrière should bring their own subjectivity to the work is to be expected. It is perhaps no mere coincidence that many of the extrapolations that go to create the bulk of their adaptation resonate with Shakespearean themes. After all, it was with his justly praised Shakespeare productions that Brook attained worldwide prominence. And although I am in favour of inter-textual readings on the stage, I also believe that such disjunctive devices work only when the primary text itself, on some level, has been apprehended by an audience. Contemporary stagings of episodes from *The Mahabharata* within India do take on inter-textual guises. I recall once seeing a Marxist revisioning that brought to the fore and questioned the alarmingly revisionist high-priest and royal-caste ethics embedded in the text. Its impact on the rural audience was considerable, and the reason for it obviously rested on their prior familiarity with the story.

The inter-textual elements in Brook's production, most significantly the

Shakespearean ones (Dhritarashtra comes across as King Lear; Krishna as Prospero; Kunti, Gandhari and Draupadi as Lear's daughters), may have served as easy referents to his western audience, but they fail to do justice to specific traits of these characters, traits that stem from a complex underpinning of Brahmanic and Vedic precepts. It is perhaps impossible to embrace the various threads of philosophical lore that this epic possesses in the course of a few hours; none the less, the responsibility to confront them is a grave one. One should not, under cover of universality of theme or character, undercut the intrinsic core of how *The Mahabharata*'s characters function within the worlds of which they are a part.

It is then understandable, perhaps, why Brook and Carrière chose to omit stories that, for the Indian viewer, belong to the heart of *The Mahabharata*. Why, for instance, were the legends of Rama and Sita, Savitri, Manu, Bhagiratha, Nala, Damayanti, Garuda, Soma, and others ignored? If time was a factor, surely some of the more drawn out sequences, particularly in the last third of the production – which resemble in scope the battle sequences of Shakespeare's history plays – could have been sacrificed for tales that would round out for a western audience a fuller sense of the Hindu world-view.

It is, of course, entirely conceivable that such was not the intent of Brook and Carrière. Given the internationalist cast and the quixotic admixture of costumes and musical instruments, it seems obvious that coherence was not their primary concern. Unfortunately, however, despite the elegance of Brook's staging, the arresting theatrical effects and, for the most part, the seductive pacing of the production, the intentional hodgepodge of diverse accents and downright poor acting in a few crucial instances did little to alleviate the lack of theatrical coherence as well. It would indeed be sad if the restrictions imposed by the cast forced Carrière's hand in rendering the stately poetic lines of *The Mahabharata* in prose. The sixteen-syllable line, the *Sloka* meter of the original Sanskrit, lends The Epic a noble tread and adds to the grandeur of its theme. The prose adaptation achieves a poetic intensity in longer passages and in the narrative sections, but when it occurs at the level of everyday dialogue, it seems oddly commonplace and at variance with the characters who mouth them.

If, as I have suggested, Brook's *Mahabharata* falls short of the essential Indianness of The Epic by staging predominantly its major incidents and failing to adequately emphasize its coterminous philosophical precepts, it does however raise the spectre, in no uncertain terms, of the fate that awaits us in the event of a nuclear holocaust. The play is completed on a note of cosmic desolation, with corpses littering the field of battle (an arena referred to in the original as the Field of Righteousness, or Law) and Yudishthira's descent into hell. (This penultimate sequence is billed as 'The Last Illusion', and the play ends with all the characters reunited, although this seems rather arbitrary and does not quite follow from all that has gone on previously.) It is also not the actual ending of The Epic. In the *Aswa-Medha*, or the Sacrifice of the Horse, which is the proper ending, harmony once again is restored to the universe through a series of sacrificial rituals. The tragic *rasa* or mode, which the Brook productions suggests, is inimical to Hindu norms of aesthetic decorum and religious beliefs. The tragic is irreversible, it is definite. It has no place in the endless cycle of birth and rebirth, the crux of Hindu thought.

Brook's tragic coda is appended to a body of prophetic writings that give daily sustenance to millions of Hindus the world over. Here again we might possibly glimpse another aspect of 'orientalism'. But now that even India possesses the bomb, *The Mahabharata*, yes, Peter Brook's and Jean-Claude Carrière's *Mahabharata*, apocalyptic ending in place, should be performed in the land from which it originated. The eternal cycle will be completed, for today both India and the west possess the ultimate weapon, the *pasupata* which Shiva bestows as a gift to Arjuna.

NOTE

Originally published in *Performing Arts Journal*, no. 30, 10 (3), 1987. A shorter version of this article appeared in the *Village Voice*, 27 October 1987.

19

BROOK'S SIX DAYS

Theatre as the Meeting Place Between the Visible and the Invisible

Georges Banu

Georges Banu, one of France's foremost theatre scholars, teaches at the University of Paris. He is an editor of *Alternatives Théâtrales* and *Les Voies de la Création Théâtrale* (he compiled vol. XIII on Brook), and is the author of a number of books and published articles on modern theatre.

As one enters the Bouffes du Nord, one notices that, stage right, on the carpets from *Conference of the Birds* and *The Cherry Orchard*, stands a pile of cardboard boxes of the kind taken on the journeys to Iran and Africa. Meanwhile the river from *The Mahabharata* runs alongside this imaginary landscape, in which one can detect traces of the various pathways followed by Peter Brook over the last fifteen years and more. They run from high to low, from carpets to boxes, from *holy theatre* to *rough*: the space itself reflects an itinerary. All the more so given the fact that for these '*Meetings*'[1] (which contain echoes of public demonstrations organized at the Théâtre Récamier in 1973 during the Centre's early days in Paris) some of the actors who had moved away from Brook have come back to join the group currently performing *The Mahabharata*. I notice Jean-Louis Hourdin and Jean-Claude Perrin, both of whom played in *Timon of Athens*, as well as Zehava Gal and Veronique Dietschy from *Carmen*. Also present are Jean-Claude Penchenat and other members of the Théâtre du Campagnol, and actors from the Théâtre du Soleil.

With lights on full, we wait until silence fills this multi-faceted theatre, and one of the boxes begins to move, to jump and twist like some cartoon shellfish. People start to relax, even some laughter here and there as the tension dissolves. Then Brook stands up and, with a twinkle in his eye, frees Yoshi Oida from the box. 'One can make theatre anywhere, starting with the simplest of elements,' he says. 'What one has to be wary of is the danger of theorizing . . . By organizing these meetings we are responding to a demand, because necessarily throughout the rehearsal period we work by ourselves, in private. This is not a training course, nor is it a

268

series of lectures or demonstrations. It is to be an exploration during which we will share our work. Everything can be shown, except for the actual time spent working.' The journey will be complete, but at an accelerated speed. Hold tight. 'We have six days: each of them will have its own particular focus.'

THREE KINDS OF FIDELITY

We get under way with simple exercises, Bruce Myers in the middle. In silence, he does absolutely nothing. As Brook suggests afterwards, 'silence can become palpable. Something intensifies, focuses and one can taste the silence. But this kind of silence doesn't last very long. One must learn that different levels of silence exist: if an actor is able to open himself to them, to recognize them, then he can plug into the quality of an audience's attention.'

Brook suggests some movements for the actors to perform first, before inviting the entire audience to follow suit: extend the index finger, as if pointing, then turn the hand over and twist it up into a claw. You have to move from one gesture to the other because the movement itself contains 'a whole story'. Brook asks whether it is possible for the body to accomplish what a hand can do. For the time being, his only concern is with *doing*, action free of any motivation or purpose: walking, moving forward, stopping, maintaining one's balance. 'Use only your bodies to communicate. This is the exercise we do more often than any other. It is inexhaustible because it never finally resolves any problems: you come up against the same ones every time.' Through these simple clear movements, which neither contain a message nor require a technique, in fact we are looking for a *starting point*, an equivalent for a writer's opening sentence. 'If one can't open up, one will not be able to engage in a dialogue. Above all the starting point has to be perfectly natural.'

Brook demonstrates some straightforward movements for us all to try out. There is no hint of manipulation here, no suggestion of revelation of secret knowledge to initiates. This is the opening step of a collective exploration, the seed of a relationship, liberating shared activity affectively uniting those present in some way. Brook advises us: 'First make the gesture, then read what it has to say. You are your own audience. At this moment five hundred wonderful stories are being told at the very same time. Learn to be your own theatre.' Then he suggests that we try repeating the same movement while modifying the tension it contains, in order to explore the mutability, even polarity of meaning that can stem from a simple variation in intensity. Brook likes to start with the minutiae, the infinitely fine detail.

The actors bring in some bamboo sticks, objects charged with associations with past work, as far back as his celebrated *Midsummer Night's*

Dream at Stratford, and the earliest exercises at the Centre in Paris, then in Africa. Brook has used them ever since, for they bring 'something so simple. There is no need to introduce anything anecdotal, a narrative. The exercise works in a similar way to a pure sound. In order to start one must always create a space, both internally and externally. The emptier the better. One has to keep coming back to the basic imperative of having nothing at all to start with. In an empty space, everything can become an event.'

The actors manipulate the sticks with such precision and sensitivity that they seem to reflect inner impulses. From there we move on to sounds. Primal sounds first created some fifteen years before for *Orghast* at the Shiraz Festival in Iran, when an invented hybrid language had combined ancient Greek, Latin, an Iranian ritual language called Avesta and a new language created by Ted Hughes. Natasha Parry steps forward and opens a faded prompt book from *Orghast*, a relic from years past, in order to rediscover the austere vibrations of those strange archaic words, which resonate under the vaulted ceiling of the Bouffes. 'Originally, long ago, something very rich was concentrated. If one can simply trace that original pathway, recreate it by paying close attention to the slightest detail, one is able to rediscover what was there at the start. That's why one should never start with interpretation.'

Brook sets up other exercises, which at first involve simple verbal exchanges. Then whole sentences of dialogue from a specific scene, accompanied by a ball, are thrown from actor to actor, before being tossed out into the auditorium, from where spectators are expected to return them to those on stage. A very tough exercise. As Jean-Claude Carrière subsequently points out, these two performers have been playing Kunti and Karna in this same scene from *The Mahabharata* for the past year. The fact that they now make a number of textual mistakes underlines the difficulty of an exercise which demonstrates the 'three kinds of fidelity' Brook insists an actor must possess: 'A fidelity to one's own concentration, for that is the deepest source of inspiration. A fidelity to one's partner, to whom one must adapt. And finally a fidelity to the audience, to whom an actor must be able to open himself; otherwise he turns them into enemies. These three kinds of fidelity are inseparable.'

At the end of the first afternoon, Yoshi recalls how fifteen years earlier, after a children's Christmas show, he had said to Brook: 'That's it, it's over.' 'Yes, it's over,' Brook had replied, 'so now we can start on something else.' In his theatre, he has made one law his own: the law of fresh beginnings.

THE TASTE OF IMPURITY

'Yesterday', Brook says, 'we concentrated on the invisible. But the invisible can only reveal itself through the body. And for that to happen the body must be trained to open itself up to the invisible.' Bruce Myers creates a sound, then modulates its energy and pitch with the audience following him. 'From the very beginning one must try to abandon any kind of psychological approach. To create an empty space one has to place oneself in a situation of imitation. In this way one can make oneself available to experience detail by detail echoes of something distant, to discover places one never knew existed. The body has caves, hidden passages . . . one must learn to allow energy to flow through it. This would enable an infinite series of possibilities to arise, and one could really start to listen to the invisible.' *Create an empty space.* Maurice Bénichou claims that his aim is always to come on stage as empty as possible, rather than brimming with preparation, 'laden'.

Brook asks two actors to communicate with each other in *orghast*. Then at a request for non-French speakers in the audience to make themselves known, they appear on all sides: a Spaniard, a Hungarian, an Israeli, some Africans, a Latin American. The internationalism of Brook's group on stage is reflected in its audience offstage. Actors and audience members who speak different languages are asked to endeavour to communicate in a specific situation. 'Without the support of a language, one pays more attention to the other person,' Brook suggests. 'One is therefore attentive to the slightest detail, and so one manages to extend one's own possibilities. Everyone has developed a continent within themselves. What one has lost can be relocated through a partner, who can help reclaim and reactivate those missing parts.' Brook has long believed in the potency of such a mixing of races and cultures, its utopian potential being a restoration to wholeness of a fragmented unity.

When Yoshi throws himself into a dizzying sequence of vocalizations inspired by ancient Japanese theatre, Brook suggests we try to follow him despite the mediocrity of our efforts. 'While one can never acquire the true techniques of a traditional culture through imitation, one can get a strong sense of something beyond one's everyday range. That's why we prefer to talk about experiences rather than exercises. Through such experiences, one is attempting to taste something quite different.' Brook has his sights set on the flavour of the technique; rather than the technique itself. Although the Far East attracts him, he has no aspirations to reproduce it.

To launch a question or lend support to a suggestion, Brook sometimes reconstructs scenes from his own productions, granting us the pleasure of a rare privilege in the theatre: that of quotation. So for example he restages that special moment in a scene from *Conference of the Birds* when Arabic and French are combined simultaneously, which is followed by the death of Duryodhana from *The Mahabharata*, when song and words are overlaid to coexist. Then we move on to exercises involving an actor and an instrumentalist, in which words and music are conjoined.

Brook wants to give us a taste of 'the limitless possibilities of heterogeneity, of impurity. A "pure" theatre lacks life. Impurity is a sign of life. Theatre can be a meeting place where people and races are not in conflict, but in opposition to one another. That is the source of its richness. Theatre is like a public place in which one is compelled by the disparate elements present to feel what's actually developing. But one might also suggest that theatre is like a salad: and one must not forget that there are some things that go well together, others that don't. If one learns to appreciate the flavour of a Japanese vibration or of an Indian movement, then one can come to know how to mix them effectively. Everything is possible. Nothing need be excluded, as long as one succeeds in preparing the empty space, so as to be able to open oneself up, in a sensitive way, to invisible currents.' According to Brook, the invisible is conveyed through the taste of impurity, its savour.

The afternoon comes to an end with a story about the catching of a pigeon told by Jean-Claude Carrière. When he asks both actors and spectators for suggestions, an Iranian, a Senegalese and a Peruvian take turns to describe and demonstrate how they caught birds in their own villages. Childhood rediscovered at the Bouffes. Finally, a young Yugoslav woman comes forward and in a rich mountain-dweller's voice intones a peasant song about a trapped bird. The audience is speechless with emotion. Someone comments on the song's beauty: the echo of purity in an impure place.

THE EXPERIENCE OF SPACE

This afternoon's session begins with Brook's response to a spectator who had confessed his disappointment at the weak theoretical base of the group's work. 'We have a theory', he explains, 'which is an anti-theory: that *no method exists*. Around the world there are schools with very precise methods and styles. My work has led me to believe that none of these schools is exclusive; they don't cancel each other out. If one wants theatre to provide images of life – in its most immediate as well as its invisible aspects – then nothing should be left out. Everything found in life should be found there: banal behaviour and extravagant behaviour, everyday language and strange sounds. One must maintain the natural relationship between these extremes; that is part of our particular understanding of the function of theatre.'

Brook rejects the narrowing of the field that he believes the work of some avant-garde groups entails. If exclusion repels him, choice on the other hand attracts him. Referring back to Jean-Claude's story from the previous day, Brook defends all of the possibilities suggested, as well as the indispensability of moving on to the next stage in the process: *choosing*. Just as there are three kinds of fidelity, he tells us, so there are three stages. 'First, make concrete the idea that everything is possible without the slightest concern about style. Second, starting with the visible, make the invisible appear: in order for something extraordinary to emerge, one needs to start with what's ordinary – it contains the invisible. And third, celebrate that. This is where a theatrical quality comes in. One needs something very strong to help the invisible fill the space. There is a vast range of possibilities at one's disposal, and one must choose between what one wants to see and what one doesn't want to see. To animate an empty space, one must select, one must make choices. On the one hand, every-thing is possible; on the other, one must avoid being taken in by any old thing, whatever grabs you. In the sixties and seventies, the search for freedom ended up meaning "anything goes". We are looking for absolute freedom and at the same time for absolute discipline; for the bridge that links them. For that reason we do hundreds of exercises for months on end. Taken together, these constitute a real exercise, which in turn leads on to a 'Super Exercise' – the performance. This work is part of that ultimately demanding experience. And it enables us to be as precise as archers.'

Yoshi Oida demonstrates some exercises for the audience to copy – isolated movements underscored with music. Then the habitually calm Brook allows us a glimpse of another Brook, someone excited by the infectious rhythms. He points out that 'when great energy crosses space, it is quite fascinating'. Returning to the exercises, he explains that what matters first is *imitation*, then *comparison*. 'The latter enables blocks and limitations to come to light. For an exercise to be useful, it must contain a point of evident difficulty. It makes that difficulty visible. Starting from there, one can make comparisons. And there's no way of cheating. When one is confronted with real difficulties, something is put to the test, exercised: one's own self-knowledge.'

Next Brook moves on to exercises which aim to use concrete experience of space to fill it. Some of these exercises are known thanks to Michel Rostain's *Journal des Répétitions de Carmen*.[2] Some of the actors com-municate amongst themselves using single syllables, all the while closely watched by the audience who are to react to the slightest diminution in tension. Then actors in the playing space communicate with others on the balcony, or even with musicians who answer them from the third balcony. It is a question of playing for a fullness of volume while avoiding the dangers of too great a degree of intimacy. The audience must see and hear everything. For Brook, sounds and faces must never be lost or imprecise: that is at the very root of his theatre practice.

After the exploration of space, the sticks and bricks from *Ubu aux*

Bouffes are brought in. These simple objects are used as an initial anchorage point, to focus work. 'It is fine to start with nothing, but sometimes one needs certain things: small, simple things. They enable an actor to play with what's concrete, but without filling everything in: like an incomplete equation. One must preserve these "holes" in representation in order to give spectators the possibility of completing an image for themselves. That's how one frees the imagination.'

The exercises of the first three days are intended to relax the body, to enable it to become fluid and transparent, to radiate in space. Later on, this freedom will be confronted with a 'given form'.

Before the session ends, a door is brought on stage.[3] 'Who is going to enter through this door?' Brook asks. We want to reply 'the character', but, as on the other days, he prefers to end with a question. He wants to deny us the comfort of certainties. Brook's success is inseparable from the extraordinary reserve of confidence that doubt enjoys today. Not so long ago such a discourse would have been rarely heard and little understood.

INTUITION AND INTELLIGENCE

The fourth day begins with a description of what Brook feels to be a keystone, 'the relationship between the freeing of the body, the form which opens out into the unknown, and the disciplined precision once a choice is made. There is a bridge between what is formless and what must immediately take on a form.' To find the right response, he goes on, one must follow a process which has as its starting point the decision to take on a dramatic or epic work, a decision made uniquely because of some personal desire rather than as a result of any externally imposed obligations. 'Within every text there's a subject, a history behind the signs written on paper. If one tries to perform it straight away, barriers are created: we ourselves are these obstacles. It is impossible for either our bodies or our imaginations to be fully ready to serve this subject.' So from this point actors improvise using situations inspired by the text, even actual dialogue as their starting points: the aim is as much to free them from awkwardness as to provide additional information.

'Two faculties must work in conjunction. The first is intuition: it grasps the invisible. But intuition will disappear if one becomes tense or loses concentration. Initially everything is aimed at making one available to intuition, although it would be a mistake to give oneself to it completely, blindly, in full confidence. Allowing anything to happen unchecked leads to failure. Intuition has to be permanently sustained by intelligence. One needs both, for intelligence on its own can also be destructive: it uses only the intellect. One must search incessantly for the relationship between intuition and intelligence in order to create true, living events.'

Everything starts from the smallest unit: the word. Brook breaks up a war song and gives each of the actors a single strong word: flower, song, death, world. Once they have allowed the word to work on them, they have to give voice to it, but without introducing or illustrating anything. 'In the end one must rediscover the freshness of the initial image.' Then an epithet is added: engulfed world. Brook tells them: 'Now try to taste the relationship between the word and the sensuality of the adjective' ('*monde englouti*').

Next the actors and then the spectators move on to making word-chains, with the aim of creating an unbroken flow. From there we turn to song as the outer limit of words, while trying to avoid the transition from one to the other becoming violent or aggressive. Finally we come to a phrase in which the actor 'must follow the movement of images without the slightest emotional colouring, above all avoiding that generalizing music that denies the possibility of hearing and understanding every word. If one allows it to carry one away, one gives the word no chance at all. Use detail.' Worked on in this way, sound material feeds into the reply addressed to a partner whose status and function are clearly established each time: for example, a blind king, a king who is responsible for the war. Here it is the second of Brook's three 'fidelities' that is being respected: proceed from the colour of words to the values of context.

Then Jean-Claude Carrière works with François Marthouret on a speech from *Timon of Athens*, the part he performed at the opening of the Bouffes in 1974. Brook intervenes: 'There is a dynamic movement in words, and by discovering that, one can grasp the real movement of the character. A major part of inspiration is concealed in letters and syllables, as well of course as in the placing of words, in their way of answering through a monologue.' To practice the third kind of fidelity, Marthouret is asked to address his speech out to the auditorium in such a way that after every line a spectator can respond and so engage in dialogue. Emotion runs high when Timon advises Alcibiades to 'pity not honoured age for his white beard', and a shout from the audience asks, 'What about your father?' In the end the exercise clarifies sentences, making them concrete and alive. 'One can speak directly to the audience,' Brook says, 'or one can talk to one's partner without ever forgetting the audience. Awareness of the presence of an audience enables actors to extend their range enormously.'

Next they experiment with modulations of pace, beginning with acceleration. 'Theatre is always a play of rhythms. Speeding up, slowing down, exaltant, relaxed. Both continuous tension and continuous calm are equally sterile. No rhythm, no language is complete, and one must learn to move from one to another without forgetting that there's always a guide, which is in whatever it is one is telling. It is only through lived experiences that one succeeds in grasping what is being told at any one moment.' Narrative clarity: for Brook an imperative that can never be compromised.

Further exercises follow. Whether involving either actors or audience, the aim remains primarily 'to examine, to explore. One must tenderize the meat. That's how one opens oneself up to conclusions one would never have arrived at otherwise. One must not believe that no vision of the text exists; it does exist, but only as a result of a long period of preparation. Being able to see clearly and to come up with ideas are indispensable qualities, but they must come as a natural consequence.' Listening to Brook talk, one is struck by the frequency of his use of verbs of movement: the dynamics of theatre as process inform his thought and animate his very being.

THEATRE AND LIFE

While every day has ended with a question, the fifth day opens with a statement, as if everything has to be flawlessly interwoven, without knots. Brook's trajectory is round, he traces a circle or a spiral. And in the luminous shelter of the Bouffes on this rainy afternoon, he steps forward alone in front of us: 'What is the difference between theatre and life? Theatre is life, but in order for life to become theatre, it must be present in an even stronger manner. Whereas in life the level of image can sometimes be weak, in theatre it always has to be more intense. Vitality is an essential component, for that's what leads on to the invisible.'

Completely empty movements to begin with. At first the rhythm is slow, then it is accelerated, obliged to follow the drumbeat. Occasionally Brook intervenes: 'Try not to become prisoner of the same movement for the same rhythm,' or, 'Keep some energy in reserve, don't waste it.' These meetings reveal the quality of Brook's directorial suggestions, which spotlight mistakes and outline a way forward. He is always there, close to the actors, talking to them in a gentle voice, treating them as equals, never tense. His clearsightedness and verbal precision form the basis of individual trust-based relationships: something almost private of which we have caught a glimpse over the last few days.

The movement exercises give way to improvisations with photographs as their starting points: the importance attached to similar work, for example during the preparation of *Carmen*, is well known.[4] Brook tells us that 'photos have the advantage of always having a source in reality. One can always say that existed, it happened. One doesn't know the invisible, so one tries to recover it. In order to do that, one must be inspired by the photograph by finding a way of understanding its inner life. One must imagine the photographed person immediately before and immediately after the shot is taken.' Without letting everyone in the audience see them, two photographs are shown to a number of volunteers: the image of a young Mexican general a few minutes before he was executed, and that of a young Turkish girl posing ostentatiously. The pose is the essence of the photograph, Barthes has said. After several attempts drawing on these two characters, Brook explains: 'At a particular moment we started to be afraid of imitation. That's a mistake. Sensitive, intelligent imitation can bring a lot of things to light if every detail is considered with great care. A photograph is like a telegram from the invisible. Starting with a small element, a detail [could this be Barthes' "punctum"?], one can arrive at an intuitive understanding of a character. It is the same with a mask, which one has to study for a long time in order for a true understanding to be able to develop. One shouldn't use imitation superficially, insensitively. The discipline of detail has to be respected, that's what ensures the quality of imitation.' Afterwards, Brook describes past work with models, photographs, images – of the mentally ill for the *Marat/Sade*, for example.

Next we move on to a scene from *The Cherry Orchard* – that of Lopakhin's false marriage proposal to Varya, when he is dazzled by his ability to relativize every statement, to sidestep making any concrete decision in haste or any untested judgement. 'One must discover something that cannot be named. What does it mean to be tender or violent?' Brook inspires attention to detail, then verifies the accuracy of responses. 'It's not a question of being right, but of opening up the field of questions.' Later that evening I remember a fragment of wisdom, the saying that there can be no great master without a listener.

A PATH FOR EVERYONE

Today, a change in the usual course of events, as Alain Maratrat begins the session by having everyone in the auditorium perform exercises, brushing aside any possible thought of passivity. Sounds and movements, not always correctly performed. Brook points out a danger: 'The trap with easy exercises is that of not making demands on oneself: at the end you are still the same as before. One must ask oneself every time: why are we doing this exercise? Everyone must interpret it in their own way. Furthermore I never show exercises for them to be written down. One must invent exercises according to the context and the needs.' To his mind, it is not in this way that one acquires technique or expertise. Exercises liberate and help overcome fear. In their absence one cannot reach that state of 'telepathy which enables a group to be together, to react together'.

Groups formed on the previous day present short improvisations, which are followed by comments and questions. Brook admits that for him 'the true litmus in appreciating something is one's capacity to be interested or to be bored. Boredom is an insuperable barrier'. He also talks about rhythm, about the need to be 'alert to rhythm. When one is out of focus, what rhythm is there is never any good. Rhythm is not something arbitrary. It is like a pulse, an invisible pulse.' Brook has a liking for metaphors appropriated from the processes of living organisms.

Just as at the very beginning Brook had endeavoured to prevent solemnity from dominating proceedings, now our discussions continue freely as though these sessions will go on forever. What is of utmost importance to him is to maintain grace and lightness. Eventually he stands up, to offer us some advice rather than formulate a conclusion: 'These meetings have tried to respond to wishes that have come from many different quarters. They may be of some help, but afterwards the only possible choice for each and every one of you is to follow your own path.

'The only thing I can say that may be of some use is that there are two ways of making theatre. One can make theatre because one likes neither life, oneself nor other people. So one tries to create things that improve on life. With that as a starting point, as soon as one stops performing for a while, one will become increasingly bitter. The other possibility is to use one's contact with theatre to live in a better way. This starting point, on the other hand, can enable one to live successfully both within the group and on one's own. If one is frustrated and embittered in life, that's how one will be in theatre. If you prepare yourself in your everyday life, if your work space is kept clear and uncluttered, you will know how to be happy in theatre. One must not allow oneself to be overcome by bitterness... One of my finest actors destroyed himself with drugs because he had a vision of theatre that was so towering and exalted that he couldn't bear the slightest imperfection or diminishing of quality.

'All one can do is pursue the kind of work that opens one up and makes one available. Everyone here will develop their own way forward elsewhere. Now we are together, but if we leave here with regret we will not be as strong tomorrow. There cannot be any final concluding statement. We can all feel somewhat strengthened by this meeting, while recognizing that everything remains up in the air, nothing has been resolved. One can say that the theatre is good or bad. And how does one feel that? By tasting it. The proof of the pudding.'

A fragment of *The Bone (L'Os)* is performed, but not all of it. As usual we come to an end with a question, at an unresolved point: something remains unfinished. In the wake of the achievement of *The Mahabharata*, these meetings serve as provisional conclusions. Conversations continue in the carpeted space. Someone offers Brook a bag of sweets, someone else gives him a letter, a third person offers him a book that has just been published. Bénichou wanders through the crowd, Carrière tells a story: Yoshi, Bruce, Alain, Natasha are all there. It is hot and bright.

NOTE

Translation by David Williams of unpublished account of the CICT 'Rencontres' at the Bouffes du Nord, Paris, March 1986. An English version, 'Peter Brook's Six Days', translated by Susan Bassnett, was printed in *New Theatre Quarterly*, 3(10), May 1987.

EDITOR'S NOTES

1 These 'meetings' took place at the Théâtre des Bouffes du Nord, Paris, in March 1986, with an invited audience of practitioners, academics, friends and others.
2 In Georges Banu (ed.), *Peter Brook: Les Voies de la Création Théâtrale* (Paris: CNRS 1985), vol. 13, pp. 190–218. See also David Williams' compilation *Peter Brook, A Theatrical Casebook* (London: Methuen, 1988), which contains extracts from Rostain's log in translation (pp. 340–9).
3 To my knowledge, a doorframe has been used by the Centre in this way (i.e. as a 'root' object, the only imposed given in a continuous series of improvisations) at least since the mid-1970s. Not only at the Bouffes, but also around Paris – Banu mentions a 'brilliant improvisation' at Cergy-Pontoise – and indeed throughout the world. In December 1989, I watched the identical exercise in Bangalore during a 'Theatre Day' presented by members of the Centre to a gathering of Indian practitioners. As an object, a door (like Yoshi's box) is sufficiently banal to be virtually neutral, and at the same time inexhaustibly charged, latent. It conceals a space that can be defined as the opener wishes, his/her actions literally framed, highlighted, focused. Close the door and the frame is emptied, the door returns to neutrality and potentiality: it is a new door, demanding to be opened on to a fresh reality by someone as yet unknown. Like all such improvisational work around objects, comic anecdotes and splashy effects soon pall and have to give way to something less cluttered and more resonant, something simpler.
4 See, for example, David Williams, op. cit. (n2), p. 341.

Part V

STAGING AN EPIC: *THE MAHABHARATA* IN PRODUCTION

20

MAHABHARATA PRODUCTION DETAILS

Playtext by Jean-Claude Carrière
Set and costumes designed by Chloé Obolensky
Produced by Micheline Rozan and William Wilkinson
Directed and adapted into English by Peter Brook

The play was originally a co-production of the CICT and the 29th Festival d'Avignon, with the assistance of the Ministry of Culture and the City of Paris, France. The world tour (1987–8) of the English-language version was co-produced by the Los Angeles Festival, the Brooklyn Academy of Music, the Australian Bicentennial Authority and the City of Zurich, with the additional support of the French Ministry of Culture, L'Association Française d'Action Artistique, the Indian Council for Cultural Relations, AT & T, the Ford Foundation, the Rockefeller Foundation, the National Endowment for the Arts, Pippa Scott, the Asian Cultural Council, Union Bank of Switzerland, the Handicrafts and Handlooms Exports Corporation of India, Channel 4 Television – London.

FRENCH-LANGUAGE PRODUCTION

Premiered at the Festival d'Avignon in the Carrière Callet à Boulbon, 7 July 1985, as part of the 'Year of India in France', under the auspices of Mrs Pupul Jayakar and the Festival d'Avignon. Subsequent European tour to Italy, Germany, Greece and Spain, as well as a long season at the Bouffes du Nord, Paris.

Original cast (in alphabetical order)

Joséphine Derenne	Kunti
Mireille Maalouf	Ganga, Gandhari, Gudeshna
Tam Sir Niane	Madri, Hidimbi
Pascaline Pointillart	Amba, Subhadra, Sikhandin, Urvasi
Mallika Sarabhai	Satyavati, Draupadi

283

Maurice Bénichou	Ganesha, Krishna
Ryszard Cieslak	Dhritarashtra
Clovis	Ekalavya, Uttara, Abhimanyu
Georges Corraface	Duhsassana
Jean-Paul Denizon	Nakula, Aswhattaman
Mamadou Dioume	Bhima
Matthias Habich	Yudishthira
Andreas Katsulas	Salva, Jayadratha
Sotigui Kouyate	Bhishma, Parashurama
Alain Maratrat	Vyasa, Dhryshtadyumna
Clément Masdongar	Sisupala, Ghatotkatcha, The Sun
Vittorio Mezzogiorno	Arjuna
Bruce Myers	Karna
Yoshi Oida	Drona, Kitchaka
Andrzej Seweryn	Duryodhana
Douta Seck	Shakuni, Virata, Sanjaya
Tapa Sudana	Pandu, Shiva, Salya
Mahmoud Tabrizi-Zadeh	Sahadeva
Ken Higelin/Lufti Jafkar/Nicholas Sananikone/Samon Takahashi (alternating performances)	Young Boy

Musicians, under the direction of Toshi Tsuchitori (percussion): Djamchid Chemirani (percussion), Kim Menzer (*nagaswaram*), Mahmoud Tabrizi-Zadeh (*kamantche*), Kudsi Erguner (*ney*).

Production coordinator and assistant to the director	Marie-Hélène Estienne
Technical Directors	Jean-Guy Lecat, Philippe Mulon
Musical adviser	L. Subramaniam
Artistic adviser	Rajeev Sethi
Literary adviser	Philippe Lavastine
Traditional arts consultants	Nina Soufy, Karunakaran Nair
Musicologist	Vincent Dehoux
Martial arts consultant	Dan Schwarz
Fight arranger	Alain Maratrat
Assistant to the designer	Pippa Cleator
Lighting designer	Jean Kalman
Lighting assistant/operator	Pascal Merat
Properties	Nicole Aubry, Mustapha El Amri
Wardrobe mistresses	Valérie Blais, Geneviève Humbert

ENGLISH-LANGUAGE PRODUCTION

Premiered in Zurich (August 1987) in a boat-house by the Zurichsee, followed by world tour to Los Angeles (Raleigh Studios Sound Stage 12), New York (Majestic Theatre), Perth (Boya Quarry, Mundaring Shire), Adelaide (Anstey's Hill Quarry), Copenhagen, Glasgow (Old Transport Museum) and Tokyo (Ginza Saison Theatre).

Original cast (in alphabetical order)

Miriam Goldschmidt	Kunti
Corinne Jaber	Subhadra
Mireille Maalouf	Ganga, Gandhari, Gudeshna
Hélène Patarot	Amba, Sikhandin
Mallika Sarabhai	Satyavati, Draupadi
Tam Sir Niane	Madri, Hidimbi, Urvasi
Urs Bihler	Duhsassana
Ryszard Cieslak	Dhritarashtra
Georges Corraface	Duryodhana
Mamadou Dioume	Bhima
Richard Fallon	Jayadratha, Salva
Nolan Hemmings	Ekalavya, Uttara, Abhimanyu
Ciàran Hinds	Nakula, Aswhattaman
Jeffery Kissoon	Karna
Sotigui Kouyate	Bhishma, Parashurama
Tuncel Kurtiz	Shakuni, Sanjaya, Virata, Adiratha
Robert Langdon Lloyd	Vyasa
Mavuso Mavuso	The Sun, Sisupala, Ghatotkatcha
Vittorio Mezzogiorno	Arjuna
Bruce Myers	Ganesha, Krishna
Yoshi Oida	Drona, Kitchaka
Andrzej Seweryn	Yudishthira
Tapa Sudana	Pandu, Shiva, Salya, Maya
Mahmoud Tabrizi-Zadeh	Sahadeva
Akram Khan/Leo Moriya/Mipam Thurman/Antonin Stahly-Vishwan-adan (alternating performances)	Young Boy

Musicians: as for French-language production.

Assistant to the director/fight arranger	Alain Maratrat
Tour manager	Caroline Mackay
Wardrobe mistress	Jo Kuhn
Deputy wardrobe mistresses	Lindsay Pugh, Christine Tucker

Chief electrician	Michael Calf
Assistant electrician	Tim Boyd
Properties mistress	Denny Kingsley-Symes
Properties assistants	Claude Pinout, Florence Stahly
Chaperone	Valentine Stahly
Language coach	Clifford de Spenser
Administrator	Pierre Sberro-Terrighi

All costumes and props for *The Mahabharata* were made in India, in collaboration with the Paris Workshop.

India

Central Cottage Industries Corporation, New Delhi
Asha Sarabhai (quilted coats), Ahmedabad
Anokhi, Jaipur
Archana Shah, Ahmedabad
Sheela Balaji, Madras
Jamini Ahluwalia Jewelery, Bombay
Laila Tyabji, New Delhi
Kassab, Bombay
Weavers Service Centre, Hyderabad and Madras

The CICT also extended thanks for their advice and help to the following:

Dr Jyotindra Jain, Director of the Crafts Museum, New Delhi
Theatre Arts Museum, New Delhi
The Calico Textile Museum, Ahmedabad
Komal Kothari, Jodhpur
Martand Singh, New Delhi

In addition, particular thanks were extended to the many craftsmen and women who contributed to this work, and to Mrs Maya Johar, whose help was invaluable in coordinating the project.

Paris:

Ba Higgins (workshop head)
Mary Papadakis (costume assistant)
Anne Corbière, Patricia Faget, Rozenn Honoré, Isabelle Lebreton, Annika
  Nilsson (costume artisans)
Simon Duhamel (assistant to the designer, for the sets)
Alain Baliteau (scenic artist)
Ulysse Ketselidis, Malak Khazai, Annie Tolleter (scenic artisans)
Daniel Cendron (masks)
Patricia Cameron (hair pieces)
Sean Dunbar and Partners (props construction)

MAHABHARATA FILM PRODUCTION

Cast (in alphabetical order)

Erika Alexander	Madri, Hidimbi
Amba Bihler	Virata's daughter
Miriam Goldschmidt	Kunti
Hapsari Hardjito	Abhimanyu's wife
Gisèle Hogard	First princess
Corinne Jaber	Amba, Sikhandin
Leela Mayor	Satyavati
Yumi Nara	Virata's wife
Tam Sir Niane	Urvasi
Hélène Patarot	Gandhari
Julie Romanus	Second princess
Mallika Sarabhai	Draupadi
Myriam Tadesse	Gandhari's servant
Maurice Bénichou	Kitchaka
Lou Bihler	Young Karna
Urs Bihler	Duhsassana
Ryszard Cieslak	Dhritarashtra
Georges Corraface	Duryodhana
Jean-Paul Denizon	Nakula
Mamadou Dioume	Bhima
Nolan Hemmings	Abhimanyu
Ken Higelin	Deathless boy
Cìaran Hinds	Aswhattaman
Lutfi Jafkar	Uttara
Akram Khan	Ekalavya
Jeffery Kissoon	Karna
Sotigui Kouyate	Bhishma
Joseph Kurian	Dhryshtadyumna
Tuncel Kurtiz	Shakuni
Robert Langdon Lloyd	Vyasa
Clément Masdongar	Gazelle
Vittorio Mezzogiorno	Arjuna
Bruce Myers	Ganesha, Krishna
Yoshi Oida	Drona
Abbi Patrix	Salva
Bakary Sangare	The Sun, Rakshasa, Ghatotkatcha
Andrzej Seweryn	Yudishthira
Mas Soegeng	Virata
Antonin Stahly-Vishwanadan	The young boy
Tapa Sudana	Pandu, Shiva, Salya

Mahmoud Tabrizi-Zadeh   Sahadeva
Velu Vishwanadan   The hermit

Directed by Peter Brook
Produced by Michael Propper
Screenplay by Peter Brook, Jean-Claude Carrière, Marie-Hélène Estienne
Director of Photography, William Lubtchansky
Production Designer, Chloé Obolensky

1st assistant director	Marc Guilbert
2nd assistants	Philippe Tourret, Josef Baar
Continuity	Carole Fèvre
Editor	Nicolas Gaster
Sound	Daniel Brisseau, Dominique Dalmasso
Music	Toshi Tsuchitori, Djamchid Chemirani, Kudsi Erguner, Kim Menzer, Mahmoud Tabrizi-Zadeh
Songs interpreted by	Sarmila Roy
Music production	Philippe Eidel
Original soundtrack	Real World Label (RWLP9): produced by 3ème Etage/WOMAD, published by Virgin Musique, 1990
Production superviser	Christine Raspillère
Executive producers	Michael Birkett, Harvey Lichtenstein, Michael Kustow
Co-producers	Edward Myerson, Micheline Rozan, Rachel Tabori, William Wilkinson

21

THE WORLD TOUR
Logistics and Economics

During 1977 and 1978, the English-language version of *The Mahabharata* travelled around the world, opening in Zurich, before moving on to Los Angeles, New York, Perth, Adelaide, Copenhagen, Glasgow and Tokyo: eight cities in six countries. In this chapter, I will endeavour to detail some of the practical, logistical and technical problems and solutions generated by touring a production of this complex nature and size: economic exigencies (as well as, implicitly and critically, the economics of representation), venue prerequisites, adaptations of existing and 'found' or 'constructed' theatre spaces, and implications for the production itself of staging decisions made. By focusing almost exclusively on two tour venues, the Majestic Theater in Brooklyn, and the Boya Quarry in Perth – one indoor, one outdoor space – it will become apparent why London, for example, never played host to the production, despite Brook's avowed interest in returning to England.

THE MAHABHARATA AT THE 1987 NEXT WAVE FESTIVAL: MAJESTIC THEATER, BROOKLYN, NEW YORK, OCTOBER 1987 TO JANUARY 1988[1]

Built in 1904, the Majestic Theater was first proposed to Peter Brook as a potential venue for the Paris company in 1985 by Harvey Lichtenstein, the Brooklyn Academy of Music's president and executive producer: they had also looked unsuccessfully at various piers in the East River. Although the theatre had been abandoned in a state of complete disrepair almost two decades before in 1968, and had long since been boarded up, Brook immediately recognized a space in many ways akin to the Bouffes du Nord – ravaged, scarred and abused by the passage of time, fire and water damage and vandals, but structurally sound.

Located in a fairly depressed part of Brooklyn, at 651 Fulton Street, only two blocks away from the BAM, in its past the theatre had been a vaudeville, then a cinema. The building had to be significantly remodelled and restored to accommodate *The Mahabharata*; the New York architectural firm Hardy Holzman Pfeiffer acted as coordinators. The cost of renovations came to about $5 million, of which approximately $4.2 million was supplied by the City of New York, the owners of the property; the BAM managed to raise another $600,000, with a view to establishing a new venue for subsequent programming as well as for *The Mahabharata*. (In addition, the cost of mounting this one production was to be $2.2 million; principal sponsors included AT & T, the Ford, Philip Morris and Rockefeller Foundations, and the Eleanor Naylor Dana Trust.) The seven-month building process involved removing the old orchestra floor, then raising the playing area about 2 metres, as well as extending it out as a thrust through the proscenium arch into the auditorium; removing sections of the balcony and mezzanine, and installing new upholstered seating for semi-circular rows of benches on the ground floor and on the balcony – providing a new seating capacity of 901, rather than the 1,800 it had originally held; the partial restoration and stabilization of damaged pillasters and frescoes, to arrest further decline in the decor; the installation of heating, air-conditioning and ventilation systems; the complete replacement of an irreparable electrical system and the installation of new lighting equipment (including 220 lamps); and the building of dressing rooms and laundry facilities under the former stage, the latter essential for this production with about 6,000 separate costume pieces, many of them duplicates or triplicates.[2]

For the production itself, a 10 ton, foot-deep earth floor was laid on top of the stage, Brook and his technical manager Philipe Mulon specifying grade and colour of materials used. After exhaustive samplings of local clays and sands, a Long Island supplier provided the desired blend of sand and clay, which had to be combined with water and a straw binder. Michael Sommers described the process in *Theater Crafts*: 'the recipe involves six parts of ground-up iron ore (for colour), three parts clay (with a 20% sand content), one part water, and one part straw. About 40 cubic yards of these raw materials were delivered in a cement truck to the Majestic loading dock, where it was mixed. Spread 4″ thick over a plywood base that extends far out into the house, the mixture took three weeks to dry.' This floor would have to be inspected daily during the three-month run for any damage incurred during the performance. Into the surface of the floor were constructed shallow waterproof beds for the upstage river and the downstage pool. These concrete troughs had to be coloured to blend with the surrounding earth, then covered with sand to cushion the actors' bare feet. Both bodies of water were drained and refilled three times a week, and vacuumed daily to remove incidental debris.

In accordance with Chloé Obolensky's detailed specifications, the back and side walls of the building were reworked by a team of scenic artists. In order to achieve a quality both of neutrality and of 'crumbling decay', similar

Figure 21.1 The interior of the renovated Majestic Theater, New York: frontal view of the *Mahabharata* playing space from the balcony – the musicians' area to the right of the pool, the river at the base of the back wall. (Photographer – David Epstein, BAM)

to the Bouffes with its contradictory traces of incomplete demolition/ renovation, they applied a material called Structo-Lite (a tough foam pannelling) in layers on to the back wall, before painting and mottling it with dry pigments (ochre and Venetian red). Steel rungs were also secured in the back wall, climbing points for the actors in performance. Finally the interior of the building as a whole – boxes, lobbies, halls and stairways – was finished according to the same principle of 'stabilized distress'. Certain commentators inevitably read this 'unfinished' interior as evidence of a contrived post-modernism, a 'radical chic' aesthetic inappropriate and rather distasteful in times of economic recession. Accusations that a 'ruin' had been created are inaccurate[3] – it was already there; it had simply been rendered safe and technically workable, while an innate flavour of temporal wear had been 're-constructed' and foregrounded, a self-consciousness coherent with the meta-theatrical performative idiom of the production itself. One noteworthy fact is that the new venue immediately attracted a great deal of positive attention from other creative artists, who expressed publicly an interest in using the space for their own performances: these included Teresa Stratas, Pierre Boulez and Laurie Anderson. And the renovations were never intended by the BAM to make a space uniquely for *The Mahabharata* (unlike the work undertaken on the tour's open-air spaces). Clearly the Majestic has a future, for it will continue to offer a viable addition to existing facilities for performing artists of all kinds, complementing the nearby BAM's Opera House and Lepercq Space. Although its form in some ways celebrates temporality and impermanence, it will enjoy an extended 'shelf-life'.[4]

As far as pyrotechnics were concerned, New York's stringent fire safety regulations precluded the possibility of the company continuing with their rather primitive Paris effects (these included pouring rubber cement on the bare earth before igniting it, for both the circle of flame around the pool and the serpentine fire trail in Urvasi's wake). A great deal of research was undertaken by the BAM's Fred Bucholz in conjunction with Gary Zeller, a chemist and engineer with extensive experience in pyrotechnics for theatre, TV and film (*Scanners, Amityville II*, etc.). Eventually, a propane gas system had to be installed with the steel piping running beneath the wood floor base to outlets in the earth and the valves controlled from offstage. Michael Sommers records that a specified flame height of approximately 8 inches was preset prior to rehearsals; despite the presence at each performance of two licensed pyrotechnicians to operate and ignite effects, eight fireguards were always present.

In addition to the twenty-four actors and six musicians, accommodation had to be found for twenty-seven others, taking into account individual dietary specifications (macrobiotic, vegetarian, etc.): apartments were rented in Brooklyn and Manhattan for this travelling group of fifty-seven (including eleven children). In terms of the backstage crew, Brook's company is unique. There is no stage manager to call the show: a technical supervisor forewarns the actors at the beginning of a performance, which then is self-generated and regulated. Similarly, lighting cues are taken directly from the stage action. The actors themselves manipulate simple properties during the course of the performance to re-establish location; a crew of five ASM's are concerned solely with setting and distributing the vast array of hand props – weaponry, torches, ritual paraphernalia, etc. (the supply of many of them contractually agreed with the venue: see Perth Festival details below). Five dressers facilitated the numerous costume changes, while five prep crew and laundry staff ensured that damaged or soiled costuming could be mended or dry cleaned efficiently and quickly.

Lighting designer Jean Kalman and the BAM's assistant production manager were obliged to detail brand-new lamp hanging positions in this *tabula rasa*: the possibilities were of course limitless. They decided on some concealed side-light booms offstage, with frontal light supplied by attaching lamps to the rear and front of the balcony and the ceiling. Out of a desire to explore and exploit the specificity of this particular performance space, detailed plot design and cues were evolved during a three-day tech rehearsal, rather than emerging from a pre-existent model; none the less a basic structure of 250 cues elaborated for the Zurich production was used as the starting point. For the high-volume, directional lighting effects elaborated by Brook and Kalman, the production employed a number of Mole-Richardson 5 kW lamps and Mini-Brutes (both more familiar as cinematic lighting). To replicate the French 'Découpé' and 'Svoboda' units stipulated in the original plot, both of them difficult to find outside Europe, Strand ellipsoidals and PAR 64s were found – the latter, according to Mark Loeffler in *Theater Crafts*, 'extremely narrow-beam aircraft landing lights' to match the 'Svoboda' shafts. Loeffler also details colour correction filters used, most from the range of Rosco Cinegel, all eschewing overt colouration.

After months of budgetary analysis, the BAM eventually settled on two ranges of ticket price. Those seats at the very back of the gallery balcony went on sale at $30 each for a complete cycle of *The Mahabharata*; all others were made available at $75 each, if purchased before 9 October (the opening night was 13 October), and $96 thereafter. As was the case in Paris at the Bouffes, three possible performance structures for individual spectators were elaborated: on Saturdays, commencing at 1 p.m., the 'marathon' version as a continuum, with meal breaks between the separate parts; on three consecutive weekday nights, commencing at 8 p.m.; or on any single weeknight for three consecutive weeks. A special leaflet was printed and distributed with tickets to forewarn audiences as to how they might best prepare for the experience (appropriate clothing, reading the synopsis beforehand, resting, etc.), as well as to list food outlets.

During its three-month run, the productions played to 97 per cent capacity houses, and took box-office receipts of $1.5 million. It was one of the most successful events ever staged in the annual Next Wave Festival.

THE MAHABHARATA AT THE FESTIVAL OF PERTH, WESTERN AUSTRALIA: 2–13 FEBRUARY 1988[5]

Early in 1988, *The Mahabharata* travelled from the USA to the Festival of Perth in Western Australia, then on to the Adelaide Festival of the

293

Arts. The tour was produced in association with the Australian Bicentennial Authority, the CICT, and the Royal Shakespeare Theatre. Additional financial assistance was provided in Perth by the Government of Western Australia, through the Department of the Arts, and by the Friends of the Festival.

Production schedule (as of 8 June 1987)

June 19	Receive topographical survey map from Mundaring Shire engineer
June 26	Send on to Mulon in Paris: survey map, lighting details, props details, scaffold details and schedule, letter re. suitability of quarries
July 10	Mulon to advise which quarry[6]; press release to advise of site; confirm with Shire Council, discuss signage; contact State Energy Commission, Water Authority, Chief of Explosives, bus and train companies, local caterers, Dept. of Aviation (reorganization of incoming aircraft flight paths)
Aug. 15	See marathon *Mahabharata* in Zurich
Aug. 16/17	Discuss technical details with CICT company
Early Sept.	Mulon's second site visit: Tony Reagan (site manager) involved from now on
October	Check that following are finalized: lighting, scaffolding, final site preparation crew, performance and bump-out crew, site sheds and accessories, rubbish disposal, public lighting, security caravan, council water truck and signage to venue, assistance of W. A. Fire Brigade, catering (to be located in cleared area in adjacent quarry), policing for parking etc., Ministerial suspension of Bush Fire Board's 'no burn' period, Shire to divert traffic adjacent to quarry
December	Shire grades access road, levels site, clears carpark and cuts access steps; SEC installs power; Water Authority installs water outlet
Jan. 6	Mulon arrives Perth; power on to site. Site preparation (stage – marking out rock piles, seating location, river, etc.); caravan for security
Jan. 7–9	Site preparation (stage), including delivery of materials – e.g. 40 cu. metres of small limestone aggregate and 20 cu. metres of wet sand; also large loader to move boulders for rock piles ('wings' – walls of 10m long × 2.3m high × 2.5m wide). First freight containers leave New York. One phone on
Jan. 11	First freight arrives Melbourne: fumigation, then truck to Perth (30 hrs)

Jan. 11–12	Site preparation (stage/wings); water and roll surface
Jan. 13	Second freight containers leave New York
Jan. 13–16	Site preparation (river); scaffold (seating and lighting towers)
Jan. 15	Second freight arrives Melbourne: fumigation, then truck to Perth (30 hrs)
Jan. 18–19	Security on site; continue scaffold
Jan. 20–21	Props etc. arrive (approx. 80 cu. metres); rig stage lights and public lighting
Jan. 22–23	Rig stage lights; deliver all site sheds
Jan. 24	CICT technical team arrives Perth
Jan. 25	Bump-in props; P.M. – focus lights; company leaves Paris
Jan. 26	Continue bump-in; P.M. – focus
Jan. 27	Company arrives Perth; continue bump-in; P.M. – focus
Jan. 29 – Feb. 1	Rehearsals
Jan. 30	Peter Brook arrives Perth. TV crews film rehearsals – P.M.
Jan. 31	National press conference in the quarry
Feb. 2	Part I (approx. 7.15 – 10.00 p.m.)
Feb. 3	Part II (approx. 7.15 – 10.00 p.m.)
Feb. 4	Part III (approx. 7.15 – 11.00 p.m.)
Feb. 6	Marathon (approx. 7.15 p.m. – 6.30 a.m.)*
Feb. 9	Part I (approx. 7.15 – 10.00 p.m.)
Feb. 10	Part II (approx. 7.15 – 10.00 p.m.)
Feb. 11	Part III (approx. 7.15 – 11.00 p.m.)
Feb. 13	Marathon (approx. 7.15 p.m. – 6.30 a.m.)* [*with one half-hour and one one-hour interval]
Feb. 14	Bump-out props/LX; P.M. – props to Adelaide
Feb. 15	Bump-out seating, sheds; caravan out, security off site; power off (SEC), water off (Water Authority), phones off (Telecom); main CICT group depart for Adelaide
Feb. 16	Finish bump-out

Set layout: Philippe Mulon's technical specifications

(1) We shall play in front of the rock face indicated by Philippe Mulon to Henry Boston (see plan).
(2) Clear and level the area, then aggregate 100mm deep, compact and recover with finely crushed aggregate from the quarry.
(3) Construct grandstand seating for a maximum of 1,000 persons,[7] according to the attached plan. Ensure that there is a tunnel under the grandstand for the quick crossovers of actors from one wing to the other; also access at the back for latecomers.
(4) Ensure that there is a sufficient electrical supply for the stage lighting and the ancillary services (approx. 300 KwA).

(5) Ensure that there is a water supply with a long enough pipe to water the total playing area.

(6) For the lighting, build 2 × 12m high towers, 3 × 10m high towers and 2 × 6m high towers (see plan).

(7) Layout of playing area in detail:

(a) Build two stone walls, one on each side of the stage, according to the instructions of M. Mulon. Behind these walls, we will create wings using cane fencing or other material. Behind the wings on both sides, we will need quick-change booths containing: full-length mirror; costume rack; shelving (2.2m high × 2.5m wide, 5 shelves; weapon holders; 5 × trestle tables; chairs; plastic basins (to be emptied during the day); safety lighting on a dimmer; fire extinguishers (1 × foam, 1 × water); stage weights to hold object down when it is windy.

(b) On the playing surface, build two pools (river and lake) in earth-coloured cement of about 100mm depth, in the places indicated by M. Mulon (see plan).

(c) Fix 20 metal spikes into the rock face (positions to be decided by M. Mulon) so that the actors can climb up.

(d) Ensure that you can cover the playing area with a tarpaulin in case of storm, heavy rain or burning sun (plastic to retain humidity?)

(e) Construct stage left a wooden platform for the musicians – 120mm high.

(f) Construct three bridges out of old planks which will straddle the river: 1 × 3m × 0.66m, 2 × 3m × 1.32m.

(g) Ensure that there are audio monitors in the dressing rooms and the village.

(h) Ensure that there is intercom between prompt corner and the lighting desk position.

(8) General layout arrangements:

(a) Ensure that there is public lighting between the entrance and the stage which can be controlled by the lighting board operator.

(b) Blue safety lighting all around the seating, the wings and the dressing rooms.

(c) Ensure that when the telephone is installed there is the possibility of switching from audio to visual.

(d) Put down old carpets on the offstage thoroughfares of both actors and latecomers.

(e) Provide toilets for the general public (vital given the length of performances).

(f) Change the water in the small pond every day, and in the river every three performances (you will need a water pump).

(g) Provide 50 cushions for the general public to sit on the ground in front of the grandstand seating.

296

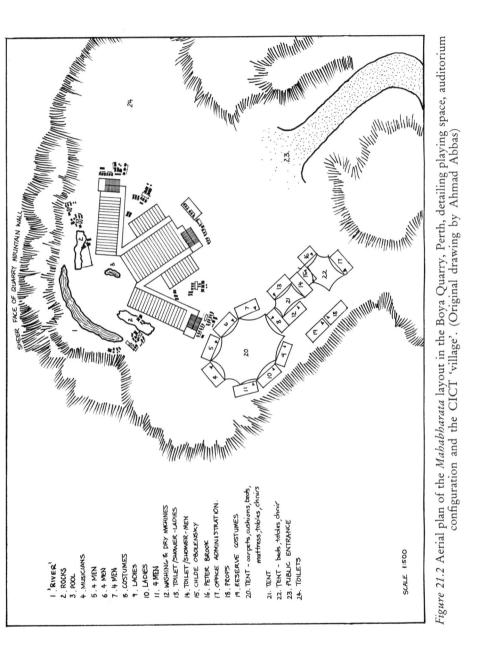

1. 'RIVER'
2. ROCKS
3. POOL
4. MUSICIANS
5. 4 MEN
6. 4 MEN
7. 4 MEN
8. COSTUMES
9. LADIES
10. LADIES
11. 4 MEN
12. WASHING & DRY MACHINES
13. TOILET /SHOWER -LADIES
14. TOILET /SHOWER-MEN
15. CHLOE OBOLENSKY
16. PETER BROOK
17. OFFICE ADMINISTRATION.
18. PROPS
19. RESERVE COSTUMES
20. TENT - carpets, cushions, beds, mattress, tables, chairs
21. TENT
22. TENT - beds, tables, chair
23. PUBLIC ENTRANCE
24. TOILETS

SCALE 1:500

Figure 21.2 Aerial plan of the *Mahabharata* layout in the Boya Quarry, Perth, detailing playing space, auditorium configuration and the CICT 'village'. (Original drawing by Ahmad Abbas)

(h) Provide cleaning for the auditorium and ancillary buildings (dressing rooms, etc.).

Figure 21.3 Aerial view of the layout for *The Mahabharata* in the Boulbon quarry, Avignon (1985), detailing the location of pool, river, rock-piles, etc.; the actors are warming up in the central playing area with Brook. (CICT photograph)

(i) Provide in each wing, under the seating, covers and plastic tarpaulins to store the musical instruments and the larger properties.

N.B. All of these constructions and arrangements must be ready when M. Mulon arrives to begin work in early January.

Lighting requirements: with additional explanatory information supplied to the Festival of Perth by BAM, New York

- 20 × 5k Fresnels (Pollux) – strong washes from all directions. Two 'effects' are installed in different areas on two of these units: the first comprising a manual colour change in the form of a curtain of lighting media drawn up in front of the unit; the second also using a 'curtain – but in this case the curtain is a piece of diffusing media which is drawn up in front of the unit, casting a moving 'shadow' across the stage.

Figure 21.4 Scenic configuration for the beginning of THE WAR, Boya Quarry, Perth. Centre stage, Tsuchitori's drum; to the left of the seating, the musicians' area. In the background, the quarry wall. (Photographer – Tony Reagan)

- 36 × 1k Fresnels (Polaris) – 'plano-convex'; also provide washes, although from shorter distances. FIND SUBSTITUTE.
- 16 × 1k zoom profiles (20/35) – 'Découpé'; cf. traditional ellipsoidal or 'Leko', with additional unique feature – a variable focal length, or 'zoom' function.
- 18 × 1k zoom profiles (7/20) – 'Découpé' (as above).
- 17 × 9 light (24V × 250W) 'Svoboda' lights – intense multi-beam shafts (similar to aircraft lights). These two-tiered units, fitted with beam projector optics, can be used to punch through strong washes and highlight action. In the Bouffes, they are hung both horizontally and vertically, from high and low positions. FIND SUBSTITUTE.
- 2 × 6 light (110V × 650W) 'Minibrutes' – 3 with 'Daylight' lamps, 3 with 'Indoor' lamps: fill lights – standard film industry unit, as booster for location and indoor shots in direct fill light or bounce light.
- 8 × 1k Cyclorama lighting – 'Horiziodes': fill lights.

Lighting control: a computer memory unit, with the capacity for 240 memories. Circuits: 25 × 5kW, 44 × 2.5kW.

Lighting positions to be determined by M. Jean Kalman according to the venue. Lighting and sound control to be installed at the rear of the centre grandstand.

Major lighting equipment eventually hired by the Festival of Perth and source

20 × 5 kW Pollux Fresnel Luminaires (spots)	ABC
10 × replacement 2.5kW lamps	ABC
8 × 2kW Fresnel spots	Perth
23 × 2kW Cadenza spots	Melbourne
5 × CCT spots	Sydney
4 × 6 light Minibrutes	Channel 9
7 × 9 light Minibrutes	Channel 7
64 × Parcans	Perth
4 × Svoboda light curtains	Adelaide Festival
12 × mini light curtains	Adelaide Festival
12 × dimmer racks	Perth
18 × 500W spots	Perth
16 × 500W floods	Perth
1 × Gemini control desk	Melbourne

Andy Ciddor, the lighting technician employed by the Festival of Perth to coordinate lighting in the Boya Quarry set-up, etc., recalls that the Minibrutes – hired from Channel 9 and Channel 7 TV, Perth – were used as broad and 'brutal' directional sources from lateral positions; they were necessary given the nature of the space and the primacy of visibility stipulated for this visually exciting production. A number of profiles were employed for lateral slashes, while others were pooled around the forestage pond. In addition to profiles on the cliff face, providing textural highlighting and diagonal slashes across the rock, there were also lamps located on the cliff top for actors (for sequences in *Exile* and *The War*) – performers had to be guided up a dangerously steep path on the stage right lip of the quarry by ASMs with torches. Two cliff-top lamps were used as backlighting for the space, to give shape and form to figures on stage. There were two unusual specials: a 'moonlight effect' on the cliff wall, and profile light reflected off the river onto the wall, producing a ripple tank effect, 'liquefying' the solid surface. Almost 300 lighting cues were specified, almost all of them visual, operated using a Gemini board with about 500 memories and at least 108 channels (controlling 66 × 2.5kW and 42 × 5kW dimmers); and in the end approximately 1.2MWs of power were needed to sustain performance, public lighting, the 'village' and catering facilities (located in the neighbouring quarry). In terms of the power required for cooking for over 800 people, refrigeration, safety lighting, cabling, etc., the catering marquees used more power than the stage space.

Problems encountered included: the need for the State Energy Commission to install a 22kV feed line from existing supply lines about 200 metres away, as well as a 10kVA transformer in the parking area (covering about 20,000 sq. metres), and two 200kVA transformers in parallel to supply the performance and catering areas (at a cost of $13,000); the obligation to refocus the plot six times during the run – the lamps were moved by strong gusting winds, which in particular caught barn doors on the Minibrutes, and on one occasion during the night blew a 2kW Fresnel right off its mountings, smashing it. Despite the initial 'intransigence' of the CICT technical management, much of the specified equipment eventually had to be replaced with equivalents, which involved searching Australia-wide, given the fact that both the Sydney and Adelaide festivals were to take place at roughly the same time. The venue was asked to provide a dozen dimmer racks 'without noise to distract the actors' (racks which Ciddor claims were inaudible anyway, given the high winds) – and finally some of these had to be replaced at the last moment as a result of recurrent 'bugs'. There were significant communications problems, in the absence of a stage manager *per se* – and with no telephones in use, four or five radio network systems had to be in simultaneous use for technical crew, FOH, catering, carparking and bus disembarkation stewards, as well as the state emergency services.[8] Finally, during plotting, some young kids decided it would be fun to hurl rocks off the cliff top at the technicians below! Ciddor remembers the event as a whole in terms of 'a crisis management situation'.

CICT costumes and props freighted to venue[9]

Costuming:

446 pairs of trousers	56 battle/war skirts
182 shirts	364 assorted pieces of cloth/fabrics
35 long shirts	1 head band
27 short shirts	1 headdress
19 quilted shirts	2 turbans
99 vests	58 black scarves
35 quilted vests	10 assorted scarves
120 assorted jackets/coats	43 pairs of leather gaiters
8 'Nagaland' raincoats	28 pairs of leather boots
36 quilted jackets/coats	54 pairs of leather shoes
9 embroidered jackets/coats	61 belts
26 battle/war coats	1 shell belt

3 waistcoats
2 large cloaks
12 dhotis
14 cholis
76 pairs of puttees/leggings
2 pairs of quilted puttees
9 saris
30 dresses
55 skirts
2 embroidered skirts
2 quilted skirts
1 'Ganga' skirt
11 hats
1 box of make-up
1 bag of assorted make-up boxes

5 pairs of gloves
5 pairs of leather gloves
2 fur masks
3 fur costumes
1 box of costume jewellery
1 bag of assorted jewellery
4 silver bracelets
1 bell necklace
2 wooden necklaces
2 strings of pearls
1 pair of bell ankle bracelets
1 pair leg bells
1 wig
5 hair pieces

Properties:

2 boxes of assorted bells, dice, shells
1 pole of bells/shaking stick
2 padded frames
12 masks
2 fur masks
1 crown
17 bags of assorted floral garlands
1 flower platter
2 cloth bundles
3 coils of red rope
2 rolls of silk
10 silk flags
4 red flags
9 carpets/rugs
2 big white carpets/rugs
5 black carpets/rugs
7 red carpets/rugs
4 small carpets/rugs (dhurries)
29 rush mats
1 straw bundle bird
1 boar
1 piece of dog fur
1 wooden ball
10 puppets
2 large books

3 wooden ladders
2 platforms
1 palanquin (Gandhari)
3 beds
2 death beds
1 bed support (Bhishma)
8 sets of bed legs
4 mattresses
15 pillows/cushions with assorted covers
2 blankets
1 silver dish
1 silver cup
1 brass bell
4 brass candle holders
1 brass bowl
9 brass cups
7 brass lamps
8 brass dishes
1 brass vase
2 copper vases
1 metal bell
4 metal bowls
5 metal bottles/jars
1 marble bowl
1 stone jar

302

2 small wooden tables
1 dice table
6 dice (for dice game)
1 wooden board game
3 conches
4 torches
12 wicker/bamboo palisades
3 umbrellas
3 umbrella heads
4 walking sticks/canes
3 wooden cartwheels

30 clay bowls
2 clay vases
9 clay plates
6 wooden bowls
1 wooden jug
4 wooden plates
1 wooden tray
5 wicker baskets
1 wicker bowl
4 skin bowls
7 oil lamps

Weaponry, etc.:

3 leather sticks/crops
5 whips
1 piece of straw armour
2 armour pieces
8 swords
1 double-bladed sword
1 sword with bendy blade
4 swords in leather sheaths
2 gold-handled swords
4 swords with bamboo handles
and bells
3 sword sheaths
4 daggers with belts
5 knives
1 knife with blood
4 bows with assorted arrows
(approx. 150)
2 targets

1 box with metal scythes (Kalarippayatt)
4 large clubs
2 wooden clubs
3 axes
9 spears/lances
1 iron bar
1 metal point-spike
1 pick handle
63 bamboo lengths
5 wooden batons/sticks
26 half-length batons/sticks
35 fighting sticks
2 red-covered sticks
2 shields
2 leather shields
1 tree trunk (Bhima)

Musical instruments:

Drums
1 maddharam
3 zarbs
1 gimbe
1 kettledrum
2 tablas
1 7-headed drum
2 dholes
3 damals

1 mridangan
1 khale
1 pakawaj
1 gatabela
1 tabor
2 gongs
1 gatam
4 other drums

1 tavil
1 talking drum

1 dovura
30 drumsticks

Others

1 harmonium
1 kamantche
1 xylophone
2 bendils
1 esrj
1 sithar
1 revanhata
1 set of bells
1 lute
1 pungi
1 flute
1 Balinese flute
1 bagpipes
1 soprano saxophone
3 stringed instruments/bows
1 wooden flute

1 santour
2 violins
1 Pan pipe
1 decorated conch
1 cow horn
2 bamboo flutes
6 nagaswarams
1 set of crotals
1 erhu
2 didgeridoos
1 wooden horn
1 trombone
1 clarinet
1 koto
8 combos

3 boxes of small instruments
4 drum stands
1 gong stand
1 percussion stool

Properties to be provided by the Festival of Perth

Unless otherwise stated, amounts are for one marathon performance:

20 'night light' candles (votive)
15 Zip firelighters
1 500g tin of carpet stain-remover powder (Pancrasol)
1 pack of cotton wool
14 pieces of camphor: 1 inch sq. blocks for burning
1 150g bag of incense
25 round charcoal burners (for the incense)
1 2kg box of Indian/Lebanese sweets (for 10 cycles)
1 2kg sack of brick dust: very fine, red
2 large sacks of vermiculite (potting mixture insulation): very fine, light-coloured bits
1 1kg tin of rubber cement for paper (for 10 cycles)
15 eucalyptus leaf candle holders
15 large candles: 3 in. round, 1½ in. high
30 torches: wound string on cardboard

20 bamboo rods for arrows: 1.2m long (to be replaced after each cycle)

15 artificial rose petals

20 artificial flowers: Frangipani (for 10 cycles)

12 fresh flowers (Marigold)

25 sheets of paper for Ganesha's book: Offset Michel Ange 100g, or Verger d'Arche 160g: 360mm × 360mm)

1 litre of kerosene for Vyasa's cotton wick (for 20 cycles)

2 small cigarette lighters (black)

2 big boxes of matches (for 5 cycles)

1 bottle of vegetable oil (for oil lamps)

1 metre of wick cotton

1 box of Bic ballpoint refills

1 kg of long grain rice

1 whole coconut

1 150g bag of big black charcoal (for incense)

1 tin of condensed milk (for 10 cycles)

Fruit: 2 mangos, 2 kg of grapes, 4 bananas, 2 kiwi fruits, dried figs, dried apricots

1 bottle of coconut oil for Mallika's cotton wicks (for 4 cycles)

25 pieces of very dry kindling wood for burning camp fire: 25 cm long, 1 stick 65 cm long

Green twigs: access to shrubs/trees for cuttings

1 large piece of tree wood for Mamadou

1 bag of small, soft, cubed vanilla liquorice candy

3 bags of straw to make torches

1 stick for fighting: hard wood (oak?), approx 2.6 cm by 2 m – must be very strong

1 bundle of straw (for Karna)

1 canister of white hair spray

2 pieces of bark

2 litres of washable blood: non-staining, non-toxic – must be able to be swallowed

1 5kg sack of sand, same colour as the stage

1 500g box of biscuits: several types, pretty looking

Pink face powder

150g of sandlewood powder

Some glitter

2kg of Fuller's earth/clay court construction material ('rassoul') for Mamadou's mud

1 box of red make-up powder and cream foundation (for 10 cycles)

Pyrotechnic specials: to be provided by the Festival of Perth (per marathon)

The following are subject to the fire officer's approval, otherwise please find substitutes:

16 ounces of Lycopode powder (dry hair shampoo powder which ignites when thrown into a flame)
1 litre of C6H12 (cyclohexane burner liquid – industrial quality)
4 boxes of Spectaflam (paste)
1 smoke bomb/canister, or mushroom cloud bomb: approx. 20 second burner [Perth Festival eventually used Electric Salutes – Howards – and Electric Smoke Clouds – Xetex.]

Pyrotechnics: details from a production report sent on to the Perth Festival by Paul King of the BAM, New York

(1) Trail of fire (cyclohexane[10])

A liquid chemical is poured out of a container by an actor over the water in the pool, and on to the earth, trailing off stage. The chemical is then lit off stage and a low-level flame travels on stage. The flame burns for 3–5 minutes and dies out as the chemical is consumed. The chemical breakdown is, as yet, unknown, but research is being done on its composition.

(2) Circle of fire (cyclohexane)

A yellow liquid chemical with a rubber cement base is poured out of a container around the perimeter of the pool. This is then ignited by an actor, and burns for 10 minutes. One quart of this material is used per cycle. An undesirable result of this effect is a black residue left on the earth that eventually gets on to the costumes. Efforts to eliminate this are being made.

(3) Fire ball (Lycopode)

'Lycopode', a commercially available pollen powder that is used extensively in film work and circus, is the ingredient in this effect. Ony one actor employs this material, although another carries the container. The actor throws a handful of the powder at a torch that he holds high overhead. He is relatively isolated from the other actors on stage. The effect forms part of a carefully devised ceremony. 500g are used per cycle.

(4) Camphor tablets

These small tablets, commonly burnt in Indian ritual, are placed on the earthen deck in a wide pattern, then lit with a torch by an actor. A small 2″ high flame is produced that burns for a short duration, and is extinguished by an actor stepping on them. About 20 tablets are used per cycle.

(5) Tube torches

These torches are constructed of 7–8″ diameter paper tubing that is wrapped with a wax-impregnated jute twine. They are 16″ long and burn for 15 minutes. Torches either burn out themselves, or are immersed in water or sand to extinguish. 30 are used per cycle. Available from Paris Festival Pyropa, 18 rue Notre Dame de Lorette, Paris 75009.

(6) Grass mat torches

Two foot length of grass matting rolled and bound around bamboo shafts. Several are used without the shafts and are grasped at one end. They are approximately 4″ in diameter: 3 of them are used per cycle. Extinguishing effected in the same way as the tube torches.

(7) Campfire

The position is pre-set on stage. An actor scoops loose earth from a masonry-based recess in the earthen deck, 'builds' the fire using 1″ diameter birch sticks (kiln-dried before use in New York, to reduce the amount of smoke), and ignites the fire using a grass mat torch. At least one actor always attends the campfire: sand is applied to extinguish. The same effect was used for *La Tragédie de Carmen*.

(8) Candles

A number of small and large candles are used at various times on stage. Large candles are inserted into eucalyptus leaf holders, in order to float on the water.

'The village': requirements for site shed arrangements (to be located near the playing area – see plan)

For the actors: 4 rooms (17 men), 2 rooms (6 women), all equipped with make-up tables, chairs, costume racks, full-length mirror, lights and power points, air conditioning.

For the musicians: 1 room (5 men), with 2 make-up tables, 2 chairs, a carpet, some cushions, 3 trestle tables, costume rack, a 2-bar heater for instruments, air conditioning.

For the costumes: 2 rooms, with 3 high tables, 5 ironing boards (3 full-length, 2 half-length), 5 steam irons (able to take tap water), 2 Bernina sewing machines, 30 costume rails, 6 laundry baskets, lights and power points. Also 1 room with 2 washing machines (minimum capacity – 6 kg), 2 tumble dryers (minimum capacity – 6 kg), 2 drying cabinets and sinks with running water.

For the props: 1 room, with 3 tables, shelving, costume rack on wheels, a fridge, air conditioning.

1 small room each for the director, the designer, the administration – each with tables, chairs, bed, light, telephone, air conditioning.

Create a carpeted area, shaded by a canopy, in the middle of the site shed layout. In this area, provide 4/5 tables to work on, eat, etc., chairs, benches, camp bed, 30 cushions, light. Also provide someone to prepare meals during the marathons.

Minimum sanitary requirements: 3 showers, 4 WCs and basins.

Staffing requirements (to be provided by the Festival of Perth)

10 mechs for bump-in and bump-out
4 electrics for rigging and hook-up before the company arrives
3 electrics for refocusing during rehearsals (includes board operator)
2 electrics during performances
2 mechs during set-up, rehearsals and performances (change water, clean stage and wings, etc.)
3 props during set-up, rehearsals and performances (includes pyro)
4 dressers to maintain costumes during the day (washing and ironing, etc.) throughout the whole season, including bump-in/out
3 dressers during rehearsals and performances
1 site manager (Tony Reagan)
Tutor and chaperone (approx. 3 hours a day for 5 days a week)
Security guard to live on site throughout run; also 2 security personnel on site during each performance
Van driver to take company to and from quarry from accommodation in Fremantle (to arrive 1½ hours prior to beginning of perform-ance)
Volunteer fire watchers on duty throughout performances.

Budgetary estimates for Australian tour (as of April 1987)

EXPENDITURE	AUSTRALIAN $
Pre-production	352,112
Fees (weekly)	414,285
Per diems	86,400 (40 days)
Accommodation (Adelaide)	72,000 (20 days)
Accommodation (Perth)	72,000 (20 days)
Advance guard	25,000
Union dues	13,500
Fares (Perth-Adelaide)	12,000
Freight (Perth-Adelaide)	12,500
Running costs	25,352
Tour management	16,000
Contingencies	72,580
SUB-TOTAL	1,171,227
INCOME	
LESS ABA GRANT	
(Bicentennial Authority)	650,000
NETT TOTAL	521,227
LESS PERTH PERFORMANCES	232,769
LESS ADELAIDE PERFORMANCES	290,961
SUB-TOTAL	523,730
TOTAL PROFIT	2,503

Festival of Perth ticket prices (cost per cycle)

General public	$90
Pensioners/unemployed	$78
Friends of the Festival	$69
Students	$60
Artcard (from Jan. 1988)	$54

NOTES

1 For some of the information connected with the New York production that follows, I am indebted to the co-authors of an article about *The Mahabharata* at the Majestic that was printed in the technical theatre journal *Theater Crafts*

('Peter Brook's Earth, Water and Fire', November 1987). The article was co-written by Michael Sommers, Mark Loeffler and Bree Burns.

2 All of these costume pieces, hand-stitched in India, had to be flameproofed at regular intervals, a process which in itself adversely affects the quality of fabrics in terms of colour and texture. The costumes used in the French-language version had to be replaced due to wear and tear. As a result of the physical exigencies of the performance and its elemental environment, some cast members were obliged to have at their disposal three to six sets each of back-up costumes for each run.

3 See, for example, 'Putting Old Wrinkles into a Theater's New Face' by Michael Kimmelman, *New York Times*, 25 October 1987. He suggests that the new space is 'the architectural equivalent of the intentionally worn look of a Ralph Lauren jacket'. Paradoxically, he felt, 'it is precisely because it works hard to evoke the past that it is all too much a building of this moment. The strong historicizing tendencies that have dominated architecture for the last two decades find a resolution here: not only are decorative elements from the past employed, but an artificial impasto of time lays across the entire design. The theater harks back to the follies that British aristocrats built on the hills of their country estates roughly two centuries ago . . . The Majestic's "timeless" concept may soon seem woefully dated.'

4 In February 1988, the Majestic played host to a three-month run of Brook's English-language production of Chekhov's *The Cherry Orchard*, starring Natasha Parry. The transition between the two productions evinced Brook and Lichtenstein's claims for the new space's versatility. It has subsequently been used for concert performances during the '*651*' music festival, and for theatre and dance in the Next Wave Festival, both in 1990. The Majestic has also housed community events such as Burl Hash's annual Celebrate Brooklyn festival.

5 I am indebted to the Festival of Perth – and in particular to Mr Henry Boston – for granting me free access to their records; the bulk of material in this section comes from that source, with additional information from interviews, correspondence, etc.

6 A disused quarry off Hudman Road in Boya, West of Perth, was eventually chosen after a long search in the Perth area.

7 The scaffold seating, with a capacity of 801, as well as the scaffold lighting towers, were hired from Rapid Metal Development, Perth, at a cost of $21,600; risers were at 300mm increments and of 800mm depth, with the width of the front of the performing area at 14 metres. See plan for configuration.

8 State Fire Brigade water trucks were present at every performance, understandably wary of this mid-summer tinder-box environment and the potential hazards caused by caterers, spectators smoking, etc.: one crew was located in the graded catering area, another at a look-out on the cliff top. And late in the afternoon of February 9, a small fire did break out around an SEC pole-mounted transformer installation which had shorted; the fire was extinguished within 30 minutes by the CICT company and crew using sand before the water trucks and a fire engine arrived. Full power was restored, enabling the performance to start with only a minimal delay. A full inquiry was undertaken by the Festival.

9 From an inventory submitted to French Customs, August 1987, with insurance valuations. The inventory lists almost 3,000 articles *in toto*, and records an estimated value of FFr 488,738.

10 According to *The Merck Index: An Encyclopedia of Chemicals and Drugs*

(Rahway, New Jersey, 1976, p. 2728), cyclohexane – C6H12 – is usually employed as a solvent for lacquers and resins, or as a paint and varnish remover: insoluble in water, it is obtained in the distillation of petrol or by hydrogenation of benzene. It is not listed as a carcinogen, which appears to have been the worry here.

BIBLIOGRAPHY

PETER BROOK, THE CICT AND CRITICAL MATERIAL RELATING TO THE CICT *MAHABHARATA*

For a fuller bibliographical listing, please refer to David Williams' *Peter Brook: A Theatrical Casebook*.

Amos, Stephen (1988) 'An epic in a quarry' (review of *The Mahabharata* in Perth), *The Australian* 4(2).

Banu, Georges (ed.) (1985) *Peter Brook: Les Voies de la Création Théâtrale*, vol. XIII, Paris, Editions du CNRS.

—— (ed.) (1985) *Le Mahabharata* – Special Edition, *Alternatives Théâtrales* 24, July.

—— (1986) 'Les six jours de Brook': an account of the CICT 'Recontres' at the Bouffes du Nord, Paris, in March – never published in French; an English version, translated by Susan Bassnett, 'Peter Brook's Six Days', was printed in *New Theatre Quarterly* 3(10), May 1987.

——, and Martinez, Alessandro (eds) (1990) *Gli anni di Peter Brook*, Milan, Ubulibri.

Barber, John (1985) 'Brook's epic contest' (review of *Le Mahabharata* in Avignon), *Daily Telegraph*, 16 July.

Behr, Edward (1985) 'A three-night epic play' (review of *Le Mahabharata* in Avignon), *Newsweek*, 19 August.

Bernard, Kenneth (1980) 'Some observations in the theatre of Peter Brook', *Theater*, Fall/Winter.

Bharucha, Rustom (1988) 'Peter Brook's *Mahabharata*: A view from India', *Theater* 19(2), Spring.

Billington, Michael (1985) 'Krishna comes to the city of the Popes' (review of *Le Mahabharata* in Avignon), *Guardian*, 16 July.

—— (1985) 'A Fire snake in the sand' (review of *Le Mahabharata* in Avignon), *Théâtre en Europe* 8, October.

—— (1987) 'Dawning glory' (review of *The Mahabharata* in Zurich), *Guardian*, 18 August.

—— (1988) 'Peter Brook: practical optimist rather than hermetic visionary', *Bicentennial Arts Guide*, Sydney.

—— (1989) 'Brook at the R.S.C.', paper presented at a conference in Taormina, Sicily, on the occasion of Brook's award of the Premio Europa per il Teatro, May.

Billington, Michael and Hebert, Hugh (1989) 'The realm of grand illusion' (review of *The Mahabharata* film), *Guardian*, 11 December.

Bose, Mihir (1989) 'Religion without responsibility' (review of *The Mahabharata* film), *Daily Telegraph*, 9 December.

Bradby, David and Williams, David (1989) *Directors' Theatre*, Basingstoke, Macmillan.

Bramwell, Murray (1988) 'Day for night' (review of *The Mahabharata* in Adelaide), *The Adelaide Review*, February.

Brennan, Mary (1988) 'Dazzling tale of life and death' (review of *The Mahabharata* in Glasgow), *Glasgow Herald*, 19 April.

Britton, David (1987) 'Theatre, popular and special: and the perils of cultural piracy' (interview with Peter Brook), *Westerly* 32(4), December.

— — (1988) 'Message of hope in nine-hour epic play' (review of *The Mahabharata* in Perth), *The West Australian*, 4 February and 6 February.

Brook, Peter (1968) *The Empty Space*, Harmondsworth, Penguin.

— — (1987) *The Shifting Point*, New York, Harper & Row.

Brookman, Rob (1987) Review of *The Mahabharata* in Zurich, *Adelaide Advertiser*, 12 September.

Brown, Jonathon (1989) 'A human perspective' (review of *The Mahabharata* film), *The Times Literary Supplement*, 22–28 December.

Burdett-Coutts, William (1988) Review of *The Mahabharata* in Adelaide, *The Scotsman*, 11 April.

Calder, Angus (1988) 'Nice one Peter? Reflections on Peter Brook's *Mahabharata* in Glasgow', *Cencrastus* 30, Summer.

Campbell, Lance (1988) 'A nocturnal awakening' (review of *The Mahabharata* in Perth), *Adelaide Advertiser*, 20 February.

Cannan, Denis, and Higgins, Colin (1975) *Les Iks* (Paris: CICT; French translation by Jean-Claude Carrière).

Carrière, Jean-Claude (1985) *Le Mahabharata* (theatre adaptation), Paris, CICT, 3 volumes: 'La Partie de Dès', 'L'Exil dans la Forêt', 'La Guerre'.

— — (1987) *The Mahabharata* (theatre adaptation translated from the French by Peter Brook), New York, Harper & Row; London, Methuen, 1988.

Chaikin, Joseph (1980) *The Presence of the Actor*, New York, Atheneum.

Champagne, Lenora (1987) 'West from India with Brook and Carrière', *American Theater*, December.

Cody, Gabrielle (1988) 'Art for Awe's Sake', *Theater* 19(2), Spring.

Conway, Anne-Marie (1988) 'Life, the universe and (nearly) everything' (review of *The Mahabharata* in Glasgow), *Times Higher Educational Supplement*, 27 April.

Coveney, Michael (1988) Review of *The Mahabharata* in Glasgow, *Financial Times*, 19 April.

Croyden, Margaret (1980) *The Center: A Narrative*, Paris, CICT.

— — (1985) 'Peter Brook transforms an Indian Epic for the stage' (review of *Le Mahabharata* in Avignon), *New York Times*, 25 August.

— — (1987) 'Peter Brook creates a nine-hour epic' (interview with Peter Brook, re. *The Mahabharata* in New York), *New York Times*, 4 October.

Curtis, Anthony (1985) Review of *The Mahabharata* in Avignon, *Financial Times*, 16 July.

Curtiss, Thomas Quinn (1985) Review of *Le Mahabharata* in Avignon, *Herald Tribune*, 23 July.

Dasgupta, Gautam (1987) '*The Mahabharata*: Peter Brook's orientalism', *Performing Arts Journal* 30, Volume 10(3).

—— (1987) 'Rites and Wrongs' (review of *The Mahabharata* in New York), *The Village Voice*, 27 October.

Devereaux, Kent (1989) 'Peter Brook's production of *The Mahabharata* at the Brooklyn Academy of Music', *Asian Theatre Journal* 5(2), Fall.

Drake, Sylvie (1987) 'The longest story ever told' (interview with Peter Brook), *Los Angeles Times*, 16 August.

Dumézil, Georges (1985) 'Repercussions of a lie' (interview re. the CICT *Mahabharata*), *Théâtre en Europe* 8, October.

Edwardes, Jane (1988) Review of *The Mahabharata* in Glasgow, *Time Out*, 20 April.

Edwards, Christopher (1988) 'Epic grandeur' (review of *The Mahabharata* in Glasgow), *Spectator*, 23 April.

Elsom, John (1985) 'Brook's latest' (interview with Peter Brook re. *Le Mahabharata* in Avignon), *Plays International*, September.

—— (1989) 'Letting go lightly: an appreciation of Peter Brook', paper presented at a conference in Taormina, Sicily, on the occasion of Brook's award of the Premio Europa per il Teatro, May.

Evans, Bob (1988) 'Three incomparable nights' (review of *The Mahabharata* in Perth), *Sydney Morning Herald*, 8 February.

Feingold, Michael (1987) 'Brook of life' (review of *The Mahabharata* in New York), *The Village Voice*, 27 October.

Gibson, Michael (1973) 'Brook's Africa' (interview with Peter Brook), *Drama Review* 17(3), September.

Gore-Langton, Robert (1988) Review of *The Mahabharata* in Glasgow, *Plays and Players*, June.

Grande, Maurizio (1989) 'La regia come scrittura di scena', paper presented at a conference in Taormina, Sicily, on the occasion of Brook's award of the Premio Europa per il Teatro, May.

Harris, Samela (1988) 'Not mere entertainment' (review of *The Mahabharata* in Adelaide), *Adelaide Advertiser*, 22 February.

Harvey, Andrew (1987) 'Peter Brook makes believers of us all' (review of *Le Mahabharata* in Paris), *Vogue*, October.

Hayman, Ronald (1988) 'Rebel in a theatrical cause' (re. *The Mahabharata* in Glasgow), *Independent*, 7 April.

Heilpern, John (1979) *Conference of the Birds: the Story of Peter Brook in Africa*, Harmondsworth, Penguin.

Hemming, Sarah (1988) 'Ninety-nine per cent inspiration' (interview with Peter Brook), *Independent*, 20 April.

Henderson, Liza (1988) 'Brook's point', *Theater* 19(2), Spring.

Henry, William A. (1987) 'An epic journey through myth' (review of *The Mahabharata* in Los Angeles), *Time*, 19 October.

Hewison, Robert (1985) 'Universal meanings revealed' (review of *Le Mahabharata* in Avignon), *Sunday Times*, 18 July.

Hiley, Jim (1988) 'Once is enough' (review of *The Mahabharata* in Glasgow), *The Listener*, 28 April.

Hill, Diane (1985) 'Brook goes quarrying for eternal verities' (review of *Le Mahabharata* in Avignon), *The Stage*, 15 August.

Hoad, Brian (1988) 'Cosmic explosion sows the seeds of dharma' (review of *The Mahabharata* in Perth), *The Bulletin*, 16 February.

Hunt, Albert (1988) 'Brook's poem of the world' (re. *The Mahabharata* in Glasgow), *New Society*, 15 April.

Jackson, Kevin (1989) 'Family feuding' (review of *The Mahabharata* film), *Independent*, 11 December.

Jayakar, Pupul (1985) 'A bush swaying in the wind' (review of *Le Mahabharata* in Avignon), *Théâtre en Europe* 8, October.

Jones, Edward Trostle (1985) *Following Directions: A Study of Peter Brook*, New York, Lang.

Kemp, Peter (1988) 'Dharma drama' (review of *The Mahabharata* in Glasgow), *Independent*, 19 April.

Kimmelman, Michael (1987) 'Putting old wrinkles into a theater's new face', *New York Times*, 25 October.

King, Francis (1988) Review of *The Mahabharata* in Glasgow, *Sunday Telegraph*, 24 April.

Kingston, Jeremy (1988) 'Image overwhelms word' (review of *The Mahabharata* in Glasgow), *The Times*, 19 April.

Koehler, Robert (1987) 'Indians applaud Festival's *The Mahabharata*', *Los Angeles Times*, 30 September.

Kothari, Sunil (1985) 'Peter Brook's *Mahabharata*' (review of Avignon premiere), *Sunday Statesman*, 28 July.

Kothari, Sunil and Sethi, Sunil (1985) 'An epic endeavour' (review of *Le Mahabharata* in Avignon), *India Today*, 31 July.

Kroll, Jack (1987) 'An epic saga of India' (review of *The Mahabharata* in Los Angeles), *Newsweek*, 21 September.

Kurcfeld, Michael (1987) 'Magic carpet ride' (review of *The Mahabharata* in Los Angeles, and interviews with Brook, Carriére and Obolensky), *L.A. Weekly*, 28 August – 3 September.

Kustow, Michael (1985) Review of *Le Mahabharata* at Avignon, *London Review of Books*, 3 October.

Levin, Bernard (1988) 'Man, monsters – and magic' (review of *The Mahabharata* in Glasgow), *The Times*, 25 April.

Lockerbie, Catherine (1988) 'Epic spell-binder' (review of *The Mahabharata* in Glasgow), *The Scotsman*, 19 April.

Loney, Glenn (1988) 'Myth and music: resonances across the continents and centuries', *Theater* 19(2), Spring.

Long, Roger (1989) 'Peter Brook's *The Mahabharata*: A personal reaction', *Asian Theatre Journal* 5(2), Fall.

McAlpine, Maureen (1988) Review of *The Mahabharata* in Glasgow, *The Tribune*, 29 April.

McMillan, Joyce (1988) 'The wisest story ever told' (review of *The Mahabharata* in Glasgow), *Guardian*, 19 April.

Mambrino, Jean (1985) 'Une histoire de l'humanité: *Le Mahabharata* conçu par Peter Brook', *Etudes* 363(5), November.

Marotti, Ferruccio (1989) 'Brook come artigiano del teatro', paper presented at a conference in Taormina, Sicily, on the occasion of Brook's award of the Premio Europa per il Teatro, May.

Menon, Sadanand (1989) 'Giving a bad name to interculturalism', *The Hindu*, 29 December.

Miller, Judith G. (1986) 'Peter Brook's *Mahabharata*', *Theater* 17(2).

Mishra, Vijay (1988) 'The Great Indian Epic and Peter Brook', *Meanjin* 47(2), Winter.

Moore, James (1976) 'A subject that is complete' (interview with Peter Brook), *Guardian*, 20 July.

315

O'Connor, Garry (1989) *The Mahabharata: Peter Brook's Epic in the Making*, London, Hodder & Stoughton; photographs by Gilles Abegg.

Oliver, Roger *et al.* (1987) '*The Mahabharata*: Peter Brook's earth, water and fire', *Theater Crafts*, November.

Ortolani, Olivier (1988) *Peter Brook: Regie im Theater*, Frankfurt am Mein, Fischer.

Osborne, Charles (1988) 'Doubts about the guru' (review of *The Mahabharata* in Perth), *Daily Telegraph*, 21 March.

Pronko, Leonard C. (1989) 'Los Angeles Festival: Peter Brook's *The Mahabharata*', *Asian Theatre Journal* 5(2), Fall.

Provvedini, Claudia (1985) 'Tutti intorno al *Mahabharata*', *Sipario*, August/September.

Radic, Leonard (1988) 'Peter Brook's mighty *Mahabharata*', *The Age* (Melbourne), 27 February.

Radin, Victoria (1988) 'War and peace' (review of *The Mahabharata* in Glasgow), *New Statesman*, 29 April.

Ratcliffe, Michael (1985) 'Hindu magic in Provence' (review of *Le Mahabharata* in Avignon), *Observer*, 14 July.

—— (1986) 'Radical magician', *Observer Magazine*, 11 May.

—— (1987) Review of *The Mahabharata* in New York, *Observer*, 1 November.

—— (1988) 'Transports of delight' (review of *The Mahabharata* in Glasgow), *Observer*, 24 April.

Raymond, Gerard (1987) 'A storyteller's point of view' (interview with Jean-Claude Carriére), *Theaterweek* 1(10), 19–25 October.

Rich, Frank (1987) Review of *The Mahabharata* in New York, *New York Times*, 19 October.

Robertson, Nan (1987) 'Making way for *The Mahabharata*', *New York Times*, 30 September.

Rockwell, John (1987) 'The cultural "global village" ', *International Herald Tribune*, 16 October.

Schechner, Richard (ed.) (1985) *The Mahabharata*: interviews etc., *Drama Review* 30(1), October.

Selbourne, David (1982) *The Making of a Midsummer Night's Dream*, London, Methuen.

Sethi, Sunil (1982) 'Stage presence', *India Today*, 15 March.

Shorter, Eric (1988) 'A passage from India' (review of *The Mahabharata*), *Daily Telegraph*, 19 April.

Shulman, Milton (1988) 'The nine hour wonder' (review of *The Mahabharata* in Glasgow), *London Evening Standard*, 21 April.

Singh, Santa Serbjeet (1985) 'The second coming of *The Mahabharata*' (review of the première in Avignon), *Indian Express*, Bombay, 1 September.

Smith A. C. H. (1972) *Orghast at Persepolis*, London, Eyre Methuen.

Smith, John D. (1988) 'Destinies and deities' (review of *The Mahabharata* in Glasgow), *Times Literary Supplement*, 13 May.

Sommers, Michael *et al.* (1987) 'Peter Brook's earth, water and fire' (re. *The Mahabharata* at the Majestic Theatre, New York), *Theater Crafts*, November.

Sullivan, Dan (1987) 'A trip like no other' (review of *The Mahabharata* in Los Angeles), *Los Angeles Times*, 7 September.

—— (1987) 'The scope of *Mahabharata*' (review of *The Mahabharata* in Los Angeles), *Los Angeles Times*, 13 September.

Théâtre en Europe (1985) 'Shakespeare et *Le Mahabharata*' (interview with Jean-Claude Carrière and Peter Brook), *Théâtre en Europe* 7, June.

Théâtre en Europe (1985) *The Mahabharata* (many interviews and photographs of the French-language version in Avignon and Paris), *Théâtre en Europe* 8, October.

Tinker, Jack (1988) Review of *The Mahabharata* in Glasgow, *Daily Mail*, 20 April.

Tonkin, Boyd (1988) 'The reluctant hero comes home' (an interview with Peter Brook re. *The Mahabharata* in Glasgow), *New Statesman*, 22 April.

Tonkin, Boyd and Colvin, Clare (1986) 'Maha marathon' (review of *The Mahabharata* in Avignon and Paris), *Drama* 159, Winter.

Trewin, John C. (1971) *Peter Brook: A Biography*, London, Macdonald.

Tynan, Kenneth (1977) 'Director as misanthropist: on the moral neutrality of Peter Brook', *Theatre Quarterly* 7(25), Spring, 20–8.

Wardle, Irving (1982) 'The Indian pilgrimage of Peter Brook', *The Times*, 5 May.

— — (1985) 'Images of tenderness, triumph and death' (review of *The Mahabharata* in Avignon), *The Times*, 13 July.

— — (1989) 'Brook and Shakespeare', paper presented at a conference in Taormina, Sicily, on the occasion of Brook's award of the Premio Europa per il Teatro, May.

Willbourn, Hugh (1985) Review of *The Mahabharata* in Avignon, *Plays and Players*, October.

Williams, David (1983) 'Theatre of Innocence and Experience: Peter Brook, 1964–80', MA thesis, University of Kent.

— — (1985) ' "A place marked by life": Peter Brook at the Bouffes du Nord', *New Theatre Quarterly* 1(1), February.

— — (1986) *In Search of a Lost Theatre: The Story of Peter Brook's Centre*, Paris, CICT.

— — (ed.) (1988) *Peter Brook: A Theatrical Casebook*, London, Methuen.

— — (1988) ' "The Great Poem of the World": Peter Brook's *Mahabharata*', *New Theatre Australia* 3, February.

— — (1988) 'An enigmatic, surreal fable', *Canberra Times*, 10 January.

— — (1988) 'A journey towards life . . .' Adelaide Festival Programme, February.

— — (1989) *The Mahabharata*, paper presented at a conference in Taormina, Sicily, on the occasion of Brook's award of the Premio Europa per il Teatro, May.

Williams, Gary Jay (1988) 'From the *Dream* to *The Mahabharata*', *Theater* 19(2), Spring.

Wilson, Peter (1973) 'Sessions in the U.S.A.: A chronicle', Paris, CICT, unpublished.

Wright, Allen (1988) 'Glasgow goes for the epic accolade' (review of *The Mahabharata* in Glasgow), *The Scotsman*, 18 April.

Zarrilli, Phillip (ed.) (1986) 'The aftermath: when Peter Brook came to town' (discussion with Probir Guha and Deborah Neff), *Drama Review* 30(1), Spring.

— — *et al.* (1988) 'More aftermath after Peter Brook', *Drama Review* 32(2), Summer.

ADDITIONAL MATERIAL CONSULTED RE. *THE MAHABHARATA*, ETC.

Ashton, Martha Bush, and Christie, Bruce (1977) *Yakshagana, a Dance-Drama of India*, New Delhi, Abhivan.

Bailey, Greg (1986) 'Suffering in the *Mahabharata*', in Kapil N. Tiwari (ed.), *Suffering: Indian Perspectives*, Delhi, Motilal Banarsidass, pp. 38–60.

Barthes, Roland (1973) *Le Plaisir du texte*, Paris, Seuil.

Basham, A. L. (ed.) (1975) *A Cultural History of India*, Oxford, Oxford University Press.

Bhattacharyya, S. (1971) *Imagery in The Mahabharata*, Calcutta, Sanskrit Pustak Bhandar.

Bose, Buddhadeva (1986) *The Book of Yudhishthir*, translated by Sujit Mukherjee, Hyderabad, Sangam Books.

Buck, William (1973) *Mahabharata*, Berkeley and Los Angeles, University of California Press.

Campbell, Joseph (1962) *The Masks of God: Oriental Mythology*, New York, Viking Press.

Chaitanya, Krishna (1985) 'The Mahabharata and the creative use of imagery', *Indian Horizons* 34(1–2).

Chakravarti, A. C. (1976) *The Story of Krishna in Indian Literature*, Calcutta, Indian Associated Publishing Co.

Chakravarti, P. C. (1941) *The Art of War in Ancient India*, Dacca, University of Dacca.

Chandrasekhar, B. S. (1983) 'Mahabharata in modern idiom', *Indian Literature* 26(3), May/June.

Coomeraswamy, Ananda and Duggirala, Gopala K. (1977) *The Mirror of Gesture*, New Delhi, Munshiram Manoharlal.

Courtright, Paul B. (1985) *Ganesha: Lord of Obstacles, Lord of Beginnings*, Oxford, Oxford University Press.

Creel, Austin B. (1977) *Dharma in Hindu Ethics*, Calcutta, Firma KLM.

Dange, S. A. (1969) *Legends in The Mahabharata*, Delhi, Motilal Banarsidass.

Deshpande, C. R. (1978) *Transmission of the Mahabharata Tradition*, Simla, Indian Institute of Advanced Study.

Dimock, Edward C. Jr *et al.* (1974) *The Literatures of India: An Introduction*, Chicago, University of Chicago Press.

Drekmeier, Charles (1962) *Kingship and Community in Early India*, Stanford, University of California Press.

Dumézil, Georges (1968) *Mythe et Epopée*, Vol. 1, Paris, Gallimard.

—— (1971) *Mythe et Epopée*, Vol. 2, Paris, Gallimard.

—— (1968) *The Destiny of the Warrior*, translated by Alf Hiltebeitel, Chicago, University of Chicago Press.

Dutt, Ramesh C. (1976) *The Great Epics of India*, Delhi, Ess Ess Publications.

Eck, Diane L. (1983) *Banaras, City of Lights*, London, Routledge & Kegan Paul.

Eliade, Mircea (1982) *A History of Religious Ideas*, Vol. 2, translated by Willard R. Trask, Chicago, University of Chicago Press.

Fergusson, Francis (1949) *The Idea of a Theater*, Princeton, Princeton University Press.

Gargi, Balwant (1966) *Folk Theater of India*, Seattle, University of Washington Press.

Gehrts, Heino (1975) *Mahabharata, Das Geschehen und seine Bedeutung*, Bonn, Bouvier.

George, David E. R. (1986) *India: Three Ritual Dance-Dramas*, Cambridge, Chadwyck-Healey.

Getty, Alice (1971) *Ganesha: A Monograph on the Elephant-Faced God*, New Delhi, Munshiram Manoharlal.

Giteau, Madeleine (1965) *Khmer Sculpture and the Angkor Civilisation*, London, Thames & Hudson.

Godine, David R. (undated) *Krishna, the Divine Lover: Myth and Legend through Indian Art*, London, Serindia Publications.

Gould, Eric (1981) *Mythical Intentions in Modern Literature*, Princeton, NJ, Princeton University Press.

Gupta, S. P. and Ramachandran, K. S. (eds) (1976) *Mahabharata: Myth and Reality – Differing Views*, Delhi, Agam Prakashan.

Hatto, A. T. (ed.) (1980) *Traditions of Heroic and Epic Poetry*, London, MHRA.

Hawley, John Stratton (1983) *Krishna, The Butter Thief*, Princeton, NJ, Princeton University Press.

Held, Gerrit Jan (1935) *The Mahabharata, An Ethnological Study*, London, Kegan Paul/Trench/Truber.

Hiltebeitel, Alf (1976) *The Ritual of Battle*, Ithaca, NY, and London, Cornell University Press.

—— (1980) 'Siva, the goddess, and the disguises of the Pandavas and Draupadi', *History of Religions* 20, 147–74.

—— (1980) 'Draupadi's garments', *Indo-Iranian Journal* 22(2), April.

—— (1981) 'Draupadi's hair', *Purasartha* 5, 179–214.

Hopkins, E. W. (1969) *Epic Mythology*, New York, Biblo and Tannen.

—— (1978) *The Great Epic of India: Its Character and Origin*, Calcutta, Punthi Pustak.

Ions, Veronica (1967) *Indian Mythology*, London, Newnes Books.

Jayal, Shakambari (1966) *The Status of Women in the Epics*, Delhi, Motilal Benarsidass.

Jung, C. G. (1977) *Memories, Dreams, Reflections*, ed. Aniela Jaffe, London, Collins Fount.

Kakar, Sudhir (1982) *The Inner World*, New Delhi, Oxford University Press.

Kale, M. R. (1967) *The Hitopadesa of Narayana*, Delhi, Motilal Banarsidass.

Karanth, Shivarama K. (1975) *Yakshagana*, Mysore, Institute of Kannada Studies, University of Mysore.

Karve, Irawati (1969) *Yuganta, the End of an Epoch*, Poona, Deshmukh Prakashan.

Kinsley, David R. (1975) *The Sword and the Flute: Kali and Krishna*, Berkeley, University of California Press.

—— (1979) *The Divine Player*, Delhi, Motilal Banarsidass.

Klaes, Norbert (1975) *Conscience and Consciousness: Ethical Problems of The Mahabharata*, Bangalore, Dharmaram College.

Kramrisch, Stella (1981) *The Presence of Shiva*, Princeton, NJ, Princeton University Press.

Kunjunni Raja, K. (1969) *Indian Theories of Meaning*, Madras, Adyar Library and Research Centre.

Lannoy, Richard (1971) *The Speaking Tree: A Study of Indian Culture and Society*, Oxford, Oxford University Press.

Lingat, Robert (1973) *The Classical Law of India*, translated by J. D. M. Derrett, Berkeley, University of California Press.

Lukács, Georg (1971) *The Theory of the Novel*, translated by Anna Bostok, London, Merlin Press.

Monier-Williams, M. (1976) *Sanskrit – English Dictionary*, Delhi, Munshiram Manoharlal.

Narayan, R. K. (1965) *Gods, Demons and Others*, London, Heinemann.

Newby, Eric and Singh, Raghubir (1974) *Ganga: Sacred River of India*, Hong Kong, The Perennial Press.

O'Flaherty, Wendy Doniger (1973) *Asceticism and Eroticism in the Mythology of Siva*, Oxford, Oxford University Press.

—— (1975) *Hindu Myths*, Penguin, Harmondsworth.

—— (1976) *The Origins of Evil in Hindu Mythology*, Berkeley, University of California Press.

O'Flaherty, Wendy Doniger and Derrett, J. Duncan M. (eds) (1978) *The Concept of Duty in South Asia*, Delhi, Vikas Publishing House.

Parkhill, Thomas (1986) 'Going to the forest: the case of the Pandavas', *Annals of the Bhandarkar Oriental Research Institute* 47(1–4).

Peter, John (1987) *Vladimir's Carrot*, London, Methuen.

Ramanujan, A. K. (trans. and ed.) (1973) *Speaking of Shiva*, Harmondsworth, Penguin.

Rea, Kenneth (1978) 'Theatre in India: The old and the new, Parts 1 and 2', *Theatre Quarterly* 8(30), Summer, 9–23, and 8(31), Autumn, 45–60.

Roy, B. P. (1975) *Political Ideas and Institutions in The Mahabharata*, Calcutta, Punthi Pustak.

Ryan, Dennis R. (1976) 'The Myth of Yudhisthira in *The Mahabharata*', PhD, Fordham University.

Said, Edward W. (1985) *Orientalism*, Harmondsworth, Penguin.

Sarabhai, Mrinalini (1979) *The Sacred Dance of India*, Bombay, Bharatiya Vidya Bhavan.

Schechner, Richard (1982) 'Intercultural performance', *The Drama Review*, 26(2), Summer, pp. 3–4.

—— (1983) *Performative Circumstances from the Avant-Garde to Ramlila*, Calcutta, Seagull Books.

—— (1985) *Between Theater and Anthropology*, Philadelphia, University of Pennsylvania Press.

—— (1988) *Performance Theory* (revised edn), London, Routledge.

Scheuer, Jacques (1982) *Siva dans Le Mahabharata*, Paris, Presses Universitaires de France.

Scott, A. C. (1972) *The Theatre in Asia*, London, Weidenfeld & Nicolson.

Sharma, R. K. (1964) *Elements of Poetry in the Mahabharata*, Berkeley, University of California Press.

Shulman, David Dean (1985) *The King and the Clown in South Indian Myth and Poetry*, Princeton, NJ, Princeton University Press.

Singer, Milton (ed.) (1971) *Krishna: Myths, Rites and Attitudes*, Chicago, University of Chicago Press.

Sinha, J. P. (1977) *The Mahabharata: A Literary Study*, New Delhi, Meharchand Lachhmandas.

Smith, John D. (1980) 'The two Sanskrit epics', in A. T. Hatto (ed.), *Traditions of Heroic and Epic Poetry*, London, Modern Humanities Research Association.

Steiner, George (1979) *Language and Silence*, London, Penguin.

Stutley, Margaret and James (1977) *A Dictionary of Hinduism*, London, Routledge & Kegan Paul.

Subramaniam, M. V. (1967) *Vyasa and Variations*, Madras, Higginbothams.

Sukhtankar, V. S. (1957) *On the Meaning of The Mahabharata*, Bombay, Asiatic Society of Bombay.

Sullivan, Bruce M. (1984) 'The seer of the Fifth Veda: Krsna Dvaipayana Vyasa in *The Mahabharata*', *Dissertation Abstracts International* 45(4), October.

Tarlekar, G. H. (1975) *Studies in the Natyasastra*, Delhi, Motilal Banarsidass.

Thorp, Burt M. (1986) 'Krsna Vasudeva and the art of ambiguity in *The Mahabharata*', *Dissertation Abstracts International* 47(6), December.

Tolstoi, Tatiana (1985) '*Le Mahabharata*: récit fondateur', *La Quinzaine Littéraire* 449, October.

Trikha, Dr Urmila R. (1980) *The Concepts of Religion in The Mahabharata*, Delhi, Nag Publishers.

Turner, Victor (1982) *From Ritual to Theater: The Human Seriousness of Play*, New York, PAJ.

van Buitenen (1982) *The Bhagavadgita in The Mahabharata: Text and Translation*, Chicago, University of Chicago Press.

van Nooten, Barend, A. (1971) *The Mahabharata*, New York, Twayne Publishers.

Vitsaxis, Vassilis G. (1977) *Hindu Epics, Myths and Legends*, Oxford, Oxford University Press.

Zaehner, R. C. (1962) *Hinduism*, Oxford, Oxford University Press.

Zarrilli, Phillip (1984) *The Kathakali Complex*, New Delhi, Abhinav.

Zimmer, Heinrich (1969) *Philosophies of India*, Princeton, NJ, Princeton University Press.

PRINCIPAL EDITIONS OF *THE MAHABHARATA*

*English-language versions

The Mahabharata: an epic poem (1839) Calcutta, 1834–39, 5 volumes.

Mahabharata (1863) Edited by Atmarama Khadilkar, Bombay, Ganpat Krsnaji Press.

Le Mahabharata, poème épique (1870) French translation by T. Fauche, up to the *Karnaparvan*, Paris, 1863–70, 10 volumes.

* *The Mahabharata* (1896) Edited by P. C. Roy, translated by Kisari Mohan Ganguli, Calcutta, Bharata Press, 18 volumes.

* *The Mahabharata, translated into English Prose with esoteric commentary* (1899) Translation by S. C. Mukhopadhay, Calcutta.

* *A Prose English Translation of The Mahabharata* (1905) Translated by M. N. Dutt, Calcutta, H. S. Dass, 1895–1905, 6 volumes.

* *The Mahabharata: A Summary* (1921) Translation by John M. Macfie, Madras, Christian Literary Society for India.

* *The Maha Bharata* (1922) Translation by Jagadisa Ayyay, Madras.

Mahabharata (1933) Edited by Ramachandra S. Kinjavadekar, Poona, 1929–33.

Mahabharata: Southern Recension (1936) Edited by P. P. S. Shastri, Madras, 1931–6, 18 volumes.

Il Mahabharata (1939) Free verse Italian translation by Michele Kerbaker, Rome, 5 volumes.

* *Mahabharata* (1951) English version by C. Rajagopalachari, Bombay, Bharatiya Vidya Bhavan.

* *The Mahabharata* (1956) Edited by S. C. Nott, London, Janus Press.

Mahabharata (1959) The 'Critical Edition', edited by Vishnu S. Sukthankar *et al.*, Poona, Bhandarkar Oriental Research Institute, 1933–66, 19 volumes.

* *Mahabharata* (1965) Translation by Kamala Subramaniam, Bombay, Bharatiya Vidya Bhavan.

* *The Mahabharata* (1965) English version by V. Narasimhan, New York, Columbia University Press.

Mahabharata (1968–90) Translation into English by P. Lal, Calcutta, Writers' Workshop, individual fascicules.

* *The Mahabharata* (1973, 1975, 1978) Translated by J. A. B. van Buitenen, Chicago, University of Chicago Press. Volume 1, 1973; Volume 2, 1975; Volume 3, 1978.

* *The Mahabharata*: a shortened modern prose version (1978) English version by R. K. Narayan, London, Heinemann.
* *The Ramayana and The Mahabharata* (1976) English versions by Romesh C. Dutt, London, Everyman's Library; first edition 1898, London, J. M. Dent.

Le Mahabharata (1985) Theatre adaptation by Jean-Claude Carrière, Paris, CICT; 3 volumes: 'La Partie de Dès', 'L'Exil dans la Forêt', 'La Guerre'.

Le Mahabharata (1986) Extracts translated from the Sanskrit by Jean-Michel Peter-falvi, introduction and commentary by Madeleine Biardeau, Paris, Flammarion.

* *The Mahabharata* (1987) Jean-Claude Carrière's theatre adaptation, translated from the French by Peter Brook, New York, Harper & Row; also London, Methuen, 1988.

INDEX